PHILOSOPHIES
OF
RELIGION

The multitude — ever prone to superstition, and caring more for the shreds of antiquity than for eternal truths — pays homage to the Books of the Bible, rather than to the Word of God.

(Spinoza: A Theologico-Political Treatise)

PHILOSOPHIES
OF
RELIGION

William S. Sahakian, Ph.D.

88460

SCHENKMAN PUBLISHING COMPANY, INC.

Cambridge, Massachusetts

Copyright © 1965

Schenkman Publishing Company, Inc.
Cambridge, Massachusetts 02138

Printed in the United States of America
Library of Congress Catalog Card Number: 65-20304

TOPICAL TABLE OF CONTENTS

PART THREE
AGNOSTICISM: *A Noncommittal Position*

PART FOUR
CONCEPTS OF GOD: *The Nature of God*

PART FIVE
THE SOUL: *Its Nature and Freedom*

PART SIX

IMMORTALITY: *The Survival of the Soul*

PART SEVEN

EVIL: *The Problem of Its Origin*

PART EIGHT

MIRACLES: *Their Nature and the Question of Their Validity*

PART NINE

PRAYER: *Communion with the Divine*

PART TEN

RELIGIOUS FAITH AND KNOWLEDGE: *The Problem of Religious Knowledge*

CHRONOLOGICAL AND BIBLIOGRAPHICAL TABLE OF CONTENTS

FOREWORD

Philosophy of religion is not, as so many of the uninitiated fancy, theology, that is, the study of various doctrines of faith entertained by diverse religious bodies. The philosopher's concept of faith is not unquestioned acceptance of dogmatic beliefs, as is true in the theological community, but commitment. Blind belief, acceptance of articles of revelation or authority, is the province of divine theology or revealed theology, while the spirit of rational inquiry, constructive doubt, and critical investigation is the hallmark of philosophy of religion.

Philosophy, defined, is the critical evaluation of all the facts of experience; applied to philosophy of religion, it is a critical evaluation of all the facts of *religious* experience. The major areas of religious experience are: (*a*) God, (*b*) the soul, (*c*) immortality, (*d*) natural evil, (*e*) prayer, and (*f*) miracles, (*g*) the knowledge of God. Each is an important area, and worthy of our attention; accordingly, each has been treated in the present work.

(1) The question of *God's existence,* or nonexistence, has early commanded the attention of philosophical speculation and continues to the present as one of the most perplexing and persistent problems of philosophy. It seems appropriate that a work devoted to philosophy of religion should open with a treatment of this area. The three major positions assumed by philosophers (Theism, Atheism, and Agnosticism) have been discussed by their most influential proponents, and the appearance of each man in the body of the text has been arranged chronologically within a given topic.

(2) Some philosophers are of the opinion that debate regarding God does not pertain to whether or not he exists, but to the more serious issue of what is meant by the term, that is, what conception is entertained when the word is employed. What is predicated of God becomes the critical issue; hence the reason for the section in the volume devoted to *Concepts of God.*

(3) Philosophical attention related to the human *soul* centers prin-

cipally upon its nature, freedom, and ability to survive death to immortality. Here questions regarding fatalism, indeterminism, predestinarianism, determinism, etc. are raised and deliberated.

(4) Closely related to the topic of the nature and freedom of the soul is *immortality*, the question as to whether the soul exists, and if so, whether it is capable of surviving bodily death. The possibility or impossibility of the soul's existence and survival is discussed in the light of scientific inquiry philosophically interpreted.

(5) Thought regarding the problem of *evil* gravitates toward natural evil, more so than moral evil for which humanity is responsible. The latter topic falls properly within the circumscribed bounds of ethics. Philosophical debate engaged in the topic of natural evil inquires as to the origin and *why* of evil's presence in the world.

(6) Revealed theology uncritically accepts the validity of *miracles*, and raises the fundamental question: Which revelation claims are true? But the philosopher's quest drives him to a critical examination in the light of reason and scientific data as to any possibility of the existence or even desirability of miracles.

(7) The next topic treated in the text relates to the problem of *prayer;* here, the issue centers on its definition, validity, effectuality, and meaning. Again, here as elsewhere in philosophy, the topic permits of no bias, but is approached from a rational standpoint.

(8) The final section is devoted to the troublesome question as to the nature and possibility of the knowledge of God. The attempt here is to resolve such questions as: Is knowledge of God possible? What is the nature of faith? Is faith a valid form of knowledge? What is the value of faith? This section is dominated by the contributions of contemporary philosophers of religion, who apparently consider it the most important of the current issues to which philosophers of religion address themselves.

. . . . .

A book of readings, particularly in the area of philosophy of religion where there is such a wide diversity of conflicting positions, has much to commend it. First of all, there is the wide scope of ideas, presented from differing points of view, which acts as a deterrent to dogmatism; secondly, it avoids the imposition of the instructor's biases upon the student, yet on the other hand, allows the instructor complete freedom in expressing his own ideas without the burden of guilt that he is slanting discussion in his own favor, since other points of view are readily available in the text. Thirdly, it gives the instructor the opportunity of presenting his own lectures on the subject, as a supplement to the material

FOREWORD

already presented, without the instructor and text competing against each other, as often is the case in the use of the traditional type of text. Fourthly, the student is exposed to the thought of mankind's most influential philosophers, and receives a first hand acquaintance with the ideas which the world's titans have sired.

Being true to the philosophical spirit, the author does not seek to impose his own position on the reader, but rather places the classical writers at the reader's disposal with the expectation that the reader, in the genuine spirit of philosophy, will arrive at his own conclusions in the various areas of religious values.

Prefaced to each reading, the author has provided an introduction to the philosopher in question, with pertinent data regarding his biography, writings, philosophical position and influence. Where the reader seeks to pursue the thought of a particular philosopher further, these introductory remarks will aid him in that respect. In certain instances in which more than a single selection of a given philosopher has been used, editorial material will be found accompanying the initial selection only.

To Dr. Mabel Lewis Sahakian of Northeastern University, my wife and colleague, I wish to express my gratitude for her reading of and commenting on the manuscript.

William S. Sahakian

Beacon Hill,
Boston, Massachusetts

DEDICATED TO THE MEMORY OF

the family I once shared and lost:
my parents and my sister Peg.

Part One: THEISM

Arguments for God's Existence

ST. ANSELM

ST. ANSELM (1033-1109), Archbishop of Canterbury, originally from Aosta in Piedmont, was for an extended period of time at the monastery at Bec, Normandy, where he became Abbot in 1078. From 1093 to his death, he assumed the archbishopric of Canterbury.

His works consist of: **De Veritae** (c. 1080), a tract in which his epistemological views are formulated; **Monologium** (1077), an attempt to prove God's existence on a Platonic foundation; his masterpiece, **Cur Deus Homo** (1094-1098), a theological treatise dealing with Christology and Soteriology; and his philosophic classic, **Proslogium** (1078), the work containing his celebrated Ontological Argument for the existence of God, an argument which accorded him fame in his own day, and assured him an unmistakable niche in the history of philosophy. The influential Ontological Argument commanded the attention and interest of Descartes, Spinoza, Locke, Leibniz, Kant, Hegel, Lotze, and others of lesser rank. The **Proslogium** should be read in conjunction with the reply by Gaunilon in his **Liber pro Insipiente** and Anselm's rebuttal in his **Liber Apologeticus.** Selections from all three have been knitted into an integral unit in the text for the convenience of the reader.

Anselm's Ontological Argument for God's existence is predicated on the theory that a concept of a perfect Being must exist in reality as well as in the understanding, otherwise it could not be regarded as perfect. Initial opposition to this thesis was met by Guanilon, who, assuming the cudgels of the fool and Atheist, attacked the argument on the grounds that a mere idea of some object grants no assurance of its existence in reality. If it did, then it would be possible to prove the existence of a nonexistent island merely on the basis of having a conception of a perfect island, that is to say, the argument proves too much. Anselm's apologetic against Gaunilon is: although the Ontological Argument does not hold true in the case of a perfect island, it does maintain in reference to God, inasmuch as in the case of God, a perfect Being, existence is necessary.

ST. ANSELM

The Ontological Argument[1]

And so, Lord, do thou, who dost give understanding to faith, give me, so far as thou knowest it to be profitable, to understand that thou art as we believe; and that thou art that which we believe. And indeed, we believe that thou art a being than which nothing greater can be conceived. Or is there no such nature, since the fool hath said in his heart, there is no God? (Psalms xiv. 1). But, at any rate, this very fool, when he hears of this being of which I speak — a being than which nothing greater can be conceived — understands what he hears, and what he understands is in his understanding; although he does not understand it to exist.

For, it is one thing for an object to be in the understanding, and another to understand that the object exists. When a painter first conceives of what he will afterwards perform, he has it in his understanding, but he does not yet understand it to be, because he has not yet performed it. But after he has made the painting, he both has it in his understanding, and he understands that it exists, because he has made it.

Hence, even the fool is convinced that something exists in the understanding, at least, than which nothing greater can be conceived. For, when he hears of this, he understands it. And whatever is understood, exists in the understanding. And assuredly that, than which nothing greater can be conceived, cannot exist in the understanding alone. For, suppose it exists in the understanding alone: then it can be conceived to exist in reality; which is greater.

Therefore, if that, than which nothing greater can be conceived, exists in the understanding alone, the very being, than which nothing greater can be conceived, is one, than which a greater can be conceived. But

[1] St. Anselm, *Proslogium*, tr. Sidney Norton Deane (LaSalle, Illinois: Open Court Publishing Co., 1903); excerpts from chapters 2-4.

3

obviously this is impossible. Hence, there is no doubt that there exists a being, than which nothing greater can be conceived, and it exists both in the understanding and in reality.

. . . . .

And it assuredly exists so truly, that it cannot be conceived not to exist. For, it is possible to conceive of a being which cannot be conceived not to exist; and this greater than one which can be conceived not to exist. Hence, if that, than which nothing greater can be conceived, can be conceived not to exist, it is not that than which nothing greater can be conceived. But this is an irreconcilable contradiction. There is, then, so truly a being than which nothing greater can be conceived to exist, that it cannot even be conceived not to exist; and this being thou art, O Lord, our God.

So truly, therefore, dost thou exist, O Lord, my God, that thou canst not be conceived not to exist; and rightly. For, if a mind could conceive of a being better than thee, the creature would rise above the Creator; and this is most absurd. And, indeed, whatever else there is, except thee alone, can be conceived not to exist. To thee alone, therefore, it belongs to exist more truly than all other beings, and hence in a higher degree than all others. For, whatever else exists does not exist so truly, and hence in a less degree it belongs to it to exist. Why, then, has the fool said in his heart, there is no God (Psalms xiv. 1), since it is so evident, to a rational mind that thou dost exist in the highest degree of all? . . .

. . . . .

But how has the fool said in his heart what he could not conceive; or how is it that he could not conceive what he said in his heart? since it is the same to say in the heart, and to conceive.

But, if really, nay, since really, he both conceived, because he said in his heart; and did not say in his heart, because he could not conceive; there is more than one way in which a thing is said in the heart or conceived. For, in one sense, an object is conceived, when the word signifying it is conceived; and in another, when the very entity, which the object is, is understood.

In the former sense, then, God can be conceived not to exist; but in the latter, not at all. For no one who understands what fire and water are can conceive fire to be water, in accordance with the nature of the facts themselves, although this is possible according to the words. So, then, no one who understands what God is can conceive that God does not exist; although he says these words in his heart, either without any, or with some foreign, signification. For, God is that than which a greater cannot be conceived. And he who thoroughly understands this, assuredly understands that this being so truly exists, that not even in concept can it be non-existent. Therefore, he who understands that God so exists, cannot conceive that he does not exist. . . .

GAUNILON, A MONK OF MARMOUTIER:
In Behalf of the Fool [2]

1. If one doubts or denies the existence of a being of such a nature that nothing greater than it can be conceived, he receives this answer:

The existence of this being is proved, in the first place, by the fact that he himself, in his doubt or denial regarding this being, already has it in his understanding; for in hearing it spoken of he understands what is spoken of. It is proved, therefore, by the fact that what he understands must exist not only in his understanding, but in reality also.

And the proof of this is as follows: — It is a greater thing to exist both in the understanding and in reality than to be in the understanding alone. And if this being is in the understanding alone, whatever has even in the past existed in reality will be greater than this being. And so that which was greater than all beings will be less than some being, and will not be greater than all: which is a manifest contradiction.

And hence, that which is greater than all, already proved to be in the understanding, must exist not only in the understanding, but also in reality: for otherwise it will not be greater than all other beings.

2. The fool might make this reply:

This being is said to be in my understanding already, only because I understand what is said. Now could it not with equal justice be said that I have in my understanding all manner of unreal objects, having absolutely no existence in themselves, because I understand these things if one speaks of them, whatever they may be?

Unless indeed it is shown that this being is of such a character that it cannot be held in concept like all unreal objects, or objects whose existence is uncertain: and hence I am not able to conceive of it when I hear of it, or to hold it in concept; but I must understand it and have it in my understanding; because, it seems, I cannot conceive of it in any other way than by understanding it, that is, by comprehending in my knowledge its existence in reality.

But if this is the case, in the first place there will be no distinction be-

[2] Gaunilon, *In Behalf of the Fool*, tr. Sidney Norton Deane (LaSalle, Illinois: Open Court Publishing Co., 1903); excerpts.

tween what has precedence in time — namely, the having of an object in the understanding — and what is subsequent in time — namely, the understanding that an object exists; as in the example of the picture, which exists first in the mind of the painter, and afterwards in his work.

Moreover, the following assertion can hardly be accepted: that this being, when it is spoken of and heard of, cannot be conceived not to exist in the way in which even God can be conceived not to exist. For if this is impossible, what was the object of this argument against one who doubts or denies the existence of such a being? . . .

3.   . . . The painter who already has in his understanding what he is to paint cannot agree with this argument. For the picture, before it is made, is contained in the artificer's art itself; and any such thing, existing in the art of an artificer, is nothing but a part of his understanding itself . . . .

.   .   .   .   .

5.   . . . How, then, is the veritable existence of that being proved to me from the assumption, by hypothesis, that it is greater than all other beings? For I should still deny this, or doubt your demonstration of it, to this extent, that I should not admit that this being is in my understanding and concept even in the way in which many objects whose real existence is uncertain and doubtful, are in my understanding and concept. For it should be proved first that this being itself really exists somewhere; and then, from the fact that it is greater than all, we shall not hesitate to infer that it also subsists in itself.

6. For example: it is said that somewhere in the ocean is an island, which, because of the difficulty, or rather the impossibility, of discovering what does not exist, is called the lost island. And they say that this island has an inestimable wealth of all manner of riches and delicacies in greater abundance than is told of the Islands of the Blest; and that having no owner or inhabitant, it is more excellent than all other countries, which are inhabited by mankind, in the abundance with which it is stored.

Now if some one should tell me that there is such an island, I should easily understand his words, in which there is no difficulty. But suppose that he went on to say, as if by a logical inference: "You can no longer doubt that this island which is more excellent than all lands exists somewhere, since you have no doubt that it is in your understanding. And since it is more excellent not to be in the understanding alone, but to exist both in the understanding and in reality, for this reason it must exist. For if it does not exist, any land which really exists will be more excellent than it; and so the island already understood by you to be more excellent will not be more excellent."

If a man should try to prove to me by such reasoning that this island truly exists, and that its existence should no longer be doubted, either I should believe that he was jesting, or I know not which I ought to regard as the greater fool: myself, supposing that I should allow this proof; or him, if he should suppose that he had established with any certainty the existence of this island. For he ought to show first that the hypothetical excellence of this island exists as a real and indubitable fact, and in no wise as any unreal object, or one whose existence is uncertain, in my understanding. . . .

ANSELM'S APOLOGETIC — *In Reply to Gaunilon's Answer*[3]

It was a fool against whom the argument of my Proslogium was directed. Seeing, however, that the author of these objects is by no means a fool, and is a Catholic, speaking in behalf of the fool, I think it sufficient that I answer the Catholic.

. . . In answer to this, I maintain positively: if that being can be even conceived to be, it must exist in reality. For that than which a greater is inconceivable cannot be conceived except as without beginning. But whatever can be conceived to exist, and does not exist, can be conceived to exist through a beginning. Hence what can be conceived to exist, but does not exist, is not the being than which a greater cannot be conceived. Therefore, if such a being can be conceived to exist, necessarily it does exist.

Furthermore: if it can be conceived at all, it must exist. For no one who denies or doubts the existence of a being than which a greater is inconceivable, denies or doubts that if it did exist, its non-existence, either in reality or in the understanding, would be impossible. For otherwise it would not be a being than which a greater cannot be conceived. But as to whatever can be conceived, but does not exist — if there were such a being, its non-existence, either in reality or in the understanding, would be possible. Therefore if a being than which a greater is inconceivable can be even conceived, it cannot be non-existent.

But let us suppose that it does not exist, even if it can be conceived. Whatever can be conceived, but does not exist, if it existed, would not be a being than which a greater is inconceivable. If, then, there were a being a greater than which is inconceivable, it would not be a being than which a greater is inconceivable: which is most absurd. Hence, it is false

[3] Anselm, *Apologetic*, tr. Sidney Norton Deane (LaSalle, Illinois: Open Court Publishing Co.); excerpts from chapters 1, 5, and 9.

to deny that a being than which a greater cannot be conceived exists, if it can be even conceived; much the more, therefore, if it can be understood or can be in the understanding.

Moreover, I will venture to make this assertion: without doubt, whatever at any place or at any time does not exist — even if it does exist at some place or at some time — can be conceived to exist nowhere and never, as at some place and at some time it does not exist. For what did not exist yesterday, and exists to-day, as it is understood not to have existed yesterday, so it can be apprehended by the intelligence that it never exists. And what is not here, and is elsewhere, can be conceived to be nowhere, just as it is not here. So with regard to an object of which the individual parts do not exist at the same places or times: all its parts and therefore its very whole can be conceived to exist nowhere or never.

For, although time is said to exist always, and the world everywhere, yet time does not as a whole exist always, nor the world as a whole everywhere. And as individual parts of time do not exist when others exist, so they can be conceived never to exist. And so it can be apprehended by the intelligence that individual parts of the world exist nowhere, as they do not exist where other parts exist. Moreover, what is composed of parts can be dissolved in concept, and be non-existent. Therefore, whatever at any place or at any time does not exist as a whole, even if it is existent, can be conceived not to exist.

But that than which a greater cannot be conceived, if it exists, cannot be conceived not to exist. Otherwise, it is not a being than which a greater cannot be conceived: which is inconsistent. By no means, then, does it at any place or at any time fail to exist as a whole: but it exists as a whole everywhere and always.

Do you believe that this being can in some way be conceived or understood, or that the being with regard to which these things are understood can be in concept or in the understanding? For if it cannot, these things cannot be understood with reference to it. But if you say that it is not understood and that it is not in the understanding, because it is not thoroughly understood; you should say that a man who cannot face the direct rays of the sun does not see the light of day, which is none other than the sunlight. Assuredly a being than which a greater cannot be conceived exists, and is in the understanding, at least to this extent — that these statements regarding it are understood.

· · · · ·

. . . You often repeat that I assert that what is greater than all other beings is in the understanding; and if it is in the understanding, it exists also in reality, for otherwise the being which is greater than all would not be greater than all.

Nowhere in all my writings is such a demonstration found. For the real existence of a being which is said to be *greater than all other beings* cannot be demonstrated in the same way with the real existence of one that is said to be *a being than which a greater cannot be conceived.*

If it should be said that a being than which a greater cannot be conceived has no real existence, or that it is possible that it does not exist, or even that it can be conceived not to exist, such an assertion can be easily refuted. For the non-existence of what does not exist is possible, and that whose non-existence is possible can be conceived not to exist. But whatever can be conceived not to exist, if it exists, is not a being than which a greater cannot be conceived; but if it does not exist, it would not, even if it existed, be a being than which a greater cannot be conceived. But it cannot be said that a being than which a greater is inconceivable, if it exists, is not a being than which a greater is inconceivable; or that if it existed, it would not be a being than which a greater is inconceivable.

It is evident, then, that neither is it non-existent, nor is it possible that it does not exist, nor can it be conceived not to exist. For otherwise, if it exists, it is not that which it is said to be in the hypothesis; and if it existed, it would not be what it is said to be in the hypothesis.

But this, it appears, cannot be so easily proved of a being which is said to be *greater than all other beings.* For it is not so evident that what can be conceived not to exist is not greater than all existing beings, as it is evident that it is not a being than which a greater cannot be conceived. Nor is it so indubitable that if a being greater than all other beings exists, it is no other than the being than which a greater cannot be conceived; or that if it were such a being, some other might not be this being in like manner; as it is certain with regard to a being which is hypothetically posited as one than which a greater cannot be conceived.

For consider: if one should say that there is a being greater than all other beings, and that this being can nevertheless be conceived not to exist; and that a being greater than this, although it does not exist, can be conceived to exist: can it be so clearly inferred in this case that this being is therefore not a being greater than all other existing beings, as it would be most positively affirmed in the other case, that the being under discussion is not, therefore, a being than which a greater cannot be conceived?

For the former conclusion requires another premise than the predication, *greater than all other beings.* In my argument, on the other hand, there is no need of any other than this very predication, *a being than which a greater cannot be conceived.*

If the same proof cannot be applied when the being in question is predicated to be greater than all others, which can be applied when it is predicated to be a being than which a greater cannot be conceived, you have unjustly censured me for saying what I did not say; since such a predication differs so greatly from that which I actually made. If, on the other hand, the other argument is valid, you ought not to blame me so for having said what can be proved.

Whether this can be proved, however, he will easily decide who recognises that this being than which a greater cannot be conceived is demonstrable. For by no means can this being than which a greater cannot be conceived be understood as any other than that which alone is greater than all. Hence, just as that than which a greater cannot be conceived is understood, and is in the understanding, and for that reason is asserted to exist in the reality of fact: so what is said to be greater than all other beings is understood and is in the understanding, and therefore it is necessarily inferred that it exists in reality.

You see, then, with how much justice you have compared me with your fool, who, on the sole ground that he understands what is described to him, would affirm that a lost island exists.

⋅   ⋅   ⋅   ⋅   ⋅

But even if it were true that a being than which a greater is inconceivable cannot be conceived or understood; yet it would not be untrue that a being than which a greater cannot be conceived is conceivable and intelligible. There is nothing to prevent one's saying *ineffable*, although what is said to be ineffable cannot be spoken of. *Inconceivable* is conceivable, although that to which the word *inconceivable* can be applied is not conceivable. So, when one says, *that than which nothing greater is conceivable,* undoubtedly what is heard is conceivable and intelligible, although that being itself, than which a greater is inconceivable, cannot be conceived or understood.

Or, though there is a man so foolish as to say that there is no being than which a greater is inconceivable, he will not be so shameless as to say that he cannot understand or conceive of what he says. Or, if such a man is found, not only ought his words to be rejected, but he himself should be contemned.

Whoever, then, denies the existence of a being than which a greater cannot be conceived, at least understands and conceives of the denial which he makes. But this denial he cannot understand or conceive of without its component terms; and a term of this statement is *a being than which a greater cannot be conceived.* Whoever, then, makes this denial, understands and conceives of that than which a greater is inconceivable.

Moreover, it is evident that in the same way it is possible to conceive of and understand a being whose non-existence is impossible; but he who conceives of this conceives of a greater being than one whose non-existence is possible. Hence, when a being than which a greater is inconceivable is conceived, if it is a being whose non-existence is possible that is conceived, it is not a being than which a greater cannot be conceived. But an object cannot be at once conceived and not conceived. Hence he who conceives of a being than which a greater is inconceivable, does not conceive of that whose non-existence is possible, but of that whose non-existence is impossible. Therefore, what he conceives of must exist; for anything whose non-existence is possible, is not that of which he conceives.

ST. THOMAS AQUINAS

ST. THOMAS AQUINAS (1225-1274), born in Roccasicca (lower Italy), received his training at Monte Cassino Abbey, Naples, Cologne, and Paris. In addition to teaching at the last three mentioned universities, Thomas instructed at Rome and Bologna. On March 7, 1274, he died en route to the council of Lyons at Fossanuova Abbey.

Equally adept at philosophy and theology, he was accorded the titles **Doctor communis** and **Doctor angelicus.** The most influential of all Roman Catholic thinkers, his philosophy was officially endorsed by two papal encyclicals, that of Leo XIII (**Aeterni Patris,** 1879) and Pius XI (**Studiorum Ducem,** 1923).

Most of Thomas' works are lectures prepared for the various courses which he offered, but two have become philosophical classics: **Summa contra Gentiles** (1259-1264) and **Summa Theologiae,** currently simply referred to as **Theologica** (1266-1273). From the latter work, his famous **Quinque Viae** (five ways of proving God's existence) have been excerpted, and from the same book, his treatment of miracles.

Thomas, regarded as the greatest Scholastic of all, sought to harmonize natural theology (philosophy and science) with revealed theology (revelation), by showing that God reveals himself in a dual mode: through the Bible and through nature (the book of life). The **angelic doctor,** a Realist and Intellectualist, ascribed a relative rank of superiority of God's intellect over his will, that is, the divine will is subject to the dictates of divine wisdom; God's wisdom determines what is good and his will chooses accordingly.

Aquinas, dissatisfied with Anselm's Ontological Argument, dismisses it on the grounds that a mental idea cannot emerge into objective reality; definition does not generate into existence. Aquinas replaces the Ontological Argument with his **Quinque Viae** (five ways of proving God's existence): (1) The Way of Motion, (2) The Way of Efficient Causality, (3) The Way of Possibility and Necessity, (4) The Way of Degrees of Perfection, and (5) The Way of Purposiveness.

The first, The Way of Motion, is the Aristotelian First or Prime Mover argument, an Aetiological Argument predicated on the necessity of the universe requiring an Initial Mover, namely God. The inadequacy of this argument is its inability to prove the God revealed in the Judeo-Christian sacred writings. At best, it proves what has been termed a 'trigger-God,' some Being or principle which started the world going.

Thomas' second argument, The Way of Efficient Cause, also is a form of the Aetiological Argument, that is, it traces objects of nature back to their Original Cause. This argument is often termed First Cause, and is classified as a subdivision of the Cosmological. The shortcoming of the argument, like its predecessor, lies in its inability to prove a Theistic God, a personal Being, rather than an impersonal one.

The third, The Way of Possibility and Necessity, is predicated on the empirical fact of all things coming into being at a specific point in time and subsequently perishing, a fact indicative of all contingent objects. The principle is: only that which is absolute or self-existing is eternal; since all nature is dependent, requiring something other than self for existence, a noncontingent Being must have been responsible for the initial coming into being of all things. This is evidenced by the fact that natural objects exist at the present time, incapable of self-existence, hence there must have been a time when nothing existed — and if nothing existed at some given time in the past, it is impossible for anything to be at the present time — unless a self-existing Being (God) is postulated. Therefore, since the world, a contingent entity, exists, it necessarily follows that God, an absolute eternal Being, must exist to effect the consequence we call the world.

The Way of Degrees of Perfection, Aquinas' fourth argument, reasons that things exist which are more or less good, true, etc. because they participate in truth, goodness, etc., hence necessitate a Supreme Being who is the ground or cause of each participating being with its relative degree of perfection. This fourth argument must be understood in the light of the Platonic doctrine of Participation.

The fifth way, The Way of Purposiveness, Aquinas' finest, is a Teleological Argument, predicated on the existence of purpose present in the world. This argument, however, has been refined to a sophisticated level in the treatment of Paley and others.

2

ST. THOMAS AQUINAS

Quinque Viae[1]

... The existence of God can be proved in five ways.

The first and more manifest way is the argument from motion. It is certain, and evident to our senses, that in the world some things are in motion. Now whatever is moved is moved by another, for nothing can be moved except it is in potentiality to that towards which it is moved; whereas a thing moves inasmuch as it is in act. For motion is nothing else than the reduction of something from potentiality to actuality. But nothing can be reduced from potentiality to actuality, except by something in a state of actuality. Thus that which is actually hot, as fire, makes wood, which is potentially hot, to be actually hot, and thereby moves and changes it. Now it is not possible that the same thing should be at once in actuality and potentiality in the same respect, but only in different respects. For what is actually hot cannot simultaneously be potentially hot; but it is simultaneously potentially cold. It is therefore impossible that in the same respect and in the same way a thing should be both mover and moved, i.e., that it should move itself. Therefore, whatever is moved must be moved by another. If that by which it is moved be itself moved, then this also must needs be moved by another, and that by another again. But this cannot go on to infinity, because then there would be no first mover, and, consequently, no other mover, seeing that subsequent movers move only inasmuch as they are moved by the first mover; as the staff moves only because it is moved by the hand. Therefore it is necessary to arrive at a first mover, moved by no other; and this everyone understands to be God.

[1] St. Thomas Aquinas, *The Summa Theologica*, from the *Basic Writings of Saint Thomas Aquinas*, tr. by Laurence Shapcote, edited and annotated by Anton C. Pegis. (London: Burns & Oates, Ltd., and New York: Random House, Inc., 1945), Q. 2, Art. 3.

The second way is from the nature of efficient cause. In the world of sensible things we find there is an order of efficient causes. There is no case known (neither is it, indeed, possible) in which a thing is found to be the efficient cause of itself; for so it would be prior to itself, which is impossible. Now in efficient causes it is not possible to go on to infinity, because in all efficient causes following in order, the first is the cause of the intermediate cause, and the intermediate is the cause of the ultimate cause, whether the intermediate cause be several, or one only. Now to take away the cause is to take away the effect. Therefore, if there be no first cause among efficient causes, there will be no ultimate, nor any intermediate, cause. But if in efficient causes it is possible to go on to infinity, there will be no first efficient cause, neither will there be an ultimate effect, nor any intermediate efficient causes; all of which is plainly false. Therefore it is necessary to admit a first efficient cause, to which everyone gives the name of God.

The third way is taken from possibility and necessity, and runs thus. We find in nature things that are possible to be and not to be, since they are found to be generated, and to be corrupted, and consequently, it is possible for them to be and not to be. But it is possible for these always to exist, for that which can not-be at some time is not. Therefore, if everything can not-be, then at one time there was nothing in existence. Now if this were true, even now there would be nothing in existence, because that which does not exist begins to exist only through something already existing. Therefore, if at one time nothing was in existence, it would have been impossible for anything to have begun to exist; and thus even now nothing would be in existence — which is absurd. Therefore, not all beings are merely possible, but there must exist something the existence of which is necessary. But every necessary thing either has its necessity caused by another, or not. Now it is impossible to go on to infinity in necessary things which have their necessity caused by another, as has been already proved in regard to efficient causes. Therefore we cannot but admit the existence of some being having of itself its own necessity, and not receiving it from another, but rather causing in others their necessity. This all men speak of as God.

The fourth way is taken from the gradation to be found in things. Among beings there are some more and some less good, true, noble, and the like. But *more* or *less* are predicated of different things according as they resemble in their different ways something which is the maximum, as a thing is said to be hotter according as it more nearly resembles that which is hottest; so that there is something which is truest, something best, something noblest, and, consequently, something which is most being, for those things that are greatest in truth are greatest in being, as it is written in *Metaph.* ii. [18]. Now the maximum in any genus is the cause of all in that genus, as fire, which is the maximum of heat, is the cause of all hot things, as is said in the same book. Therefore there must also be something which is to all beings the cause of the being, goodness, and every other perfection; and this we call God.

The fifth way is taken from the governance of the world. We see that things which lack knowledge, such as natural bodies, act for an end, and this is evident from their acting always, or nearly always, in the same way, so as to obtain the best result. Hence it is plain that they achieve their end, not fortuitously, but designedly. Now whatever lacks knowledge cannot move towards an end, unless it be directed by some being endowed with knowledge and intelligence; as the arrow is directed by the archer. Therefore some intelligent being exists by whom all natural things are directed to their end; and this being we call God.

RENÉ   DESCARTES

RENÉ DESCARTES (1596-1650), born at La Haye, Touraine on March 31, 1596, was educated at the Jesuit school at La Flèche, in Anjou, where he was trained in logic, ethics, mathematics, and physics. He distinguished himself in both philosophy and mathematics, contributing his analytic geometry to the latter study. Leaving the Jesuit school in 1612, he studied law from 1613 to 1616 at the University of Poiters. There followed a few years of indecisiveness until 1618, when he left France for Holland where he flirted with a military career, and in 1619, he took a trip throughout several parts of Europe, but the year 1622 found him back in France again. Due to controversy generated by his doctrines, he abandoned the disagreeable atmosphere of Paris, and later the Netherlands for the same reason, for Stockholm, Sweden, where, at the invitation of its Queen Christine, he found respite; he died the following year.

Descartes is considered France's greatest philosopher as well as the father of modern metaphysics; he initiated the philosophy of Continental Rationalism, the attempt to apply geometric method to philosophical disciplines. The Twentieth Century schools of Phenomenology and Existentialism find their roots in his famous **cogito,** which has been included in the present readings. His principal works are: **Discourse on Method** (1637), **Meditations on the First Philosophy** (1641), and **Principles of Philosophy** (1644).

Although famous for many philosophical and mathematical contributions, Descartes is especially well known for his **cogito,** originating with St. Augustine. The **cogito,** or preferably **cogito, ergo sum** (I think, therefore I am) is an argument for the existence of the soul based on the premise that the indubitability of the soul is proof of its existence. That is to say, each time I doubt my own existence, I find myself, in effect, proving it. Or, as St. Augustine put it: doubting is an aspect of thinking; thinking implies existence; hence to doubt necessarily entails existence. Accordingly, the existence of the soul is proved with intuitive certainty.

A Rationalist who is convinced that all truth is derived through reason (clear ideas), Descartes maintains the existence of **innate ideas,** knowledge at birth. The **cogito** is one such innate idea, but so is the idea of God, since it is not a derivative of experience or prior ideas. The Cartesian proof for God's existence, an Ontological one, stems from the conception of an absolutely perfect Being, Anselm's **ens perfectissimum,** who must be responsible for instilling the idea of himself in us, inasmuch as the senses are the source of human knowledge (and since God is not sensed — yet we have an idea of him), God must have instilled the idea in us. Furthermore, the integrity of God (a corollary of his perfection) assures his not deceiving humans in this regard. "For this proof gives the charter for acknowledging with complete certainty as true all propositions which manifest themselves in clear and distinct light before the reason. Here belong, firstly, all truths of mathematics, but here belongs also the **ontological** proof for the existence of God. For with the same necessity of thought — thus Descartes takes up Anselm's argument — with which the geometrical propositions with regard to a triangle follow from the definition of the triangle, it follows from the mere definition of the most Real being that the attribute of existence belongs to him. The possibility of thinking God suffices to prove his existence."[1] Thus, the Rationalist's criterion of truth, a clear and distinct idea, is applicable to God's existence as well as mathematics and empirical facts of experience.

[1] W. Windelband, **A History of Philosophy,** tr. James H. Tufts (1893, 1901), 393.

3

RENÉ DESCARTES

The Innateness of God (The Ontological Argument)[1]

Of my thoughts some are, as it were, images of things and to these alone properly belongs the name *idea;* as when I think [represent to my mind] a man, chimera, the sky, an angel, or God. Others, again, have certain other forms; as when I will, fear, affirm, or deny, I always, indeed, apprehend something as the object of my thought, but I also embrace in thought something more than the representation of the object; and of this class of thoughts some are called volitions or affections, and others judgments. . . .

But, among these ideas, some appear to me to be innate, others adventitious, and others to be made by myself (factitious); for, as I have the power of conceiving what is called a thing, or a truth, or a thought, it seems to me that I hold this power from no other source than my own nature; but if I now hear a noise, if I see the sun, or if I feel heat, I have all along judged that these sensations proceeded from certain objects existing out of myself; and, in fine, it appears to me that sirens, hippogryphs, and the like, are inventions of my own mind. But I may even perhaps come to be of opinion that all my ideas are of the class which I call adventitious, or that they are all innate, or that they are all factitious, for I have not yet clearly discovered their true origin; and what I have here principally to do is to consider, with reference to those that appear to come from certain objects without me, what grounds there are for thinking them like these objects. . . .

But, among these my ideas, besides that which represents myself, respecting which there can be here no difficulty, there is one that represents a God; others that represent corporeal and inanimate things; others angels; others animals; and, finally, there are some that represent men

[1] René Descartes, *Meditations on the First Philosophy,* tr. John Veitch (1853); excerpts from Meditation III, "Of God: That He Exists;" (original French version 1641).

like myself. But with respect to the ideas that represent other men, or animals, or angels, I can easily suppose that they were formed by the mingling and composition of the other ideas which I have of myself, of corporeal things, and of God, although there were, apart from myself, neither men, animals, nor angels. And with regard to the ideas of corporeal objects, I never discovered in them anything so great or excellent which I myself did not appear capable of originating; for, by considering these closely and scrutinising them individually, in the same way that I yesterday examined the idea of wax, I find that there is but little in them that is clearly and distinctly perceived. As belonging to the class of things that are clearly apprehended, I recognise the following, viz., magnitude or extension in length, breadth, and depth; figure, which results from termination of extension; situation, which bodies of diverse figures preserve with reference to each other; and motion of the change of situation; to which may be added substance, duration, and number. But with regard to light, colours, sounds, odours, tastes, heat, cold and the other tactile qualities, they are thought with so much obscurity and confusion, that I cannot determine even whether they are true or false; in other words, whether or not the ideas I have of these qualities are in truth the ideas of real objects. For although I before remarked that it is only in judgments that formal falsity, or falsity properly so called, can be met with, there may nevertheless be found in ideas a certain material falsity, which arises when they represent what is nothing as if it were something. Thus, for example, the ideas I have of cold and heat are so far from being clear and distinct, that I am unable from them to discover whether cold is only the privation of heat, or heat the privation of cold; or whether they are or are not real qualities: and since, ideas being as it were images, there can be none that does not seem to us to represent some object, the idea which represents cold as something real and positive will not improperly be called false, if it be correct to say that cold is nothing but a privation of heat; and so in other cases. To ideas of this kind, indeed, it is not necessary that I should assign any author besides myself: for if they are false, that is, represent objects that are unreal, the natural light teaches me that they proceed from nothing; in other words, that they are in me only because something is wanting to the perfection of my nature; but if these ideas are true, yet because they exhibit to me so little reality that I cannot even distinguish the object represented from non-being, I do not see why I should not be the author of them.

With reference to those ideas of corporeal things that are clear and distinct, there are some which, as appears to me, might have been taken from the idea I have of myself, as those of substance, duration, number, and the like. For when I think that a stone is a substance, or a thing

capable of existing of itself, and that I am likewise a substance, although
I conceive that I am a thinking and non-extended thing, and that the
stone, on the contrary, is extended and unconscious, there being thus
the greatest diversity between the two concepts, — yet these two ideas
seem to have this in common that they both represent substances. In
the same way, when I think of myself as now existing, and recollect besides that I existed some time ago, and when I am conscious of various
thoughts whose number I know, I then acquire the ideas of duration and
number, which I can afterwards transfer to as many objects as I please.
With respect to the other qualities that go to make up the ideas of
corporeal objects, viz., extension, figure, situation, and motion, it is true
that they are not formally in me, since I am merely a thinking being; but
because they are only certain modes of substance, and because I myself
am a substance, it seems possible that they may be contained in me eminently.

There only remains, therefore, the idea of God, in which I must consider whether there is anything that cannot be supposed to originate
with myself. By the name God, I understand a substance infinite [eter-
nal, immutable], independent, all-knowing, all-powerful, and by which
I myself, and every other thing that exists, if any such there be, were
created. But these properties are so great and excellent, that the more
attentively I consider them the less I feel persuaded that the idea I have
of them owes its origin to myself alone. And thus it is absolutely necessary to conclude, from all that I have before said, that God exists: for
though the idea of substance be in my mind owing to this, that I myself
am a substance, I should not, however, have the idea of an infinite substance, seeing I am a finite being, unless it were given me by some substance in reality infinite.

And I must not imagine that I do not apprehend the infinite by a true
idea, but only be the negation of the finite, in the same way that I comprehend repose and darkness by the negation of motion and light: since,
on the contrary, I clearly perceive that there is more reality in the infinite
substance than in the finite, and therefore that in some way I possess the
perception (notion) of the infinite before that of the finite, that is, the
perception of God before that of myself, for how could I know that I
doubt, desire, or that something is wanting to me, and that I am not
wholly perfect, if I possessed no idea of a being more perfect than myself, by comparison of which I knew the deficiences of my nature?

And it cannot be said that this idea of God is perhaps materially false,
and consequently that it may have arisen from nothing [in other words,
that it may exist in me from my imperfection], as I before said of the
ideas of heat and cold, and the like: for, on the contrary, as this idea is

very clear and distinct, and contains in itself more objective reality than any other, there can be no one of itself more true, or less open to the suspicion of falsity.

The idea, I say, of a being supremely perfect, and infinite, is in the highest degree true; for although, perhaps, we may imagine that such a being does not exist, we cannot, nevertheless, suppose that his idea represents nothing real, as I have already said of the idea of cold. It is likewise clear and distinct in the highest degree, since whatever the mind clearly and distinctly conceives as real or true, and as implying any perfection, is contained entire in this idea. And this is true, nevertheless, although I do not comprehend, nor perhaps even compass by thought in any way; for it is of the nature of the infinite that it should not be comprehended by the finite; and it is enough that I rightly understand this, and judge that all which I clearly perceive, and in which I know there is some perfection, and perhaps also an infinity of properties of which I am ignorant, are formally or eminently in God, in order that the idea I have of him may become the most true, clear, and distinct of all the ideas in my mind.

But perhaps I am something more than I suppose myself to be, and it may be that all those perfections which I attribute to God, in some way exist potentially in me, although they do not yet show themselves, and are not reduced to act. Indeed, I am already conscious that my knowledge is being increased [and perfected] by degrees; and I see nothing to prevent it from thus gradually increasing to infinity, nor any reason why, after such increase and perfection, I should not be able thereby to acquire all the other perfections of the Divine nature; nor, in fine, why the power I possess of acquiring those perfections, if it really now exist in me, should not be sufficient to produce the ideas of them. Yet, on looking more closely into the matter, I discover that this cannot be; for, in the first place, although it were true that my knowledge daily acquired new degrees of perfection, and although there were potentially in my nature much that was not as yet actually in it, still all these excellences make not the slightest approach to the idea I have of the Deity, in whom there is not perfection merely potentially [but all actually] existent; for it is even an unmistakable token of imperfection in my knowledge, that it is augmented by degrees. Further, although my knowledge increase more and more, nevertheless I am not, therefore, induced to think that it will ever be actually infinite, since it can never reach that point beyond which it shall be incapable of further increase. But I conceive God as actually infinite, so that nothing can be added to his perfection. And, in fine, I readily perceive that the objective being of an idea cannot be produced by a being that is merely potentially existent, which, properly speaking, is nothing, but only by a being existing formally or actually.

And, truly, I see nothing in all that I have now said which it is not easy for any one, who shall carefully consider it, to discern by the natural light; but when I allow my attention in some degree to relax, the vision of my mind being obscured, and, as it were, blinded by the images of sensible objects, I do not readily remember the reason why the ideas of a being more perfect than myself, must of necessity have proceeded from a being in reality more perfect. On this account I am here desirous to inquire further, whether I, who possess this idea of God could exist supposing there were no God. And I ask, from whom could I, in that case derive my existence? Perhaps from myself, or from my parents, or from some other causes less perfect than God; for anything more perfect, even equal to God, cannot be thought or imagined. But if I [were independent of every other existence, and] were myself the author of my being, I should doubt of nothing, I should desire nothing, and, in fine, no perfection would be awanting to me; for I should have bestowed upon myself every perfection of which I possess the idea, and I should thus be God. And it must not be imagined that what is now wanting to me is perhaps of more difficult acquisition than that of which I am already possessed; for, on the contrary, it is quite manifest that it was a matter of much higher difficulty that I, a thinking being, should arise from nothing, than it would be for me to acquire the knowledge of many things of which I am ignorant, and which are merely the accidents of a thinking substance; and certainly, if I possessed of myself the greater perfection of which I have now spoken [in other words, if I were the author of my own existence], I would not at least have denied to myself things that may be more easily obtained [as that infinite variety of knowledge of which I am at present destitute]. I could not, indeed, have denied to myself any property which I perceive is contained in the idea of God, because there is not of these that seems to me to be more difficult to make or acquire; and if there were any that should happen to be more difficult to acquire, they would certainly appear so to me (supposing that I myself were the source of the other things I possess), because I should discover in them a limit to my power. And though I were to suppose that I always was as I now am, I should not, on this ground, escape the force of these reasonings, since it would not follow, even on this supposition, that no author of my existence needed to be sought after. For the whole time of my life may be divided into an infinity of parts, each of which is in no way dependent on any other; and, accordingly, because I was in existence a short time ago, it does not follow that I must now exist, unless in this moment some cause create me anew, as it were, — that is, conserve me. In truth, it is perfectly clear and evident to all who will attentively consider the nature of duration that the conservation of a substance, in each moment of its duration, requires the same power and act that would be necessary to create it, supposing it were not yet in existence; so that it is manifestly a dictate of the natural light that conservation and creation differ merely in respect of our mode of thinking [and not in reality]. All that is here required, therefore, is that I interrogate myself to discover whether I possess any power by means of which I can bring it about that I, who now am, shall exist a moment afterwards; for, since I am merely a thinking thing (or since, at least, the precise question, in the meantime, is only of that part of myself), if such a power resided in me, I should, without doubt, be conscious of it; but I am conscious of no such power, and thereby I manifestly know that I am dependent upon some being different from myself. . . .

There remains only the inquiry as to the way in which I received this idea from God; for I have not drawn it from the senses, nor is it even presented to me unexpectedly, as is usual with the ideas of sensible objects, when these are presented or appear to be presented to the external organs of the senses; it is not even a pure production or fiction of my mind, for it is not in my power to take from or add to it; and consequently there but remains the alternative that it is innate, in the same way as is the idea of myself. And, in truth, it is not to be wondered at that God, at my creation, implanted this idea in me, that it might serve, as it were, for the mark of the workman impressed on his work; and it is not alone necessary that the mark should be something different from the work itself; but considering only that God is my creator, it is highly probable that he in some way fashioned me after his own image and likeness, and that I perceive this likeness, in which is contained the idea of God, by the same faculty by which I apprehend myself, — in other words, when I make myself the object of reflection, I not only find that I am an incomplete [imperfect] and dependent being, and one who unceasingly aspires after something better and greater than he is; but, at the same time, I am assured likewise that he upon whom I am dependent possesses in himself all the goods after which I aspire [and the ideas of which I find in my mind], and that not merely indefinitely and potentially, but infinitely and actually, and that he is thus God. And the whole force of the argument of which I have here availed myself to establish the existence of God, consists in this, that I perceive I could not possibly be of such a nature as I am, and yet have in my mind the idea of a God, if God did not in reality exist, — this same God, I say, whose idea is in my mind — that is, a being who possesses all those lofty perfections, of which the mind may have some slight conception, without, however, being able fully to comprehend them, — and who is wholly superior to all defect [and has nothing that marks imperfection]: whence it is sufficiently manifest that he cannot be a deceiver, since it is a dictate of the natural light that all fraud and deception spring from some defect.

BLAISE PASCAL

Blaise Pascal (1623-1662), French philosopher, scientist, and author, from Port Royal and Paris, was born in Clermont-Ferrand on June 19, 1623. At the young age of twelve, he wrote a treatise on sounds; at sixteen, an essay on conic sections, and before he was twenty, he constructed an arithmetical machine. Later, he advanced a theory of probability, invented the hydraulic press, instruments for measuring atmospheric pressure, and other appliances, but his fame lies in the area of religious philosophy to which he contributed his **Pensées** (1670). The selection used in the present text is Pascal's celebrated argument for God, termed the **Religious Wager.** His only other major work is his **Provincial Letters** (1656-1657).

Pascal founded his philosophy of mysticism on Skepticism, arguing on the premise that science and philosophy are incapable of mathematical certainty and evidence; consequently man must rest content with accepting the dictates of his heart (the heart has its reasons that the mind cannot know); the heart's impulses or feelings direct human conduct, not logical reasoning.

This being the case, rational proof of God's existence is neither capable nor desirable, but requires that an act of faith be exercised, and cast in favor of the existence of Deity. Pascal's argument for God's existence, the Religious Wager, asserts that man is confronted with two and only two possibilities regarding the existence of Deity: either God exists or he does not; if you accept the belief that he does exist then, you lose nothing even if the idea should turn out erroneously, but if you elect to deny God's existence and awaken from death discovering that he is very much a reality, then you may have everything to lose, eternally. The wager is a forced option; abstention from voting is impossible; your behavior marks you as either a Theist or an Atheist.

4

BLAISE PASCAL

The Religious Wager[1]

Infinite — nothing. — Our soul is cast into a body, where it finds number, time, dimension. Thereupon it reasons, and calls this nature, necessity, and can believe nothing else.

Unity joined to infinity adds nothing to it, no more than one foot to an infinite measure. The finite is annihilated in the presence of the infinite, and becomes a pure nothing. So our spirit before God, so our justice before divine justice. There is not so great a disproportion between our justice and that of God, as between unity and infinity.

The justice of God must be vast like His compassion. Now justice to the outcast is less vast, and ought less to offend our feelings than mercy towards the elect.

We know that there is an infinite, and are ignorant of its nature. As we know it to be false that numbers are finite, it is therefore true that there is an infinity in number. But we do not know what it is. It is false that it is even, it is false that it is odd; for the addition of a unit can make no change in its nature. Yet it is a number, and every number is odd or even (this is certainly true of every finite number.) So we may well know that there is a God without knowing what He is. Is there not one substantial truth, seeing there are so many things which are not the truth itself?

We know then the existence and nature of the finite, because we also are finite and have extension. We know the existence of the infinite, and are ignorant of its nature, because it has extension like us, but not limits like us. But we know neither the existence nor the nature of God, because He has neither extension nor limits.

But by faith we know His existence; in glory we shall know His nature.

[1] Blaise Pascal, *Pensées*, tr. William Finlayson Trotter (1904) from the edition of Léon Brunschvicg (1897), #233; the date of the original *Pensées* is 1670.

Now, I have already shown that we may well know the existence of a thing, without knowing its nature.

Let us now speak according to natural lights.

If there is a God, He is infinitely incomprehensible, since having neither parts nor limits, He has no affinity to us. We are then incapable of knowing either what He is or if He is. This being so, who will dare to undertake the decision of the question? Not we, who have no affinity to Him.

Who then will blame Christians for not being able to give a reason for their belief, since they profess a religion for which they cannot give a reason? They declare, in expounding it to the world, that it is a foolishness, *stultitiam;* and then you complain that they do not prove it! If they proved it, they would not keep their word; it is in lacking proofs, that they are not lacking in sense. "Yes, but although this excuses those who offer it as such, and takes away from them the blame of putting it forward without reason, it does not excuse those who receive it." Let us then examine this point, and say, "God is, or He is not." But to which side shall we incline? Reason can decide nothing here. There is an infinite chaos which separated us. A game is being played at the extremity of this infinite distance where heads or tails will turn up. What will you wager? According to reason, you can do neither the one thing nor the other; according to reason, you can defend neither of the propositions.

Do not then reprove for error those who have made a choice; for you know nothing about it. "No, but I blame them for having made, not this choice, but a choice; for again both he who chooses heads and he who chooses tails are equally at fault, they are both in the wrong. The true course is not to wager at all."

Yes; but you must wager. It is not optional. You are embarked. Which will you choose then? Let us see. Since you must choose, let us see which interests you least. You have two things to lose, the true and the good; and two things to stake, your reason and your will, your knowledge and your happiness; and your nature has two things to shun, error and misery. Your reason is no more shocked in choosing one rather than the other, since you must of necessity choose. This is one point settled. But your happiness? Let us weigh the gain and the loss in wagering that God is. Let us estimate these two chances. If you gain, you gain all; if you lose, you lose nothing. Wager, then, without hesitation that He is. — "That is very fine. Yes, I must wager; but I may perhaps wager too much." — Let us see. Since there is an equal risk of gain and of loss, if you had only to gain two lives, instead of one, you might wager. But if there were three lives to gain, you would have to play (since you are under the necessity of playing), and you would be imprudent, when you are forced to play, not to chance your life to gain three at a game where there is an equal risk of loss and gain. But there is an eternity of life and happiness. And this being so, if there were an infinity of chances, of which one only would be for you, you would still be right in wagering one to win two, and you would act stupidly, being obliged to play, by refusing to stake one life against three at a game in which out of an infinity of chances there is one for you, if there were an infinity of an infinitely happy life to gain. But there is here an infinity of an infinitely happy life to gain, a chance of gain against a finite number of chances of loss, and what you stake is finite. It is all divided; wherever the infinite is and there is not time to hesitate, you must give all. And thus, when one is forced to play, he must renounce reason to preserve his life, rather than risk it for infinite gain, as likely to happen as the loss of nothingness.

For it is no use to say it is uncertain if we will gain, and it is certain that we risk, and that the infinite distance between the *certainty* of what is staked and the *uncertainty* of what will be gained, equals the finite good which is certainly staked against the uncertain infinite. It is not so, as every player stakes a certainty to gain an uncertainty, and yet he stakes a finite certainty to gain a finite uncertainty, without transgressing against reason. There is not an infinite distance between the certainty staked and the uncertainty of the gain; that is untrue. In truth, there is an infinity between the certainty of gain and the certainty of loss. But the uncertainty of the gain is proportioned to the certainty of the stake according to the proportion of chances of gain and loss. Hence it comes that, if there are as many risks on the one side as on the other, the course is to play even; and then the certainty of the stake is equal to the uncertainty of the gain, so far is it from fact that there is an infinite distance between them. And so our proposition is of infinite force, when there is the finite to stake in a game where there are equal risks of gain and of loss, and the infinite to gain. This is demonstrable; and if men are capable of any truths, this is one.

"I confess it, I admit it. But, still, is there no means of seeing the faces of the cards?" — Yes, Scripture and the rest, etc. "Yes, but I have my hands tied and my mouth closed; I am forced to wager, and am not free. I am not released, and am so made that I cannot believe. What, then, would you have me do?"

True. But at least learn your inability to believe, since reason brings you to this, and yet you cannot believe. Endeavour then to convince yourself, not by increase of proofs of God, but by the abatement of your passions. You would like to attain faith, and do not know the way; you would like to cure yourself of unbelief, and ask the remedy for it. Learn of those who have been bound like you, and who now stake all their possessions. These are people who know the way which you would follow, and who are cured of an ill of which you would be cured. Follow the way by which they began; by acting as if they believed, taking the holy water, having masses said, etc. Even this will naturally make you believe, and deaden your acuteness. — "But this is what I am afraid of." — And why? What have you to lose?

But to show you that this leads you there, it is this which will lessen the passions, which are your stumbling-blocks.

The end of this discourse. — Now, what harm will befall you in taking this side? You will be faithful, honest, humble, grateful, generous, a sincere friend, truthful. Certainly you will not have those poisonous pleasures, glory and luxury; but will you not have others? I will tell you that you will thereby gain in this life, and that, at each step you take on this road, you will see so great certainty of gain, so much nothingness in what you risk, that you will at last recognise that you have wagered for something certain and infinite, for which you have given nothing.

"Ah! This discourse transports me, charms me," etc.

If this discourse pleases you and seems impressive, know that it is made by a man who has knelt, both before and after it, in prayer to that Being, infinite and without parts, before whom he lays all he has, for you also to lay before Him all you have for your own good and for His glory, that so strength may be given to lowliness.

ISAAC NEWTON

Isaac Newton (1642-1727), English natural philosopher and mathematician, was born in Woolsthorpe, Lincolnshire on Christmas day, 1642. For two years he attended the free grammar school of Grantham, and later another school, in preparation for Cambridge, matriculating at Trinity College in 1661. He graduated with the Bachelor of Arts degree in 1665, the same year in which he discovered the binomial theorem, and in the following year, he discovered the differential and integral calculus (an honor which he shares with Leibniz). He then proceeded to the discovery of the law of gravity, and began work on optics and color, all within the years 1665 and 1666, "the prime of life" (as he put it) at only twenty-three to twenty-four years of age. The year 1667 found him a fellow of Trinity at Cambridge, and in 1672, a Fellow of the Royal Society, where in 1703, he became its president with Queen Anne knighting him in 1705.

Among his works are the immortal **Philosophiae Naturalis Principia Mathematica** (1687), **Optics** (1704), **Arithmetica Universalis** (1707-1712), **Methodus Differentialism** (1711), **Chronology of the Ancient Kingdoms Amended** (1728), and **Observation or Daniel and the Apocalypse** (1733),

Newton's argument for the existence of God is established on the presence of order in the cosmos, including the behavior of the solar system and animal nature. For Newton, the world was constructed as if it knew geometry and the science of mechanics. Respecting this point, he writes: "To make this system, therefore, with all its motions, required a cause which understood and compared together the quantities of matter in the several bodies of the sun and planets and the gravitating powers resulting from thence, the several distances of the primary planets from the sun and of the secondary ones from Saturn, Jupiter, and the earth, and the velocities with which these planets could revolve about those quantities of matter in the central bodies; and to compare and adjust all these things together, in so great a variety of bodies, argues that cause to be, not blind and fortuitous, but very well skilled in mechanics and geometry." [1] Newton felt each time he discovered a new scientific law that he was thinking God's thoughts after him.

[1] Isaac Newton, **Opera Omnia**, letter to Rev. Richard Bentley.

31

5

ISAAC NEWTON

The Teleological Argument for God's Existence[1]

. . . When I wrote my treatise about our system, I had an eye upon such principles as might work with considering men for the belief of a Deity; and nothing can rejoice me more than to find it useful for that purpose. But if I have done the public any service this way, it is due to nothing but industry and patient thought.

As to your first query, it seems to me that if the matter of our sun and planets and all the matter of the universe were evenly scattered throughout all the heavens, and every particle had an innate gravity toward all the rest, and the whole space throughout which this matter was scattered was but finite, the matter on the outside of this space would, by its gravity, tend toward all the matter on the inside and, by consequence, fall down into the middle of the whole space and there compose one great spherical mass. But if the matter was evenly disposed throughout an infinite space, it could never convene into one mass; but some of it would convene into one mass and some into another, so as to make an infinite number of great masses, scattered at great distances from one to another throughout all that infinite space. And thus might the sun and fixed stars be formed, supposing the matter were of a lucid nature. But how the matter should divide itself into two sorts, and that part of it which is fit to compose a shining body should fall down into one mass and make a sun and the rest which is fit to compose an opaque body should coalesce, not into one great body, like the shining matter, but into many little ones; or if the sun at first were an opaque body like the planets or the planets lucid bodies like the sun, how he alone should be changed into opaque ones whilst he remains unchanged, I do not think explicable by mere natural causes, but am forced to ascribe it to the counsel and contrivance of a voluntary Agent.

[1] Isaac Newton, *Opera Omnia* (1779-1785); letter to the Reverend Richard Bentley, at the Bishop of Worcester's House, in Park Street, Westminster.

The same Power, whether natural or supernatural, which placed the sun in the center of the six primary planets, placed Saturn in the center of the orbs of his five secondary planets and Jupiter in the center of his four secondary planets, and the earth in the center of the moon's orb; and therefore, had this cause been a blind one, without contrivance or design, the sun would have been a body of the same kind with Saturn, Jupiter, and the earth, that is, without light and heat. Why there is one body in our system qualified to give light and heat to all the rest, I know no reason but because the Author of the system thought it convenient; and why there is but one body of this kind, I know no reason but the Cartesian hypothesis of suns losing their light and then turning into comets, and comets into planets, can have no place in my system and is plainly erroneous; because it is certain that, as often as they appear to us, they descend into the system of our planets, lower than the orb of Jupiter and sometimes lower than the orbs of Venus and Mercury, and yet never stay here, but always return from the sun with the same degrees of motion by which they approached him.

To your second query, I answer that the motions which the planets now have could not spring from any natural cause alone, but were impressed by an intelligent Agent. For since comets descend into the region of our planets and here move all manner of ways, going sometimes the same way with the planets, sometimes the contrary way, and sometimes in crossways, in places inclined to the plane of the ecliptic and at all kinds of angles, it is plain that there is no natural cause which could determine all the planets, both primary and secondary, to move the same way and in the same plane, without any considerable variation; this must have been the effect of counsel. Nor is there any natural cause which could give the planets those just degrees of velocity, in proportion to their distances from the sun and other central bodies, which were requisite to make them move in such concentric orbs about those bodies. Had the planets been as swift as comets, in proportion to their distances from the sun (as they would have been had their motion been caused by their gravity, whereby the matter, at the first formation of the planets, might fall from the remotest regions toward the sun), they would not move in concentric orbs, but in such eccentric ones as the comets move in. Were all the planets as swift as Mercury or as slow as Saturn or his satellites, or were their several velocities otherwise much greater or less than they are, as they might have been had they arose from any other cause than their gravities, or had the distances from the centers about which they move been greater or less than they are, with the same velocities, or had the quantity of matter in the sun or in Saturn, Jupiter, and the earth, and by consequence their gravitating power, been greater or less that it is, the primary planets could not have revolved about the sun nor the secondary ones about Saturn, Jupiter, and the earth, in concentric circles, as they do, but would have moved in hyperbolas or parabolas or in ellipses very eccentric. To make this system, therefore, with all its motions, required a cause which understood and compared together the quantities of matter in the several bodies of the sun and planets and the gravitating powers resulting from thence, the several distances of the primary planets from the sun and of the secondary ones from Saturn, Jupiter, and the earth, and the velocities with which these planets could revolve about those quantities of matter in the central bodies; and to compare and adjust all these things together, in so great a variety of bodies, argues that cause to be, not blind and fortuitous, but very well skilled in mechanics and geometry.

To your third query, I answer that it may be represented that the sun may, by heating those planets most of which are nearest to him, cause them to be better concocted and more condensed by that concoction. But when I consider that our earth is much more heated in its bowels below the upper crust by subterraneous fermentations of mineral bodies that by the sun, I see not why the interior parts of Jupiter and Saturn might not be as much heated, concocted, and coagulated by those fermentations as our earth is; and therefore this various density should have some other cause than the various distances of the planets from the sun. And I am confirmed in this opinion by considering that the planets of Jupiter and Saturn, as they are rarer than the rest, so they are vastly greater and contain a far greater quantity of matter, and have many satellites about them; which qualifications surely arose, not from their being placed at so great a distance from the sun, but were rather the cause why the Creator placed them at great distance. For, by their gravitating powers, they disturb one another's motions very sensibly, as I find by some late observations of Mr. Flamsteed; and had they been placed much nearer to the sun and to one another, they would, by the same powers, have caused a considerable disturbance in the whole system.

To your fourth query, I answer that, in the hypothesis of vortices, the inclination of the axis of the earth might, in my opinion, be ascribed to the situation of the earth's vortex before it was absorbed by the neighboring vortices and the earth turned from a sun to a comet; but this inclination ought to decrease constantly in compliance with the motion of the earth's vortex, whose axis is much less inclined to the ecliptic, as appears by the motion of the moon carried about therein. If the sun by his rays could carry about the planets, yet I do not see how he could thereby effect their diurnal motions.

ISAAC NEWTON: *The Teleological Argument for God's Existe*

Lastly, I see nothing extraordinary in the inclination of the earth's ax for proving a Deity, unless you will urge it as a contrivance for winter and summer, and for making the earth habitable toward the poles; and that the diurnal rotations of the sun and planets, as they could hardly arise from any cause purely mechanical, so by being determined all the same way with the annual and menstrual motions they seem to make up that harmony in the system which, as I explained above, was the effect of choice rather than chance.

There is yet another argument for a Deity, which I take to be a very strong one; but till the principles on which it is grounded are better received, I think it more advisable to let it sleep. . . .

IMMANUEL KANT

IMMANUEL KANT (1724-1804), a man of Scot-German ancestry, was born in Königsberg, Germany and died there on Feb. 12, 1804. His education was limited to the schools of Königsberg, its Collegium Fredericianum and its university. When Kant's father died, he took to tutoring as a means of livelihood from 1746 to 1755. While tutoring the family of Count Kayserling, he was permitted to pursue his university career which earned him his doctorate and certification as **Privatdozent.** As **Privatdozent,** his fame grew, owing to his writings and lectures, but he had definitely arrived when, in 1770, he acquired the Chair of Logic and Metaphysics at his **alma mater.** Eleven years later, he revolutionized the philosophical world with the appearance of his **Critique of Pure Reason** (1781), which earned him a permanent place in the philosophical hall of fame. His philosophy dominated the German scene, and later the entire philosophical world. His popularity grew to the point of approaching deification by the young students who flocked to Königsberg as a shrine of philosophy. His views on philosophy of religion divided the Christian community; Frederick William II issued a mandate that Kant should desist from writing any further on religious philosophy to which the philosopher adhered until the king's demise.

The selection chosen as representative of Kant's thought, Kantian Agnosticism, is from his celebrated **Critique of Pure Reason,** and the selection favoring the existence of Deity from his classic **The Critique of Practical Reason** (1788). Other important works of his are: **Prolegomena to Any Future Metaphysic** (1783), **Foundations of the Metaphysics of Ethics** (1785), **Religion within the Limits of Pure Reason** (1784), **Perpetual Peace** (1795), **Critique of Judgment** (1790).

Kantian Agnosticism repudiates the traditional arguments for God's existence: (1) He rejects the Ontological Argument, asserting that existence does not follow from mere conception. (2) The reasoning of the Cosmological Argument is circular, for it derives a First Cause of contingent objects in an absolutely necessary Being. (3) The Teleological Argument (or as Kant terms it, the Physico-Theological Argument), by postulating harmony, beauty, adaptation, and purposiveness in the world, does prove the existence of a God, but not a **Creator** God, rather an **Architect** of the world. The failure of the traditional arguments is that they are supersensuous, transcending the bounds of legitimate experience, thereby becoming illicit forms of knowledge. The Idea of God is an Ideal of Reason, a regulative principle by which to make incomplete data of science coherent.

The only valid justification of God's existence stems not from proof, but from moral grounds, or faith. The moral order of the universe postulates the being of Deity. "Ethical consciousness requires the **reality of the highest good,** faith must reach beyond the empirical life of man, and beyond the order of Nature, on into the supersensuous. It postulates a reality of personality which extends beyond the temporal existence — the **immortal life** — and a **moral order of the universe,** which is grounded in a Supreme Reason — in God." [1] God is a necessary postulate to guarantee harmony between morality and happiness, if not now then in a life to come, the purpose being to right the wrongs of this world in a future life. The will postulates God's existence: when I will, I will as if God existed. When I will, I create not only my freedom and immortality, but God's existence as well.

[1] W. Windelband, **A History of Philosophy** (New York: The Macmillan Co., 1893), 556.

6

IMMANUEL KANT

The Moral Argument for God's Existence (The Axiological Argument)[1]

The Existence of God As a Postulate of Pure Practical Reason [1]

In the foregoing analysis the moral law led to a practical problem which is prescribed by pure reason alone, without the aid of any sensible motives, namely, that of the necessary completeness of the first and principal element of the *summum bonum,* viz. Morality; and as this can be perfectly solved only in eternity, to the postulate of *immortality.* The same law must also lead us to affirm the possibility of the second element of the *summum bonum,* viz. Happiness proportioned to that morality, and this on grounds as disinterested as before, and solely from impartial reason; that is, it must lead to the supposition of the existence of a cause adequate to this effect; in other words, it must postulate the *existence of God,* as the necessary condition of the possibility of the *summum bonum* (an object of the will which is necessarily connected with the moral legislation of pure reason). We proceed to exhibit this connexion in a convincing manner.

Happiness is the condition of a rational being in the world with whom *everything goes according to his wish and will;* it rests, therefore, on the harmony of physical nature with his whole end, and likewise with the essential determining principle of his will. Now the moral law as a law of freedom commands by determining principles, which ought to be quite independent on nature and on its harmony with our faculty of desire (as springs). But the acting rational being in the world is not the cause of the world and of nature itself. There is not the least ground, therefore, in the moral law for a necessary connexion between morality and proportionate happiness in a being that belongs to the world as part of it, and

[1] Immanuel Kant, *Critique of Practical Reason,* tr. T. K. Abbott (1898, 5th ed.), original German edition, 1788; selection from bk. II, ch. 2, sect. 5.

therefore dependent on it, and which for that reason cannot by his will be a cause of this nature, nor by his own power make it thoroughly harmonize, as far as his happiness is concerned, with his practical principles. Nevertheless, in the practical problem of pure reason, *i.e.* the necessary pursuit of the *summum bonum,* such a connexion is postulated as necessary: we ought to endeavour to promote the *summum bonum,* which, therefore, must be possible. Accordingly, the existence of a cause of all nature, distinct from nature itself, and containing the principle of this connexion, namely, of the exact harmony of happiness with morality, is also *postulated.* Now, this supreme cause must contain the principle of the harmony of nature, not merely with a law of the will of rational beings, but with the conception of this *law,* in so far as they make it the *supreme determining principle of the will, and* consequently not merely with the form of morals, but with their morality as their motive, that is, with their moral character. Therefore, the *summum bonum* is possible in the world only on the supposition of a supreme Being having a causality corresponding to moral character. Now a being that is capable of acting on the conception of laws is an *intelligence* (a rational being), and the causality of such a being according to this conception of laws is his will; therefore the supreme cause of nature which must be presupposed as a condition of the *summum bonum,* is a being which is the cause of nature by *intelligence* and *will,* consequently its author, that is God. It follows that the postulate of the possibility of the *highest derived good* (the best world) is likewise the postulate of the reality of a *highest original good,* that is to say, of the existence of God. Now it was seen to be a duty for us to promote the *summum bonum;* consequently it is not merely allowable, but it is a necessity connected with duty as a requisite, that we should presuppose the possibility of this *summum bonum;* and as this is possible only on condition of the existence of God, it inseparably connects the supposition of this with duty; that is, it is morally necessary to assume the existence of God.

· · · · · ·

The Moral Proof of the Existence of God [2]

Theoretical reflective judgment is quite justified in supposing, on the ground of a *physical teleology,* that there is an intelligent cause of the world. Now, in our own moral consciousness, and still more in the general conception of a rational being who is endowed with free causality, there is implied a *moral teleology.* But as the relation to ends, together

[2] Immanuel Kant, *Critique of Judgment,* tr. John Watson (1888), section 87 and 88.

with the laws connected with them, is determined *a priori* in ourselves, and therefore is known to be necessary, this internal conformity to law does not require for its explanation the supposition of an intelligent cause outside of ourselves. At the same time moral teleology has to do with man as a being in the world, and therefore with man as connected with other things in the world. For, in the conception of ourselves as beings under moral law, we find the standard by reference to which those other things are judged either to be ends, or to be objects subordinate to ourselves as the ultimate end. Moral teleology, then, has to do with the relation of our own causality to ends, and even to an ultimate end necessarily set up by us as our goal in the world, as well as with the possibility of realizing that end, the external world being what it is. Hence the question necessarily arises, whether reason compels us to seek, in a supreme intelligence outside of the world, for a principle which shall explain to us even the purpose in nature relatively to the law of morality within us. There is therefore a moral teleology, which is concerned on the one hand with the *nomothetic* of freedom, and on the other hand with that of nature.

If we suppose certain things, or even certain forms of things, to be contingent, and therefore to depend upon something else which is their cause, we may seek for this supreme cause, or unconditioned ground of the conditioned, either in the physical or in the teleological order. That is to say, we may either ask, what is the supreme productive cause of those things, or what is their supreme and absolutely unconditioned end, that is, the ultimate end of that cause in its production of those things, or even of all things. In the latter case it is plainly implied that the cause in question is capable of setting an end before itself, that is, is an intelligence, or at least must be thought of as acting in accordance with the laws of an intelligence.

From the teleological point of view, it is a *fundamental proposition* admitted by every one, that there can be no *ultimate end* at all presupposed by reason *a priori*, unless that end is *man as under moral laws*. A world consisting of mere lifeless things, or even containing living but unintelligent beings, would have no meaning or value, because there would be in it no intelligent being to appreciate its value. Again, suppose that in the world there are intelligent beings, whose reason enables them to value existing things for the pleasure they bring, but who have not themselves any power of imparting a value to things by means of freedom; then, there will indeed be relative ends, but there will be no absolute or ultimate end, for the existence in the world of such intelligent beings can never have an end. Moral laws, however, are of this peculiar character, that they prescribe for reason something as an end apart from all conditions, and therefore exactly as the conception of an ultimate end requires. The existence of a reason which can be for itself the supreme law in the relation of ends, in other words the existence of rational beings under moral laws, can alone be conceived as the ultimate end of the existence of a world. On any other supposition its existence does not imply a cause acting from any end, or it implies ends but no ultimate end.

The moral law, as the formal condition in reason of the use of our freedom, lays its commands on us entirely on its own authority, without appealing to any material condition as an end; but it nevertheless determines for us, and indeed *a priori* an ultimate end as the goal to which our efforts ought to be directed; and that end is the *highest good* possible *in the world* through freedom.

The subjective condition which entitles man to set before himself an ultimate end subordinate to the moral law is happiness. Hence the highest physical good possible in the world is *happiness,* and this end we must seek to advance, as far as in us lies, but always under the objective condition of the harmony of man with the law of *morality* as worthiness to be happy.

But it is impossible, in consistency with all the faculties of our intelligence, to regard the two requisites of the ultimate end presented to us through the moral law as *connected* by merely natural causes, and yet as conforming to the idea of that ultimate end. If, therefore, nature is the only cause which is connected with freedom as a means, the conception of the *practical necessity* of the ultimate end through the application of our powers, does not harmonize with the theoretical conception of the *physical possibility* of the realization of that end.

Accordingly, we must suppose a moral cause or author of the world, in order to set before ourselves an ultimate end that is conformable with the moral law; and in so far as the latter is necessary, in the same degree, and on the same ground, the former also must necessarily be admitted; it must, in other words, be admitted that there is a God.

Limitation of the Moral Proof

The ultimate end, as merely a conception of our practical reason, is not an inference from data of experience for the theoretical explanation of nature, nor can it be applied in the knowledge of nature. Its only possible use is for practical reason in relation to moral laws; and the ultimate end of creation is that constitution of the world which harmonizes with the only end which we can definitely present to ourselves as conforming to laws, namely, the ultimate end of our pure practical reason, in so far as it is the nature of reason to be practical. Now, we have in the moral law, which enjoins on us practically, the application of our powers to the realization of the ultimate end, a ground for supposing the possibility and practicability of that end, and therefore also a ground for supposing a nature of things harmonious with it. Hence we have a moral ground for representing in the world an ultimate end of creation.

So far we have not advanced from moral teleology to theology, that is, to the existence of a moral author of the world, but have merely concluded to an ultimate end of creation determined in that way. But, in order to account for this creation, that is, for the existence of things that are adapted to an *ultimate end,* in the first place an intelligent being, and in the second place not only an intelligent but a *moral* being or author of the world, that is, a God, must be admitted to exist. But this conclusion is of the judgment according to conceptions of practical reason, and as such for the reflective not the determinant judgment. It is true that in us morally practical reason is essentially different in its principles from technically practical reason. But we cannot assume that in the Supreme Cause of the world, conceived of as an intelligence, the same contrast exists, and that a peculiar kind of causality is required for the ultimate end, different in its character from that which is required merely for ends of nature. We cannot assume, therefore, that in an ultimate end we have a reason for admitting not merely a *moral ground* or ultimate end of creation as an effect, but also a *moral being* as the original ground of creation. But we may certainly say, that, *according to the constitution of our reason,* we cannot make intelligible to ourselves the possibility of an adaptation relative to the *moral law,* and to its object as it is in this ultimate end, apart from an author and ruler of the world, who is also a moral lawgiver.

Physical teleology sufficiently proves for theoretical reflective judgment an intelligent cause of the world; moral teleology proves it for the practical judgment, through the conception of an ultimate end, which must be attributed to creation when we view it in relation to action. It is true that the objective reality of the idea of God, as the moral author of the world, cannot be shown from a consideration of physical ends *alone.* But, it is a maxim of pure reason to secure unity of principles, so far as that is possible; and hence the knowledge of physical ends, when it is brought into relation with the knowledge of the moral end, greatly aids us in connecting the practical reality of the idea of God with its theoretical reality as already existing for judgment. . . .

WILLIAM PALEY

WILLIAM PALEY (1743-1805), a native of Peterborough, England, was educated at Giggleswick School where his father was headmaster; from there he attended Christ's College, Cambridge, where, upon graduation, he became a fellow in 1766, and tutor in 1768, offering courses in moral philosophy. These courses laid the foundation of his book, **View of the Evidences in Christianity** (1784); in 1785, his lectures were published under the title of **The Principles of Moral and Political Philosophy,** an attempt to synthesize Utilitarianism with Authoritarianism. Other writings of his are: **Horae Paulinae** (1790), and **Natural Theology** (1802), the work which furnishes the present text with his classic "Watch Argument" for the existence of God. Paley's genius is neither in originality nor profundity, but in the cogency of his reasoning and the lucidity of his argument.

In Paley's **Natural Theology,** we find vividly depicted by the analogy of a 'watch,' a classic and superlative presentation of the Teleological Argument for God's existence. The text permits of a dual division: (1) the proof of the existence of God as the designer of the world, and (2) proof of the attributes of Deity. Paley's argument is essentially: A watch, an instrument of many parts working harmoniously together for the resultant purpose of telling time, must be an object requiring a designer, some mind which contrived the entire mechanical feat. Accordingly, the cosmos, a mechanical apparatus expressing design of far greater magnitudinal proportions and mechanical complexities than anything like a watch, and extending beyond man's capability of creating, must have (analogous to a watch) been created by a Designer, namely God. This argument is beautifully presented by Paley, and to be appreciated fully, must be read as offered by the original author himself.

7

WILLIAM PALEY

The Classic Watch Argument
(The Teleological Argument)[1]

In crossing a heath, suppose I pitched my foot against a *stone*, and were asked how the stone came to be there; I might possibly answer, that, for any thing I knew to the contrary, it had lain there for ever nor; would it perhaps be very easy to show the absurdity of this answer. But suppose I had found a *watch* upon the ground, and it should be inquired how the watch happened to be in that place; I should hardly think of the answer which I had before given, that, for any thing I knew, the watch might have always been there. Yet why should not this answer serve for the watch as well as for the stone? why is it not as admissible in the second case, as in the first? For this reason, and for no other, viz. that, when we come to inspect the watch, we perceive (what we could not discover in the stone) that its several parts are framed and put together for a purpose, *e.g.* that they are so formed and adjusted as to produce motion, and that motion so regulated as to point out the hour of the day; that, if the different parts had been differently shaped from what they are, of a different size from what they are, or placed after any other manner, or in any other order, than that in which they are placed, either no motion at all would have been carried on in the machine, or none which would have answered the use that is now served by it. To reckon up a few of the plainest of these parts, and of their offices, all tending to one result: — We see a cylindrical box containing a coiled elastic spring, which, by its endeavour to relax itself, turns round the box. We next observe a flexible chain (artificially wrought for the sake of flexure), communicating the action of the spring from the box to the fusee. We then find a series of wheels, the teeth of which catch in, and apply to, each other, conducting the motion from the fusee to the balance, and from

---

[1] William Paley, *Natural Theology* (1802), chapters 1 and 2.

the balance to the pointer: and at the same time, by the size and shape of those wheels, so regulating that motion, as to terminate in causing an index, by an equable and measured progression, to pass over a given space in a given time. We take notice that the wheels are made of brass in order to keep them from rust; the springs of steel, no other metal being so elastic; that over the face of the watch there is placed a glass, a material employed in no other part of the work, but in the room of which, if there had been any other than a transparent substance, the hour could not be seen without opening the case. This mechanism being observed (it requires indeed an examination of the instrument, and perhaps some previous knowledge of the subject, to perceive and understand it; but being once, as we have said, observed and understood), the inference, we think, is inevitable, that the watch must have had a maker: that there must have existed, at some time, and at some place or other, an artificer or artificers who formed it for the purpose which we find it actually to answer: who comprehended its construction, and designed its use.

I. Nor would it, I apprehend, weaken the conclusion, that we had never seen a watch made; that we had never known an artist capable of making one; that we were altogether incapable of executing such a piece of workmanship ourselves, or of understanding in what manner it was performed; all this being no more than what is true of some exquisite remains of ancient art, of some lost arts, and, to the generality of mankind, of the more curious productions of modern manufacture. Does one man in a million know how oval frames are turned? Ignorance of this kind exalts our opinion of the unseen and unknown artist's skill, if he be unseen and unknown, but raises no doubt in our minds of the existence and agency of such an artist, at some former time, and in some place or other. Nor can I perceive that it varies at all the inference, whether the question arise concerning a human agent, or concerning an agent of a different nature.

II. Neither, secondly, would it invalidate our conclusion, that the watch sometimes went wrong, or that it seldom went exactly right. The purpose of the machinery, the design, and the designer, might be evident, and in the case supposed would be evident, in whatever way we accounted for the irregularity of the movement, or whether we could account for it or not. It is not necessary that a machine be perfect, in order to show with what design it was made: still less necessary, where the only question is, whether it were made with any design at all.

III. Nor, thirdly, would it bring any uncertainty into the argument, if there were a few parts of the watch, concerning which we could not discover, or had not yet discovered, in what manner they conduced to the general effect; or even some parts, concerning which we could not ascertain, whether they conduced to that effect in any manner whatever. For, as to the first branch of the case; if by the loss, or disorder, or decay of the parts in question, the movement of the watch were found in fact to be stopped, or disturbed, or retarded, no doubt would remain in our minds as to the utility or intention of these parts, although we should be unable to investigate the manner according to which, or the connexion by which, the ultimate effect depended upon their action or assistance: and the more complex is the machine, the more likely is this obscurity to arise. Then, as to the second thing supposed, namely, that there were parts which might be spared, without prejudice to the movement of the watch, and that we had proved this by experiment, — these superfluous parts, even if we were completely assured that they were such, would not vacate the reasoning which we had instituted concerning other parts. The indication of contrivance remained, with respect to them, nearly as it was before.

IV. Nor, fourthly, would any man in his senses think the existence of the watch, with its various machinery, accounted for, by being told that it was one out of possible combinations of material forms; that whatever he had found in the place where he found the watch, must have contained some internal configuration or other; and that this configuration might be the structure now exhibited, viz. of the works of a watch, as well as a different structure.

V. Nor, fifthly, would it yield his inquiry more satisfaction to be answered, that there existed in things a principle of order, which had disposed the parts of the watch into their present form and situation. He never knew a watch made by the principle of order; nor can he even form to himself an idea of what is meant by a principle of order, distinct from the intelligence of the watch-maker.

VI. Sixthly, he would be surprised to hear that the mechanism of the watch was no proof of contrivance, only a motive to induce the mind to think so.

VII. And not less surprised to be informed, that the watch in his hand was nothing more than the result of the laws of *metallic* nature. It is a perversion of language to assign any law, as the efficient, operative cause of any thing. A law presupposes an agent; for it is only the mode, according to which an agent proceeds: it implies a power; for it is the order, according to which that power acts. Without this agent, without this power, which are both distinct from itself, the *law* does nothing; is nothing. The expression, "the law of metallic nature," may sound strange and harsh to a philosophic ear; but it seems quite as justifiable as some others which are more familiar to him, such as "the law of vegetable nature," "the law of animal nature," or indeed as "the law of nature" in general, when assigned as the cause of phaenomena, in exclusion of agency and power; or when it is substituted into the place of these.

VIII. Neither, lastly, would our observer be driven out of his conclusion, or from his confidence in its truth, by being told that he knew nothing at all about the matter. He knows enough for his argument: he knows the utility of the end: he knows the subserviency and adaptation of the means to the end. These points being known, his ignorance of other points, his doubts concerning other points, affect not the certainty of his reasoning. The consciousness of knowing little need not beget a distrust of that which he does know.

· · · · ·

Suppose, in the next place, that the person who found the watch, should, after some time, discover, that, in addition to all the properties which he had hitherto observed in it, it possessed the unexpected property of producing, in the course of its movement, another watch like itself (the thing is conceivable); that it contained within it a mechanism, a system of parts, a mould for instance, or a complex adjustment of lathes, files, and other tools, evidently and separately calculated for this purpose; let us inquire, what effect ought such a discovery to have upon his former conclusion.

I. The first effect would be to increase his admiration of the contrivance, and his conviction of the consummate skill of the contriver. Whether he regarded the object of the contrivance, the distinct apparatus, the intricate, yet in many parts intelligible mechanism, by which it was carried on, he would perceive, in this new observation, nothing but an additional reason for doing what he had already done, — for referring the construction of the watch to design, and to supreme art. If that construction *without* this property, or which is the same thing, before this property had been noticed, proved intention and art to have been employed about it; still more strong would the proof appear, when he came to the knowledge of this farther property, the crown and perfection of all the rest.

II. He would reflect, that though the watch before him were, *in some sense,* the maker of the watch, which was fabricated in the course of its movements, yet it was in a very different sense from that, in which a carpenter, for instance, is the maker of a chair; the author of its contrivance, the cause of the relation of its parts to their use. With respect to these, the first watch was no cause at all to the second; in no such sense as this was it the author of the constitution and order, either of the parts which the new watch contained, or of the parts by the aid and instrumentality of which it was produced. We might possibly say, but with great latitude of expression, that a stream of water ground corn: but no latitude of expression would allow us to say, no stretch of conjecture could lead us to think, that the stream of water built the mill, though it were too ancient for us to know who the builder was. What the stream of water does in the affair, is neither more nor less that this; by the application of an unintelligent impulse to a mechanism previously arranged, arranged independently of it, and arranged by intelligence, an effect is produced, viz. the corn is ground. But the effect results from the arrangement. The force of the stream cannot be said to be the cause or author of the effect, still less of the arrangement. Understanding and plan in the formation of the mill were not the less necessary, for any share which the water has in grinding the corn: yet is this share the same, as that which the watch would have contributed to the production of the new watch, upon the supposition assumed in the last section. Therefore,

III. Though it be now no longer probable, that the individual watch, which our observer had found, was made immediately by the hand of an artificer, yet doth not this alteration in anywise affect the inference, that an artificer had been originally employed and concerned in the production. The argument from design remains as it was. Marks of design and contrivance are no more accounted for now, than they were before. In the same thing, we may ask for the cause of different properties. We may ask for the cause of the colour of a body, of its hardness, of its heat; and these causes may be all different. We are now asking for the cause of that subservience to a use, that relation to an end, which we have remarked in the watch before us. No answer is given to this question, by telling us that a preceding watch produced it. There cannot be design without a designer; contrivance, without a contriver; order, without choice; arrangement, without any thing capable of arranging; subserviency and relation to a purpose, without that which could intend a purpose; means suitable to an end, and executing their office in accomplishing that end, without the end ever having been contemplated, or the means accommodated to it. Arrangement, disposition of parts, subserviency of means to an end, relation of instruments to a use, imply the presence of intelligence and mind. No one, therefore, can rationally believe, that the insensible, inanimate watch, from which the watch before us issued, was the proper cause of the mechanism we so much admire in it; — could be truly said to have constructed the instrument, disposed its parts, assigned their office, determined their order, action, and mutual dependency, combined their several motions into one result, and that also a result connected with the utilities of other beings. All these properties, therefore, are as much unaccounted for, as they were before.

IV. Nor is any thing gained by running the difficulty farther back, *i.e.*

by supposing the watch before us to have been produced from another watch, that from a former, and so on indefinitely. Our going back ever so far, brings us no nearer to the least degree of satisfaction upon the subject. Contrivance is still unaccounted for. We still want a contriver. A designing mind is neither supplied by this supposition, nor dispensed with. If the difficulty were diminished the farther we went back, by going back indefinitely we might exhaust it. And this is the only case to which this sort of reasoning applies. Where there is a tendency, or, as we increase the number of terms, a continual approach towards a limit, *there,* by supposing the number of terms to be what is called infinite, we may conceive the limit to be attained: but where there is no such tendency, or approach, nothing is effected by lengthening the series. There is no difference as to the point in question (whatever there may be as to many points), between one series and another; between a series which is finite, and a series which is infinite. A chain, composed of an infinite number of links, can no more support itself, than a chain composed of a finite number of links. And of this we are assured (though we never *can* have tried the experiment), because, by increasing the number of links, from ten for instance to a hundred, from a hundred to a thousand, &c. we make not the smallest approach, we observe not the smallest tendency, towards self-support. There is no difference in this respect (yet there may be a great difference in several respects) between a chain of a greater or less length, between one chain and another, between one that is finite and one that is infinite. This very much resembles the case before us. The machine which we are inspecting, demonstrates, by its construction, contrivance and design. Contrivance must have had a contriver; design, a designer; whether the machine immediately proceeded from another machine or not. That circumstance alters not the case. That other machine may, in like manner, have proceeded from a former machine: nor does that alter the case; contrivance must have had a contriver. That former one from one preceding it: no alteration still; a contriver is still necessary. No tendency is perceived, no approach towards a diminution of this necessity. It is the same with any and every succession of these machines; a succession of ten, of a hundred, of a thousand; with one series, as with another; a series which is finite, as with a series which is infinite. In whatever other respects they may differ, in this they do not. In all equally, contrivance and design are unaccounted for.

The question is not simply, How came the first watch into existence? which question, it may be pretended, is done away by supposing the series of watches thus produced from one another to have been infinite, and consequently to have had no such *first,* for which it was necessary to provide a cause. This, perhaps, would have been nearly the state of the

question, if nothing had been before us but an unorganised, unmechan-
ised substance, without mark or indication of contrivance. It might be
difficult to show that such substance could not have existed from eternity,
either in succession (if it were possible, which I think it is not, for unorganised bodies to spring from one another), or by individual perpetui-
ty. But that is not the question now. To suppose it to be so, is to suppose
that it made no difference whether he had found a watch or a stone. As it
is, the metaphysics of that question have no place; for, in the watch
which we are examining, are seen contrivance, design; and end, a purpose; means for the end, adaptation to the purpose. And the question
which irresistibly presses upon our thoughts, is, whence this contrivance
and design? The thing required is the intending mind, the adapting hand,
the intelligence by which that hand was directed. This question, this
demand, is not shaken off, by increasing a number or succession of substances, destitute of these properties; nor the more, by increasing that
number to infinity. If it be said, that, upon the supposition of one watch
being produced from another in the course of that other's movements,
and by means of the mechanism within it, we have a cause for the watch
in my hand, viz. the watch from which it proceeded; I deny, that for
the design, the contrivance, the suitableness of means to an end, the
adaptation of instruments to a use (all which we discover in the watch),
we have any cause whatever. It is in vain, therefore, to assign a series of
such causes, or to allege that a series may be carried back to infinity;
for I do not admit that we have yet any cause at all of the phaenomena,
still less any series of causes either finite or infinite. Here is contrivance,
but no contriver; proofs of design, but no designer.

V. Our observer would farther also reflect, that the maker of the
watch before him, was, in truth and reality, the maker of every watch
produced from it; there being no difference (except that the latter manifests a more exquisite skill) between the making of another watch with
his own hands, by the mediation of files, lathes, chisels, &c. and the disposing, fixing, and inserting of these instruments, or of others equivalent
to them, in the body of the watch already made in such a manner, as to
form a new watch in the course of the movements which he had given to
the old one. It is only working by one set of tools, instead of another.

The conclusion which the *first* examination of the watch, of its works,
construction, and movement, suggested, was, that it must have had, for
the cause and author of that construction, an artificer, who understood its
mechanism, and designed its use. This conclusion is invincible. A *second*
examination presents us with a new discovery. The watch is found, in
the course of its movement, to produce another watch, similar to itself;
and not only so, but we perceive in it a system or organization, separately

calculated for that purpose. What effect would this discovery have, or ought it to have, upon our former inference? What, as hath already been said, but to increase, beyond measure, our admiration of the skill, which had been employed in the formation of such a machine? Or shall it, instead of this, all at once turn us round to an opposite conclusion, viz. that no art or skill whatever has been concerned in the business, although all other evidences of art and skill remain as they were, and this last and supreme piece of art be now added to the rest? Can this be maintained without absurdity? Yet this is atheism.

JOHN STUART MILL

JOHN STUART MILL (1806-1872), an English philosopher, born in London on May 20, 1806, was exclusively educated by his famous father, James Mill. John Stuart Mill knew classical Greek at three years of age, Latin at eight, logic at twelve, political economy at thirteen, and was writing articles for the **Westminster Review** at seventeen, but in consequence of his intense over-education, he suffered a breakdown at twenty. At ten, he was reading Plato in the original Greek with ease, and the same for Aristotle at twelve years of age. He accepted an appointment as examiner with the East India Company in 1823, a post he retained for thirty-five years.

Mill's influence in the philosophical world has been manifold, encompassing such broad areas as, philosophy of religion, logic, ethics, and political philosophy. His **canons**, defining scientific method relating to causation, continue to reign supreme as **the** scientific method for determining causes. His major works are: **System of Logic** (1843), **Essays on Some Unsettled Questions of Political Economy** (1844), **Principles of Political Economy** (1848), **Memorandum of the Improvements in the Administration of India** (1858), **On Liberty** (1859), **Thoughts on Parliamentary Reform** (1859), **Considerations on Representative Government** (1861), **Utilitarianism** (1863), **Examination of Sir William Hamilton's Philosophy** (1865), **Auguste Comte and Positivism** (1865), **England and Ireland** (1868), **Subjection of Women** (1869), **Autobiography** (1873), **Nature, the Utility of Religion and Theism** (1874, posthumously).

Mill was a Theist, but technically one designated a Theistic Finitist, that is, a person who believes in a benevolent though limited God involved in a world which he designed or fashioned, yet did not create. Dissatisfied with traditional arguments for God, Mill repudiates as fallacious the Ontological Argument and the Aetiological Argument (First Cause) for God, but like Hume and Kant, he accorded respect to the Teleological Argument (the Argument from Design) to such an extent that he dismisses as inconclusive the Darwinian doctrine of the Survival of the Fittest (Natural Selection) as an insufficient explanation of adaptations prevalent in nature.

For Mill, if God were an omnipotent Creator, he would be a malevolent Being for creating a world adulterated with evil, and "whatever power such a being may have over me," he writes, "there is one thing which he shall not do: compel me to worship him. I will call no being good, who is not what I mean when I apply that epithet to my fellow-creatures; and if such a being can sentence me to hell for not so calling him, then to hell I will go." But Mill is convinced that God is the benevolent Author of the "Sermon on the Mount," a morally perfect being, whose limitations of power incapacitated him from creating a world of his uninhibited choice, consequently the world was formed out of substance which he never made, or chose to use.

As to belief in immortality, Mill bases his belief in it on his theory of substance, namely "permanent possibilities of sensations" or experience. If the stuff of the world is composed of permanent possibilities of experience, then the doctrine of Materialism is destroyed and the way open for belief in the survival of a human being beyond bodily death.

Respecting miracles, particularly Hume's view of them, Mill notes that Hume did not prove the nonexistence of miracles, but rather the inadequacy of proofs offered in their support; hence, Hume's position is both negative and presumptuous. Hume's position is analogous to saying that a certain soldier did not die on a battle field because most of us did not see the man die, and the testimony of the person who did witness the death is to be rejected.

8

JOHN STUART MILL

The Argument from Design
(The Teleological Argument)[1]

We now at last reach an argument of a really scientific character,
which does not shrink from scientific tests, but claims to be judged by the
established canons of induction. The design argument is wholly grounded
on experience. Certain qualities, it is alleged, are found to be characteristic of such things as are made by an intelligent mind for a purpose. The
order of nature, or some considerable part of it, exhibit these qualities in
a remarkable degree. We are entitled, from this great similarity in the
effects, to infer similarity in the cause, and to believe that things which
it is beyond the power of man to make, but which resemble the works
of man in all but power, must also have been made by Intelligence armed
with a power greater than human.

I have stated this argument in its fullest strength, as it is stated by its
most thoroughgoing ancestors. A very little consideration, however, suffices to show that though it has some force, its force is very generally
overrated. Paley's illustration of a watch puts the case much too strongly.
If I found a watch on an apparently desolate island, I should, indeed, infer that it had been left there by a human being; but the inference would
not be from marks of design, but because I already knew by direct experience that watches are made by men. I should draw the inference no
less confidently from a footprint or from any relic, however insignificant,
which experience has taught me to attribute to man: as geologists infer
the past existence of animals from coprolites, though no one sees marks
of design in a coprolite. The evidence of design in creation can never
reach the height of direct induction; it amounts only to the inferior kind
of inductive evidence called analogy. Analogy agrees with induction in

---

[1] John Stuart Mill, *Three Essays on Religion* (1875, 4th ed.); posthumously published, first edition appeared in 1874. Mill died May 8, 1873.

this, that they both argue that a thing known to resemble another in certain circumstances (call those circumstances A and B) will resemble it in another circumstance (call it C). But the difference is that in induction A and B are known, by a previous comparison of many instances, to be the very circumstances on which C depends or with which it is in some way connected. When this has not been ascertained, the argument amounts only to this, that since it is not known with which of the circumstances existing in the known case C is connected, they may as well be A and B as any others; and therefore there is a greater probability of C in case where we know that A and B exist than in cases of which we know nothing at all. This argument is of a weight very difficult to estimate at all, and impossible to estimate precisely. It may be very strong when the known points of agreement A and B, etc., are numerous and the known points of difference few, or very weak when the reverse is the case; but it can never be equal in validity to a real induction. The resemblances between some of the arrangements in nature and some of those made by man are considerable, and even as mere resemblances afford a certain presumption of similarity of cause, but how great that presumption is it is hard to say. All that can be said with certainty is that these likenesses make creation by intelligence considerably more probable than if the likenesses had been less, or than if there had been no likeness at all.

This mode, however, of stating the case does not do full justice to the evidence of theism. The design argument is not drawn from mere resemblances in nature to the works of human intelligence, but from the special character of those resemblances. The circumstances in which it is alleged that the world resembles the works of man are not circumstances taken at random, but are particular instances of a circumstance which experience shows to have a real connection with an intelligent origin — the fact of conspiring to an end. The argument therefore is not one of mere analogy. As mere analogy it has its weight, but it is more than analogy. It surpasses analogy as induction surpasses it. It is an inductive argument.

This, I think, is undeniable, and it remains to test the argument by the logical principles applicable to induction. For this purpose it will be convenient to handle, not the argument as a whole, but some one of the most impressive cases of it, such as the structure of the eye or of the ear. It is maintained that the structure of the eye proves a designing mind. To what class of inductive arguments does this belong, and what is its degree of force?

The species of inductive arguments are four in number, corresponding to the four inductive methods: the methods of agreement, of difference, of residues, and of concomitant variations. The argument under consideration falls within the first of these divisions, the method of agreement. This is, for reasons known to inductive logicians, the weakest of the four, but the particular argument is a strong one of the kind. It may be logically analyzed as follows:

The parts of which the eye is composed, and the collocations which constitute the arrangement of those parts, resemble one another in this very remarkable property, that they all conduce to enabling the animal to see. These things being as they are, the animal sees: if any one of them were different from what it is, the animal, for the most part, would either not see or would not see equally well. And this is the only marked resemblance that we can trace among the different parts of this structure beyond the general likeness of composition and organization which exists among all other parts of the animal. Now the particular combination of organic elements called an eye had, in every instance, a beginning in time and must therefore have been brought together by a cause or causes. The number of instances is immeasurably greater than is, by the principles of inductive logic, required for the exclusion of a random concurrence of independent causes; or, speaking technically, for the elimination of chance. We are therefore warranted by the canons of induction in concluding that what brought all these elements together was some cause common to them all; and in as much as the elements agree in the single circumstance of conspiring to produce sight there must be come connection by way of causation between the cause which brought those elements together, and the fact of sight.

This I conceive to be legitimate inductive inference, and the sum and substance of what induction can do for theism. The natural sequel of the argument would be this: Sight, being a fact not precedent but subsequent to the putting together of the organic structure of the eye, can only be connected with the production of that structure in the character of a final, not an efficient, cause; that is, it is not sight itself but an antecedent idea of it that must be the efficient cause. But this at once marks the origin as proceeding from an intelligent will.

I regret to say, however, that this latter half of the argument is not so inexpugnable as the former half. Creative forethought is not absolutely the only link by which the origin of the wonderful mechanism of the eye may be connected with the fact of sight. There is another connecting link on which attention has been greatly fixed by recent speculations, and the reality of which cannot be called in question, though its adequacy to account for such truly admirable combinations as some of those in nature is still and will probably long remain problematical. This is the principle of "the survival of the fittest."

This principle does not pretend to account for the commencement of sensation or of animal or vegetable life. But assuming the existence of some one or more very low forms of organic life in which there are no complex adaptations nor any marked appearances of contrivance, and supposing, as experience warrants us in doing, that many small variations from those simple types would be thrown out in all directions, which would be transmissible by inheritance, and of which some would be advantageous to the creature in its struggle for existence and others disadvantageous, the forms which are advantageous would always tend to survive and those which are disadvantageous to perish. And thus there would be a constant though slow general improvement of the type as it branched out into many different varieties, adapting it to different media and modes of existence until it might possibly, in countless ages, attain to the most advanced examples which now exist.

It must be acknowledged that there is something very startling, and *prima facie* improbable in this hypothetical history of nature. It would require us, for example, to suppose that the primeval animal of whatever nature it may have been could not see and had at most such slight preparation for seeing as might be constituted by some chemical action of light upon its cellular structure. One of the accidental variations which are liable to take place in all organic beings would at some time or other produce a variety that could see in some imperfect manner, and this peculiarity being transmitted by inheritance, while other variations continued to take place in other directions, a number of races would be produced who, by the power of even imperfect sight, would have a great advantage over all other creatures which could not see and would in time extirpate them from all places, except, perhaps, a few very peculiar situations underground. Fresh variations supervening would give rise to races with better and better seeing powers until we might at last reach as extraordinary a combination of structures and functions as are seen in the eye of man and of the more important animals. Of this theory when pushed to this extreme point, all that can now be said is that it is not so absurd as it looks, and that the analogies which have been discovered in experience, favorable to its possibility, far exceed what anyone could have supposed beforehand. Whether it will ever be possible to say more than this is at present uncertain. The theory if admitted would be in no way whatever inconsistent with creation. But it must be acknowledged that it would greatly attenuate the evidence for it.

Leaving this remarkable speculation to whatever fate the progress of discovery may have in store for it, I think it must be allowed that in the present state of our knowledge the adaptations in nature afford a large balance of probability in favor of creation by intelligence. It is equally certain that this is no more than a probability, and that the various other arguments of natural theology which we have considered add nothing to its force. Whatever ground there is, revelation apart, to believe in an Author of Nature is derived from the appearances in the universe. Their mere resemblance to the works of man, or to what man could do if he had the same power over the materials of organized bodies which he has over the materials of a watch, is of some value as an argument of analogy: but the argument is greatly strengthened by the properly inductive considerations which establish that there is some connection through causation between the origin of the arrangements of nature and the ends they fulfill — an argument which is in many cases slight, but in others, and chiefly in the nice and intricate combinations of vegetable and animal life, is of considerable strength.

JOHN FISKE

JOHN FISKE (1842-1901) was born in Hartford, Conn. on March 30, 1842. In 1869, he began teaching at Harvard University in Cambridge, Mass., from which school he was graduated in 1863, and remained there until his death at Gloucester, Mass., July 4, 1901. Trained in law, as well as philosophy, history, and languages, he practiced law in Boston, but his attention was centered on writing and lecturing in philosophy. At Harvard, he taught philosophy and history, and later assumed responsibilities as assistant librarian at its Widener Library.

Fiske's beautiful and free flowing style of writing earned him recognition as America's greatest interpreter of the Theory of Evolution; he has done more than any other American writer to diffuse the Evolutionary Naturalism of Charles Darwin and Herbert Spencer in the United States, rendering them palatable and consonant with religious belief. His important works are: **Outlines of Cosmic Philosophy** (1874), **The Unseen World** (1876), **Darwinianism and Other Essays** (1879), **The Destiny of Man** (1884), **The Idea of God** (1885), **Through Nature to God** (1899), **Life Everlasting** (1901).

A confirmed Evolutionist, Fiske viewed the world of events, animate and human, as the efforts of an immanent God actively engaged in a world of his own creation. God, basically personal in nature, consciously concerned for results of his handiwork, especially his highest creative activity, man, takes special pains to insure the conservation of these values, namely the survival of man to immortality. God's activity in the world of nature indicates a decided tendency toward the highest possible development of man, ethically and spiritually.

Fiske depicts God's relationship to the world, not as artificer in the sense of Paley's contriver in the designing of watches, but as the responsible quasi-personal Being developing a living, progressive, active, vital process which is yet in the making, and tending toward its designed objective, higher psychic life of superior spiritual and ethical qualities.

9

JOHN FISKE

The Evolutionary Argument for God
(The Teleological Argument)[1]

Simile of the Watch Replaced by Simile of the Flower

It was in its own chosen stronghold that this once famous argument was destined to meet its doom. It was in the adaptations of the organic world, in the manifold harmonies between living creatures and surrounding circumstances, that it had seemed to find its chief support; and now came the Darwinisn theory of natural selection, and in the twinkling of an eye knocked all this support from under it. It is not that the organism and its environment have been adapted to each other by an exercise of creative intelligence, but it is that the organism is necessarily fitted to the environment because in the perennial slaughter that has gone on from the beginning only the fittest have survived. Or, as it has been otherwise expressed, "the earth is suited to its inhabitants because it has produced them, and only such as suit it live." In the struggle for existence no individual peculiarity, however slight, that tends to the preservation of life is neglected. It is unerringly seized upon and propagated by natural selection, and from the cumulative action of such slight causes have come the beautiful adaptations of which the organic world is full. The demonstration of this point, through the labours of a whole generation of naturalists, has been one of the most notable achievements of modern science, and to the theistic arguments of Paley and the Bridgewater treatises it has dealt destruction.

But the Darwinian theory of natural selection does not stand alone. It is part of a greater whole. It is the most conspicuous portion of that doctrine of evolution in which all the results hitherto attained by the great modern scientific movement are codified and which Herbert Spencer had already begun to set forth in its main outlines before the Darwinian

[1] John Fiske, *The Idea of God As Affected by Modern Knowledge* (1885), selections from Chapters 10 and 14.

theory had been made known to the world. This doctrine of evolution so far extends the range of our vision through past and future time as entirely to alter our conception of the universe. Our grandfathers, in common with all preceding generations of men, could and did suppose that at some particular moment in the past eternity the world was created in very much the shape which it has at present. But our modern knowledge does not allow us to suppose anything of the sort. We can carry back our thoughts through a long succession of great epochs, some of them many millions of years in duration, in each of which the innumerable forms of life that covered the earth were very different from what they were in all the others, and in even the nearest of which they were notably different from what they are now . . . . And through the vast sweep of time, from the simple primeval vapour down to the multifarious world we know to-day, we see the various forms of Nature coming into existence one after the other in accordance with laws of which we are already beginning to trace the character and scope. Paley's simile of the watch is no longer applicable to such a world as this. It must be replaced by the simile of the flower. The universe is not a machine, but an organism, with an indwelling principle of life. It was not made, but it has grown.

That such a change in our conception of the universe marks the greatest revolution that has ever taken place in human thinking need scarcely be said. But even in this statement we have not quite revealed the depth of the change. Not only has modern science made it clear that the varied forms of Nature which make up the universe have arisen through a process of evolution, but it has also made it clear that what we call the laws of Nature have been evolved through the self-same process. The axiom of the persistence of force, upon which all modern science has come to rest, involves as a necessary corrollary the persistence of the relations between forces; so that, starting with the persistence of force and the primary qualities of matter, it can be shown that all those uniformities of coexistence and succession which we call natural laws have arisen one after the other in connection with the forms which have afforded the occasions for their manifestation. The all-pervading harmony of Nature is thus itself a natural product, and the last inch of ground is cut away from under the theologians who suppose the universe to have come into existence through a supernatural process of manufacture at the hands of a Creator outside of itself.

The Power That Makes for Righteousness

Although it was the Darwinian theory of natural selection which overthrew the argument from design, yet . . . when thoroughly understood it will be found to replace as much teleology as it destroys. Indeed, the doctrine of evolution, in all its chapters, has a certain teleological aspect, although it does not employ those methods which in the hands of the champions of final causes have been found so misleading. The doctrine of evolution does not regard any given arrangement of things as scientifically explained when it is shown to subserve some good purpose, but it seeks its explanation in such antecedent conditions as may have been competent to bring about the arrangement in question. Nevertheless, the doctrine of evolution is not only perpetually showing us the purposes which the arrangements of Nature subserve, but throughout one large section of the ground which it covers it points to a discernible dramatic tendency, a clearly-marked progress of events toward a mighty goal. Now it especially concerns us to note that this large section is just the one, and the only one, which our powers of imagination are able to compass. The astronomic story of the universe is altogether too vast for us to comprehend in such wise as to tell whether it shows any dramatic tendency or not. But in the story of the evolution of life upon the surface of our earth, where alone we are able to compass the phenomena, we see all things working together, through countless ages of toil and trouble, toward one glorious consummation. It is therefore a fair inference, though a bold one, that if our means of exploration were such that we could compass the story of all the systems of worlds that shine in the spacious firmament, we should be able to detect a similar meaning. At all events, the story which we can decipher is sufficiently impressive and consoling. It clothes our theistic belief with moral significance, reveals the intense and solemn reality of religion, and fills the heart with tidings of great joy.

The glorious consummation toward which organic evolution is tending is the production of the highest and most perfect psychical life. Already the germs of this conclusion existed in the Darwinian theory as originally stated, though men were for a time too busy with other aspects of the theory to pay due attention to them. In the natural selection of such individual peculiarities as conduce to the survival of the species, and in the evolution by this process of higher and higher creatures endowed with capacities for a richer and more varied life, there might have been seen a well-marked dramatic tendency, toward the *dénouement* of which every one of the myriad little acts of life and death during the entire series of geologic aeons was assisting. The whole scheme was teleological, and each single act of natural selection had a teleological meaning. Herein lies the reason why the theory so quickly destroyed that of Paley. It did not merely refute it, but supplanted it with explanations which had the merit of being truly scientific, while at the same time they hit the mark at which natural theology had unsuccessfully aimed.

Such was the case with the Darwinian theory as first announced. But since it has been more fully studied in its application to the genesis of Man, a wonderful flood of light has been thrown upon the meaning of evolution, and there appears a reasonableness in the universe such as had not appeared before. It has been shown that the genesis of Man was due to a change in the direction of the working of natural selection, whereby physical variations were selected to the neglect of physical variations. It has been shown that one chief result of this change was the lengthening of infancy, whereby Man appeared on the scene as a plastic creature capable of unlimited psychical progress. It has been shown that one chief result of the lengthening of infancy was the origination of the family and of human society endowed with rudimentary moral ideas and moral sentiments. It has been shown that through these coöperating processes the difference between Man and all lower creatures has come to be a difference in kind transcending all other differences; that his appearance upon the earth marked the beginning of the final stage in the process of development, the last act in the great drama of creation; and that all the remaining work of evolution must consist in the perfecting of the creature thus marvellously produced. It has been further shown that the perfecting of Man consists mainly in the ever-increasing predominance of the life of the soul over the life of the body. And lastly, it has been shown that, whereas the earlier stages of human progress have been characterized by a struggle for existence like that through which all lower forms of life have been developed, nevertheless the action of natural selection upon Man is coming to an end, and his future development will be accomplished through the direct adaptation of his wonderfully plastic intelligence to the circumstances in which it is placed. Hence it has appeared that war and all forms of strife, having ceased to discharge their normal function, and having thus become unnecessary, will slowly die out; that the feelings and habits adapted to ages of strife will ultimately perish from disuse; and that a stage of civilization will be reached in which human sympathy shall be all in all, and the spirit of Christ shall reign supreme throughout the length and breadth of the earth.

These conclusions, with the grounds upon which they are based, have been succinctly set forth in my little book entitled "The Destiny of Man Viewed in the Light of his Origin." Startling as they may have seemed to some, they are no more so than many of the other truths which have been brought home to us during this unprecedented age. They are the fruit of a wide induction from the most vitally important facts which the doctrine of evolution has set forth; and they may fairly claim recognition as an integral body of philosophic doctrine fit to stand the test of time. Here they are summarized as the final step in my argument concerning the true nature of theism. They add new meanings to the idea of God, as it is affected by modern knowledge, while at the same time they do but give articulate voice to time-honoured truths which it was feared the skepticism of our age might have rendered dumb and powerless. For if we express in its most concentrated form the meaning of these conclusions regarding Man's origin and destiny, we find that it affords the full justification of the fundamental ideas and sentiments which have animated religion at all times. We see Man still the crown and glory of the universe and the chief object of divine care, yet still the lame and halting creature, loaded with a brute-inheritance of original sin, whose ultimate salvation is slowly to be achieved through ages of moral discipline. We see the chief agency which produced him — natural selection which always works through strife — ceasing to operate upon him, so that, until human strife shall be brought to an end, there goes on a struggle between his lower and his higher impulses, in which the higher must finally conquer. And in all this we find the strongest imaginable incentive to right living, yet one that is still the same in principle with that set forth by the great Teacher who first brought men to the knowledge of the true God.

As to the conception of Deity, in the shape impressed upon it by our modern knowledge, I believe I have now said enough to show that it is no empty formula or metaphysical abstraction which we would seek to substitute for the living God. The infinite and eternal Power that is manifested in every pulsation of the universe is none other than the living God. We may exhaust the resources of metaphysics in debating how far his nature may fitly be expressed in terms applicable to the psychical nature of Man; such vain attempts will only serve to show how we are dealing with a theme that must ever transcend our finite powers of conception. But of some things we may feel sure. Humanity is not a mere local incident in an endless and aimless series of cosmical changes. The events of the universe are not the work of chance, neither are they the outcome of blind necessity. Practically there is a purpose in the world whereof it is our highest duty to learn the lesson, however well or ill we may fare in rendering a scientific account of it. When from the dawn of life we see all things working together toward the evolution of the highest spiritual attributes of Man, we know, however the words may stumble in which we try to say it, that God is in the deepest sense a moral Being. The everlasting source of phenomena is none other than the infinite Power that makes for righteousness. . . .

JOSIAH ROYCE

JOSIAH ROYCE (1855-1916), America's foremost Hegelian Absolute Idealist, was born in Grass Valley, California on Nov. 20, 1855, and died in Cambridge, Mass. on Sept. 14, 1916. Royce's higher education began at the University of California, where, on graduation in 1875, he continued graduate studies at Leipzig and Göttingen, Germany in 1876; the school year of 1877-1878 was spent at Johns Hopkins University. His professional career began at the University of California in 1878, but in 1882, William James was instrumental in his appointment as Instructor in Philosophy at Harvard University, where he stayed for the remainder of his career, but not without a promotion in 1885 to Assistant Professor, and, in 1892, to Professor of History of Philosophy.

Royce, one of philosophy's most articulate spokesmen, attained literary reputation for his distinguished style and lucidity of writing. His philosophical works comprise: **A Primer of Logical Analysis** (1881), **The Religious Aspect of Philosophy** (1885), **The Spirit of Modern Philosophy** (1892), **The Conception of God** (1897), **Studies of Good and Evil** (1898), **The Conception of Immortality** (1900, the Ingersoll lecture for 1899), **The World and the Individual** (1900-1901, the Gifford Lectures for 1899-1900), **Outlines of Psychology** (1903), **Herbert Spencer** (1904), **The Philosophy of Loyalty** (1908), **William James and Other Essays on the Philosophy of Life** (1911), **Sources of Religious Insight** (1912), **The Problem of Christianity** (1913, 2 vols.), **War and Insurance** (1914), **The Hope of the Great Community** (1917, posthumously), **Lectures on Modern Idealism** (1919, posthumously).

The essence of Royce's Absolute Idealism is found in chapter eleven of his **The Religious Aspect of Philosophy** (a portion of which is here included), and again in lecture eleven of **The Spirit of Modern Philosophy.** Royce repudiates Materialism on the grounds that it is indefinable, unknowable, inconceivable, hence impossible, and thus opens the way to Idealism. The presence in the world of error and truth imply an Absolute Mind because "both error and truth are possible only if an idea can aim at its special object and that an Absolute Mind is needed to bring the aiming relation about." [1] Regarding the problem of evil, Royce, like the Pantheist Spinoza before him, treats evil as an illusion. A Pantheist is compelled to dismiss evil either as ignorance or illusion, otherwise God, being the sum total of all which exists, including humanity, would be implicated in evil.

[1] Julius Seelye Bixler, **Encyclopedia of Religion** (New York: Philosophical Library, Inc., 1945), article entitled: "Josiah Royce."

10

JOSIAH ROYCE

The Argument from Abstract Truth[1]

Now that our argument is completed as an investigation, let us review it in another way. We started from the fact of Error. That there is error is indubitable. What is, however, an error? The substance of our whole reasoning about the nature of error amounted to the result that in and of itself alone, no single judgment is or can be an error. Only as actually included in a higher thought, that gives to the first its completed object, and compares it therewith, is the first thought an error. It remains otherwise a mere mental fragment, a torso, a piece of drift-wood, neither true nor false, objectless, no complete act of thought at all. But the higher thought must include the opposed truth, to which the error is compared in that higher thought. The higher thought is the whole truth, of which the error is by itself an incomplete fragment.

Now, as we saw with this as a starting-point, there is no stopping-place short of an Infinite Thought. The possibilities of error are infinite. Here is this stick, this brickbat, this snow-flake: there is an infinite mass of error possible about any one of them, and notice, not merely possible is it, but actual. All the infinite series of blunders that you could make about them not only would be blunders, but in very truth now are blunders, though you personally could never commit them all. You cannot in fact *make* a truth or a falsehood by your thought. You only *find* one. From all eternity that truth was true, that falsehood false. Very well then, that infinite thought must somehow have had all that in it from the beginning. If a man doubts it, let him answer our previous difficulties. Let him show us how he can make an error save through the presence of an actual inclusive thought for which the error always was error and never became such at all. If he can do that, let him try. We

---

[1] Josiah Royce, *The Religious Aspect of Philosophy* (Boston: Houghton Mifflin and Co., 1885); from section IX, "Absolute Idealism As the Result of the Chapter," of chapter XI, "The Possibility of Error."

should willingly accept the result if he could show it to us. But he cannot. We have rambled over those barren hills already too long. Save for Thought there is no truth, no error. Save for inclusive Thought, there is no truth, no error, in separate thoughts. Separate thoughts as such cannot then know or have the distinction between their own truth and their own falsity in themselves, and apart from the inclusive thought. There is then nothing of truth or of error to be found in the world of separate thoughts as such. All the thoughts are therefore in the last analysis actually true or false, only for the all-including Thought, the Infinite.

We could have reached the same result had we set out from the problem, *What is Truth?* We chose not to do so because our skepticism had the placid answer ready: "No matter *what* truth is, for very likely there is little or no truth at all to be had. Why trouble one's mind to define what a fairy or a brownie is?" "Very well, then," we said to our skepticism, "if that is thy play, we know a move that thou thinkest not of. We will not ask thee of truth, if thou thinkest there is none. We will ask thee of error, wherein thou revelest." And our skepticism very cheerfully, if somewhat incoherently, answers, that, "if there be little or no truth here below, there is at least any amount of error, which as skeptics we have all been detecting ever since we first went to school." "We thank thee for the word, oh friend, but now, what is an error?" Blessed be Socrates for that question. Upon that rock philosophy can, if it wants, build we know not yet how much.

It is enough for the moment to sum up the truth that we have found. It is this: "*All reality must be present to the Unity of the Infinite Thought.*" There is no chance of escape. For all reality is reality because true judgments can be made about it. And all reality, for the same reason, can be the object of false judgments. Therefore, since the false and the true judgments are all true or false as present to the infinite thought, along with their objects, no reality can escape. You and I and all of us, all good, all evil, all truth, all falsehood, all things actual and possible, exist as they exist, and are known for what they are, in and to the absolute thought; are therefore all judged as to their real character at this everlasting throne of judgment.

This we have found to be true, because we tried to doubt everything. We shall try to expound in the coming chapter the religious value of the conception.[2] We can however at once see this in it: The Infinite Thought must, knowing all truth, include also a knowledge of all wills, and of their conflict. For him all this conflict, and all the other facts of the moral world, take place. He then must know the outcome of the con-

---

[2] See the excerpts by Royce on the chapters treating "Concepts of God," and "Evil."

flict, that Moral Insight of our first book. In him then we have the Judge of our ideals, and the Judge of our conduct. He must know the exact value of the Good Will, which for him, like all other possible truth, must be an actually realized Fact. And so we cannot pause with a simply theoretical idealism. Our doctrine is practical too. We have found not only an infinite Seer of physical facts, but an infinite Seer of the Good as well as of the Evil. He knows what we have and what we lack. In looking for goodness we are in no wise looking for what the real world does not contain.

This, we say, we have found as a truth, because we tried to doubt everything. We have taken the wings of the morning, and we have fled; but behold, we are in the midst of the Spirit. Truly the words that some people have thought so fantastic ought henceforth to be put in the text-books as commonplaces of logical analysis: —

> "They reckon ill that leave me out;
> When me they fly, I am the wings,
> I am the doubter and the doubt." —

Everything finite we can doubt, but not the Infinite. That eludes even our skepticism. The world-builders, and the theodicies that were to justify them, we could well doubt. The apologetic devices wearied us. All the ontologies of the realistic schools were just pictures, that we could accept or reject as we chose by means of postulates. We tried to escape them all. We forsook all those gods that were yet no gods; but here we have found something that abides, and waxes not old, something in which there is no variableness, neither shadow of turning. No power it is to be resisted, no planmaker to be foiled by fallen angels, nothing finite, nothing striving, seeking, losing, altering, growing weary; the All-Enfolder it is, and we know its name. Not Heart, nor Love, though these also are in it and of it; Thought it is, and all things are for Thought, and in it we live and move.

WILLIAM JAMES

WILLIAM JAMES (1842-1910), born in New York City on Jan. 11, 1842, a brother of the noted novelist Henry James, trained for a career in medicine at Harvard Medical School. From 1867 to 1868, he interrupted his medical school career to study psychology with Helmholtz in Germany; while there he came under the influence of the philosophy of Renouvier, particularly his concept of free-will. Returning home, he earned his degree in medicine from Harvard in 1870, and there accepted an appointment as Instructor of Physiology from 1872 to 1876. Then followed a period of psychological interests which climaxed in his world renowned **Principles of Psychology** (1890) and a professorship in psychology at Harvard. In the 1890's his interest turned to philosophy; Harvard appointed him Professor of Philosophy; he delivered the celebrated Gifford Lectures (1899-1901), the Lowell Lectures (1906), and the Hibbert Lectures at Oxford (1909).

Some authorities regard James as the foremost of all American philosophers. As one of the founders of Pragmatism, he infused it into every aspect of his philosophy, characterizing his philosophy of religion as well, as the selections from his **The Will to Believe** (1897) will indicate. Other influential philosophical writings are: **Human Immortality** (1898), **Talks to Teachers on Psychology and to Students on Some of Life's Ideals** (1899), **The Varieties of Religious Experience** (1902, the Gifford Lectures), **Pragmatism** (1906), **Essays in Radical Empiricism** (1912), **A Pluralistic Universe** (1909), **Some Problems of Philosophy** (1911), **The Meaning of Truth** (1909).

Pragmatism is a philosophy which lays stress on the practical consequences regarding any issue; the test of an idea is determined in the light of its workability. If an idea does not work, then it cannot be true. The Pragmatist and Radical Empiricist, James, caring more for practical purposes and what a thing is experienced as, rather than its metaphysical reality per se, either dismisses metaphysics entirely or remains content with an incomplete metaphysics. **The Will to Believe** particularly illustrates this point by indicating the necessary choices which a person must make

70

in everyday practical living, particularly in matters pertaining to religion. Religion, and the concomitant choices relating thereto, cannot be ignored; for all practical purposes we must recognize and accept them as facts of experience, and deal with them accordingly.

James' position pertaining to the problem of immortality is that of removing the greatest obstacle to its acceptance, namely assuming the cause of the soul to be the body. James contends that the mind is not a **productive** function (causal) of the body, but only a **transmissive** one, hence when the veil of the soul, viz. the body, is removed, the soul is liberated.

11

WILLIAM JAMES

The Will to Believe (The Pragmatic Argument)[1]

. . . I have brought with me to-night something like a sermon on justification by faith to read to you, — I mean an essay in justification *of* faith, a defence of our right to adopt a believing attitude in religious matters, in spite of the fact that our merely logical intellect may not have been coerced. 'The Will to Believe,' accordingly, is the title of my paper. . . .

I.

Let us give the name of *hypothesis* to anything that may be proposed to our belief; and just as the electricians speak of live and dead wires, let us speak of any hypothesis as either *live* or *dead*. A live hypothesis is one which appeals as a real possibility to him to whom it is proposed. If I ask you to believe in the Mahdi, the notion makes no electric connection with your nature, — it refuses to scintillate with any credibility at all. As an hypothesis it is completely dead. To an Arab, however (even if he be not one of the Mahdi's followers), the hypothesis is among the mind's possibilities: it is alive. This shows that deadness and liveness in an hypothesis are not intrinsic properties, but relations to the individual thinker. They are measured by his willingness to act. The maximum of liveness in an hypothesis means willingness to act irrevocably. Practically, that means belief; but there is some believing tendency wherever there is willingness to act at all.

Next, let us call the decision between two hypotheses an *option*. Options may be of several kinds. They may be — 1, *living* or *dead*; 2, *forced* or *avoidable*; 3, *momentous* or *trivial*; and for our purposes we may call an option a *genuine* option when it is of the forced, living, and momentous kind.

[1] William James, *The Will To Believe* (1897).

1. A living option is one in which both hypotheses are live ones. If I say to you: "Be a theosophist or be a Mohammedan," it is probably a dead option, because for you neither hypothesis is likely to be alive. But if I say: "Be an agnostic or be a Christian," it is otherwise: trained as you are, each hypothesis makes some appeal, however small, to your belief.

2. Next, if I say to you: "Choose between going out with your umbrella or without it," I do not offer you a genuine option, for it is not forced. You can easily avoid it by not going out at all. Similarly, If I say, "Either love me or hate me," "Either call my theory true or call it false," your option is avoidable. You may remain indifferent to me, neither loving nor hating, and you may decline to offer any judgment as to my theory. But if I say, "Either accept this truth or go without it," I put on you a forced option, for there is no standing place outside of the alternative. Every dilemma based on a complete logical disjunction, with no possibility of not choosing, is an option of this forced kind.

3. Finally, if I were Dr. Nasen and proposed to you to join my North Pole expedition, your option would be momentous; for this would probably be your only similar opportunity, and your choice now would either exclude you from the North Pole sort of immortality altogether or put at least the chance of it into your hands. He who refuses to embrace a unique opportunity loses the prize as surely as if he tried and failed. *Per contra,* the option is trivial when the opportunity is not unique, when the stake is insignificant, or when the decision is reversible if it later prove unwise. Such trivial options abound in the scientific life. A chemist finds an hypothesis live enough to spend a year in its verification: he believes in it to that extent. But if his experiments prove inconclusive either way, he is quit for his loss of time, no vital harm being done.

It will facilitate our discussion if we keep all these distinctions well in mind.

II.

The next matter to consider is the actual psychology of human opinion. When we look at certain facts, it seems as if our passional and volitional nature lay at the root of all our convictions. When we look at others, it seems as if they could do nothing when the intellect had once said its say. Let us take the latter facts up first.

Does it not seem preposterous on the very fact of it to talk of our opinions being modifiable at will? Can our will either help or hinder our intellect in its perceptions of truth? Can we, by just willing it, believe that Abraham Lincoln's existence is a myth, and that the portraits of

him in McClure's Magazine are all of some one else? Can we, by any
effort of our will, or by any strength of wish that it were true, believe
ourselves well and about when we are roaring with rheumatism in bed,
or feel certain that the sum of the two one-dollar bills in our pocket
must be a hundred dollars? We can *say* any of these things, but we are
absolutely impotent to believe them; and of just such things is the
whole fabric of the truths that we do believe in made up, — matters of
fact, immediate or remote, as Hume said, and relations between ideas,
which are either there or not there for us if we see them so, and which
if not there cannot be put there by any action of our own.

In Pascal's Thoughts there is a celebrated passage known in literature
as Pascal's wager. In it he tries to force us into Christianity by reasoning
as if our concern with truth resembled our concern with the stakes in a
game of chance. Translated freely his words are these: You must either
believe or not believe that God is — which will you do? Your human
reasons cannot say. A game is going on between you and the nature of
things which at the day of judgment will bring out either heads or tails.
Weigh what your gains and your losses would be if you should stake all
you have on heads, or God's existence: if you win in such case, you gain
eternal beatitude; if you lose, you lose nothing at all. If there were an
infinity of chances, and only one for God in this wager, still you ought to
stake your all on God; for though you surely risk a finite loss by this procedure, and finite loss is reasonable, even a certain one is reasonable, if
there is but the possibility of infinite gain. Go, then, and take holy water,
and have masses said; belief will come and stupefy your scruples, — *Cela
vous fera croire et vous abêtira.* Why should you not? At bottom, what
have to lose?

You probably feel that when religious faith expresses itself thus, in the
language of the gaming-table, it is put to its last trumps. Surely Pascal's
own personal belief in masses and holy water had far other springs; and
this celebrated page of his is but an argument for others, a last desperate
snatch at a weapon against the hardness of the unbelieving heart. We
feel that a faith in masses and holy water adopted wilfully after such a
mechanical calculation would lack the inner soul of faith's reality; and
if we were ourselves in the place of the Deity, we should probably take
particular pleasure in cutting off believers of this pattern from their infinite reward. It is evident that unless there be some pre-existing tendency to believe in masses and holy water, the option offered to the will
by Pascal is not a living option. Certainly no Turk ever took to masses
and holy water on its account; and even to us Protestants these means of
salvation seem such foregone impossibilities that Pascal's logic, invoked
for them specifically, leaves us unmoved. As well might the Mahdi write to

us saying, "I am the Expected One whom God has created in his efful-gence. You shall be infinitely happy if you confess me; otherwise you shall be cut off from the light of the sun. Weigh, then, your infinite gain if I am genuine against your finite sacrifice if I am not!" His logic would be that of Pascal; but he would vainly use it on us, for the hypothesis he offers us is dead. No tendency to act on it exists in us to any degree. . . .

III.

. . . Evidently, then, our non-intellectual nature does influence our convictions. There are passional tendencies and volitions which run be-fore and others which come after belief, and it is only the latter that are too late for the fair; and they are not too late when the previous passional work has been already in their own direction. Pascal's argument, instead of being powerless, then seems a regular clincher, and is the last stroke needed to make our faith in the masses and holy water complete. The state of things is evidently far from simple; and pure insight and logic, whatever they might do ideally, are not the only things that really do produce our creeds.

IV.

Our next duty, having recognized this mixed-up state of affairs, is to ask whether it be simply reprehensible and pathological, or whether, on the contrary, we must treat it as a normal element in making up our minds. The thesis I defend is, briefly stated, this: *Our passional nature not only lawfully may, but must, decide an option between propositions, whenever it is a genuine option that cannot by its nature be decided on intellectual grounds; for to say, under such circumstances, "Do not decide, but leave the question open," is itself a passional decision, — just like deciding yes or no, — and is attended with the same risk of losing the truth.* The thesis thus abstractly expressed will, I trust, soon become quite clear. . . .

·   ·   ·   ·   ·

IX.

Moral questions immediately present themselves as questions whose solution cannot wait for sensible proof. A moral question is a question not of what sensibly exists, but of what is good, or would be good if it did exist. Science can tell us what exists; but to compare the *worths*, both of what exists and of what does not exist, we must consult not science, but what Pascal calls our heart. Science herself consults her heart when she lays it down that the infinite ascertainment of fact and correction of false belief are the supreme goods for man. Challenge the statement, and science can only repeat it oracularly, or else prove it by showing that such ascertainment and correction bring man all sorts of other goods which man's heart in turn declares. The question of having moral beliefs at all or not having them is decided by our will. Are our moral preferences true or false, or are they only odd biological phenomena, making things good or bad for *us,* but in themselves indifferent. How can your pure intellect decide? If your heart does not *want* a world of moral reality, your head will assuredly never make you believe in one. Mephistophelian scepticism, indeed, will satisfy the head's play-instincts much better than any rigorous idealism can. Some men (even at the student age) are so naturally cool-hearted that the moralistic hypothesis never has for them any pungent life, and in their supercilious presence the hot young moralist always feels strangely ill at ease. The appearance of knowingness is on their side, of *naïveté* and gullibility on his. Yet, in the inarticulate heart of him, he clings to it that he is not a dupe, and that there is a realm in which (as Emerson says) all their wit and intellectual superiority is no better than the cunning of a fox. Moral scepticism can no more be refuted or proved by logic than intellectual scepticism can. When we stick to it that there *is* truth (be it of either kind), we do so with our whole nature, and resolve to stand or fall by the results. The sceptic with his whole nature adopts the doubting attitude; but which of us is the wiser, Omniscience only knows.

Turn now from these wide questions of good to a certain class of questions of fact, questions concerning personal relations, states of mind between one man and another. *Do you like me or not?* — for example. Whether you do or not depends, in countless instances, on whether I meet you half-way, am willing to assume that you must like me, and show you trust and expectation. The previous faith on my part in your liking's existence is in such cases what makes your liking come. But if I stand aloof, and refuse to budge an inch until I have objective evidence, until you shall have done something apt, as the absolutists say, *ad extorquendum assensum meum,* ten to one your liking never comes. How many women's hearts are vanquished by the mere sanguine insistence of some man that they *must* love him! he will not consent to the hypothesis that they cannot. The desire for a certain kind of truth here brings about that special truth's existence; and so it is in innumerable cases of other sorts. Who gains promotions, boons, appointments, but the man in whose life they are seen to play the part of live hypotheses, who discounts them, sacrifices other things for their sake before they have come, and takes risks for them in advance? His faith acts on the powers above him as a claim, and creates its own verification.

A social organism of any sort whatever, large or small, is what it is because each member proceeds to his own duty with a trust that the other members will simultaneously do theirs. Wherever a desired result is achieved by the co-operation of many independent persons, its existence as a fact is a pure consequence of the precursive faith in one another of those immediately concerned. A government, an army, a commercial system, a ship, a college, an athletic team, all exist on this condition, without which not only is nothing achieved, but nothing is even attempted. A whole train of passengers (individually brave enough) will be looted by a few highwaymen, simply because the latter can count on one another, while each passenger fears that if he makes a movement of resistance, he will be shot before any one else backs him up. If we believed that the whole car-full would rise at once with us, we should each severally rise, and train-robbing would never even be attempted. There are, then, cases where a fact cannot come at all unless a preliminary faith exists in its coming. *And where faith in a fact can help create the fact,* that would be an insane logic which should say that faith running ahead of scientific evidence is the 'lowest kind of immorality' into which a thinking being can fall. Yet such is the logic by which our scientific absolutists pretend to regulate our lives!

X.

In truths dependent on our personal action, then, faith based on desire is certainly a lawful and possibly an indispensable thing.

But now, it will be said, these are all childish human cases, and have nothing to do with great cosmical matters, like the question of religious faith. Let us then pass on to that. Religions differ so much in their accidents that in discussing the religious question we must make it very generic and broad. What then do we now mean by the religious hypothesis? Science says things are; morality says some things are better than other things; and religion says essentially two things.

First, she says that the best things are the more eternal things, the overlapping things, the things in the universe that throw the last stone, so to speak, and the final word. "Perfection is eternal," — this phrase of Charles Secrétan seems a good way of putting this first affirmation of religion, an affirmation which obviously cannot yet be verified scientifically at all.

The second affirmation of religion is that we are better off even now if we believe her first affirmation to be true.

Now, let us consider what the logical elements of this situation are *in case the religious hypothesis in both its branches be really true.* (Of course, we must admit that possibility at the outset. If we are to discuss the question at all, it must involve a living option. If for any of you religion be a hypothesis that cannot, by any living possibility be true, then you need go no farther. I speak to the 'saving remnant' alone.) So proceeding, we see, first, that religion offers itself as a *momentous* option. We are supposed to gain, even now, by our belief, and to lose by our nonbelief, a certain vital good. Secondly, religion is a *forced* option, so far as that good goes. We cannot escape the issue by remaining sceptical and waiting for more light, because, although we do avoid error in that way *if religion be untrue,* we lose the good, *if it be true,* just as certainly as if we positively chose to disbelieve. It is as if a man should hesitate indefinitely to ask a certain woman to marry him because he was not perfectly sure that she would prove an angel after he brought her home. Would he not cut himself off from that particular angel-possibility as decisively as if he went and married some one else? Scepticism then, is not avoidance of option; it is option of a certain particular kind of risk. *Better risk loss of truth than chance of error,* — that is your faith-vetoer's exact position. He is actively playing his stake as much as the believer is; he is backing the field against the religious hypothesis, just as the believer is backing the religious hypothesis against the field. To preach scepticism to us as a duty until 'sufficient evidence' for religion be found, is tantamount therefore to telling us, when in presence of the religious hypothesis, that to yield to our fear of its being error is wiser and better than to yield to our hope that it may be true. It is not intellect against all passions, then; it is only intellect with one passion laying down its law. And by what, forsooth, is the supreme wisdom of this passion warranted? Dupery for dupery, what proof is there that dupery through hope is so much worse than dupery through fear? I, for one, can see no proof; and I simply refuse obedience to the scientist's command to imitate his kind of option, in a case where my own stake is important enough to give me the right to choose my own form of risk. If religion be true and the evidence for it be still insufficient, I do not wish, by putting your extinguisher upon my nature (which feels to me as if it had after all some business in this matter), to forfeit my sole chance in life of getting upon the winning side, — that chance depending, of course, on my willingness to run the risk of acting as if my passional need of taking the world religiously might be prophetic and right.

All this is on the supposition that it really may be prophetic and right, and that, even to us who are discussing the matter, religion is a live hypothesis which may be true. Now, to most of us religion comes in a still further way that makes a veto on our active faith even more illogical. The more perfect and more eternal aspect of the universe is represented in our religions as having personal form. The universe is no longer a mere *It* to us, but a *Thou,* if we are religious; and any relation that may be possible from person to person might be possible here. For instance, although in one sense we are passive portions of the universe, in another we show a curious autonomy, as if we were small active centres on our own account. We feel, too, as if the appeal of religion to us were made to our own active good-will, as if evidence might be forever withheld from us unless we met the hypothesis half-way. To take a trivial illustration: just as a man who in a company of gentlemen made no advances, asked a warrant for every concession, and believed no one's word without proof, would cut himself off by such churlishness from all the social rewards that a more trusting spirit would earn, — so here, one who should shut himself up in a snarling logicality and try to make the gods extort his recognition willy-nilly, or not get it at all, might cut himself off forever from his only opportunity of making the god's acquaintance. This feeling, forced on us we know not whence, than by obstinately believing that there are gods (although not to do so would be so easy both for our logic and our life) we are doing the universe the deepest service we can, seems part of the living essence of the religious hypothesis. If the hypothesis *were* true in all its parts, including this one, then pure intellectualism, with its veto on our making willing advances, would be an absurdity; and some participation of our sympathetic nature would be logically required. I, therefore, for one, cannot see my way to accepting the agnostic rules for truth-seeking, or wilfully agree to keep my willing nature out of the game. I cannot do so for this plain reason, that *a rule of thinking which would absolutely prevent me from acknowledging certain kinds of truth if those kinds of truth were really there, would be an irrational rule.* That for me is the long and the short of the formal logic of the situation, no matter what the kinds of truth might materially be.

I confess I do not see how this logic can be escaped. But sad experience makes me fear that some of you may still shrink from radically saying with me, *in abstracto,* that we have the right to believe at our own risk any hypothesis that is live enough to tempt our will. I suspect, however, that if this is so, it is because you have got away from the abstract logical point of view altogether, and are thinking (perhaps without realizing it) of some particular religious hypothesis which for you is dead. The freedom to 'believe what we will' you apply to the case of some patent superstition; and the faith you think of is the faith defined by the schoolboy when he said, "Faith is when you believe something that you know ain't true." I can only repeat that this is misapprehension. *In concreto,* the freedom to believe can only cover living options which the intellect of the individual cannot by itself resolve; and living options never seem absurdities to him who has them to consider. When I look at the religious question as it really puts itself to concrete men, and when I think of all the possibilities which both practically and theoretically it involves, then this command that we shall put a stopper on our heart, instincts, and courage, and wait — acting of course meanwhile more or less as if religion were *not* true[2] — till doomsday, or till such time as our intellect and senses working together may have raked in evidence enough, — this command, I say, seems to me the queerest idol ever manufactured in the philosophic cave. Were we scholastic absolutists, there might be more excuse. If we had an infallible intellect with its objective certitudes, we might feel ourselves disloyal to such a perfect organ of knowledge in not trusting to it exclusively, in not waiting for its releasing word. But if we are empiricists, if we believe that no bell in us tolls to let us know for certain when truth is in our grasp, then it seems a piece of idle fantasticality to preach so solemnly our duty of waiting for the bell. Indeed we *may* wait if we will, — hope you do not think that I am denying that, — but if we do so, we do so at our peril as much as if we believed. In either case we *act*, taking our life in our hands. No one of us ought to issue vetoes to the other, nor should we bandy words of abuse. We ought, on the contrary, delicately and profoundly to respect one another's mental freedom: then only shall we bring about the intellectual republic; then only shall we have that spirit of inner tolerance without which all our outer tolerance is soulless, and which is empiricism's glory; then only shall we live and let live, in speculative as well as in practical things.

I began by a reference to Fitz James Stephen, let me end by a quotation from him. "What do you think of yourself? What do you think of the world? . . . These are questions with which all must deal as it seems good to them. They are riddles of the Sphinx, and in some way or other we must deal with them. . . . In all important transactions of life we have to take a leap in the dark . . . If we decide to leave the riddles unanswered, that is a choice; if we waver in our answer, that, too, is a choice: but whatever choice we make, we make it at our peril. If a man

[2] Since belief is measured by action, he who forbids us to believe religion to be true, necessarily also forbids us to act as we should if we did believe it to be true. The whole defence of religious faith hinges upon action. If the action required or inspired by the religious hypothesis is in no way different from that dictated by the naturalistic hypothesis, then religious faith is a pure superfluity, better pruned away, and controversy about its legitimacy is a piece of idle trifling, unworthy of serious minds. I myself believe, of course, that the religious hypothesis gives to the world an expression which specifically determines our reactions, and makes them in a large part unlike what they might be on a purely naturalistic scheme of belief.

chooses to turn back altogether on God and the future, no one can prevent him; no one can show beyond reasonable doubt that he is mistaken. If a man thinks otherwise and acts as he thinks, I do not see that any one can prove that *he* is mistaken. Each must act as he thinks best; and if he is wrong, so much the worse for him. We stand on a mountain pass in the midst of whirling snow and blinding mist, through which we get glimpses now and then of paths which may be deceptive. If we stand still we shall be frozen to death. If we take the wrong road we shall be dashed to pieces. We do not certainly know whether there is any right one. What must we do? 'Be strong and of a good courage.' Act for the best, hope for the best, and take what comes. . . . If death ends all, we cannot meet death better." [3]

[3] Liberty, Equality, Fraternity, p. 353, 2d edition. London, 1874.

HASTINGS RASHDALL and WILLIAM RITCHIE SORLEY

HASTINGS RASHDALL (1858-1924) was a British philosopher and theologian who belonged to the school of Personal Idealism, and is credited with being one of its founders. He also founded the school of ethics termed Ideal Utilitarianism, a philosophy which seeks to synthesize the better aspects of both Idealism and Utilitarianism, the Idealism of Thomas Hill Green (particularly his concept of the infinite intrinsic value of persons), and the Utilitarianism of Henry Sidgwick (particularly the aspect which emphasizes the determination of moral value judgments in the light of ensuing consequences). Rashdall is known principally for his classic two volume work, **Theory of Good and Evil** (1907), from which the present text derives its Axiological Argument for the existence of God, an argument expanded upon by William R. Sorley. An earlier work of his, which gave him reputable standing, was his multivolume book, **The Universities of Europe in the Middle Ages** (1895); a third work, giving him stature in the field of theology, comprised his Bampton Lectures for the year 1919, **Idea of Atonement in Christian Theology.**

Rashdall, like Mill before him, maintained a Theistic Finitism, a limited God — one who is not coincidentally omnipotent and all-good. In his Axiological Argument for God, Rashdall shares the same view as Sorley, believing in the objective existence of moral ideals, basing their presence on the existence of a personal God.

WILLIAM RITCHIE SORLEY (1885-1935), British philosopher, was born on Nov. 4, 1885, and died at Cambridge on July 28, 1935. His higher education began at the University of Edinburgh and his graduate studies took him to Tübingen, Berlin, and Cambridge Universities. Strong strains of the influence of the philosophers James Ward and Henry Sidgwick can be found in him. Ward later was to become Sorley's colleague when in 1900 Sorley assumed the Knightbridge Professor of Moral Philosophy at Cambridge, a chair vacated by Sidgwick. The early development of Sorley's career began when he was elected fellow of Trinity College, Cambridge, in 1883; in 1888 he accepted an appointment as Professor of Philosophy at Cardiff, a post he retained until 1894 when he became Regius Professor of Moral Philosophy at Aberdeen. He terminated his position at Aberdeen in 1900 to accept a similar appointment at Cambridge, the tenure of which he enjoyed until his retirement in 1933, two years prior to his death.

Among his writings are the classic **Moral Values and the Idea of God** (Gifford Lectures, 1914-1915), the source which provides the present text with his celebrated Axiological Argument for God's existence; **A History of English Philosophy** (1920), **The Ethics of Naturalism** (1885), **Recent Tendencies in Ethics** (1904), **The Moral Life and Moral Worth,** and numerous articles in support of the philosophy of Theism.

Sorley, a severe critic of naturalistic ethics and an outspoken adherent of the Moral Argument for God's existence (The Axiological Argument), founds his theory of moral value on the fact or experience of **obligation.** The "ought" experience, being irreducible and ultimate, furnishes us with an insight into existence. The experience of obligation is an objective value, a valid experience of a moral nature. "The coherent interpretation of these in relation to natural existence, and the human realization of values, leads reasonably to a personal God in whom these values have their being as ends of existence." [1]

[1] Peter A. Bertocci, "William Sorley" in **Encyclopedia of Religion,** ed., Vergilius Ferm (New York: Philosophical Library, 1945).

12

HASTINGS RASHDALL
and
WILLIAM RITCHIE SORLEY

The Axiological Argument

Hastings Rashdall: [1]

So long as the ultimate reality of things is regarded as purely material, so long as material process is regarded as the sole cause or source or ground of mind and all its contents, there is always the possibility of scepticism as to the knowledge of which this material world has somehow delivered itself. Our knowledge may be conceived of as representing, not the real truth of things, but the way in which it is most conducive to the survival of the race that we should think of them. Error and delusion may be valuable elements in Evolution; to a certain extent it is undeniable, from any metaphysical standpoint, that they have actually been so. But on the naturalistic view of things the doubt arises not merely whether this or that particular belief of ours is a delusion, but whether human thought in general may not wholly fail to correspond with Reality, whether thought *qua* thought may not be a delusion, whether (to put it still more paradoxically) the more rational a man's thought becomes, the more faithfully the individual adheres to the canons of human Reason, the wider may be the gulf between his thinking and the facts. Arguments might no doubt be found for putting away such an 'unmotived' doubt as to the trustworthiness of our knowledge about ordinary matters of fact — its self-consistency, the constant correspondence of the predictions which it makes with subsequent experience, the practical serviceableness for the purposes of life of its assumed validity, and the uselessness of entertaining doubts as to the trustworthiness of our faculties which from the nature of the case can be neither confirmed nor refuted; though after all such arguments at bottom assume the validity of thought. But these considerations do not apply in the same degree to moral knowledge. It is

[1] Hastings Rashdall, *The Theory of Good and Evil* (Oxford: University Press, 1907), 209 ff.

often possible to explain in a sense this or that particular ethical belief by the history of the race, the environment of the individual, and the like. Such considerations do not shake belief in the ultimate validity of moral distinctions for an Idealist who believes that the Universe owes its very existence to the Mind which assures him of these distinctions (though he is aware that the evolution of his individual mind has been conditioned by physical processes and social environment); but they wear a totally different aspect for one who has no general *a priori* reason for assuming a correspondence of thought with things. The Idealist has every reason for believing the ultimate moral ideas to be true that he has for believing any other ideas to be true, though he realizes that he does not know the whole truth, and that his knowledge of this or ignorance of that element in the moral ideal (like his knowledge or ignorance of ordinary scientific truth) is in part explicable by the accident of antecedents or environment. But to the man who regards all spiritual life as a mere inexplicable incident in the career of a world which is essentially material (were it not produced) and as a whole essentially purposeless, there is not conclusive reason why all moral ideas — the very conception of 'value,' the very notion that one thing is intrinsically better than another, the very conviction that there is something which a man ought to do — may not be merely some strange illusion due to the unaccountable freaks of a mindless process or to the exigencies of natural selection. It cannot be said that a man who allowed such doubts to shake or modify his allegiance to the dictates of Morality, where they do not happen to coincide with his actual desires or inclination, would be doing anything essentially unreasonable. Reasonable conduct would for him mean merely 'conduct conformable to his own private reason'; intrinsically or absolutely reasonable or unreasonable conduct could not exist in a world which was not itself the product of Reason or governed by its dictates.

Another way of putting much the same difficulty is this. We say that the Moral Law has a real existence, that there is such a thing as an absolute Morality, that there is something absolutely true or false in ethical judgements, whether we or any number of human beings at any given time actually think so or not. Such a belief is distinctly implied in what we mean by Morality. The idea of such an unconditional, objectively valid, Moral Law or ideal undoubtedly exists as a psychological fact. The question before us is whether it is capable of theoretical justification. We must then face the question *where* such an ideal exists, and what manner of existence we are to attribute to it. Certainly it is to be found, wholly and completely, in no individual human consciousness. Men actually think differently about moral questions, and there is no empirical reason for supposing that they will ever do otherwise. Where then and how does the moral ideal really exist? As regards matters of fact or physical law, we have no difficulty in satisfying ourselves that there is an objective reality which is what it is irrespective-of our beliefs or disbeliefs about it. For the man who supposes that objective reality resides in the things themselves, our ideas about them are objectively true or false so far as they correspond or fail to correspond with this real and independent archetype, though he might be puzzled to give a metaphysical account of the nature of this 'correspondence' between experience and a Reality whose *esse* is something other than to be experienced. In the physical region the existence of divergent ideas does not throw doubt upon the existence of a reality independent of our ideas. But in the case of moral ideals it is otherwise. On materialistic or naturalistic assumptions the moral ideal can hardly be regarded as a real thing. Nor could it well be regarded as a property of any real thing: it can be no more than an aspiration, a product of the imagination, which may be useful to stimulate effort in directions in which we happen to want to move, but which cannot compel respect when we feel no desire to act in conformity with it. An absolute Moral Law or moral ideal cannot exist *in* material things. And it does not (we have seen) exist in the mind of this or that individual. Only if we believe in the existence of a Mind for which the true moral ideal is already in some sense real, a Mind which is the source of whatever is true in our own moral judgements, can we rationally think of the moral ideal as no less real than the world itself. Only so can we believe in an absolute standard of right and wrong, which is as independent of this or that man's actual ideas and actual desires as the facts of material nature. The belief in God, though not (like the belief in a real and an active self) a postulate of there being any such thing as Morality at all, is the logical presupposition of an 'objective' or absolute Morality. A moral ideal can exist nowhere and nohow but in a mind; an absolute moral ideal can only claim objective validity in so far as it can rationally be regarded as the revelation of a moral ideal eternally existing in the mind of God.

We may be able, perhaps, to give some meaning to Morality without the postulate of God, but not its true or full meaning. If the existence of God is not a postulate of all Morality, it is a postulate of a sound Morality; for it is essential to that belief which vaguely and implicitly underlies all moral beliefs, and which forms the very heart of Morality in its highest, more developed, more explicit forms. The truth that the moral ideal is what it is whether we like it or not is the most essential element in what the popular consciousness understands by 'moral obligation.' Moral obligation means moral objectivity. That *at least* seems to be implied in any legitimate use of the term: at least it implies the existence of an absolute, objective moral ideal. And such a belief we have seen imperatively to demand an explanation of the Universe which shall be idealistic or at least spiritualistic, which shall recognize the existence of a Mind whose thoughts are the standard of truth and falsehood alike in Morality and in respect of all other existence. In other words, objective Morality implies the belief in God. The belief in God, if not so obviously and primarily a postulate of Morality as the belief in a permanent spiritual and active self, is still a postulate of a Morality which shall be able fully to satisfy the demands of the moral consciousness. It may conveniently be called the secondary postulate of Morality.

William R. Sorley: [2]

This means that it is possible to regard God as the author and ruler of the world, as it appears in space and time, and at the same time to hold that the moral values of which we are conscious and the moral ideal which we come to apprehend with increasing clearness express his nature. But the question remains, Are we to regard morality — its values, laws, and ideal — as belonging to a Supreme Mind, that is, to God? It is as an answer to this question that the specific Moral Argument enters. And here I cannot do better than give the argument in the words of Dr. Rashdall. . . .[3]

The argument as thus put may be looked upon as a special and striking extension of the cosmological argument. In its first and most elementary form the cosmological argument seeks a cause for the bare existence of the world and man: to account for them there must be something able to bring them into being: God is the First Cause. The order of nature impresses us by its regularity, and we come by degrees to understand the principles of its working and the laws under which the material whole maintains its equilibrium and the ordered procession of its changes: these laws and this order call for explanation, and we conceive God as the Great Lawgiver. But beyond this material world, we understand relations and principles of a still more general kind; and the intellect of man recognizes abstract truths so evident that, once understood, they cannot be questioned, while inferences are drawn from these which only the more expert minds can appreciate and yet which they recognise as eternally valid. To what order do these belong and what was their home when man as yet was unconscious of them? Surely if their validity is eternal they must have had existence somewhere, and we can only suppose them

---

[2] William R. Sorley, *Moral Values and the Idea of God* (New York: The Macmillan Co., 1924), 347-349.

[3] At this point, Sorley quotes a portion of the above by Rashdall.

to have existed in the one eternal mind: God is therefore the God of Truth. Further, persons are conscious of values and of an ideal of goodness, which they recognise as having undoubted authority for the direction of their activity; the validity of these values or laws and of this ideal, however, does not depend upon their recognition: it is objective and eternal; and how could this eternal validity stand alone, not embodied in matter and neither seen nor realised by finite minds, unless there were an eternal mind whose thought and will were therein expressed? God must therefore exist and his nature be goodness.

Part Two: ATHEISM

The Case against God's Existence

FRIEDRICH NIETZSCHE

FRIEDRICH WILHELM NIETZSCHE (1844-1900), a German poet philosopher, was born on Oct. 15, 1844 in Röcken, a Prussian province of Saxony, and died in Weimar on Aug. 25, 1900. His father, a Protestant pastor, died prematurely of an accident when the philosopher was yet a boy of tender years. Nietzsche's academic training was in theology and classical philosophy at the University of Bonn, where he studied under the gifted Ritschl. During this period, he came under the influence of Schopenhauer's philosophy, the profound effect of which led him away both from theological studies and Christianity. At twenty-five years of age, in consequence of Ritschl's recommendation, Nietzsche was granted a professorship at Basle, a post he held until his resignation (owing to ill health) in 1879. A modest pension received from the University of Basle permitted him to leave Germany and live in northern Italy, the Engadine, and the French Riviera, where some improvement in health saw the production of many of his greatest works. In 1888-1889, Nietzsche's health broke down critically owing to a syphilitic infection which produced psychosis; a dozen years later, he died.

Among his work are: **The Birth of Tragedy** (1872), **Untimely Meditations** (1873-1876), **Human, All-too-Human** (1878-1879), **The Wanderer and his Shadow** (1880), **The Dawn** (1881), **Joyful Wisdom** (1882), **Thus Spake Zarathustra** (1883-1885), **Beyond Good and Evil** (1886), **Genealogy of Morals** (1887), **The Wagner Case** (1888), **The Twilight of the Idols** (1889), **The Antichrist** (1895), **Ecco Homo** (1908), **Nietzsche contra Wagner** (1895).

13

FRIEDRICH NIETZSCHE

God as Dead[1]

After Buddha was dead people showed his shadow for centuries after-wards in a cave, — an immense frightful shadow. God is dead: but as the human race is constituted, there will perhaps be caves for millenniums yet, in which people will show his shadow. — And we — we have still to overcome his shadow!

WHAT OUR CHEERFULNESS SIGNIFIES.[2]

The most important of more recent events — that "God is dead," that the belief in the Christian God has become unworthy of belief — already begins to cast its first shadows over Europe. To the few at least whose eye, whose *suspecting* glance, is strong enough and subtle enough for this drama, some sun seems to have set, some old, profound confidence seems to have changed into doubt: our old world must seem to them daily more darksome, distrustful, strange and "old." In the main, how-ever, one may say that the event itself is far too great, too remote, too much beyond most people's power of apprehension, for one to suppose that so much as the report of it could have *reached* them; not to speak of many who already knew *what* had taken place, and what must all col-lapse now that this belief had been undermined, — because so much was built upon it, so much rested on it, and had become one with it: for example, our entire European morality. This lengthy, vast and uninter-rupted process of crumbling, destruction, ruin and overthrow which is now imminent: who has realised it sufficiently to-day to have to stand up as the teacher and herald of such a tremendous logic of terror, as the prophet of a period of gloom and eclipse, the like of which has probably never taken place on earth before? . . . Even we, the born riddle-readers,

<hr />

[1]Friedrich Nietzsche, *Joyful Wisdom*, tr. Thomas Common, 108, "New Struggles", translated from the German *Die fröhliche Wissenschaft* (1882).
[2] *Ibid.*, 343, "What Our Cheerfulness Signifies."

who wait as it were on the mountains posted 'twixt to-day and to-morrow, and engirt by their contradiction, we, the firstlings and premature children of the coming century, into whose sight especially the shadows which must forthwith envelop Europe *should* already have come — how is it that even we, without genuine sympathy for this period of gloom, contemplate its advent without any *personal* solitude or fear? Are we still, perhaps, too much under the *immediate effects* of the event — and are these effects, especially as regards *ourselves*, perhaps the reverse of what was to be expected — not at all sad and depressing, but rather like a new and indescribable variety of light, happiness, relief, enlivenment, encouragement, and dawning day? . . . In fact, we philosophers and "free spirits" feel ourselves irradiated as by a new dawn by the report that the "old God is dead"; our hearts overflow with gratitude, astonishment, presentiment and expectation. At last the horizon seems open once more, granting even that it is not bright; our ships can at last put out to sea in face of every danger; every hazard is again permitted to the discerner; the sea, *our* sea, again lies open before us; perhaps never before did such an "open sea" exist. —

Let[3] us be on our guard against thinking that the world is a living being. Where could it extend itself? What could it nourish itself with? How could it grow and increase? We know tolerably well what the organic is; and we are to reinterpret the emphatically derivative, tardy, rare and accidental, which we only perceive on the crust of the earth, into the essential, universal and eternal, as those do who call the universe an organism? That disgusts me. Let us now be on our guard against believing that the universe is a machine; it is assuredly not constructed with a view to *one* end; we invest it with far too high an honour with the word "machine." Let us be on our guard against supposing that anything so methodical as the cyclic motions of our neighbouring stars obtains generally and throughout the universe; indeed a glance at the Milky Way induces doubt as to whether there are not many cruder and more contradictory motions there, and even stars with continuous, rectilinearly gravitating orbits, and the like. The astral arrangement in which we live is an exception; this arrangement, and the relatively long durability which is determined by it, has again made possible the exception of exceptions, the formation of organic life. The general character of the world, on the other hand, is to all eternity chaos; not the absence of necessity, but in the sense of the absence of order, structure, form, beauty, wisdom, and whatever else our aesthetic humanities are called. Judged by our reason, the unlucky casts are far oftenest the rule, the exceptions are not the

---

[3] *Ibid.*, 109, "Let Us Be on Our Guard."

secret purpose; and the whole musical box repeats eternally its air, which can never be called a melody, — and finally the very expression, "unlucky cast" is already an anthropomorphising which involves blame. But how could we presume to blame or praise the universe! Let us be on our guard against ascribing to it heartlessness and unreason, or their opposites; it is neither perfect, nor beautiful, nor noble; nor does it seek to be anything of the kind, it does not at all attempt to imitate man! It is altogether unaffected by our aesthetic and moral judgments! Neither has it any self-preservative instinct, nor instinct at all; it also knows no law. Let us be on our guard against saying that there are laws in nature. There are only necessities: there is no one who commands, no one who obeys, no one who transgresses. When you know that there is no design, you know also that there is no chance: for it is only where there is a world of design that the word "chance" has a meaning. Let us be on our guard against saying that death is contrary to life. The living being is only a species of dead being, and a very rare species. — Let us be on our guard against thinking that the world eternally creates the new. There are no eternally enduring substances; matter is just another such error as the God of the Eleatics. But when shall we be at an end with our foresight and precaution! When will all these shadows of God cease to obscure us? When shall we have nature entirely undeified! When shall we be permitted to *naturalise* ourselves by means of the pure, newly discovered, newly redeemed nature?

THE MADMAN.[4]

Have you ever heard of the madman who on a bright morning lighted a lantern and ran to the market-place calling out unceasingly: "I seek God! I seek God!" — As there were many people standing about who did not believe in God, he caused a great deal of amusement. Why! is he lost? said one. Has he strayed away like a child? said another. Or does he keep himself hidden? Is he afraid of us? Has he taken a sea-voyage? Has he emigrated? — the people cried out laughingly, all in a hubbub. The insane man jumped into their midst and transfixed them with his glances. "Where is God gone?" he called out. "I mean to tell you! *We have killed him,* — you and I! We are all his murderers! But how have we done it? How were we able to drink up the sea? Who gave us the sponge to wipe away the whole horizon? What did we do when we loosened this earth from its sun? Whither does it now move? Whither do we move? Away from all suns? Do we not dash on unceasingly? Backwards, sideways, forwards, in all directions? Is there still an above and below? Do

---

[4] *Ibid.,* 125, "The Madman."

we not stray, as through infinite nothingness? Does not empty space breathe upon us? Has it not become colder? Does not night come on continually, darker and darker? Shall we not have to light lanterns in the morning? Do we not hear the noise of the grave-diggers who are burying God? Do we not smell the divine putrefaction? — for even Gods putrefy! God is dead! God remains dead! And we have killed him! How shall we console ourselves, the most murderous of all murderers? The holiest and the mightiest that the world has hitherto possessed, has bled to death under our knife, — who will wipe the blood from us? With what water could we cleanse ourselves? What lustrums, what sacred games shall we have to devise? Is not the magnitude of this deed too great for us? Shall we not ourselves have to become Gods, merely to seem worthy of it? There never was a greater event, — and on account of it, all who are born after us belong to a higher history than any history hitherto!" — Here the madman was silent and looked again at his hearers; they also were silent and looked at him in surprise. At last he threw his lantern on the ground, so that it broke in pieces and was extinguished. "I come too early." he then said, "I am not yet at the right time. This prodigious event is still on its way, and is travelling, — it has not yet reached men's ears. Lightning and thunder need time, the light of the stars needs time, deeds need time, even after they are done, to be seen and heard. This deed is as yet further from them than the furthest star, — *and yet they have done it!*" — It is further stated that the madman made his way into different churches on the same day, and there intoned his *Requiem aeternam deo*. When led out and called to account, he always gave the reply: "What are these churches now, if they are not the tombs and monuments of God?" —

KARL MARX

KARL HEINRICH MARX (1818-1883) was born in Prussia at Treves, on May 5, 1818, of Jewish parents who embraced Christianity in 1824. After a secondary school education at Treves, Marx went to the universities of Bonn and Berlin, where he studied philosophy, history, and law, his doctoral degree being conferred in 1841. Marx early came under the influence of Hegelian philosophy which was dominant at the time; his Hegelian bent was accentuated as a result of his close association with the Bauer brothers, Bruno and Edgar, and the entire Hegelian **Freien.**

Turning to a career of journalism in 1842, Marx became editor of the **Rheinische Zeitung,** a Democratic journal, but was compelled to leave for Paris the following year due to his radical socialistic articles. In Paris, he became an editor of the **Deutsch-Französische-Jahrbücher,** until he was expelled from France in 1845, and went to Brussels, where he was active in the Communist League. In 1847, in collaboration with Engels, he wrote the **Manifesto of the Communist Party.** In 1848, he left Brussels for Germany; there, he founded the **Neue Rheinische Zeitung,** but owing to his revolutionary activities in 1849, he was expunged from Germany. Then he went to London via Paris, and applied himself to serious study, earning his living as London correspondent for the New York **Tribune.**

Marx's more influential writings are: **Manifesto of the Communist Party** (with Engels, 1847), **Das Kapital** (1867 ff.), **Contribution to the Critique of Hegel's Philosophy of Right** (1844), **Theses on Feuerbach** (1845), **Critique of the Gotha Program** (1875), **The German Ideology** (1845-1846, with Engels), **The Holy Family, or Critique of Critical Criticism** (1844, with Engels).

Marx drew his philosophy of Dialectical Materialism from Hegel and Feuerbach; from the former he obtained the dialectic technique of logic and a philosophy of history, from the latter, a philosophy of Materialism. Marx was also influenced by the philosophy of Evolutionary Naturalism and Positivism.

Marx sought to establish ethics on a scientific basis in order to derive a synthesis, a "Scientific Socialism," one which depicted a deliberate historical course of man and nature as headed ultimately toward Communistic Socialism. This ultimate course is augmented by the belief that each period of history contains "the germs of its own destruction."

Friedrich Engels considers as the most important contribution of Marx's discoveries the doctrine of history as being essentially one of class struggle, an inherent class war ensuing between proletariat and capitalist. The outcome of such a class struggle is Communism, but in the interim transpires a series of struggles, revolutions, generated out of the conflicting interest of each group. Herein is the Church, entailed with its vested interests, sided with the bourgeoisie, a defender of the status quo, hence a supporter of Capitalism. Accordingly, the Church, its ideas and interests must be abolished since it is merely the tool of the capitalist, functioning as a "police force" designed to keep the people "in check," prohibiting them from uprising and insurrection. As to theology **per se**, it is the "opium of the people," designed to keep the masses in a stupor, insensed from the oppression of the capitalist.

14

KARL MARX

Religion as the Opium of the Masses[1]

For Germany the *criticism of religion* is in the main complete, and criticism of religion is the premise of all criticism.

The *profane* existence of error is discredited after its *heavenly oratio pro et focis* has been rejected. Man, who looked for a superman in the fantastic reality of heaven and found nothing there but the *reflexion* of himself, will no longer be disposed to find but the *semblance* of himself, the non-human [*Unmensch*] where he seeks and must seek his true reality.

The basis of irreligious criticism is: *Man makes religion,* religion does not make man. In other words, religion is the self-consciousness and self-feeling of man who has either not yet found himself or has already lost himself again. But *man* is no abstract being squatting outside the world. Man is *the world of man,* the state, society. This state, this society, produce religion, a *reversed world-consciousness,* because they are a *reversed world.* Religion is the general theory of that world, its encyclopaedic compendium, its logic in a popular form, its spiritualistic *point d'honneur,* its enthusiam, its moral sanction, its solemn completion, its universal ground for consolation and justification. It is *the fantastic realization* of the human essence because the *human essence* has no true reality. The struggle against religion is therefore mediately the fight against *the other world,* of which religion is the spiritual *aroma.*

Religious distress is at the same time the *expression* of real distress and the *protest* against real distress. Religion is the sigh of the oppressed creature, the heart of a heartless world, just as it is the spirit of a spiritless situation. It is the *opium* of the people.

The abolition of religion as the *illusory* happiness of the people is required for their *real* happiness. The demand to give up the illusions about its condition is the *demand to give up a condition which needs illusions.*

[1] Karl Marx, *Contribution to the Critique of Hegel's Philosophy of Right* (Moscow: Foreign Languages Publishing House, 1955); excerpts from the "Introduction."

The criticism of religion is therefore *in embryo the criticism of the vale of woe,* the *halo* of which is religion.

Criticism has plucked the imaginary flowers from the chain not so that man will wear the chain without any fantasy or consolation but so that he will shake off the chain and cull the living flower. The criticism of religion disillusions man to make him think and act and shape his reality like a man who has been disillusioned and has come to reason, so that he will revolve round himself and therefore round his true sun. Religion is only the illusory sun which revolves round man as long as he does not revolve round himself.

The task of history, therefore, once the *world beyond the truth* has disappeared, is to establish the *truth of this world.* The immediate *task of philosophy,* which is at the service of history, once the *saintly form* of human self-alienation has been unmasked, is to unmask self-alienation in its *unholy forms.* Thus the criticism of heaven turns into the criticism of the earth, the *criticism of religion* into the *criticism of right* and the *criticism of theology* into the *criticism of politics.* . . .

The weapon of criticism cannot, of course, replace criticism of the weapon, material force must be overthrown by material force; but theory also becomes a material force as soon as it has gripped the masses. Theory is capable of gripping the masses as soon as it demonstrates *ad hominem,* and it demonstrates *ad hominem* as soon as it becomes radical. To be radical is to grasp the root of the matter. But for man the root is man himself. The evident proof of the radicalism of German theory, and hence of its practical energy, is that it proceeds from a resolute *positive* abolition of religion. The criticism of religion ends with the teaching that *man is the highest essence for man,* hence with the *categoric imperative to overthrow all relations* in which man is debased, enslaved, abandoned, despicable essence, relations which cannot be better described than by the cry of a Frenchman when it was planned to introduce a tax on dogs: Poor dogs! They want to treat you as human beings!

Even historically, theoretical emancipation has specific practical significance for Germany. For Germany's *revolutionary* past is theoretical, it is the *Reformation.* As the revolution then began in the brain of the *monk,* so now it begins in the brain of the *philosopher.*

Luther, we grant, overcame bondage out of *devotion* by replacing it by bondage out of *conviction.* He shattered faith in authority because he restored the authority of faith. He turned priests into laymen because he turned laymen into priests. He freed man from outer religiosity because he made religiosity the inner man. He freed the body from chains because he enchained the heart.

But if Protestantism was not the true solution of the problem it was at least the true setting of it. It was no longer a case of the layman's struggle against his own *priest outside himself* but of his struggle against *his own priest inside himself*, his *priestly nature*. And if the Protestant transformation of the German laymen into priests emancipated the lay popes, the *princes*, with the whole of their priestly clique, the privileged and philistines, the philosophical transformation of priestly Germans into men will emancipate the people. But *secularization* will not stop at the *confiscation of church estates* set in motion mainly by hypocritical Prussia any more than emancipation stops at princes.

SIGMUND FREUD

SIGMUND FREUD (1856-1939) was born on May 6, 1856 at Freiberg in Moravia, but since the age of four, he lived in Vienna until his expulsion by Hitler in 1938 because of his Jewish ancestry. He moved to London where, upon landing on British soil, he was granted English citizenship. The Royal society elected him into membership in 1936. The greatest influences upon Freud were a Viennese physician, Josef Breuer, who showed him how to relieve symptoms of conversion hysteria by catharsis, and J. M. Charcot, the noted Parisian neurologist. Several Freudian ideas were anticipated in the philosophy of Arthur Schopenhauer and Friedrich Nietzsche, though Freud repudiates drawing material from either of these sources.

The influence of Freud on the academic world is legion: he revolutionized psychology and psychiatry, founded the psychological school of Psychoanalysis, developed a theory of personality, and applied Psychoanalysis to philosophy and religion.

Freud regarded religion as "a universal, obsessional neurosis of mankind," a father complex, a wish-fulfillment, an infantile desire to control a hostile nature, and a neurosis to be overcome. God, a being man created in his own image, is a father ideal, a childish wish to protect himself from the hostilities of nature, a regression to a state of infantilism, the halcyon days of childhood. On the other hand, the healthy mind shuns the crutch of religion, and lives a life of independence.

Freudian psychology of religion and his philosophy of religion are criticized on two major issues: (1) the fact that Freud was dealing with mentally disturbed minds and drew his data from this biased and narrow source almost exclusively, and (2) the fact that his philosophical ideas pertaining to religion, such as those found in **Moses and Monotheism,** are naive, ridden with inconsistencies from which he was never able to extricate himself. In regard to the first objection, in fairness to Freud, it should be noted that he did valuable service to the field of philosophy of religion by differentiating wholesome religion from that entertained by the sick mind.

Freud's important books pertaining to religion are: **Civilization and Its Discontents** (1930), a work in which he discusses man's consciousness of the feeling of being immortal, as well as the price of civilization being almost too costly to bear (in terms of guilt feelings); **The Future of an Illusion** (1928), in which he points out that religious ideas are spawned out of man's intolerable helplessness and need for security. Here, he views man as a helpless child seeking a father, and creating a God as a father complex; religion is essentially a wish-fulfillment, "a universal, obsessional neurosis of mankind." In **Moses and Monotheism** (1939), something of a biography of Moses, Freud seizes the opportunity to work out his own theory of religion by casting doubt on the authenticity of Moses being a Hebrew (claiming Moses to be an Egyptian), setting himself up as a modern Moses by establishing a new religion, Psychoanalysis. In **Totem and Taboo** (1913), Freud notes the place played by the father in primitive religions, particularly the ambivalency with which a father is both respected and feared; this father relationship is transferred to God, the creation of man's mind, a father ideal.

15

SIGMUND FREUD

Religion as an Illusion, Wish-Fulfilment, and a Father Complex[1]

An enquiry that proceeds uninterruptedly, like a monologue, is not altogether without its dangers. One is not too easily tempted to push aside thoughts that would interrupt it, and in exchange one is left with a feeling of uncertainty which one will drown in the end by over-decisiveness. I shall therefore imagine an opponent who follows my arguments with mistrust, and I shall let him interject remarks here and there.

I hear him saying: 'You have repeatedly used the expressions "culture creates these religious ideas", "culture places them at the disposal of its members", which sounds strange to me somehow. I could not say why myself, but it does not sound so natural as to say that culture has made regulations about distributing the products of labour or about the rights over women and children.'

I think, nevertheless, that one is justified in expressing oneself thus. I have tried to show that religious ideas have sprung from the same need as all other achievements of culture: from the necessity for defending itself against the crushing supremacy of nature. And there was a second motive: the eager desire to correct the so painfully felt imperfections of culture. Moreover, there is something particularly apposite in saying that culture gives the individual these ideas, for he finds them at hand, they are presented to him ready-made; he would not be in a position to find them by himself. It is the heritage of many generations which he enters into and which he takes over as he does the multiplication table, geometry, etc. There is certainly a distinction in this, but it lies elsewhere, and I cannot examine it at this point. The feeling of strangeness that you mention may be partly accounted for by the fact that this stock of religious ideas is generally offered as a divine revelation. But that is

[1] From *The Future of an Illusion* by Sigmund Freud. By permission of Liveright Publishing Corp., New York. Excerpts from chapters 4, 6, and 10.

in itself a part of the religious system, and entirely leaves out of account the known historical development of these ideas and their variations in different ages and cultures.

'Another point which seems to me more important. You would derive the humanization of nature from the desire to put an end to human perplexity and helplessness in the face of nature's dreaded forces. But this explanation seems to be superfluous. For primitive man has no choice, he has no other way of thinking. It is natural to him, as if innate, to project his existence outwards into the world, and to regard all events that come under his observation as the manifestations of beings who fundamentally resemble himself. It is his only method of comprehension. And it is by no means self-evident, on the contrary it is a remarkable coincidence, that he should succeed in satisfying one of his great wants by thus indulging his natural disposition.'

I do not find that so striking. For do you suppose that men's thought-processes have no practical motives, that they are simply the expression of a disinterested curiosity? That is surely very improbable. I believe, rather, that when he personifies the forces of nature man is once again following an infantile prototype. He has learnt from the persons of his earliest environment that the way to influence them is to establish a relationship with them, and so, later on, with the same end in view, he deals with everything that happens to him as he dealt with those persons. Thus I do not contradict your descriptive observation; it is, in point of fact, natural to man to personify everything that he wishes to comprehend, in order that later he may control it — the psychical subjugation as preparation for the physical — but I provide in addition a motive and genesis for this peculiarity of human thought.

'And now yet a third point. You have dealt with the origin of religion once before, in your book *Totem und Tabu*. But there it appears in a different light. Everything is the son-father relationship; God is the exalted father, and the longing for the father is the root of the need for religion. Since then, it seems, you have discovered the factor of human weakness and helplessness, to which indeed the chief part of the formation of religion is commonly assigned, and you now transfer to helplessness everything that was formerly father complex. May I ask you to enlighten me on this transformation?'

With pleasure. I was only waiting for this invitation. But is it really a transformation? In *Totem und Tabu* it was not my purpose to explain the origin of religions, but only of totemism. Can you from any standpoint known to you explain the fact that the first form in which the protecting deity revealed itself to men was that of an animal, that a prohibition existed against killing or eating this animal, and that yet it was the solemn custom to kill it and eat it communally once a year? It is just this that takes place in totemism. And it is hardly to the purpose to argue whether totemism should be called a religion. It has intimate connections with the later god-religions; the totem animal become the sacred animals of the gods; and the earliest, and the most profound, moral restrictions — the murder prohibition and the incest prohibition — originate in totemism. Whether or not you accept the conclusions of *Totem und Tabu*, I hope you will admit in that book a number of very remarkable isolated facts are brought together into a consistent whole.

Why in the long run the animal god did not suffice and why it was replaced by the human — that was hardly discussed in *Totem und Tabu*, and other problems of the formation of religion find no mention there at all. But do you regard such a limitation as identical with a denial? My work is a good example of the strict isolation of the share that psycho-analytic observation can contribute to the problem of religion. If I am now trying to add to it the other, less deeply hidden, part, you should not accuse me of inconsistency, just as before I was accused of being one-sided. It is of course my business to point out the connecting links between what I said before and what I now put forward, between the deeper and the manifest motivation, between the father complex and man's helplessness and need for protection.

These connections are not difficult to find. They consist in the relation of the child's helplessness to the adult's continuation of it, so that, as was to be expected, the psycho-analytic motivation of the forming of religion turns out to be the infantile contribution to its manifest motivation. Let us imagine ourselves the mental life of the small child. You remember the object-choice after the anaclitic type, which psycho-analysis talks about? The libido follows the paths of narcissistic needs, and attaches itself to the objects that ensure their satisfaction. So the mother, who satisfies hunger, becomes the first love-object, and certainly also the first protection against all the undefined and threatening dangers of the outer world; becomes, if we may so express it, the first protection against anxiety.

In this function the mother is soon replaced by the stronger father, and this situation persists from now on over the whole of childhood. But the relation to the father is affected by a peculiar ambivalence. He was himself a danger, perhaps just because of that earlier relation to the mother; so he is feared no less than he is longed for and admired. The indications of this ambivalence are deeply imprinted in all religions, as is brought out in *Totem und Tabu*. Now when the child grows up and finds that he is destined to remain a child for ever, and that he can never do without protection against unknown and mighty powers, he invests these with the traits of the father-figure; he creates for himself the gods, of whom he is afraid, whom he seeks to propitiate, and to whom he nevertheless entrusts the task of protecting him. Thus the longing-for-the-father explanation is identical with the other, the need for protection against the consequences of human weakness; the child's defensive re-action to his helplessness gives the characteristic features to the adult's reaction to his own sense of helplessness, *i.e.* the formation of religion. But it is not our intention to pursue further the development of the idea of God; we are concerned here with the matured stock of religious ideas as culture transmits them to the individual.

. . . . .

. . . We must ask where the inherent strength of these doctrines lies and to what circumstances they own their efficacy, independent, as it is, of the acknowledgment of the reason. . . .

I think we have sufficiently paved the way for the answer to both these questions. It will be found if we fix our attention on the psychical origin of religious ideas. These, which profess to be dogmas, are not the residue of experience or the final result of reflection; they are illusions, fulfil-ments of the oldest, strongest and most insistent wishes of mankind; the secret of their strength is the strength of these wishes. We know already that the terrifying effect of infantile helplessness aroused the need for protection — protection through love — which the father relieved, and that the discovery that this helplessness would continue through the whole of life made it necessary to cling to the existence of a father — but this time a more powerful one. Thus the benevolent rule of divine provi-dence allays our anxiety in face of life's dangers, the establishment of a moral world order ensures the fulfilment of the demands of justice, which within human culture have so often remained unfulfilled, and the pro-longation of earthly existence by a future life provides in addition the local and temporal setting for these wish-fulfilments. Answers to the questions that tempt human curiosity, such as the origin of the universe and the relation between the body and soul, are developed in accordance with the underlying assumptions of this system; it betokens a tremendous relief for the individual psyche if it is released from the conflicts of childhood arising out of the father complex, which are never wholly overcome, and if these conflicts are afforded a universally accepted solu-tion.

When I say that they are illusions, I must define the meaning of the word. An illusion is not the same as an error, it is indeed not necessarily an error . . . . In the delusion we emphasize as essential the conflict with reality; the illusion need not be necessarily false, that is to say, unrealizable or incompatible with reality. For instance, a poor girl may have an illusion that a prince will come and fetch her home. It is possible; some such cases have occurred. That the Messiah will come and found a golden age is much less probable; according to one's personal attitude one will classify this belief as an illusion or as analogous to a delusion. Examples of illusions that have come true are not easy to discover, but the illusion of the alchemists that all metals can be turned into gold may prove to be one. The desire to have lots of gold, as much gold as possible, has been considerably damped by our modern insight into the nature of wealth, yet chemistry no longer considers a transmutation of metals into gold as impossible. Thus we call a belief an illusion when wish-fulfilment is a prominent factor in its motivation, while disregarding its relations to reality, just as the illusion itself does.

If after this survey we turn again to religious doctrines, we may reiterate that they are all illusions, they do not admit of proof, and no one can be compelled to consider them as true or to believe in them. Some of them are so improbable, so very incompatible with everything we have laboriously discovered about the reality of the world, that we may compare them — taking adequately into account the psychological differences — to delusions. Of the reality value of most of them we cannot judge; just as they cannot be proved neither can they be refuted. . . .

· · · · ·

. . . I know how difficult it is to avoid illusions; perhaps even the hopes I have confessed to are of an illusory nature. But I hold fast to one distinction. My illusions — apart from the fact that no penalty is imposed for not sharing them — are not, like the religious ones, incapable of correction, they have no delusional character. If experience should show — not to me, but to others after me who think as I do — that we are mistaken, then we shall give up our expectations. Take my endeavour for what it is. A psychologist, who does not deceive himself about the difficulty of finding his bearings in this world, strives to review the development of mankind in accord with what insight he has won from studying the mental processes of the individual during his development from childhood to manhood. In this connection the idea forces itself upon him that religion is comparable to a childhood neurosis, and he is optimistic enough to assume that mankind will overcome this neurotic phase, just as so many children grow out of their similar neuroses. . . .

GEORGE SANTAYANA

GEORGE SANTAYANA (1863-1952), an American philosopher, poet, and novelist, was born in Madrid, Spain, on Dec. 16, 1863. Born of Spanish parents, he migrated with them to the United States in 1872, where he attended Boston Latin School and Harvard University, and was graduated from the latter institution in 1886. From 1889 to 1912, he taught at Harvard as Professor of Philosophy, but resigned in order to devote full time to writing. He travelled extensively throughout Europe, living chiefly in England, but early in World War II, he settled in a nunnery in Rome where he remained until his death on Sept. 26, 1952.

Although English was not Santayana's native tongue, he attained a degree of mastery in it which accorded him a permanent place in American literature. His **magnum opus** is the five volume **Life of Reason** (1905-1906), a portion of which has been excerpted for the present text. Other works of his include: **The Sense of Beauty** (1896), **Scepticism and Animal Faith** (1923), the four volume work, **The Realms of Being: (The Realm of Essence**, 1927-1928; **The Realm of Matter**, 1930; **The Realm of Truth**, 1937; **The Realm of Science**, 1940), **Winds of Doctrine** (1926), **Egotism in German Philosophy** (1916), **Philosophical Opinion in America** (1918), **The Unknowable** (1923), **Dialogues in Limbo** (1925), **Platonism and the Spiritual Life** (1927), **Some Turns of Thought in Modern Philosophy** (1933), **The Last Puritan** (1936), **Obiter Scripta** (1936), **Persons and Places** (2 vols., 1944-1945), **The Idea of Christ in the Gospels** (1946), **Dominations and Powers** (1951).

Despite his never abandoning the religion of his birth, Roman Catholicism, and retiring in Italy in a nunnery, Santayana was intellectually an Atheist. As a Metaphysical Materialist, Santayana regards all spiritual and mental qualities as mere epiphenomena, by-products of matter, which perish with the demise of the physical body. Consequently, God, the soul, and its immortality are precluded from any possible existence, as are all so-called spiritual realities. Religion, nevertheless, does have value, not literal in the sense of its being objectively real, but in the symbolic or poetic sense. Prayer, particularly, has value; merely because something is false does not imply that it is not good., **i.e.,** lacks value. Religion, although false, is most valuable, and serves handsomely as an escape, for religion is essentially the work of a constructive imagination.

16

GEORGE SANTAYANA

Religion as Poetry, Symbolism, and Escape[1]

How Religion May Be an Embodiment of Reason:
Religion Certainly Significant

Experience has repeatedly confirmed that well-known maxim of Bacon's, that "a little philosophy inclineth man's mind to atheism, but depth in philosophy bringeth men's minds about to religion." In every age the most comprehensive thinkers have found in the religion of their time and country something they could accept, interpreting and illustrating that religion so as to give it depth and universal application. Even the heretics and atheists, if they have had profundity, turn out after a while to be forerunners of some new orthodoxy. What they rebel against is a religion alien to their nature; they are atheists only by accident, and relatively to a convention which inwardly offends them, but they yearn mightily in their own souls after the religious acceptance of a world interpreted in their own fashion. So it appears in the end that their atheism and loud protestation were in fact the hastier part of their thought, since what emboldened them to deny the poor world's faith was that they were too impatient to understand it. Indeed, the enlightenment common to young wits and worm-eaten old satirists, who plume themselves on detecting the scientific ineptitude of religion — something which the blindest half see — is not nearly enlightened enough; it points to notorious facts incompatible with religious tenets literally taken, but it leaves unexplored the habits of thought from which those tenets sprang, their original meaning, and their true function. Such studies would bring the sceptic face to face with the mystery and pathos of mortal existence. They would make him understand why religion is so profoundly moving and in a sense so profoundly just. There must needs

[1] George Santayana, *The Life of Reason*, vol. III, *Reason in Religion* (New York: Charles Scribner's Sons, 1905); excerpts from chapter 1.

be something humane and necessary in an influence that has become the most general sanction of virtue, the chief occasion for art and philosophy, and the source, perhaps, of the best human happiness. If nothing, as Hooker said, is "so malapert as a splenetic religion," a sour irreligion is almost as perverse.

But Not Literally True

At the same time, when Bacon penned the sage epigram we have quoted he forgot to add that the God to whom depth in philosophy brings back men's minds is far from being the same from whom a little philosophy estranges them. It would be pitiful indeed if mature reflection bred no better conceptions than those which have drifted down the muddy stream of time, where tradition and passion have jumbled everything together. Traditional conceptions, when they are felicitous, may be adopted by the poet, but they must be purified by the moralist and disintegrated by the philosopher. Each religion, so dear to those whose life it sanctifies, and fulfilling so necessary a function in the society that has adopted it, necessarily contradicts every other religion, and probably contradicts itself. What religion a man shall have is a historical accident, quite as much as what language he shall speak. In the rare circumstances where a choice is possible, he may, with some difficulty, make an exchange; but even then he is only adopting a new convention which may be more agreeable to his personal temper but which is essentially as arbitrary as the old.

All Religion Is Positive And Particular

The attempt to speak without speaking any particular language is not more hopeless that the attempt to have a religion that shall be no religion in particular. A courier's or a dragoman's speech may indeed be often unusual and drawn from disparate sources, not without some mixture of personal originality; but that private jargon will have a meaning only because of its analogy to one or more conventional languages and its obvious derivation from them. So travellers from one religion to another, people who have lost their spiritual nationality, may often retain a neutral and confused residuum of belief, which they may egregiously regard as the essence of all religion, so little may they remember the graciousness and naturalness of that ancestral accent which a perfect religion should have. Yet a moment's probing of the conceptions surviving in such minds will show them to be nothing but vestiges of old beliefs, creases which thought, even if emptied of all dogmatic tenets, has not been able to smooth away at its first unfolding. Later generations, if they have any religion at all, will be found either to revert to ancient authority, or to attach themselves spontaneously to something wholly novel and immensely positive, to some faith promulgated by a fresh genius and passionately embraced by a converted people. Thus every living and healthy religion has a marked idiosyncrasy. Its power consists in its special and surprising message and in the bias which that revelation gives to life. The vistas it opens and the mysteries it propounds are another world to live in; and another world to live in — whether we expect ever to pass wholly into it or no — is what we mean by having a religion.

It Aims at the Life of Reason

What relation, then, does this great business of the soul, which we call religion, bear to the Life of Reason? That the relation between the two is close seems clear from several circumstances. The Life of Reason is the seat of all ultimate values. Now the history of mankind will show us that whenever spirits at once lofty and intense have seemed to attain the highest joys, they have envisaged and attained them in religion. Religion would therefore seem to be a vehicle or a factor in rational life, since the ends of rational life are attained by it. Moreover, the Life of Reason is an ideal to which everything in the world should be subordinated; it establishes lines of moral cleavage everywhere and makes right eternally different from wrong. Religion does the same thing. It makes absolute moral decisions. It sanctions, unifies, and transforms ethics. Religion thus exercises a function of the Life of Reason. And a further function which is common to both is that of emancipating man from his personal limitations. In different ways religions promise to transfer the soul to better conditions. A supernaturally favoured kingdom is to be established for posterity upon earth, or for all the faithful in heaven, or the soul is to be freed by repeated purgations from all taint and sorrow, or it is to be lost in the absolute, or it is to become an influence and an object of adoration in the places it once haunted or wherever the activities it once loved may be carried on by future generations of its kindred. Now reason in its way lays before us all these possibilities: it points to common objects, political and intellectual, in which an individual may lose what is mortal and accidental in himself and immortalise what is rational and human; it teaches us how sweet and fortunate death may be to those whose spirit can still live in their country and in their ideas; it reveals the radiating effects of action and the eternal objects of thought.

Yet the difference in tone and language must strike us, so soon as it is philosophy that speaks. That change should remind us that even if the function of religion and that of reason coincide, this function is performed in the two cases by very different organs. Religions are many, reason one. Religion consists of conscious ideas, hopes, enthusiasms, and objects of worship; it operates by grace and flourishes by prayer. Reason, on the other hand, is a mere principle or potential order, on which, indeed, we may come to reflect, but which exists in us ideally only, without variation or stress of any kind. We conform or do not conform to it; it does not urge or chide us, nor call for any emotions on our part other than those naturally aroused by the various objects which it unfolds in their true nature and proportion. Religion brings some order into life by weighting it with new materials. Reason adds to the natural materials only the perfect order which it introduces into them. Rationality is nothing but a form, an ideal constitution which experience may more or less embody. Religion is a part of experience itself, a mass of sentiments and ideas. The one is an inviolate principle, the other a changing and struggling force. And yet this struggling and changing force of religion seems to direct man toward something eternal. It seems to make for an ultimate harmony within the soul and for an ultimate harmony between the soul and all the soul depends upon. So that religion, in its intent, is a more conscious and direct pursuit of the Life of Reason than is society, science, or art. For these approach and fill out the ideal life tentatively and piecemeal, hardly regarding the goal or caring for the ultimate justification of their instinctive aims. Religion also has an instinctive and blind side, and bubbles up in all manner of chance practices and intuitions; soon, however, it feels its way toward the heart of things, and, from whatever quarter it may come, veers in the direction of the ultimate.

But Largely Fails to Attain It

Nevertheless, we must confess that this religious pursuit of the Life of Reason has been singularly abortive. Those within the pale of each religion may prevail upon themselves to express satisfaction with its results, thanks to a fond partiality in reading the past and generous draughts of hope for the future; but any one regarding the various religions at once and comparing their achievements with what reason requires, must feel how terrible is the disappointment which they have one and all prepared for mankind. Their chief anxiety has been to offer imaginary remedies for mortal ills, some of which are incurable essentially, while others might have been really cured by well-directed effort. The Greek oracles, for instance, pretended to heal our natural ignorance, which has its appropriate though difficult cure, while the Christian vision of heaven pretended to be an antidote to our natural death, the inevitable correlate of birth and of a changing and conditioned existence. By methods of this sort little can be done for the real betterment of life. To confuse intelligence and dislocate sentiment by gratuitous fictions is a short-sighted way of pursuing happiness. Nature is soon avenged. An unhealthy exaltation and a one-sided morality have to be followed by regrettable reactions. When these come, the real rewards of life may seem vain to a relaxed vitality, and the very name of virtue may irritate young spirits untrained in any natural excellence. Thus religion too often debauches the morality it comes to sanction, and impedes the science it ought to fulfil.

Its Imaginative Approach

What is the secret of this ineptitude? Why does religion, so near to rationality in its purpose, fall so far short of it in its texture and in its results? The answer is easy: Religion pursues rationality through the imagination. When it explains events or assigns causes, it is an imaginative substitute for science. When it gives precepts, insinuates ideals, or remoulds aspiration, it is an imaginative substitute for wisdom — I mean for the deliberate and impartial pursuit of all good. The conditions and the aims of life are both represented in religion poetically, but this poetry tends to arrogate to itself literal truth and moral authority, neither of which it possesses. Hence the depth and importance of religion become intelligible no less than its contradictions and practical disasters. Its object is the same as that of reason, but its method is to proceed by intuition and by unchecked poetical conceits. These are repeated and vulgarised in proportion to their original fineness and significance, till they pass for reports of objective truth and come to constitute a world of faith, superposed upon the world of experience and regarded as materially enveloping it, if not in space at least in time and in existence. The only truth of religion comes from its interpretation of life, from its symbolic rendering of that moral experience which it springs out of and which it seeks to elucidate. Its falsehood comes from the insidious misunderstanding which clings to it, to the effect that these poetic conceptions are not merely representations of experience as it is or should be, but are rather information about experience or reality elsewhere — an experience and reality which, strangely enough, supply just the defects betrayed by reality and experience here.

When Its Poetic Method Is Denied Its Value Is Jeopardised

Thus religion has the same original relation to life that poetry has; only poetry, which never pretends to literal validity, adds a pure value to existence, the value of a liberal imaginative exercise. The poetic value of religion would initially be greater than that of poetry itself, because religion deals with higher and more practical themes, with sides of life which are in greater need of some imaginative touch and ideal interpretation than are those pleasant or pompous things which ordinary poetry dwells upon. But this initial advantage is neutralised in part by the abuse to which religion is subject, whenever its symbolic rightness is taken for scientific truth. Like poetry, it improves the world only by imagining it improved, but not content with making this addition to the mind's furniture — an addition which might be useful and ennobling — it thinks to confer a more radical benefit by persuading mankind that, in spite of appearances, the world is really such as that rather arbitrary idealisation has painted it. This spurious satisfaction is naturally the prelude to many a disappointment, and the soul has infinite trouble to emerge again from the artificial problems and sentiments into which it is thus plunged. The value of religion becomes equivocal. Religion remains an imaginative achievement, a symbolic representation of moral reality which may have a most important function in vitalising the mind and in transmitting, by way of parables, the lessons of experience. But it becomes at the same time a continuous incidental deception; and this deception, in proportion as it is strenuously denied to be such, can work indefinite harm in the world and in the conscience.

JEAN-PAUL SARTRE

JEAN-PAUL SARTRE (1905-   ), cousin of the celebrated Albert Schweitzer, was born in Paris on June 21, 1905. His father, a polytechnician, died in Cochin-China when Sartre was but a child. After his mother's second marriage, Sartre was reared by his stepfather in La Rochelle where the boy, at eleven years of age, attended school. His training in philosophy took him to Paris; in 1925, he matriculated at the École Normale Supérieure, and in 1928, his degree in philosophy was conferred upon him. After discharging his military obligation of 16 months of service, he pursued his studies further in Germany where he came under the influence of Husserl. Returning to France, he assumed a career as teacher in Le Havre, then at Paris. The year 1939 found him again in military service involved in World War II; during the war he spent a period of time as a German prisoner of war, but was released to return to Paris owing to ill health.

Sartre's successful literary career began at the age of 33 with the publication of his classic fiction **Nausea** in 1938; he gained fame at 38 with the publication of two dramatic works: **No Exit** and **The Flies.** By 1943, his classic **Being and Nothingness** appeared, and in 1946, his popularized version of existential philosophy, **Existentialism is Humanism.** The post war years found him the most discussed philosopher of Europe and Atheistic Existentialism's foremost spokesman. Other philosophical writings of his are: **Psychology and Imagination** (1936), **Transcendence of the Ego** (1937), **The Emotions, Outline of a Theory** (1939), **Psychology of Imagination** (1940), **Descartes** (1946), **Critique of Dialectical Reason** (1960).

17

JEAN-PAUL SARTRE

Existential Atheism: (God's Absence as Abandonment)[1]

The question [regarding existentialism] is only complicated because there are two kinds of existentialists. There are, on the one hand, the Christians, amongst whom I shall name Jaspers and Gabriel Marcel, both professed Catholics; and on the other the existential atheists, amongst whom we must place Heidegger as well as the French existentialists and myself. What they have in common is simply the fact that they believe that *existence* comes before *essence* — or, if you will, that we must begin from the subjective. What exactly do we mean by that?

If one considers an article of manufacture — as, for example, a book or a paper-knife — one sees that it has been made by an artisan who had a conception of it; and he has paid attention, equally, to the conception of a paper-knife and to the pre-existent technique of production which is a part of that conception and is, at bottom, a formula. Thus the paper-knife is at the same time an article producible in a certain manner and one which, on the other hand, serves a definite purpose, for one cannot suppose that a man would produce a paper-knife without knowing what it was for. Let us say, then, of the paper-knife that its essence — that is to say the sum of the formulae and the qualities which made its production and its definition possible — precedes its existence. The presence of such-and-such a paper-knife or book is thus determined before my eyes. Here, then, we are viewing the world from a technical standpoint, and we can say that production precedes existence.

When we think of God as the creator, we are thinking of him, most of the time, as a supernal artisan. Whatever doctrine we may be considering, whether it be a doctrine like that of Descartes, or of Leibniz himself, we always imply that the will follows, more or less, from the understand-

[1] Jean-Paul Sartre, *Existentialism and Humanism* (London: Methuen & Co. Ltd., 1948), 26-35; translated by Philip Mairet from the French, *L'Existentialisme est un humanisme* (Paris: Les Editions Nagel, 1946). Reprinted by permission.

ing or at least accompanies it, so that when God creates he knows precisely what he is creating. Thus, the conception of man in the mind of God is comparable to that of the paper-knife in the mind of the artisan: God makes man according to a procedure and a conception, exactly as the artisan manufactures a paper-knife, following a definition and a formula. Thus each individual man is the realisation of a certain conception which dwells in the divine understanding. In the philosophic atheism of the eighteenth century, the notion of God is suppressed, but not, for all that, the idea that essence is prior to existence; something of that idea we still find everywhere, in Diderot, in Voltaire and even in Kant. Man possesses a human nature; that "human nature," which is the conception of human being, is found in every man; which means that each man is a particular example of an universal conception, the conception of Man. In Kant, this universality goes so far that the wild man of the woods, man in the state of nature and the bourgeois are all contained in the same definition and have the same fundamental qualities. Here again, the essence of man precedes that historic existence which we confront in experience.

Atheistic existentialism, of which I am a representative, declares with greater consistency that if God does not exist there is at least one being whose existence comes before its essence, a being which exists before it can be defined by any conception of it. That being is man or, as Heidegger has it, the human reality. What do we mean by saying that existence precedes essence? We mean that man first of all exists, encounters himself, surges up in the world — and defines himself afterwards. If man as the existentialist sees him is not definable, it is because to begin with he is nothing. He will not be anything until later, and then he will be what he makes of himself. Thus, there is no human nature, because there is no God to have a conception of it. Man simply is. Not that he is simply what he conceives himself to be, but he is what he wills, and as he conceives himself after already existing — as he wills to be after that leap towards existence. Man is nothing else but that which he makes of himself. That is the first principle of existentialism. And this is what people call its "subjectivity," using the word as a reproach against us. But what do we mean to say by this, but that man is of a greater dignity than a stone or a table? For we mean to say that man primarily exists — that man is, before all else, something which propels itself towards a future and is aware that it is doing so. Man is, indeed, a project which possesses a subjective life, instead of being a kind of moss, or a fungus or a cauliflower. Before that projection of the self nothing exists; not even in the heaven of intelligence: man will only attain existence when he is what he purposes to be. Not, however, what he may wish to be. For what we usually understand by wishing or willing is a conscious decision taken

— much more often that not — after we have made ourselves what we are. I may wish to join a party, to write a book or to marry — but in such a case what is usually called my will is probably a manifestation of a prior and more spontaneous decision. If, however, it is true that existence is prior to essence, man is responsible for what he is. Thus, the first effect of existentialism is that it puts every man in possession of himself as he is, and places the entire responsibility for his existence squarely upon his own shoulders. And, when we say that man is responsible for himself, we do not mean that he is responsible only for his own individuality, but that he is responsible for all men. The word "subjectivism" is to be understood in two senses, and our adversaries play upon only one of them. Subjectivism means, on the one hand, the freedom of the individual subject and, on the other, that man cannot pass beyond human subjectivity. It is the latter which is the deeper meaning of existentialism. When we say that man chooses himself, we do mean that every one of us must choose himself; but by that we also mean that in choosing for himself he chooses for all men. For in effect, of all the actions a man may take in order to create himself as he wills to be, there is not one which is not creative, at the same time, of an image of man such as he believes he ought to be. To choose between this or that is at the same time to affirm the value of that which is chosen; for we are unable ever to choose the worse. What we choose is always the better; and nothing can be better for us unless it is better for all. If, moreover, existence precedes essence and we will to exist at the same time as we fashion our image, that image is valid for all and for the entire epoch in which we find ourselves. Our responsibility is thus much greater than we had supposed, for it concerns mankind as a whole. If I am a worker, for instance, I may choose to join a Christian rather than a Communist trade union. And if, by that membership, I choose to signify that resignation is, after all, the attitude that best becomes a man, that man's kingdom is not upon this earth, I do not commit myself alone to that view. Resignation is my will for everyone, and my action is, in consequence, a commitment on behalf of all mankind. Or if, to take a more personal case, I decide to marry and to have children, even though this decision proceeds simply from my situation, from my passion or my desire, I am thereby committing not only myself, but humanity as a whole, to the practice of monogamy. I am thus responsible for myself and for all men, and I am creating a certain image of man as I would have him to be. In fashioning myself I fashion man.

This may enable us to understand what is meant by such terms — perhaps a little grandiloquent — as anguish, abandonment and despair. As you will soon see, it is very simple. First, what do we mean by anguish?

The existentialist frankly states that man is in anguish. His meaning is as follows — When a man commits himself to anything, fully realising that he is not only choosing what he will be, but is thereby at the same time a legislator deciding for the whole of mankind — in such a moment a man cannot escape from the sense of complete and profound responsibility. There are many, indeed, who show no such anxiety. But we affirm that they are merely disguising their anguish or are in flight from it. Certainly, many people think that in what they are doing they commit no one but themselves to anything: and if you ask them, "What would happen if everyone did so?" they shrug their shoulders and reply, "Everyone does not do so." But in truth, one ought always to ask oneself what would happen if everyone did as one is doing; nor can one escape from that disturbing thought except by a kind of self-deception. The man who lies in self-excuse, by saying "Everyone will not do it" must be ill at ease in his conscience, for the act of lying implies the universal value which it denies. By its very disguise his anguish reveals itself. This is the anguish that Kierkegaard called "the anguish of Abraham." You know the story: An angel commanded Abraham to sacrifice his son: and obedience was obligatory, if it really was an angel who had appeared and said, "Thou, Abraham, shalt sacrifice thy son." But anyone in such a case would wonder, first, whether it was indeed an angel and secondly, whether I am really Abraham. Where are the proofs? A certain mad woman who suffered from hallucinations said that people were telephoning to her, and giving her orders. The doctor asked, "But who is it that speaks to you?" She replied: "He says it is God." And what, indeed, could prove to her that it was God? If an angel appears to me, what is the proof that it is an angel; or, if I hear voices, who can prove that they proceed from heaven and not from hell, or from my own subconsciousness or some pathological condition? Who can prove that they are really addressed to me?

Who, then, can prove that I am the proper person to impose, by my own choice, my conception of man upon mankind? I shall never find any proof whatever; there will be no sign to convince me of it. If a voice speaks to me, it is still I myself who must decide whether the voice is or is not that of an angel. If I regard a certain course of action as good, it is only I who choose to say that it is good and not bad. There is nothing to show that I am Abraham; nevertheless I also am obliged at every instant to perform actions which are examples. Everything happens to every man as though the whole human race had its eyes fixed upon what he is doing and regulated its conduct accordingly. So every man ought to say, "Am I really a man who has the right to act in such a manner that humanity regulates itself by what I do." If a man does not say that, he is

dissembling his anguish. Clearly, the anguish with which we are concerned here is not one that could lead to quietism or inaction. It is anguish pure and simple, of the kind well known to all those who have
borne responsibilities. When, for instance, a military leader takes upon
himself the responsibility for an attack and sends a number of men to
their death, he chooses to do it and at bottom he alone chooses. No doubt
he acts under a higher command, but its orders, which are more general,
require interpretation by him and upon that interpretation depends the
life of ten, fourteen or twenty men. In making the decision, he cannot but
feel a certain anguish. All leaders know that anguish. It does not prevent
their acting, on the contrary it is the very condition of their action, for
the action presupposes that there is a plurality of possibilities, and in
choosing one of these, they realise that it has value only because it is
chosen. Now it is anguish of that kind which existentialism describes,
and moreover, as we shall see, makes explicit through direct responsibility towards other men who are concerned. Far from being a screen
which could separate us from action, it is a condition of action itself.

And when we speak of "abandonment" — a favorite word of Heidegger — we only mean to say that God does not exist, and that it is necessary to draw the consequences of his absence right to the end. The
existentialist is strongly opposed to a certain type of secular moralism
which seeks to suppress God at the least possible expense. Towards 1880,
when the French professors endeavoured to formulate a secular morality,
they said something like this: — God is a useless and costly hypothesis, so
we will do without it. However, if we are to have morality, a society and
law-abiding world, it is essential that certain values should be taken
seriously; they must have an *à priori* existence ascribed to them. It must
be considered obligatory *à priori* to be honest, not to lie, not to beat one's
wife, to bring up children and so forth; so we are going to do a little
work on this subject, which will enable us to show that these values exist
all the same, inscribed in an intelligible heaven although, of course,
there is no God. In other words — and this is, I believe, the purport of
all that we in France call radicalism — nothing will be changed if God
does not exist; we shall re-discover the same norms of honesty, progress
and humanity, and we shall have disposed of God as an out-of-date
hypothesis which will die away quietly of itself. The existentialist, on
the contrary, finds it extremely embarrassing that God does not exist,
for there disappears with Him all possibility of finding values in an intelligible heaven. There can no longer be any good *à priori*, since there is
no infinite and perfect consciousness to think it. It is nowhere written
that "the good" exists, that one must be honest or must not lie, since we
are now upon the plane where there are only men. Dostoievsky once

wrote "If God did not exist, everything would be permitted"; and that, for existentialism, is the starting point. Everything is indeed permitted if God does not exist, and man is in consequence forlorn, for he cannot find anything to depend upon either within or outside himself. He discovers forthwith, that he is without excuse. For if indeed existence precedes essence, one will never be able to explain one's action by reference to a given and specific human nature; in other words, there is no determinism — man is free, man *is* freedom. Nor, on the other hand, if God does not exist, are we provided with any values or commands that could legitimise our behaviour. Thus we have neither behind us, nor before us in a luminous realm of values, any means of justification or excuse. We are left alone, without excuse. That is what I mean when I say that man is condemned to be free. Condemned, because he did not create himself, yet is nevertheless at liberty, and from the moment that he is thrown into this world he is responsible for everything he does. The existentialist does not believe in the power of passion. He will never regard a grand passion as a destructive torrent upon which a man is swept into certain actions as by fate, and which, therefore, is an excuse for them. He thinks that man is responsible for his passion. Neither will an existentialist think that a man can find help through some sign being vouchsafed upon earth for his orientation: for he thinks that the man himself interprets the sign as he chooses. He thinks that every man, without any support or help whatever, is condemned at every instant to invent man. As Ponge has written in a very fine article, "Man is the future of man." That is exactly true. Only, if one took this to mean that the future is laid up in Heaven, that God knows what it is, it would be false, for then it would no longer even be a future. If, however, it means that whatever man may now appear to be, there is a future to be fashioned, a virgin future that awaits him — then it is a true saying. But in the present one is forsaken. . . .

. . . An [2] existentialist will never take man as the end, since man is still to be determined. And we have no right to believe that humanity is something to which we could set up a cult, after the manner of Auguste Comte. The cult of humanity ends in Comtian humanism, shut-in upon itself, and — this must be said — in Fascism. We do not want a humanism like that.

But there is another sense of the word, of which the fundamental meaning is this: Man is all the time outside of himself: it is in projecting and losing himself beyond himself that he makes man to exist; and, on the other hand, it is by pursuing transcendent aims that he himself is able

[2] *Ibid.*, 55-66.

to exist. Since man is thus self-surpassing, and can grasp objects only in relation to his self-surpassing, he is himself the heart and centre of his transcendence. There is no other universe except the human universe, the universe of human subjectivity. This relation of transcendence as constitutive of man (not in the sense that God is transcendent, but in the sense of self-surpassing) with subjectivity (in such a sense that man is not shut up in himself but forever present in a human universe) — it is this that we call existential humanism. This is humanism, because we remind man that there is no legislator but himself; that he himself, thus abandoned, must decide for himself; also because we show that it is not by turning back upon himself, but always by seeking, beyond himself, an aim which is one of liberation or of some particular realisation, that man can realise himself as truly human.

You can see from these few reflections that nothing could be more unjust than the objections people raise against us. Existentialism is nothing else but an attempt to draw the full conclusions from a consistently atheistic position. Its intention is not in the least that of plunging men into despair. And if by despair one means — as the Christians do — any attitude of unbelief, the despair of the existentialists is something different. Existentialism is not atheist in the sense that it would exhaust itself in demonstrations of the non-existence of God. It declares, rather, that even if God existed that would make no difference from its point of view. Not that we believe God does exist, but we think that the real problem is not that of His existence; what man needs is to find himself again and to understand that nothing can save him from himself, not even a valid proof of the existence of God. In this sense existentialism is optimistic, it is a doctrine of action, and it is only by self-deception, by confusing their own despair with ours that Christians can describe us as without despair.

Part Three: AGNOSTICISM

A Noncommittal Position

THOMAS H. HUXLEY

THOMAS HENRY HUXLEY (1825-1895) was born at Ealing, England, the son of a schoolmaster, but without formal education. At 17, he matriculated at Charing Cross Hospital to undertake medical studies; he graduated at 20, then passed the requisite examinations qualifying him for the Royal College of Surgeons. At 25, he was elected Fellow of the Royal Society; at 26, he received the royal medal and election to the council. Like Darwin, he too went on ocean voyages, gathering material which led him to adopt the philosophical thought of Evolutionary Naturalism. In 1854, he accepted the assignment as lecturer at the School of Mines, and the following year, the year of his marriage, he became a naturalist for the Geological Survey. Scientific research subsided sharply after 1870, when he became active in the Royal Society, and in 1881 to 1885, its president. In 1892, he accepted the position of Privy Councillorship, but his health steadily weakening, he became predominantly engaged in controversial writing and addresses defending the Theory of Evolution as a result of attacks on him and Darwin.

Huxley coined the term **Agnosticism,** the position of one who professes ignorance respecting the existence of God, and the term **Epiphenomenalism,** the theory that mind is the by-product of bodily functions. His writings include: **Evidence as to Man's Place in Nature** (1863) **Lay Sermons, Addresses and Reviews** (1870), **Science and Morals** (1886), **Agnosticism** (1889), **Agnosticism and Christianity** (1889), **Evolution and Ethics** (1893).

18

THOMAS H. HUXLEY

Agnosticism[1]

. . . When I reached intellectual maturity and began to ask myself whether I was an atheist, a theist, or a pantheist; a materialist or an idealist; a Christian or a freethinker; I found that the more I learned and reflected, the less ready was the answer; until, at last, I came to the conclusion that I had neither art nor part with any of these denominations, except the last. The one thing in which most of these good people were agreed was the one thing in which I differed from them. They were quite sure they had attained a certain "gnosis," — had, more or less successfully, solved the problem of existence; while I was quite sure I had not, and had a pretty strong conviction that the problem was insoluble. And, with Hume and Kant on my side, I could not think myself presumptuous in holding fast by that opinion. On the contrary, I had, and have, the firmest conviction that I never left the "verace via" — the straight road; and that this road led nowhere else but into the dark depths of a wild and tangled forest. And though I have found leopards and lions in the path; though I have made abundant acquaintance with the hungry wolf, that "with privy paw devours apace and nothing said," as another great poet says of the ravening beast; and though no friendly specter has even yet offered his guidance, I was, and am, minded to go straight on, until I either come out on the other side of the wood, or find there is no other side to it, at least, none attainable by me.

This was my situation when I had the good fortune to find a place among the members of that remarkable confraternity of antagonists, long since deceased, but of green and pious memory, the Metaphysical Society. Every variety of philosophical and theological opinion was represented there, and expressed itself with entire openness; most of my colleagues were -ists of one sort or another; and, however, kind and

---

[1] Thomas H. Huxley, *Science and Christian Tradition* (1894); excerpts from the chapter on "Agnosticism."

friendly they might be, I, the man without a rag of a label to cover himself with, could not fail to have some of the uneasy feelings which must have beset the historical fox when, after leaving the trap in which his tail remained, he presented himself to his normally elongated companions. So I took thought, and invented what I conceived to be the appropriate title of "agnostic." It came into my head as suggestively antithetic to the "gnostic" of Church history, who professed to know so much about the very things of which I was ignorant; and I took the earliest opportunity of parading it at our Society, to show that I, too, had a tail, like the other foxes. To my great satisfaction, the term took; and when the *Spectator* has stood godfather to it, any suspicion in the minds of respectable people, that a knowledge of its parentage might have awakened, was, of course, completely lulled. . . .

It appears that Mr. Gladstone some time ago asked Mr. Laing if he could draw up a short summary of the negative creed; a body of negative propositions, which have so far been adopted on the negative side as to be what the Apostles' and other accepted creeds are on the positive; and Mr. Laing at once kindly obliged Mr. Gladstone with the desired articles — eight of them.

If any one had preferred this request to me I should have replied that, if he referred to agnostics, they have no creed; and, by the nature of the case, can not have any. Agnosticism, in fact, is not a creed, but a method, the essence of which lies in the rigorous application of a single principle. That principle is of great antiquity; it is as old as Socrates; as old as the writer who said, "Try all things, hold fast by that which is good"; it is the foundation of the Reformation, which simply illustrated the axiom that every man should be able to give a reason for the faith that is in him; it is the great principle of Descartes; it is the fundamental axiom of modern science. Positively the principle may be expressed: In matters of the intellect follows your reason as far as it will take you without regard to any other consideration. And negatively: In matters of the intellect do not pretend that conclusions are certain which are not demonstrated or demonstrable. That I take to be the agnostic faith, which if a man keep whole and undefiled, he shall not be ashamed to look the universe in the face, whatever the future may have in store for him.

The results of the working out of the agnostic principle will vary according to individual knowledge and capacity, and according to the general condition of science. That which is unproved today may be proved by the help of new discoveries tomorrow. The only negative fixed points will be those negations which flow from the demonstrable limitation of our faculties. And the only obligation accepted is to have the mind always open to conviction. Agnostics who never fail in carrying out their principles are, I am afraid, as rare as other people of whom the same consistency can be truthfully predicted. But, if you were to meet with such a phoenix and to tell him that you had discovered that two and two make five, he would patiently ask you to state your reasons for that conviction, and express his readiness to agree with you if he found them satisfactory. The apostolic injunction to "suffer fools gladly" should be the rule of life of a true agnostic. I am deeply conscious how far I myself fall short of this ideal, but it is my personal conception of what agnostics ought to be.

19

IMMANUEL KANT

Kantian Agnosticism[1]

The Arguments of Speculative Reason in Proofs of the Existence of a Supreme Being

... There are only three kinds of proofs of the existence of God from speculative reason.

All the paths that can be followed to this end begin either from definite experience and the peculiar nature of the world of sense, known to us through experience, and ascend from it, according to the laws of causality, to the highest cause, existing outside the world; or they rest on indefinite experience only, that is, on any experience which is empirically given; or lastly, they leave all experience out of account, and conclude, entirely *a priori* from mere concepts, the existence of a supreme cause. The first proof is the *physico-theological,* the second the *cosmological,* the third the *ontological* proof. There are no more, and there can be no more.

I shall show that neither on the one path, the empirical, nor on the other, the transcendental, can reason achieve anything, and that it stretches its wings in vain, if it tries to soar beyond the world of sense by the mere power of speculation. With regard to the order in which these three arguments should be examined, it will be the opposite of that, followed by reason in its gradual development, in which we placed them also at first ourselves. For we shall be able to show that, although experience gives the first impulse, it is the transcendental concept only which guides reason in its endeavours, and fixes the last goal which reason wishes to retain. I shall therefore begin with the examination of the transcendental proof, and see afterwards how far it may be strengthened by the addition of empirical elements.

[1] Immanuel Kant, *The Critique of Pure Reason,* tr. F. Max Müller (1891), original German edition, 1781, 1787; selections from bk. II, ch. 3, sect. 3-6.

The Ontological Proof

... I might have hoped to put an end to this subtle argumentation, without many words, and simply by an accurate definition of the concept of existence, if I had not seen that the illusion, in mistaking a logical predicate for a real one (that is the predicate which determines a thing), resists all correction. Everything can become a *logical predicate*, even the subject itself may be predicated of itself, because logic takes no account of any contents of concepts. Determination, however, is a predicate, added to the concept of the subject, and enlarging it, and it must not therefore be contained in it.

Being is evidently not a real predicate, or a concept of something that can be added to the concept of a thing. It is merely the admission of a thing, and of certain determinations in it. Logically, it is merely the copula of a judgment. The proposition, *God is almighty,* contains two concepts, each having its object, namely, God and almightiness. The small word *is,* is not an additional predicate, but only serves to put the predicate *in relation* to the subject. If, then, I take the subject (God) with all its predicates (including that of almightiness), and say, *God is* or there is a God, I do not put a new predicate to the concept of God, but only put the subject by itself, with all its predicates, in relation to my concept, as its object. Both must contain exactly the same kind of thing, and nothing can have been added to the concept, which expresses possibility only, by my thinking its object as simply given and saying, it is. And thus the real does not contain more than the possible. A hundred real dollars do not contain a penny more than a hundred possible dollars. For as the latter signify the concept, the former the object and its position by itself, it is clear that, in case the former contained more than the latter, my concept would not express the whole object, and would not therefore be its adequate concept. In my financial position no doubt there exists more by one hundred real dollars, than by their concept only (that is their possibility), because in reality the object is not only contained analytically in my concept, but is added to my concept (which is a determination of my state), synthetically; but the conceived hundred dollars are not in the least increased through the existence which is outside my concept.

By whatever and however many predicates I may think a thing (even in completely determining it), nothing is really added to it, if I add that the thing exists. Otherwise, it would not be the same that exists, but something more than was contained in the concept, and I could not say that the exact object of my concept existed. ...

The concept of a Supreme Being is, in many respects, a very useful idea, but, being an idea only, it is quite incapable of increasing, by itself alone, our knowledge with regard to what exists. It cannot even do so much as to inform us any further as to its possibility. The analytical characteristic of possibility, which consists in the absence of contradiction in mere positions (realities), cannot be denied to it; but the connection of all real properties in one and the same thing is a synthesis the possibility of which we cannot judge *a priori* because these realities are not given to us as such, and because, even if this were so, no judgment whatever takes place, it being necessary to look for the characteristic of the possibility of synthetical knowledge in experience only, to which the object of an idea can never belong. Thus we see that the celebrated Leibnitz is far from having achieved what he thought he had, namely, to understand *a priori* the possibility of so sublime an ideal Being.

Time and labour therefore are lost on the famous ontological (Cartesian) proof of the existence of a Supreme Being from mere concepts; and a man might as well imagine that he could become richer in knowledge by mere ideas, as a merchant in capital, if, in order to improve his position, he were to add a few thoughts to his cash account.

The Cosmological Proof

... The *cosmological proof*, which we have now to examine, retains the connection of absolute necessity with the highest reality, but instead of concluding, like the former, from the highest reality necessity in existence, it concludes from the given unconditioned necessity of any being, its unlimited reality. It thus brings everything at least into the groove of a natural, though I know not whether of a really or only apparently rational syllogism, which carries the greatest conviction, not only for the common, but also for the speculative understanding, and has evidently drawn the first outline of all proofs of natural theology, which have been followed at all times, and will be followed in future also, however much they may be hidden and disguised. We shall now proceed to exhibit and to examine this cosmological proof which Leibnitz calls also the proof *a contingentia mundi*.

It runs as follows: If there exists anything, there must exist an absolutely necessary Being also. Now I, at least, exist; therefore there exists an absolutely necessary Being. The minor contains an experience, the major the conclusion from experience in general to the existence of the necessary. This proof therefore begins with experience, and is not entirely *a priori*, or ontological; and, as the object of all possible experience is called the world, this proof is called the *cosmological proof*. As it takes no account of any peculiar property of the objects of experience, by which this world of ours may differ from any other possible world, it is distinguished, in its name also, from the physico-theological proof, which employs as arguments, observations of the peculiar property of this our world of sense.

The proof then proceeds as follows: The necessary Being can be determined in one way only, that is, by one only of all possible opposite predicates; it must therefore be determined completely by its own concept. Now, there is only one concept of a thing possible, which *a priori* completely determines it, namely, that of the *ens realissimum*. It follows, therefore, that the concept of the *ens realissimum* is the only one by which a necessary Being can be thought, and therefore it is concluded that a highest Being exists by necessity. . . .

I said before that a whole nest of dialectical assumptions was hidden in that cosmological proof, and that transcendental criticism might easily detect and destroy it. I shall here enumerate them only, leaving it to the experience of the reader to follow up the fallacies and remove them.

We find, first, the transcendental principle of inferring a cause from the accidental. This principle, that everything contingent must have a cause, is valid in the world of sense only, and has not even a meaning outside it. For the purely intellectual concept of the contingent cannot produce a synthetical proposition like that of causality, and the principle of causality has no meaning and no criterion of its use, except in the world of sense, while here it is meant to help us beyond the world of sense.

Secondly. The inference of a first cause, based on the impossibility of an infinite ascending series of given causes in this world of sense, — an inference which the principles of the use of reason do not allow us to draw even in experience, while here we extend that principle beyond experience, whither that series can never be prolonged.

Thirdly. The false self-satisfaction of reason with regard to the completion of that series, brought about by removing in the end every kind of condition, without which, nevertheless, no concept of necessity is possible, and by then, when any definite concepts have become impossible, accepting this as a completion of our concept.

Fourthly. The mistaking the logical possibility of a concept of all united reality (without any internal contradiction) for the transcendental, which requires a principle for the practicability of such a synthesis, such principle however being applicable to the field of possible experience only, etc. . . .

The Physico-Theological Proof

If, then, neither the concept of things in general, nor the experience of any *existence in general*, can satisfy our demands, there still remains one way open, namely, to try whether any *definite experience,* and consequently that of things in the world as it is, their constitution and disposition, may not supply a proof which could give us the certain conviction of the existence of a Supreme Being. Such a proof we should call *physico-theological.* . . .

The principle points of the physico-theological proof are the following.

1st. There are everywhere in the world clear indications of an intentional arrangement carried out with great wisdom, and forming a whole indescribably varied in its contents and infinite in extent.

2dly. The fitness of this arrangement is entirely foreign to the things existing in the world, and belongs to them contingently only; that is, the nature of different things could never spontaneously, by the combination of so many means, co-operate towards definite aims, if these means had not been selected and arranged on purpose by a rational disposing principle, according to certain fundamental ideas.

3dly. There exists, therefore, a sublime and wise cause (or many), which must be the cause of the world, not only as a blind and all-powerful nature, by means of unconscious *fecundity,* but as an intelligence, by *freedom.*

4thly. The unity of that cause may be inferred with certainty from the unity of the reciprocal relation of the reciprocal relation of the parts of the world, as portions of a skilful edifice, so far as our experience reaches, and beyond it, with plausibility, according to the principles of analogy.

According to this argument, the fitness and harmony existing in so many works of nature might prove the contingency of the form, but not of the matter, that is, the substance in the world, because, for the latter purpose, it would be necessary to prove in addition, that the things of the world were in themselves incapable of such order and harmony, according to general laws, unless there existed, even in their *substance,* the product of a supreme wisdom. For this purpose, very different arguments would be required from those derived from the analogy of human art. The utmost, therefore, that could be established by such a proof would be an *architect of the world,* always very much hampered by the quality of the material with which he has to work, not a *creator,* to whose idea everything is subject. This would by no means suffice for the purposed aim of proving an all-sufficient original Being. If we wished to prove the contingency of matter itself, we must have recourse to a transcendental argument, and this is the very thing which was to be avoided. . . .

CHARLES DARWIN

CHARLES ROBERT DARWIN (1809-1882) was born in Shrewsbury, England on February 12, 1809 and died in Down, Kent, on April 19, 1882. His childhood schooling was at the Shrewsbury School, and in 1825 he went to study medicine at the University of Edinburgh, and later theology at Christ's College, Cambridge, where he was granted his degree in 1831. From the year of his graduation to 1836, his voyages on the **H.M.S. Beagle** carried him the world over; it was on this journey, from the facts acquired and observations made, that Darwin first formulated his classic Theory of Biological Evolution.

Darwin was for many years a Theist who accepted belief in revelation, and notwithstanding the appearance of his monumental work, **The Origin of Species** (1859-1872), he remained a Theist, but when his **Autobiography** was published in 1879, it declared him to be an Agnostic, the position of one who suspends judgment regarding the existence of God. It is interesting that Darwin employs the term **Agnostic,** the creation of his former student, Thomas H. Huxley, who coined the term in 1859. In addition to the two books mentioned above, Darwin's works include: **The Descent of Man** (1871), **Variations of Animals and Plants under Domestication** (1868), **Expression of the Emotions in Men and in Animals** (1872). The excerpt pertaining to the doctrine of Natural Selection and Survival of the Fittest has been taken from his **Origin of Species;** the sale of the first edition was exhausted the day of publication.

Intrigued by the prevalence of forms and qualities in species corresponding with the environment most suited for purposes of a satisfactory adjustment or adaptation to life, and obsessed with the possible cause of such phenomena, Darwin set out in search of them. Influenced by Malthusian ideas, particularly that living creatures survive to numbers beyond their means of subsistence, Darwin concluded that "living beings must mutually co-operate, must struggle or contend with one another in order to procure the necessities of life. Life is and must be a struggle for existence, and that individual or group of individuals which, from one reason or another, possess a faculty or an organ which the rest lack, and which corresponds to the environment, is more likely than others to succeed in the struggle. The propagation of the race will be carried on chiefly by them, and such forms as are wanting in this faculty or this organ will gradually die out. And when a group of living beings have to live within a limited space they can do so more easily the greater the difference which exists between the forms comprising this group, for in that case their different requirements can be more easily satisfied. If they all require the same food it is clear that not so many can find sustenance as when they feed on different things. In the struggle for existence, then, it is an advantage to any species to possess the faculty of variation." [1] Herein we find the seeds of the Theory of Evolution.

Darwin, unable to reconcile himself to the fact that the cruelties and sufferings of nature were deigned by the hand of God, relegated such behavior to a struggle for existence, Natural Selection, the doctrine of the Survival of the Fittest. Biological nature today, claims Darwin, is the product of an extended developmental process originating from meager beginnings to the sophisticated levels of today under the continual influence of environmental factors.

Whereas the expression: "struggle for existence" refers to the ability of the organism to adapt to its environment, both animate and vegetative, Darwin employs the term Natural Selection to signify the environmental factor in its tendency to prefer certain qualities, **i.e.,** the preservation of qualities useful to individual preservation. That organism which is fitting or suitable to preservation, the enhancement of life, or adaptation to environment, is preserved, while that whose utility is diminished until it serves its purpose poorly, or can be replaced with a better, dies out. "Purposive variations are preserved, the others die out." Only that which significantly contributes in a definite manner to the whole economy of life can possibly exist, develop, or come into being initially.

The major failure of Darwinian Evolution is its inability to explain the "arrival of the fittest" without postulating the existence of Deity; subsequent Evolutionary Naturalists have philosophized that a principle, such as God, is a necessary hypothesis.

In the **Descent of Man,** Darwin offered the radical view that man's origin is not as traditional theology taught, a fallen angel, but from lower forms of existence; yet in the mind of Darwin, man's stature suffered no diminution owing to this humble beginning — the fact that man developed into a spiritual being is both awesome and wonderful.

[1] Harald Hoffding, **A History of Modern Philosophy,** tr. B.E. Meyer (London: Macmillan and Co., 1900), bk. 9, ch 1. sect. (a).

20

CHARLES DARWIN

Natural Selection (Survival of the Fittest)[1]

How will the struggle for existence . . . act in regard to variation? Can the principle of selection, which we have seen is so potent in the hands of man, apply under nature? I think we shall see that it can act most efficiently. Let the endless number of slight variations and individual differences occurring in our domestic productions, and in a lesser degree, in those under nature, be borne in mind; as well as the strength of the hereditary tendency. Under domestication, it may truly be said that the whole organization becomes in some degree plastic. But the variability, which we almost universally meet with in our domestic productions is not directly produced, as Hooker and Asa Gray have well remarked, by man; he can neither originate varieties nor prevent their occurrence; he can only preserve and accumulate such as do occur. Unintentionally he exposes organic beings to new and changing conditions of life, and variability ensues; but similar changes of conditions might and do occur under nature. Let it also be borne in mind how infinitely complex and close-fitting are the mutual relations of all organic beings to each other and to their physical conditions of life; and consequently what infinitely varied diversities of structure might be of use to each being under changing conditions of life. Can it then be thought improbable, seeing that variations useful to man have undoubtedly occurred, that other variations useful in some way to each being in the great and complex battle of life, should occur in the course of many successive generations? If such do occur, can we doubt (remembering that many more individuals are born than can possibly survive) that individuals having any advantage, however slight, over others, would have the best chance of surviving and procreating their kind? On the other hand, we may feel sure that any variation in the least degree injurious would be rigidly de-

[1] Charles Darwin, *The Origin of Species* (1859-1872); selections from chapter 4.

stroyed. This preservation of favorable individual differences and variations, and the destruction of those which are injurious, I have called
Natural Selection, or the Survival of the Fittest. Variations neither useful
nor injurious would not be affected by natural selection, and would be left
either a fluctuating element, as perhaps we see in certain polymorphic
species, or would ultimately become fixed, owing to the nature of the
organism and the nature of the conditions.

Several writers have misapprehended or objected to the term Natural
Selection. Some have even imagined that natural selection induces variability, whereas it implies only the preservation of such variations as arise
and are beneficial to the being under its conditions of life. No one objects
to agriculturists speaking of the potent effects of man's selection; and in
this case the individual differences given by nature, which man for some
object selects, must of necessity first occur. Others have objected that the
term selection implies conscious choice in the animals which become
modified; and it has even been urged that, natural selection is a false
term; but who ever objected to chemists speaking of the elective affinities
of the various elements? — and yet an acid cannot strictly be said to
elect the base with which it in preference combines. It has been said that
I speak of natural selection as an active power or Deity; but who objects
to an author speaking of the attraction of gravity as ruling the movements
of the planets? Every one knows what is meant and is implied by such
metaphorical expressions; and they are almost necessary for brevity. So
again it is difficult to avoid personifying the word Nature; but I mean by
nature, only the aggregate action and product of many natural laws, and
by laws the sequence of events as ascertained by us. With a little famil-
iarity such superficial objections will be forgotten.

We shall best understand the probable course of natural selection by
taking the case of a country undergoing some slight physical change, for
instance, of climate. The proportional numbers of its inhabitants will
almost immediately undergo a change, and some species will probably
become extinct. We may conclude, from what we have seen of the intimate and complex manner in which the inhabitants of each country are
bound together, that any change in the numerical proportions of the inhabitants, independently of the change of climate itself, would seriously
affect the others. If the country were open on its borders, new forms
would certainly immigrate, and this would likewise seriously disturb the
relations of some of the former inhabitants. Let it be remembered how
powerful the influence of a single introduced tree or mammal has been
shown to be. But in the case of an island, or of a country partly sur-

rounded by barriers, into which new and better adapted forms could not freely enter, we should then have places in the economy of nature which would assuredly be better filled up if some of the original inhabitants were in some manner modified; for, had the area been open to immigration, these same places would have been seized on by intruders. In such cases, slight modifications, which in any way favored the individuals of any species, by better adapting them to their altered conditions, would tend to be preserved; and natural selection would have free scope for the work of improvement.

We have good reason to believe, as shown in the first chapter, that changes in the conditions of life give a tendency to increased variability; and in the foregoing cases the conditions have changed, and this would manifestly be favorable to natural selection, by affording a better chance of profitable variations. Unless such occur, natural selection can do nothing. Under the term "variations," it must never be forgotten that mere individual differences are included. As man can produce a great result with his domestic animals and plants by adding up in any given direction individual differences, so could natural selection, but far more easily from having incomparably longer time for action. Nor do I believe that any great physical change, as of climate, or an unusual degree of isolation, to check immigration, is necessary in order that new and unoccupied places should be left for natural selection to fill up by improving some of the varying inhabitants. For as all the inhabitants of each country are struggling together with nicely balanced forces, extremely slight modifications in the structure or habits of once species would often give it an advantage over others; and still further increase the advantage, as long as the species continued under the same conditions of life and profited by similar means of subsistence and defence. No country can be named in which all the native inhabitants are now so perfectly adapted to each other and to the physical conditions under which they live, that none of them could be still better adapted or improved; for in all countries the natives have been so far conquered by naturalized productions that they have allowed some foreigners to take firm possession of the land. And as foreigners have thus in every country beaten some of the natives, we may safely conclude that the natives might have been modified with advantage, so as to have better resisted the intruders.

As man can produce, and certainly has produced, a great result by his methodical and unconscious means of selection, what may not natural selection effect? Man can act only on external and visible characters; Nature, if I may be allowed to personify the natural preservation or survival of the fittest, cares nothing for appearances, except in so far as they are useful to any being. She can act on every internal organ, on every shade of constitutional difference on the whole machinery of life. Man selects only for his own good; Nature only for that of the being which she tends. Every selected character is fully exercised by her, as is implied by the fact of their selection. Man keeps the natives of many climates in the same country. He seldom exercises each selected character in some peculiar and fitting manner; he feeds a long and a short-beaked pigeon on the same food; he does not exercise a long-backed or long-legged quadruped in any peculiar manner; he exposes sheep with long and short wool to the same climate; does not allow the most vigorous males to struggle for the females; he does not rigidly destroy all inferior animals, but protects during each varying season, as far as lies in his power, all his productions. He often begins his selection by some half-monstrous form, or at least by some modification prominent enough to catch the eye or to be plainly useful to him. Under nature, the slightest differences of structure or constitution may well turn the nicely balanced scale in the struggle for life, and be preserved. How fleeting are the wishes and efforts of man! How short his time, and consequently how poor will be his results, compared with those accumulated by Nature during whole geological periods! Can we wonder, then, that Nature's productions should be far "truer" in character than man's productions; that they should be infinitely better adapted to the most complex conditions of life, and should plainly bear the stamp of far higher workmanship?

It may metaphorically be said that natural selection is daily and hourly scrutinizing, throughout the world, the slightest variations; rejecting those that are bad, preserving and adding up all that are good; silently and insensibly working, *whenever and wherever opportunity offers,* at the improvement of each organic being in relation to its organic and inorganic conditions of life. We see nothing of these slow changes in progress, until the hand of time has marked the lapse of ages, and then so imperfect is our view into long-past geological ages that we see only that the forms of life are now different from what they formerly were.

In order that any great amount of modification should be effected in a species, a variety, when once formed must again, perhaps after a long interval of time, vary or present individual differences of the same favorable nature as before; and these must again be preserved, and so onward, step by step. . . .

Although natural selection can act only through and for the good of each being, yet characters and structures, which we are apt to consider as of very trifling importance, may thus be acted on. When we see leaf-eating insects green, and bark-feeders mottled-grey; the alpine ptarmigan white in winter, the red grouse the color of heather, we must believe that these tints are of service to those birds and insects in preserving them from danger. . . .

In looking at many small points of difference between species, which, as far as our ignorance permits us to judge, seem quite unimportant, we must not forget that climate, food, etc., have no doubt produced some direct effect. It is also necessary to bear in mind that, owing to the law of correlation, when one part varies and the variations are accumulated through natural selection, other modifications, often of the most unexpected nature, will ensue. . . .

. . . . .

What[1] my own views may be is a question of no consequence to any one but myself. But, as you ask, I may state that my judgment often fluctuates. . . . In my most extreme fluctuations I have never been an Atheist in the sense of denying the existence of God. I think that generally (and more and more as I grow older), but not always, that an Agnostic would be the more correct description of my state of mind. . . .

Although I did not think much about the existence of a personal God until a considerably later period of my life, I will give the vague conclusions to which I have been driven. The old argument from design in Nature, as given by Paley, which formerly seemed to me so conclusive, fails, now that the law of natural selection has been discovered. We can no longer argue that, for instance, the beautiful hinge of a bivalve shell must have been made by an intelligent being, like the hinge of a door by man. There seems to be no more design in the variability of organic beings, and in the action of natural selection, than in the course which the wind blows. But I have discussed this subject at the end of my book on the 'Variations of Domesticated Animals and Plants,'[2] and the argument there given has never, as far as I can see, been answered.

[1] Charles Darwin, *The Life and Letters of Charles Darwin;* edited by his son, Francis Darwin (New York: D. Appleton and Co., 1889); excerpts from chapter 8.

[2] My father asks whether we are to believe that the forms are preordained of the broken fragments of rock tumbled from a precipice which are fitted together by man to build his houses. If not, why should we believe that the variations of domestic animals or plants are preordained for the sake of the breeder? "But if we give up the principle in one case, . . . no shadow of reason can be assigned for the belief that variations, alike in nature and the result of the same general laws, which have been the groundwork through natural selection of the formation of the most perfectly adapted animals in the world, man included, were intentionally and specially guided." — 'The Variation of Animals and Plants,' 1st ed. vol. II, 431. [The above footnote by Francis Darwin.]

But passing over the endless beautiful adaptations which we every-where meet with, it may be asked how can the generally beneficent ar-rangement of the world be accounted for? Some writers indeed are so much impressed with the amount of suffering in the world, that they doubt, if we look to all sentient beings, whether there is more of misery or of happiness; whether the world as a whole is a good or bad one. Ac-cording to my judgment happiness decidedly prevails, though this would be very difficult to prove. If the truth of this conclusion be granted, it harmonizes well with the effects which we might expect from natural selection. If all the individuals of any species were habitually to suffer to an extreme degree, they would neglect to propagate their kind; but we have no reason to believe that this has ever, or at least often occurred. Some other considerations, moreover, lead to the belief that all sentient beings have been formed so as to enjoy, as a general rule, happiness.

Every one who believes, as I do, that all the corporeal and mental organs (excepting those which are neither advantageous nor disadvan-tageous to the possessor) of all beings have been developed through nat-ural selection, or the survival of the fittest, together with use or habit, will admit that these organs have been formed so that their possessors may compete successfully with other beings, and thus increase in number. Now an animal may be led to pursue that course of action which is most beneficial to the species by suffering, such as pain, hunger, thirst, and fear; or by pleasure, as in eating and drinking, and in the propagation of the species, &c.; or by both means combined, as in the search for food. But pain or suffering of any kind, if long continued, causes depression and lessens the power of action, yet is well adapted to make a creature guard itself against any great or sudden evil. Pleasurable sensations, on the other hand, may be long continued without any depressing effect; on the contrary, they stimulate the whole system to increased action. Hence it has come to pass that most or all sentient beings have been developed in such a manner, through natural selection, that pleasurable sensations serve as their habitual guides. We see this in the pleasure from exertion, even occasionally from great exertion of the body or mind, — in the pleasure of our daily meals, and especially in the pleasure derived from sociability, and from loving our families. The sum of such pleasures as these, which are habitual or frequently recurrent, give, as I can hardly doubt, to most sentient beings an excess of happiness over misery, al-though many occasionally suffer much. Such suffering is quite compatible with the belief in Natural Selection, which is not perfect in its action, but tends only to render each species as successful as possible in the battle for life with other species, in wonderfully complex and changing circumstances.

That there is much suffering in the world no one disputes. Some have attempted to explain this with reference to man by imagining that it serves for his moral improvement. But the number of men in the world is as nothing compared with that of all other sentient beings, and they often suffer greatly without any moral improvement. This very old argument from the existence of suffering against the existence of an intelligent First Cause seems to me a strong one; whereas, as just remarked, the presence of much suffering agrees well with the view that all organic beings have been developed through variation and natural selection.

At the present day the most usual argument for the existence of an intelligent God is drawn from the deep inward conviction and feelings which are experienced by most persons.

Formerly I was led by feelings such as those just referred to (although I do not think that the religious sentiment was ever strongly developed in me), to the firm conviction of the existence of God, and of the immortality of the soul. In my Journal I wrote that whilst standing in the midst of the grandeur of a Brazilian forest, "it is not possible to give an adequate idea of the higher feelings of wonder, admiration, and devotion, which fill and elevate the mind." I well remember my conviction that there is more in man than the mere breath of his body. But now the grandest scenes would not cause any such convictions and feelings to rise in my mind. It may be truly said that I am like a man who has become colour-blind, and the universal belief by men of the existence of redness makes my present loss of perception of not the least value as evidence. This argument would be a valid one if all men of all races had the same inward conviction of the existence of one God; but we know that this is very far from being the case. Therefore I cannot see that such inward convictions and feelings are of any weight as evidence of what really exists. The state of mind which grand scenes formerly excited in me, and which was intimately connected with a belief in God, did not essentially differ from that which is often called the sense of sublimity; and however difficult it may be to explain the genesis of this sense, it can hardly be advanced as an argument for the existence of God, any more than the powerful though vague and similar feelings excited by music.

With respect to immortality, nothing shows me [so clearly] how strong and almost instinctive a belief it is, as the consideration of the view now held by most physicists, namely, that the sun with all the planets will in time grow too cold for life, unless indeed some great body dashes into the sun, and thus gives it fresh life. Believing as I do that man in the distant future will be a far more perfect creature than he now is, it is an intolerable thought that he and all other sentient beings are doomed to complete annihilation after such long-continued slow progress. To those who fully admit the immortality of the human soul, the destruction of our world will not appear so dreadful.

Another source of conviction in the existence of God, connected with the reason, and not with the feelings, impresses me as having much more weight. This follows from the extreme difficulty or rather impossibility of conceiving this immense and wonderful universe, including man with his capacity of looking far backwards and far into futurity, as the result of blind chance or necessity. When thus reflecting I feel compelled to look to a First Cause having an intelligent mind in some degree analogous to that of man; and I deserve to be called a Theist. This conclusion was strong in my mind about the time, as far as I can remember, when I wrote the 'Origin of Species;' and it is since that time that it has very gradually, with many fluctuations, become weaker. But then arises the doubt, can the mind of man, which has, as I fully believe, been developed from a mind as low as that possessed by the lowest animals, be trusted when it draws such grand conclusions?

I cannot pretend to throw the least light on such abstruse problems. The mystery of the beginning of all things is insoluble by us; and I for one must be content to remain an Agnostic.

Natural selection will modify the structure of the young in relation to the parent and of the parent in relation to the young. In social animals it will adapt the structure of each individual for the benefit of the whole community; if the community profits by the selected change. What natural selection cannot do, is to modify the structure of one species, without giving it any advantage, for the good of another species; and though statements to this effect may be found in works of natural history, I cannot find one case which will bear investigation. . . .

BERTRAND RUSSELL

BERTRAND ARTHUR WILLIAM RUSSELL (1872-   ), born at Trelleck, Wales, godson of John Stuart Mill, was taught by governesses and tutors until in 1890 he went to Trinity College, Cambridge. At school, he distinguished himself in philosophy by being elected a fellow in 1895, but left for Paris the previous year as an attache of the British Embassy. In 1908, he was elected fellow of the Royal Society, and, in 1910, appointed lecturer at Cambridge. Owing to his pacifistic stand during World War I, he lost his academic position, and when Harvard offered him an appointment, the British Government refused to grant him a passport, but he did lecture at Harvard in the spring of 1914. In 1920, he lectured on philosophy at Peiping University, China, and from 1927 to 1932, he operated a school for children. The school year of 1939 was spent as Professor of Philosophy at the University of California, and in 1940, when the College of the City of New York appointed him to teach, the mayor abolished the position as a means of discharging him, owing to his controversial views on morals; in 1943, his contract as lecturer for the Barnes Foundation, Merion, Penna., was cancelled for the same reason. Among the honors accorded him are: the Order of Merit in 1949, Nobel Prize for literature in 1950, Fellow of the Royal Society in 1908, and in 1931 he attained earldom.

A representative list of this prolific writer includes: **A Critical Exposition of the Philosophy of Leibniz** (1900), **The Principles of Mathematics** (1903), **Principia Mathematica** (in collaboration with A. N. Whitehead, 1910-1913, 3 vols.), **The Problems of Philosophy** (1912), **Our Knowledge of the External World** (1914), **Introduction to Mathematical Philosophy** (1918), **Mysticism and Logic** (1918), **The Analysis of Mind** (1921), **Outline of Philosophy** (1928), **Skeptical Essays** (1928), **Marriage and Morals** (1929), **Religion and Science** (1935), **An Inquiry into Meaning and Truth** (1940), **A History of Western Philosophy** (1945), **Human Knowledge: Its Scope and Limits** (1948), **Unpopular Essays** (1950), **New Hopes for a Changing World** (1952), **What Is an Agnostic?** (in **Look,** Nov. 3, 1953, vol. 17, pp. 96, 98, 100, 101; reprinted in **A Guide to the Religions of America,** ed. Leo Rosten), **Human Society in Ethics and Politics** (1954), **Logic and Knowledge** (1956), **Why I Am Not a Christian and Other Essays on Religion** (1957), **The Will**

to Doubt (1958), **My Philosophical Development** (1959), **Wisdom of the West** (1959), **Fact and Fiction** (1961).

Bertrand Russell is a most difficult man to classify philosophically, for like a honeybee that flits from flower to flower, Russell seems to sample philosophy after philosophy. His philosophical flirtations have been with Leibnizianism, Platonic Realism, Neorealism, Logical Positivism, and Behaviorism, to mention just a few. Claims later in life have been toward Agnosticism and that of 'Free-Thinker;' in theory, he sides with Agnosticism, but in practice, he leans toward Atheism. His account in the present work is a dual Russell: (1) the Agnostic, and (2) the Idealistic Humanist.

21

BERTRAND RUSSELL

Agnosticism (God as Unknowable)[1]

What Is an Agnostic?

An Agnostic thinks it impossible to know the truth in matters such as God and the future life with which Chrisitanity and other religions are concerned. Or, if not impossible, at least impossible at the present time.

Are Agnostics Atheists?

No. An atheist, like a Christian, holds that we *can* know whether or not there is a God. The Christian holds that we can know there is a God; the atheist, that we can know there is not. The Agnostic suspends judgment, saying that there are not sufficient grounds either for affirmation or for denial. At the same time, an Agnostic may hold that the existence of God, though not impossible, is very improbable; he may even hold it so improbable that it is not worth considering in practice. In that case, he is not far removed from atheism. His attitude may be that which a careful philosopher would have towards the gods of ancient Greece. If I were asked to *prove* that Zeus and Poseidon and Hera and the rest of the Olympians do not exist, I should be at a loss to find conclusive arguments. An Agnostic may think the Christian God as improbable as the Olympians; in that case, he is, for practical purposes, at one with the atheists.

The Free Man's Worship[2]

. . . How, in such an alien and inhuman world, can so powerless a creature as Man preserve his aspirations untarnished? A strange mystery it is that Nature, omnipotent but blind, in the revolutions of her secular hurryings through the abysses of space, has brought forth at last a child,

[1] Bertrand Russell, *Look* Magazine, Copyright © 1953 Cowles Magazine, Inc.
[2] Bertrand Russell, *The Free Man's Worship* (*The Independence Review*, vol. I, Dec. 1903, 415-424).

subject still to her power, but gifted with sight, with knowledge of good and evil, with the capacity of judging all the works of his unthinking Mother. In spite of Death, the mark and seal of the parental control, Man is yet free, during his brief years, to examine, to criticize, to know, and in imagination to create. To him alone, in the world with which he is acquainted, this freedom belongs; and in this lies his superiority to the resistless forces that control his outward life.

The savage, like ourselves, feels the oppression of his impotence before the powers of Nature; but having in himself nothing that he respects more than Power, he is willing to prostrate himself before his gods, without inquiring whether they are worthy of his worship. Pathetic and very terrible is the long history of cruelty and torture, of degradation and human sacrifice, endured in the hope of placating the jealous gods: surely, the trembling believer thinks, when what is most precious has been freely given, their lust for blood must be appeased, and more will not be required. The religion of Moloch — as such creeds may be generically called — is in essence the cringing submission of the slave, who dare not, even in his heart, allow the thought that his master deserves no adulation. Since the independence of ideals is not yet acknowledged, Power may be freely worshipped, and receive an unlimited respect, despite its wanton infliction of pain.

But gradually, as morality grows bolder, the claim of the ideal world begins to be felt; and worship, if it is not to cease, must be given to gods of another kind than those created by the savage. Some, though they feel the demands of the ideal, will still consciously reject them, still urging that naked Power is worthy of worship. Such is the attitude inculcated in God's answer to Job out of the whirlwind: the divine power and knowledge are paraded, but of the divine goodness there is no hint. Such also is the attitude of those who, in our own day, base their morality upon the struggle for survival, maintaining that the survivors are necessarily the fittest. But others, not content with an answer so repugnant to the moral sense, will adopt the position which we have become accustomed to regard as specially religious, maintaining that, in some hidden manner the world of fact is really harmonious with the world of ideals. Thus Man creates God, all-powerful and all-good, the mystic unity of what is and what should be.

But the world of fact, after all, is not good; and, in submitting our judgment to it, there is an element of slavishness from which our thoughts must be purged. For in all things it is well to exalt the dignity of Man, by freeing him as far as possible from the tyranny of non-human Power.

When we have realized that Power is largely bad, that man, with his knowledge of good and evil, is but a helpless atom in a world which has no such knowledge, the choice is again presented to us: Shall we worship Force, or shall we worship Goodness? Shall our God exist and be evil or shall he be recognized as the creation of our own conscience?

The answer to this question is very momentous, and affects profoundly our whole morality. The worship of Force, to which Carlyle and Nietzsche and the creed of Militarism have accustomed us, is the result of failure to maintain our own ideals against a hostile universe: it is itself a prostrate submission to evil, a sacrifice of our best to Moloch. If strength indeed is to be respected, let us respect rather the strength of those who refuse that false "recognition of facts" which fails to recognize that acts are often bad. Let us admit that, in the world we know, there are many things that would be better otherwise, and that the ideals to which we do and must adhere are not realized in the realm of matter. Let us preserve our respect for truth, for beauty, for the ideal of perfection which life does not permit us to attain, though none of these things meet with the approval of the unconscious universe. If Power is bad, as it seems to be, let us reject it from our hearts. In this lies Man's true freedom: in determination to worship only the God created by our own love of the good, to respect only the heaven which inspires the insight of our best moments. In action, in desire, we must submit perpetually to the tyranny of outside forces; but in thought, in aspiration, we are free, free from our fellow-men, free from the petty planet on which our bodies impotently crawl, free even, while we live, from the tyranny of death. Let us learn, then, that energy of faith which enables us to live constantly in the vision of the good; and let us descend, in action, into the world of fact, with that vision always before us.

When first the opposition of fact and ideal grows fully visible, a spirit of fiery revolt, of fierce hatred of the gods, seems necessary to the assertion of freedom. To defy with Promethean constancy a hostile universe, to keep its evil always in view, always actively hated, to refuse no pain that the malice of Power can invent, appears to be the duty of all who will not bow before the inevitable. But indignation is still a bondage, for it compels our thoughts to be occupied with an evil world; and in the fierceness of desire from which it is necessary there is a kind of self-assertion which it is necessary for the wise to overcome. Indignation is a submission of our thoughts, but not of our desires; the Stoic freedom in which wisdom consists is found in the submission of our desires, but not of our thoughts. From the submission of our desires springs the virtue of resignation; from the freedom of our thoughts springs the whole world of art and philosophy, and the vision of beauty by which, at last, we half reconquer the reluctant world. But the vision of beauty is possible only to unfettered contemplation, to thoughts not weighted by the load of eager wishes; and thus Freedom comes only to those who no longer ask of life that it shall yield them any of those personal goods that are subject to the mutations of Time. . . .

Except for those rare spirits that are born without sin, there is a cavern of darkness to be traversed before that temple can be entered. The gate of the cavern is despair, and its floor is paved with the gravestones of abandoned hopes. There Self must die; there the eagerness, the greed of untamed desire must be slain, for only so can the soul be freed from the empire of Fate. But out of the cavern the Gate of Renunciation leads again to the daylight of wisdom, by whose radiance a new insight, a new joy, a new tenderness, shine forth to gladden the Pilgrim's heart.

When, without the betterness of impotent rebellion, we have learnt both to resign ourselves to the outward rule of Fate and to recognize that the non-human world is unworthy of our worship, it becomes possible at last so to transform and refashion the unconscious universe, so to transmute it in the crucible of imagination, that a new image of shining gold replaces the old idol of clay. In all the multiform facts of the world — in the visual shapes of trees and mountains and clouds, in the events of the life of man, even in the very omnipotence of Death — the insight of creative idealism can find the reflection of a beauty which its own thoughts first made. In this way mind asserts its subtle mastery over the thoughtless forces of Nature. The more evil the material with which it deals, the more thwarting to untrained desire, the greater is its achievement in inducing the reluctant rock to yield up its hidden treasure, the prouder its victory in compelling the opposing forces to swell the pageant of its triumph. Of all the arts, Tragedy is the proudest, the most triumphant; for it builds its shining citadel in the very center of the enemy's country, on the very summit of his highest mountain; from its impregnable watch-towers, his camps and arsenals, his columns and forts, are all revealed; within its walls the free life continues, while the legions of Death and Pain and Despair, and all the servile captains of tyrant Fate, afford the burghers of that dauntless city new spectacles of beauty. Happy those sacred ramparts, thrice happy the dwellers on that all-seeing eminence. Honor to those brave warriors who, through countless ages of warfare, have preserved for us the priceless heritage of liberty, and have kept undefiled by sacrilegious invaders the home of the unsubdued.

But the beauty of Tragedy does but make visible a quality which, in more or less obvious shapes, is present always and everywhere in life. In the spectacle of Death, in the endurance of intolerable pain, and in the irrevocableness of a vanished past, there is a sacredness, an overpowering awe, a feeling of the vastness, the depth, the inexhaustible mystery of existence, in which, as by some strange marriage of pain, the sufferer is bound to the world by bonds of sorrow. In these moments of insight, we lose all eagerness of temporary desire, all struggling and striving for petty ends, all care for the little trivial things that, to a superficial view, make up the common life of day by day; we see, surrounding the narrow raft illumined by the flickering light of human comradeship, the dark ocean on whose rolling waves we toss for a brief hour; from the great night without, a chill blast breaks in upon our refuge; all the loneliness of humanity amid hostile forces is concentrated upon the individual soul, which must struggle alone, with what of courage it can command, against the whole weight of a universe that cares nothing for its hopes and fears. Victory, in this struggle with the powers of darkness, is the true baptism into the glorious company of heroes, the true initiation into the overmastering beauty of human existence. From that awful encounter of the soul with the outer world, renunciation, wisdom, and charity are born; and with their birth a new life begins. To take into the inmost shrine of the soul the irresistible forces whose puppets we seem to be — Death and change, the change, the irrevocableness of the past, and the powerlessness of man before the blind hurry of the universe from vanity to vanity — to feel these things and know them is to conquer them.

This is the reason why the Past has such magical power. The beauty of its motionless and silent pictures is like the enchanted purity of late autumn, when the leaves, though one breath would make them fall, still glow against the sky in golden glory. The Past does not change or strive; like Duncan, after life's fitful fever it sleeps well; what was eager and grasping, what was petty and transitory, has faded away, the things that were beautiful and eternal shine out of it like stars in the night. Its beauty, to a soul not worthy of it, is unendurable; but to a soul which has conquered Fate it is the key of religion.

The life of Man, viewed outwardly, is but a small thing in comparison with the forces of Nature. The slave is doomed to worship Time and Fate and Death, because they are greater than anything he finds in himself, and because all his thoughts are of things which they devour. But, great as they are, to think of them greatly, to feel their passionless splendor, is greater still. And such thought makes us free men; we no longer bow before the inevitable in Oriental subjection, but we absorb it, and make it a part of ourselves. To abandon the struggle for private happiness, to expel all eagerness of temporary desire, to burn with passion for eternal things — this is emancipation, and this is the free man's worship. And this liberation is effected by a contemplation of Fate; for Fate itself is subdued by the mind which leaves nothing to be purged by the purifying fire of Time.

United with his fellow-men by the strongest of all ties, the tie of a common doom, the free man finds that a new vision is with him always, shedding over every daily task the light of love. The life of Man is a long march through the night, surrounded by invisible foes, tortured by weariness and pain, towards a goal that few can hope to reach, and where none may tarry long. One by one, as they march, our comrades vanish from our sight, seized by the silent orders of omnipotent Death. Very brief is the time in which we can help them, in which their happiness or misery is decided. Be it ours to shed sunshine on their path, to lighten their sorrows by the balm of sympathy, to give them the pure joy of a never-tiring affection, to strengthen failing courage, to instill faith in hours of despair. Let us not weigh in grudging scales their merits and demerits, but let us think only of their need — of the sorrows, the difficulties, perhaps the blindnesses, that make the misery of their lives; let us remember that they are fellow-sufferers in the same darkness, actors in the same tragedy with ourselves. And so, when their day is over, when their good and their evil have become eternal by the immortality of the past, be it ours to feel that, where they suffered, where they failed, no deed of ours was the cause; but wherever a spark of the divine fire kindled in their hearts, we were ready with encouragement, with sympathy, with brave words in which high courage glowed.

Brief and powerless is Man's life; on him and all his race the slow, sure doom fails pitiless and dark. Blind to good and evil, reckless of destruction, omnipotent matter rolls on its relentless way; for Man, condemned to-day to lose his dearest, to-morrow himself to pass through the gate of darkness, it remains only to cherish, ere yet the blow falls, the lofty thoughts that ennoble his little day; disdaining the coward terrors of the slave of Fate, to worship at the shrine that his own hands have built; undismayed by the empire of chance, to preserve a mind free from the wanton tyranny that rules his outward life; proudly defiant of the irresistible forces that tolerate, for a moment, his knowledge and his condemnation, to sustain alone, a weary but unyielding Atlas, the world that his own ideals have fashioned despite the trampling march of unconscious power.

Part Four: CONCEPTS OF GOD
The Nature of God

MOSES

MOSES (c. 13th century B.C.), reared in Egypt during the nineteenth Egyptian Dynasty (after c. 1320 B.C.), reputed author of the Pentateuch (first five books of the Judeo-Christian Bible), author of the Torah (law of Judaism), and famous for the Decalogue (Ten Commandments), is the recognized founder of the Israelitish religion and nation.

The fact that Moses taught Monotheism (one universal God of all), rather than Henotheism (a supreme national God, usually accompanied with the belief in other gods as well), has been contested. Some scholars believe that Monotheism was not introduced into human thought until the Exilic Period (440 B.C.) by Isaiah. It was not until post-Exilic times that Monotheism became entrenched as a firmly established Israelitish teaching.

Nevertheless, Moses is to be credited with the teaching that God could not be localized, and lacked anthropomorphic characteristics of pagan gods, such as possessing sex or image. The God of Moses demanded his people's allegiance, ethical behavior, and obedience to his righteous will.

22

MOSES

Monotheism (The Oneness of a Supreme Personal Creator)[1]

Hear, O Israel: The Lord our God *is* one Lord.

And thou shalt love the Lord thy God with all thine heart, and with all thy soul, and with all thy might.

And these words, which I command thee this day, shall be in thine heart:

And thou shalt teach them diligently unto thy children, and shalt talk of them when thou sittest in thine house, and when thou walkest by the way, and when thou liest down, and when thou risest up.

And thou shalt bind them for a sign upon thine hand, and they shall be as frontlets between thine eyes.

And thou shalt write them upon the posts of thy house and on thy gates.

And[2] God spake all these words, saying, I *am* the Lord thy God, which have brought thee out of the land of Egypt, out of the house of bondage.

Thou shalt have no other gods before me.

Thou shalt not make unto thee any graven image, or any likeness *of any thing* that *is* in heaven above, or that *is* in the earth beneath, or that *is* in the water under the earth:

Thou shalt not bow down thyself to them, nor serve them: for I the Lord thy God *am* a jealous God, visiting the iniquity of the fathers upon the children unto the third and fourth *generation* of them that hate me; and shewing mercy unto thousands of them that love me, and keep my commandments.

[1] Moses, *Deuteronomy* 6:4-9.
[2] *Ibid., Exodus,* 20:1-6.

MOSES MAIMONIDES

MOSES MAIMONIDES (1135-1204), **Doctor Perplexorum** (owing to his celebrated **Guide of the Perplexed),** and also known as RAMBAM, the initials of Rabbi Moses Ben Maimon, was a Jewish philosopher, physician, rabbi, and man of letters. When Cordova, Spain, the city of his birth and rearing, fell in 1148 to the Mohammedans, the family settled in Egypt after a sojurn in Morocco and Palestine. Maimonides rose to a position of **nagid,** an accredited leader of Egyptian Jewry, and was also appointed court physician to Saladin.

Maimondes was influenced by Aristotelianism, a philosophy he acquired from Alfarabi and Avicenna in his early youth. At the age of sixteen, he wrote **Treatise on the Terminology of Logic,** but his **magnum opus** is **Mishneh Torah.** The selection in the present volume, typical of Monotheistic thought, is from the most famous of his writings, **Guide of the Perplexed.**

In **The Guide of the Perplexed** and in his **Book of Precepts,** he lays an Aristotelian foundation for Judaism, similar to what St. Thomas did for Christian thought, and Averroës did for the Mohammedan religious community.

According to Maimonides, God is the chief object of metaphysics; he supports belief in God by the Aristotelian argument of Prime Mover coupled with the argument distinguishing between the possible and the necessary. To these two arguments, he adds a third, peculiarly his own: God is a necessary inference from contingent and limited beings requiring an infinite Being as their ground of existence. The arguments offered by Maimonides and those advanced by Thomas share much in common.

Maimonides, a strict Monotheist, emphasizes the unity of God together with his uniquely spiritual nature. Understanding of God is gained by negative predicates, for positive concepts limit him, **i.e.,** although it cannot be said what God is in an affirmative sense, at least it can be determined what he is not. God created the world in evolutionary gradations from lower to higher beings; above man exist pure spirits superior to man but inferior to God, yet in the physical realm, man is God's chief concern. Like St. Thomas, God is known both by religious sources and philosophical ones; the two coincide.

Maimonides, the greatest Jewish philosopher of the Middle Ages, directs his **Guide of the Perplexed** to his fellow Jews, whom he considers the perplexed, troubled with doubts because they view God anthropomorphically. Religion is valuable insofar as the welfare of the masses is concerned.

23

MOSES MAIMONIDES

Monotheism (The Oneness of God)[1]

I . . . you have a desire to rise to a higher state, viz., that of reflection, and truly to hold the conviction that God is One and possesses true unity, without admitting plurality or divisibility in any sense whatever, you must understand that God has no essential attribute in any form or in any sense whatever, and that the rejection of corporeality implies the rejection of essential attributes. Those who believe that God is One, and that He has many attributes, declare the unity with their lips, and assume plurality in their thoughts. This is like the doctrine of the Christians, who say that He is one and He is three, and that the three are one. Of the same character is the doctrine of those who say that God is One, but that He has many attributes, and that He with His attributes are One. . . .

. . . For it is a self-evident truth that the attribute is not inherent in the object to which it is ascribed, but it is superadded to its essence, and is consequently an *accident;* if the attribute denoted the essence of the object, it would be either mere tautology, as if, e.g., one would say "man is man," or the explanation of a name, as, e.g., "man is a speaking animal"; for the words "speaking animal" include the true essence of man, and there is no third element besides life and speech that constitutes man; when he, therefore, is described by the attributes of life and speech, these are nothing but an explanation of the name "man," that is to say, that the thing which is called man, consists of life and speech. It will now be clear that the attribute must be one of two things, either the essence of the object described — in that case it is a mere explanation of a name, and on that account we might admit the attribute in reference to God, but we reject it from another cause as will be shown — or the attribute is something different from the object described, some extraneous superadded element; in that case the attribute would be an accident, and he

---

[1] Moses Maimonides, *Guide of the Perplexed,* tr. M. Friedländer (1885), 171 ff.

who merely rejects the appellation "accidents" in reference to the attributes of God, does not thereby alter their character; for everything superadded to the essence of an object joins it without forming part of its essential properties, and that constitutes an accident. Add to this the logical consequences of admitting many attributes, viz., the existence of many eternal beings. There cannot be any belief in the unity of God except by admitting that He is one simple substance, without any composition or plurality of elements; one from whatever side you view it, and by whatever test you examine it; not divisible into two parts in any way and by any cause, nor capable of any form of plurality either objectively or subjectively.

24

I KINGS

Henotheism (God a Personified National Spirit)[1]

And it came to pass after many days, that the word of the Lord came to Elijah in the third year, saying, Go, show thyself unto Ahab. And there was a sore famine in Samaria. And Ahab called Obadiah, which was the governor of his house. (Now Obadiah feared the Lord greatly: For it was so, when Jezebel cut off the prophets of the Lord, that Obadiah took a hundred prophets, and hid them by fifty in a cave, and fed them with bread and water.) And Ahab said unto Obadiah, Go into the land, unto all fountains of water, and unto all brooks: peradventure we may find grass to save the horses and mules alive, that we lose not all the beasts. So they divided the land between them to pass throughout it: Ahab went one way by himself, and Obadiah went another way by himself.

And as Obadiah was in the way, behold, Elijah met him: and he knew him, and fell on his face, and said, Art thou that my Lord Elijah? And he answered him, I am: go, tell thy lord, Behold, Elijah is here. So Obadiah went to meet Ahab, and told him: and Ahab went to meet Elijah.

And it came to pass, when Ahab saw Elijah, that Ahab said unto him, Art thou he that troubleth Israel? And he answered, I have not troubled Israel; but thou, and thy father's house, in that ye have forsaken the commandments of the Lord, and thou has followed Baalim. Now therefore send, and gather to me all Israel unto mount Carmel, and the prophets of Baal four hundred and fifty, and the prophets of the groves four hundred, which eat at Jezebel's table. So Ahab sent unto all the children of Israel, and gathered the prophets together unto mount Carmel.

And Elijah came unto all the people, and said, How long halt ye between two opinions? if the Lord be God, follow him: but if Baal, then follow him. And the people answered him not a word. Then said Elijah

[1] I *Kings* 18:1-39, (King James Version).

unto the people, I, even I only, remain a prophet of the Lord; but Baal's prophets are four hundred and fifty men. Let them therefore give us two bullocks; and let them choose one bullock for themselves, and cut it in pieces, and lay it on wood, and put no fire under: and I will dress the other bullock, and lay it on wood, and put no fire under: And call ye on the name of your gods, and I will call on the name of the Lord: and the God that answereth by fire, let him be God. And all the people answered and said, It is well spoken.

And Elijah said unto the prophets of Baal, Choose you one bullock for yourselves, and dress it first; for ye are many; and call on the name of your gods, but put no fire under. And they took the bullock which was given them, and they dressed it, and called on the name of Baal from morning even until noon, saying, O Baal, hear us. But there was no voice, nor any that answered. And they leaped upon the altar which was made. And it came to pass at noon, that Elijah mocked them, and said, Cry aloud: for he is a god; either he is talking, or he is pursuing, or he is in a journey, or peradventure he sleepeth, and must be awaked. And they cried aloud, and cut themselves after their manner with knives and lancets, till the blood gushed out upon them. And it came to pass, when midday was past, and they prophesied until the time of the offering of the evening sacrifice, that there was neither voice, nor any to answer, nor any that regarded.

And Elijah said unto all the people, Come near unto me. And all the people came near unto him. And he repaired the altar of the Lord that was broken down. And Elijah took twelve stones, according to the number of the tribes of the sons of Jacob, unto whom the word of the Lord came, saying, Israel shall be thy name: And with the stones he built an altar in the name of the Lord: and he made a trench about the altar, as great as would contain two measures of seed. And he put the wood in order, and cut the bullock in pieces, and laid him on the wood, and said, Fill four barrels with water, and pour it on the burnt sacrifice, and on the wood. And he said, Do it the second time. And they did it the second time. And the water ran round about the altar; and he filled the trench also with water.

And it came to pass at the time of the offering of the evening sacrifice, that Elijah the prophet came near, and said, Lord God of Abraham, Isaac, and of Israel, let it be known this day that thou art God in Israel, and that I am thy servant, and that I have done all these things at thy word. Hear me, O Lord, hear me, that this people may know that thou art the Lord God, and that thou hast turned their heart back again. Then the fire of the Lord fell, and consumed the burnt sacrifice, and the wood, and the stones, and the dust, and licked up the water that was in the trench.

And when all the people saw it, they fell on their faces: and they said, The Lord, he is the God; the Lord, he is the God. And Elijah said unto them, Take the prophets of Baal; let not one of them escape. And they took them: and Elijah brought them down to the brook Kishon, and slew them there.

PLATO

PLATO (427-347 B.C.) of Athens, born of aristocratic parents, was the most distinguished student of Socrates, and the chief exponent of Socratic philosophy. After having studied the philosophy of Heraclitus under Cratylus, he met Socrates in 407, absorbing his philosophy, method, and technique. Following the demise of Socrates in 399, Plato took refuge for a brief period of time in Megara, and there with Euclid studied Eleatic philosophy. Leaving Megara, he returned to Athens, then set out for Egypt, Cyrene, Italy and Sicily. In Cyrene, he encountered Theodorus, the mathematician; in Italy, Archytas of Taretum, the Pythagorean philosopher; and in Sicily he established a close friendship with Dion, Dionysius the Elder's brother-in-law, who was the ruler of Syracuse. Plato's criticism of the government of Syracuse caused him to be sold into slavery, but he was ransomed by Anniceris, a Cyrenaic philosopher. In 387, Plato established his Academy, as an institute for philosophical pursuit, on a parcel of land donated by generous friends, and he presided over it until his death in 347. In 367, and again in 361, Plato made journeys to Sicily, where Dionysius the Younger permitted him to conduct political experiments, both of which proved futile, endangering his life at the displeasure of Dionysius.

Plato lectured without notes, and wrote in the manner of the Socratic dialectic, in dialogues; but later in life, he lost the art and literary genius of his earlier career, and wrote dogmatically in prose. His philosophy has influenced the academic world since its inception, and still maintains a firm hold. Many contemporary philosophies have elements of Platonism imbedded in them: A. N. Whitehead's Philosophy of Organism, the metaphysics of the Neorealists, and the Phenomenology of Edmund Husserl, just to mention a few.

Although Plato's most outstanding work is the **Republic**, rich sources of his ideas may be found in the following, most of which are dialogues, with Socrates as principal spokesman: **Laws, Phaedrus, Protagoras, Symposium, Gorgias, Timaeus, Theatetus, Phaedo, Apology,** and **Crito.** The question as to the genuineness of the following writings attributed to Plato has been challenged: **Parmenides, Cratylus, Philebus,** and the **Sophist.**

161

Plato conceives of the human soul as a living element, capable of moving itself as well as other things; it perceives, knows, and wills; however, its principle characteristic is rationality. Although the soul is not equivalent in nature to the changeless, timeless, Platonic Ideals, it is capable of surviving change, particularly that of death, and attaining the sphere of immortality. The soul's knowledge of eternal Ideas attests to its eternal nature, but unlike eternal Ideas, the soul possesses an essence corresponding to the world of phenomena, **i.e.,** the sphere of perception. In the **Timaeus,** Plato allows only the soul's rational aspect to possess immortality; its sensuous nature is shed at death.

God is a demiurge, a hand-worker, a world-forming God, rather than a creator. He shapes the world according to the prescribed design of eternal Ideals, but the stuff out of which the world is made is uncreated and 'given.' From the Receptacle, God obtains unformed material substance, and fashions the world of phenomena as it is known to us. Matter, because of its imperfect nature, cannot be made into a perfect world such as the Ideals, but, at best, approximates the Ideal world; hence the physical world is an imperfect copy of the Ideal, for God is hampered by the texture or quality of the stuff with which he must work.

25

PLATO

God, a Limited Demiurge[1]

TIMAEUS. All men, Socrates, who have any degree of right feeling, at the beginning of every enterprise, whether small or great, always call upon God. And we, too, who are going to discourse of the nature of the universe, how created or how existing without creation, if we be not altogether out of our wits, must evoke the aid of gods and goddesses and pray that our words may be acceptable to them and consistent with themselves. Let this, then, be our invocation of the gods, to which I add an exhortation of myself to speak in such manner as will be most intelligible to you, and will most accord with my own intent.

First then, in my judgment, we must make a distinction and ask, What is that which always is and has no becoming; and what is that which is always becoming and never is? That which is apprehended by intelligence and reason is always in the same state; but that which is conceived by opinion with the help of sensation and without reason, is always in a process of becoming and perishing and never really is. Now everything that becomes or is created must of necessity be created by some cause, for without a cause nothing can be created. The work of the creator, whenever he looks to the unchangeable and fashions the form of nature of his work after an unchangeable pattern, must necessarily be made fair and perfect; but when he looks to the created only, and uses a created pattern, it is not fair or perfect. Was the heaven then or the world, whether called by this or by any other more appropriate name — assuming the name, I am asking a question which has to be asked at the beginning of an inquiry about anything — was the world, I say, always in existence and without beginning? or created, and had it a beginning? Created, I reply, being visible and tangible and having a body, and therefore sensible; and all sensible things are apprehended by opinion and sense and are in a process of creation and created. Now that which

[1] Plato, *Timaeus*, tr. Benjamin Jowett, 27 C ff.

is created must, as we affirm, of necessity be created by a cause. But the father and maker of all this universe is past finding out; and even if we found him, to tell of him to all men would be impossible. And there is still a question to be asked about him: Which of the patterns had the artificer in view when he made the world, — the pattern of the unchangeable, or of that which is created? If the world be indeed fair and the artificer good, it is manifest that he must have looked to that which is eternal; but if what cannot be said without blasphemy is true, then to the created pattern. Every one will see that he must have looked to the eternal; for the world is the fairest of creations and he is the best of causes. And having been created in this way, the world has been framed in the likeness of that which is apprehended by reason and mind and is unchangeable, and must therefore of necessity, if this is admitted, be a copy of something. Now it is all-important that the beginning of everything should be according to nature. And in speaking of the copy and the original we may assume that words are akin to the matter which they describe; when they relate to the lasting and permanent and intelligible, they ought to be lasting and unalterable, and, as far as their nature allows, irrefutable and immovable — nothing less. But when they express only the copy or likeness and not the eternal things themselves, they need only be likely and analogous to the real words. As being is to becoming, so is truth to belief. If, then, Socrates, amid the many opinions about the gods and the generation of the universe, we are not able to give notions which are altogether and in every respect exact and consistent with one another, do not be surprised. Enough, if we adduce probabilities as likely as any others; for we must remember that I who am the speaker, and you who are the judges, are only mortal men, and we ought to accept the tale which is probable and inquire no further.

SOCRATES. Excellent, Timaeus; and we will do precisely as you bid us. The prelude is charming, and is already accepted by us — may we beg of you to proceed to the strain?

TIMAEUS. Let me tell you then why the Creator made this world of generation. He was good, and the good can never have any jealousy of anything. And being free from jealousy, he desired that all things should be as like himself as they could be. This is in the truest sense the origin of creation and of the world, as we shall do well in believing on the testimony of wise men: God desired that all things should be good and nothing bad, so far as this was attainable. Wherefore also finding the whole visible sphere not at rest, but moving in an irregular and disorderly fashion, out of disorder he brought order, considering that this was in every way better than the other. Now the deeds of the best could never be or have been other than the fairest; and the Creator, reflecting on the things which are by nature visible, found that no unintelligent creature taken as a whole was fairer than the intelligent taken as a whole; and that intelligence could not be present in anything which was devoid of soul. For which reason, when he was framing the universe, he put intelligence in soul, and soul in body, that he might be the creator of a work was by nature fairest and best. Wherefore, using the language of probability, we may say that the world became a living creature truly endowed with soul and intelligence by the providence of God.

This being supposed, let us proceed to the next stage: In the likeness of what animal did the Creator make the world? It would be an unworthy thing to liken it to any nature which exists as a part only; for nothing can be beautiful which is like any imperfect thing; but let us suppose the world to be the very image of that whole of which all other animals both individually and in their tribes are portions. For the original of the universe contains in itself all intelligible beings, just as this world comprehends us and all other visible creatures. For the Deity, intending to make this world like the fairest and most perfect of intelligble beings, framed one visible animal comprehending within itself all other animals of a kindred nature. Are we right in saying that there is one world, or that they are many and infinite? There must be one only, if the created copy is to accord with the original. For that which includes all other intelligible creatures cannot have a second or companion; in that case there would be need of another living being which would include both, and of which they would be parts, and the likeness would be more truly said to resemble not them, but that other which included them. In order then that the world might be solitary, like the perfect animal, the Creator made not two worlds or an infinite number of them; but there is and ever will be one only-begotten and created heaven.

Such was the whole plan of the eternal God about the god that was to be, to whom for this reason he gave a body, smooth and even, having a surface in every direction equidistant from the centre, a body entire and perfect, and formed out of perfect bodies. And in the center he put the soul, which he diffused throughout the body, making it also to be the exterior environment of it; and he made the universe a circle moving in a circle, one and solitary, yet by reason of its excellence, able to converse with itself, and needing no other friendship or acquaintance. Having these purposes in view he created the world a blessed god.

Now God did not make the soul after the body, although we are speaking of them in this order; for having brought them together he would never have allowed that the elder should be ruled by the younger; but this is a random manner of speaking which we have, because somehow we ourselves too are very much under the dominion of chance. Whereas he made the soul in origin and excellence prior to and older than the body, to be the ruler and mistress, of whom the body was to be the subject. And he made her out of the following elements and on this wise: Out of the indivisible and unchangeable, and also out of that which is divisible and has to do with material bodies, he compounded a third and intermediate kind of essence, partaking of the nature of the same and of the other, and this compound he placed accordingly in a mean between the indivisible and the divisible and material. He took the three elements of the same, the other and the essence, and mingled them into one form, compressing by force the reluctant and unsociable nature of the other into the same. When he had mingled them with the essence and out of the three made one, he again divided this whole into as many portions as was fitting, each portion being a compound of the same, the other, and the essence.

Now when the Creator had framed the soul according to his will, he formed within her the corporeal universe, and brought the two together, and united them centre to centre. The soul, infused everywhere from the centre to the circumference of heaven, of which also she is the external envelopment, herself turning in herself, began a divine beginning of never-ceasing and rational life enduring throughout all time. The body of heaven is visible, but the soul is invisible, and partakes of reason and harmony, and being made by the best of intellectual and everlasting natures, is the best of things created.

When the Father and Creator saw the creature which he had made moving and living, the created image of the eternal gods, he rejoiced, and in his joy determined to make the copy still more like the original; and as this was eternal, he sought to make the universe eternal, so far as might be. Now the nature of the ideal being was everlasting, but to bestow this attribute in its fulness upon a creature was impossible. Wherefore he resolved to have a moving image of eternity, and when he set in order the heaven, he made this image eternal but moving according to number, while eternity itself rests in unity; and this image we call time. For there were no days and nights and months and years before the heaven was created, but when he constructed the heaven he created them also. They are all parts of time, and the past and future are created species of time which we unconsciously but wrongly transfer to the eternal essence; for we say that he "was," he "is," he "will be," but the truth is that "is" alone is properly attributed to him, and that "was" and "will be" are only to be spoken of becoming in time, for they are motions, but that which is immovably the same cannot become older or younger by time, nor ever did or has become, or hereafter will be, older or younger, nor is subject at all to any of those states which affect moving and sensible things and of which generation is the cause. . . .

This new beginning of our discussion of the universe requires a fuller division than the former; for then we made two classes, now a third must be revealed. The two sufficed for the former discussion; one, which we assumed, was a pattern intelligible and always the same; and the second was only the imitation of the pattern, generated and visible. There is also a third kind which we did not distinguish at the time, conceiving that the two would be enough. But now the argument seems to require that we should set forth in words another kind, which is difficult of explanation and dimly seen. What nature are we to attribute to this new kind of being? We reply, that it is the receptacle, and in a manner the nurse, of all generation.

ARISTOTLE

ARISTOTLE (384-322 B.C.), son of a Macedonian physician, was born in Stagira, Greece. Educated in Plato's Academy and its most distinguished student, he founded his own school in Athens in 335, the Lyceum, which was called the Peripatetic School; his most illustrious student was Alexander the Great. Aristotle's achievements, being of monumental proportions, led some present day scholars to conclude that the works attributed to him must have been the joint efforts of his combined faculty, for they are profound contributions encompassing not only philosophy, but psychology, biology, rhetoric, politics, logic, physics, astronomy, and literary criticism as well. The importance of his philosophical ideas is unmistakable, for they have influenced the world for over two millenia. So decisive are his conclusions, that it is said that every man is born either a Platonist or an Aristotelian. His thought dominated the second period of the Medieval Ages (1200-1453) and reached its crescendo in the philosophy of St. Thomas Aquinas, who modified it, but slightly, for use as a foundation for Christian Theistic thought, as did Averroës for the Mohammedan world, and Maimonides for the Jewish community.

Many of Aristotle's books have earned a permanent place among the classics: **Nicomachean Ethics, Politics, Organon** (logic), and **Metaphysics,** his First Philosophy, the one from which our selection is excerpted. The importance of his work, **Metaphysics,** cannot be overstressed, for it has defined the field of metaphysics. In it, he has presented, as of fundamental importance, his concept of God as Prime Mover.

According to Aristotle, a pure Form (God) is necessary to account for motion in matter, otherwise matter remains in a static state, unmoved. Motion, eternal as Being, requires Being as its source; Being is responsible for two types of motion: purposive motion and impulse. Pure Form, the First Mover, is itself unmoved, yet it is the ground, cause, purpose, of every development of matter. The Prime Mover, God, is eternal, unchangeable, immoveable, independent, incorporeal, and despite his distinct separation from every thing else, is the cause of their generation and change. God, as Prime Mover and Pure Form, a perfect Being, is at one and the same time both possibility and actuality, the superlative of all which exists. Deity, the highest and best Being, Essence, is an activity, a Pure Activity **(Actus Purus),** thought, Pure Thought, active within itself and its eternal nature. God, as perfect Being, needs nothing; hence is not wanting in any fulfillment or object, therefore as pure activity, thought of thought, self-consciousness, contemplates himself.

Thus we find in Aristotle a concept of God, not as Pantheistic but Theistic, a self-conscious Being distinct from the world, a transcendent absolute mind or spirit. Whereas all objects find their happiness in being directed toward God, the Divine Mind, since he is pure Form, requires no object; he is self-sufficient, wanting nothing, hence he finds his goal and eternal blessedness, the contemplation or knowledge of himself. Everything in the world, including material objects and their development, is a longing after God, and this constitutes God's activity (motion) in the world.

Matter, a potential object which is incapable of moving anything, though it itself is moved by God, (alone actual, who moves matter, yet himself unmoved), transpires a wide gamut or gradated series of objects which are undergoing motion, development. This process is, according to Aristotle, **nature.**

26

ARISTOTLE

God as the Unmoved Mover[1]

Since [2] as we have seen, substances are of three kinds, two belonging
to the physical world, the third being immovable, we have now to speak
of the last, and to show that of necessity there exists some eternal immovable substance.

Of things that exist substances are the first, and if they are all perishable then everything is perishable. But it is impossible that there should
be either beginning or end of motion: it is forevermore. And the same
is true of time, for it is impossible that there should be either a "before"
or an "after" if there is no time. Motion is then unceasing, just as time is,
for time is either identical with motion or else it is a certain property of
motion. And there is no motion save in space, no unceasing motion save
motion in a circle. If, however, there were something merely possessing
the power to create and to impart motion, but not actually operative,
still there is no motion. For it is conceivable that that which possesses
potentiality should not be actually operative. Nor are we any better off
if we assume eternal substances, like the "ideas" which some have assumed, unless they contain some principle that is capable of bringing
about change. And even this would not be sufficient, nor would some
other substance over and above the ideas accomplish the purpose; for
unless this principle be actually operative there will be no motion.
Moreover, even if it be actually operative, but at the same time its substance be but potentiality, it will not suffice; for still there will be no
eternal motion, for it is conceivable that what potentially is should not
come into being. It is necessary therefore that there should be a principle of such a nature that its very substance is its being actually operative.
Further, substances of this sort must be immaterial; for they must be

[1] Aristotle, *Metaphysics*, tr. Charles M. Bakewell, from his *Source Book in Ancient
Philosophy* (New York: Charles Scribner's Sons, 1907), 227ff.
[2] Aristotle, *Metaphysics*, bk. XI, ch. 6.

eternal, if anything at all is eternal. They must therefore be pure actuality. . . .

There [3] exists [1] something always moving with ceaseless motion, and its motion is cyclical. This is shown too not merely by our argument but also by the actual fact. Consequently the primal heavens are everlasting. Furthermore there exists [2] that to which these impart motion. And since that which both imparts motion and has motion imparted to it is in the mean position there exists also [3] something which imparts motion without itself having motion imparted to it — something which is eternal, which is an individual substance and wholly actual. And this is the way it imparts motion. It is like the object of desire, or the object of thought, for these impart motion without being themselves moved. Fundamentally the object of desire and the object of thought are the same. The object of desire is that which appears beautiful; the object of the will is primarily that which *is* beautiful. It is not the striving that makes a thing seem good; rather we strive after a thing because it seems good. It is the thought that comes first. And the mind moves under the instigation of the object of thought. But only the positive series is in itself the thought series, and in this series substance stands first, and substance that is pure and simple and fully actual is first of all. (We must not confound the simple with the one. The "one" signifies quantity, the "simple" a kind of relation). But surely the beautiful and that which is desirable on its own account belong in the same positive series, and here the best, or its likeness, stands first. And that the final cause belongs to the immovable order the method of division makes plain; for purpose is always a purpose which some subject *has*, and of these the one — the purpose itself — is immovable, while the other — the purpose in its relation to a subject — is not. And [this immovable final cause] draws its object unto itself as the beloved the lover; and that which is thus set in motion imparts motion to all other things. . . .

God's life is like that of which we catch a transient glimpse when our life is at its best. Thus indeed his life always is (a thing which is impossible for us), for his very self-activity is bliss. And that is why we find greatest pleasure in being awake, in feeling and in thinking, and in the hopes and memories that come through these activities. But thinking, pure thinking, has for its object that which is in itself the best, and such thinking when most perfect has for its object the supreme good. The intellect thinks itself in grasping the intelligible, for it *becomes* intelligible in laying hold upon and thinking its object. Therefore, the intellect and the intelligible are the same thing; for to be able to receive the intelligible and the real is what we mean by intellect, and the intellect

[3] Aristotle, *Metaphysics*, bk. XI, ch. 7.

actually lives in doing this. And it is this actual life of the intellect, rather than the intelligible as object, that seems to be the divine element in the intellect, and pure speculative vision is what is best and most enjoyable. If then God is always as well off as we are now and then, how wonderful it is! And if he is always better off, it is still more wonderful. But such is the fact. And life belongs to him; for the activity of the mind is life, and he is that activity. Pure self-activity of reason is God's most blessed and everlasting life. We say that God is living, eternal, perfect; and continuous and everlasting life is God's, for God is eternal life.

And they are wrong who, like Pythagoras and Speusippus, hold that the most beautiful and the best are not found in the first cause, arguing from the fact that while the first cause produces plants and animals, still it is from these that the perfect plant or animal springs. For the seed comes from a complete plant previously existing; the seed is not first, but the complete plant. Just as we should say that man is prior to the germ — not the man who springs from it, but he from whom it comes.

That there is then a substance which is eternal and immovable and separable from the objects of sense is evident from what has been said. And it has also been shown that this substance cannot have extension but is without parts and indivisible. For it imparts motion through endless time, and nothing limited has unlimited potentiality. Now since every magnitude is either limited or unlimited, for the reason given God cannot have limited magnitude; nor yet can he have unlimited magnitude because, in a word, there is no such magnitude.

And further that God is free from passion and from qualitative change has also been shown, for all other changes are subsequent to motion in space. Why these things are so is now clear.

·   ·   ·   ·   ·

With [4] regard to the divine reason certain problems arise. For while it passes for the divinest of manifestations still what its nature must be in order that it should be such is a question hard to answer. For if it thinks of nothing wherein would lie its majesty? It were just like a man asleep. On the other hand if it thinks of something and that something, being different from itself, controls its thinking, it cannot be the noblest substance — for in that case that which is its substance is not thinking but potentiality. And it is through actual thinking that it gets its noble character.

Further, whether substance be reason or thinking, what does it think about? Clearly, either itself or something else; and if something else, either always the same thing, or now one thing and now another.

[4] Aristotle, *Metaphysics,* bk XI. ch. 9.

Does it forsooth make no difference whether it thinks about what is excellent or whether it simply thinks at random? Is it not indeed absurd that it should be thinking discursively about a plurality of things? It is evident therefore that it thinks about what is most divine and most noble, and that it changes not, for it could change only for the worse, and any motion would be already such a change.

Now in the first place if the divine reason is not actual but only potential thinking, it is conceivable that it should find its everlastingness but toil and weariness. And in the second place it is evident that then something else would be nobler than reason, namely, the object of reason. For thinking, and the activity of thinking, would belong also to that which thinks the most ignoble thoughts. And consequently, if this is to be avoided — and there are some things which it is better not to see then thinking as such would not be the best thing.

The divine reason then, if it is the supremely excellent thing, has itself for its object, and its thinking is a thinking of thinking. But science, perception, opinion, discursive reasoning, seem always to have something other than themselves for their object and only incidentally to be their own object.

Again, if there is a difference between thinking and being thought, by which of the two does reason get its nobility? For [in the case supposed] thinking and being thought are in essence not the same. However, in some cases knowledge is its own object. In the case of the creative sciences it is the immaterial substance and the essential notion that is the object of knowledge; in the case of the speculative sciences it is reason itself and thinking. Since, then, the mind is not one thing and the object of the mind another, in cases where matter is not involved, the two must be identical and thinking is one with its object.

Still a puzzle remains if the object of thought is composite, for then there might be change from part to part within the whole. But the fact is everything immaterial is indivisible. And just as the human mind, which has for its object composite things, is related to its object in favored moments — for it does not then grasp the good in this or that part of its object, but rather the best in the whole of it, the object in this case being something different from itself — just so the divine thinking is itself related to itself through all eternity.

THOMAS PAINE

THOMAS PAINE (1737-1809), English-American author, humanitarian, philosopher, political and religious radical, dedicated his life and writings to the cause of Democracy in America. Born in Thetford, Norfolk, England, the son of a Quaker, he flirted with numerous jobs before embarking for America in 1774. In America, he accepted the position of editor of the **Pennsylvania Magazine,** a task which was interrupted after a brief period of a year and a half, owing to hostilities which precipitated the Revolutionary War. The war years saw such pamphlets as **Common Sense** (1776), and in 1777 the first issue of the **American Crisis,** known for its famous opening lines: "These are the times that try men's souls."

In 1787, he left for Europe, whereupon in answer to Burke's **Reflections on the French Revolution,** he wrote the **Rights of Man** (1791, 1792). When the **Age of Reason, Being an Investigation of True and Fabulous Theology** appeared in 1794, it created the greatest controversy of its period; Paine lost many friends as a result, and his public image was critically affected. Although it created much bitterness in its time as a hostile attack against religion, it is regarded today as a typical presentation of Deism. The selection chosen in this volume as representative of Deism, has been taken from Paine's **Age of Reason.**

In addition to those works listed, Paine wrote the following: **Public Good** (1780), **Dissertations on Government** (1786), **Prospects on the Rubicon** (1787), **Letter Addresses to the Addressers on the Late Proclamation** (1792), **Dissertation of First Principles of Government** (1795), **Agrarian Justice** (1797), **Discourse to the Theophilanthropists** (1797).

Deism, the belief in a transcendent God who created a mechanistic universe, but has since divorced himself from it, presently viewing the world as a disinterested bystander, is the view of many of the forefathers of this country. Their belief is that the world operates on the basis of natural law, and those persons who learn of these laws and obey them will prosper, hence in this sense 'God helps those who help themselves.' God, as an absentee landlord, peers in upon the world, but has no intentions of doing anything further with it, consequently prayer is ineffectual and miracles an impossibility. Special revelations, such as the Bible, are viewed as fables, hence unacceptable, for the only revelation God granted is the **lumen naturae** (light of nature), reason.

Deism, despite its importance as a rationalistic movement of the seventeenth and eighteenth centuries, a philosophy of the Enlightenment, today lies dormant owing to the rise and development of modern science, especially the Theory of Evolution, and nuclear physics.

27

THOMAS PAINE

Deism (God As Transcendent)[1]

It is only by the exercise of reason, that man can discover God. Take away that reason, and he would be incapable of understanding any thing; and, in this case it would be just as consistent to read even the book called the Bible to a horse as to a man. How then is it that those people pretend to reject reason?

Almost the only parts in the book called the Bible, that convey to us any idea of God, are some chapters in Job, and the 19th Psalm; I recollect no other. Those parts are true *deistical* compositions; for they treat of the *Deity* through his works. They take the book of Creation as the word of God, they refer to no other book, and all the inferences they make are drawn from that volume.

I insert, in this place, the 19th Psalm, as paraphrased into English verse by Addison. I recollect not the prose, and where I write this I have not the opportunity of seeing it.

> The spacious firmament on high,
> With all the blue etherial sky,
> And spangled heavens, a shining frame,
> Their great original proclaim.
> The unwearied sun, from day to day,
> Does his Creator's power display;
> And publishes to every land,
> The work of an Almighty hand.
> Soon as the evening shades prevail
> The moon takes up the wondrous tale,
> And nightly to the listning earth,
> Repeats the story of her birth;
> Whilst all the stars that round her burn,

[1] Thomas Paine, *The Age of Reason* (1793), excerpts.

And all the planets, in their turn,
Confirm the tidings as they roll,
And spread the truth from pole to pole.
What though in solemn silence all
Move round this dark terrestrial ball;
What though no real voice, nor sound;
Admist their radiant orbs be found,
In reason's ear they all rejoice,
And utter forth a glorious voice,
For ever singing as they shine,
THE HAND THAT MADE US IS DIVINE.

What more does man want to know, than that the hand or power, that made these things is divine, is omnipotent? Let him believe this with the force it is impossible to repel, if he permits his reason to act, and his rule of moral life will follow of course.

The allusions in Job have all of them the same tendency with this Psalm; that of deducing or proving a truth that would be otherwise unknown, from truths already known.

I recollect not enough of the passages in Job, to insert them correctly: but there is one occurs to me that is applicable to the subject I am speaking upon. "Canst thou by searching find out God? Canst thou find out the Almighty to perfection?"

I know not how the printers have pointed this passage, for I keep no Bible; but it contains two distinct questions, that admit of distinct answers.

First — Canst thou by searching find out God? Yes; because in the first place, I know I did not make myself, and yet I have existence; and by *searching* into the nature of other things, I find that no other thing could make itself; and yet millions of other things exist; therefore it is, that I know, by positive conclusion resulting from this search, that there is a power superior to all those things, and that power is God.

Secondly — Canst thou find out the Almighty to *perfection?* No; not only because the power and wisdom He has manifested in the structure of the Creation that I behold is to me incomprehensible, but because even this manifestation, great as it is, is probably but a small display of that immensity of power and wisdom, by which millions of other worlds, to me invisible by their distance, were created and continue to exist.

It is evident that both of these questions are put to the reason of the person to whom they are supposed to have been addressed; and it is only by admitting the first question to be answered affirmatively, that the second could follow. It would have been unnecessary, and even absurd, to have put a second question more difficult than the first, if the first question had been answered negatively. The two questions have different objects; the first refers to the existence of God, the second to his attributes; reason can discover the one, but it falls infinitely short in discovering the whole of the other. . . .

The true Deist has but one Deity; and his religion consists in contemplating the power, wisdom, and benignity of the Deity in his works, and in endeavoring to imitate him in every thing moral, scientifical, and mechanical. . . .

As, therefore, the Creator made nothing in vain, so also must it be believed that He organized the structure of the universe in the most advantageous manner for the benefit of man; and as we see, and from experience feel, the benefits we derive from the structure of the universe, formed as it is, which benefits we should not have had the opportunity of enjoying, if the structure, so far as relates to our system, had been a solitary globe — we can discover at least one reason why a *plurality* of worlds has been made, and that reason calls forth the devotional gratitude of man, as well as his admiration.

But it is not to us, the inhabitants of this globe, only, that the benefits arising from a plurality of worlds are limited. The inhabitants of each of the worlds of which our system is composed, enjoy the same opportunities of knowledge as we do. They behold the revolutionary motions of our earth, as we behold theirs. All the planets revolve in sight of each other; and, therefore, the same universal school of science presents itself to all.

Neither does the knowledge stop here. The system of worlds next to us exhibits, in its revolutions, the same principles and school of science, to the inhabitants of their system, as our system does to us, and in like manner throughout the immensity of space.

Our ideas, not only of the almightiness of the Creator, but of his wisdom and his beneficence, become enlarged in protection as we contemplate the extent and the structure of the universe. The solitary idea of a solitary world, rolling or at rest in the immense ocean of space, gives place to the cheerful idea of a society of worlds, so happily contrived as to administer, even by their motion, instruction to man. We see our own earth filled with abundance; but we forget to consider how much of that abundance is owing to the scientific knowledge the vast machinery of the universe has unfolded.

But, in the midst of those reflections, what are we to think of the Christian system of faith, that forms itself upon the idea of only one world, and that of no greater extent, as is before shown, than twenty-five thousand miles? An extent which a man, walking at the rate of three miles an hour, for twelve hours in the day, could he keep on in a circular direction, would walk entirely round in less than two years. Alas! what is this to the mighty ocean of space, and the almighty power of the Creator!

From whence then could arise the solitary and strange conceit, that the Almighty, who had millions of worlds equally depend on his protection, should quit the care of all the rest, and come to die in our world, because, they say, one man and one woman had eaten an apple! And, on the other hand, are we to suppose that every world in the boundless creation, had an Eve, an apple, a serpent and a redeemer? In this case, the person who is irreverently called the Son of God, and sometimes God himself, would have nothing else to do than to travel from world to world, in an endless succession of death, with scarcely a momentary interval of life.

It has been by rejecting the evidence, that the word or works of God in the creation affords to our senses, and the action of our reason upon that evidence, that so many wild and whimsical systems of faith, and of religion, have been fabricated and set up. There may be many systems of religion, that so far from being morally bad, are in many respects morally good: but there can be but ONE that is true; and that one necessarily must, as it ever will, be in all things consistent with the ever existing word of God that we behold in his works. But such is the strange construction of the Christian system of faith, that every evidence the Heavens afford to man, either directly contradicts it, or renders it absurd.

It is possible to believe, and I always feel pleasure in encouraging myself to believe it, that there have been men in the world, who persuade themselves that, what is called a *pious fraud,* might at least under particular circumstances, be productive of some good. But the fraud being once established, could not afterwards be explained; for it is with a pious fraud as with a bad action, it begets a calamitous necessity of going on.

The persons who first preached the Christian system of faith, and in some measure combined it with the morality preached by Jesus Christ, might persuade themselves that it was better than the heathen mythology that then prevailed. From the first preachers the fraud went on to the second, and to the third, till the idea of its being a pious fraud became lost in the belief of its being true! and that belief became again encouraged by the interests of those who made a livelihood by preaching it.

SÖREN KIERKEGAARD

SÖREN KIERKEGAARD (1813-1855), a Danish philosopher born in Copenhagen on May 5, 1813, attended the Borgerdydskole in Copenhagen in 1823, and in 1830 matriculated at the University of Copenhagen where he pursued theological studies, graduating in 1840. The only other aspect of his academic life was a few years of study in Berlin. He led a very uneventful life and died on Nov. 11, 1855 at the age of 42.

Kierkegaard, as a thinker, went unrecognized in America for almost one hundred years, but his fame escalated at an accelerated rate so that at the present time, great as it is, he is still growing in popularity. He is considered the greatest religious philosopher of the Nineteenth Century, and credited with being the father of contemporary Existentialism. The English speaking world has learned to appreciate him only recently, for the translations of his books into English began to appear as late as 1936, approximately a hundred years later. Among his major works in translation are: **The Journals** (1938), **Either/Or** (1944), **Eighteen Edifying Discourses** (1943-44), **Repetition** (1941), **Fear and Trembling** (1939), **Philosophical Fragments** (1936), **The Concept of Dread** (1944), **Stages on Life's Way** (1940), **Concluding Unscientific Postscript** (1941), **The Sickness unto Death** (1941), **The Point of View for My Work as an Author** (1939), **The Individual** (1939), **For Self-Examination** (1940), **Judge for Yourself!** (1941), and the work from which the present volume has taken its selection characteristic of Kierkegaard, **God's Unchangeableness** (1941).

The Existentialist, Kierkegaard, seeks to maintain the following position: Truth is subjectivity and is found in paradox. To God, truth is rational, but to earth-bound creatures, men, it appears paradoxical. The goal of life is to realize oneself through sheer efforts of will. Existence, human reality, is known through passion, not reason, and its nature is subjectivity.

Kierkegaard, a Deistic Supernaturalist, is one who believes that God is transcendent, other than the world which he created, and beyond it. However, unlike Deism, God is attainable through prayer; at times, he breaks through nature, his creation, to perform special acts (in harmony or contradictory to the laws of nature), called miracles.

28

SÖREN KIERKEGAARD:

Deistic Supernaturalism (God as the Superhuman and Supernatural Revealer of Values)[1]

God is unchangeable. In His omnipotence He created this visible world — and made Himself invisible. He clothed Himself in the visible world as in a garment; He changes it as one who shifts a garment — Himself unchanged. Thus in the world of sensible things. In the world of events He is present everywhere in every moment; in a truer sense than we can say of the most watchful human justice that it is present everywhere, in the least event as well as in the greatest, in that which can scarcely be called an event and in that which is the only event, in the death of a sparrow and in the birth of the Saviour of mankind. In each moment every actuality is a possibility in His almighty hand; He holds all in readiness, in every instant prepared to change everything: the opinions of men, their judgments, human greatness and human abasement; He changes all, Himself unchanged. When everything seems stable (for it is only in appearance that the external world is for a time unchanged, in reality it is always in flux) and in the overturn of all things, He remains equally unchanged; no change touches Him, not even the shadow of a change; in unaltered clearness He, the father of lights, remains eternally unchanged. In unaltered clearness — aye, this is precisely why He is unchanged, because He is pure clearness, a clarity which betrays no trace of dimness, and which no dimness can come near. With us men it is not so. We are not in this manner clear, and precisely for this reason we are subject to change: Now something becomes clearer in us, now something is dimmed, and we are changed; now changes take place about us, and the shadow of these changes glides over us to alter us; now there falls upon us from the surroundings an altering light, while under all this we are again changed within ourselves.

[1] Sören Kierkegaard, *The Unchangeableness of God*, tr. David F. Swenson (Princeton: Princeton University Press, 1941); original (1855). Reprinted by permission.

This thought *is terrifying, all fear and trembling.* This aspect of it is in general perhaps less often emphasized: we complain of men and their mutability, and of the mutability of all temporal things; but God is unchangeable, this is our consolation, an entirely comforting thought — so speaks even frivolity. Aye, God is in very truth unchangeable. . . .

True enough, if your will, if my will, if the will of all these many thousands happens to be not so entirely in harmony with God's will: things nevertheless take their course as best they may in the hurly-burly of the so-called actual world; it is as if God did not pay any attention. It is rather as if a just man — if there were such a man! — contemplating this world, a world which, as the Scriptures say, is dominated by evil, must needs feel disheartened because God does not seem to make Himself felt. But do you believe of that account that God has undergone any change? Or is the fact that God does not seem to make Himself felt any the less a terrifying fact, as long as it is nevertheless certain that He is eternally unchangeable? To me it does not seem so. Consider the matter, and then tell me which is the more terrible to contemplate: the picture of one who is infinitely the stronger, who grows tired of letting himself be mocked, and rises in his might to crush the refractory spirits — a sight terrible indeed, and so represented when we say that God is not mocked, pointing to the times His annihilating punishments were visited upon the human race — but is this really the most terrifying sight? Is not this other sight still more terrifying: one infinitely powerful, who — eternally unchanged! — sits quite still and sees everything, without altering a feature, almost as if He did not exist; while all the time, as the just man must needs complain, lies achieve success and win to power, violence and wrong gain the victory, to such an extent as even to attempt man to think if he hopes to accomplish anything for the good he must in part use the same means; so that it is as if God were being mocked, God the infinitely powerful, the eternally unchangeable, who none the less is neither mocked nor changed — is not this the most terrifying sight? For why, do you think, is He so quiet? Because He knows with Himself that He is eternally unchangeable. Anyone not eternally sure of Himself could not keep so still, but would rise in His strength. Only one who is eternally immutable can be in this manner so still. . . .

LUDWIG FEUERBACH

LUDWIG ANDREAS FEUERBACH (1804-1872), a German philosopher, was born at Landshut, Bavaria on the twenty-eighth of July. Notwithstanding the fact that he studied under the Idealist Hegel, he became a 'left-wing' Hegelian, that is, a Materialist or Naturalist. His post-Hegelian studies in 1828 at Erlangen were in the field of natural science.

Feuerbach's influence was the greatest among the anti-Christian theologians and philosophers, such as D. F. Strauss who wrote **The Life of Jesus,** and Karl Marx who is indebted to Feuerbach for his Materialism. Feuerbach sought to humanize theology, and presented his Humanism most forcefully in what is considered his most important work, **The Essence of Christianity** (1841), which was translated by George Eliot a dozen years later. From this translation of **The Essence of Christianity,** the Humanism of Feuerbach is presented. Other of his writings are **The Philosophy of the Future** (1843) and **The Essence of Religion** (1851).

The Humanist Feuerbach asserted the belief that religion and God are man's projection of his own nature and ideals, the product of human imagination. For him, man is God, without man God cannot be; to become man is to make God. "Man has his highest being, his God, in himself;" God is part of man's nature.

29

LUDWIG FEUERBACH

Humanism (God as Man's Highest Aspiration)[1]

Speculation makes religion say only what it has *itself* thought, and expressed far better than religion; it assigns a meaning to religion without any reference to the actual meaning of religion; it does not look beyond itself. I, on the contrary, let religion itself speak; I constitute myself only its listener and interpreter, not its prompter. Not to invent, but to discover, "to unveil existence," has been my sole object; to *see* correctly, my sole endeavour. It is not I, but religion that worships man, although religion, or rather theology, denies this; it is not I, an insignificant individual, but religion itself that says: God is man, man is God; it is not I, but religion that denies the God who is not man, but only an *ens-rationis,* — since it makes God become man, and then constitutes this God, not distinguished from man, having a human form, human feelings, and human thoughts, the object of its worship and veneration. I have only found the key to the cipher of the Christian religion, only extricated its true meaning from the web of contradictions and delusions called theology; — but in doing so I have certainly committed a sacrilege. If therefore my work is negative, irreligious, atheistic, let it be remembered that atheism — at least in the sense of this work — is the secret of religion itself, not indeed on the surface, but fundamentally, not in intention or according to its own supposition, but in its heart, in its essence, believes in nothing else than the truth and divinity of human nature. . . .

The object of any subject is nothing else than the subject's own nature taken objectively. Such as are a man's thoughts and dispositions, such is his God; so much worth as a man has, so much and no more has his God. Consciousness of God is self-consciousness, knowledge of God is self-knowledge. By his God thou knowest the man, and by the man his God;

[1] Ludwig Feuerbach, *The Essence of Christianity,* (1843), tr. George Eliot (Marian Evans), 2nd. ed.; excerpts from the Preface to the second edition and chapter 1.

the two are identical. Whatever is God to a man, that is his heart and soul; and conversely, God is the manifested inward nature, the expressed self of a man, — religion the solemn unveiling of a man's hidden treasures, the revelation of his intimate thoughts, the open confession of his love-secrets. . . .

That which is to man the self-existent, the highest being, to which he can conceive nothing higher — that is to him the Divine Being. How then should he inquire concerning this being, what he is in himself? If God were an object to the bird, he would be a winged being: the bird knows nothing higher, nothing more blissful, than the winged condition. How ludicrous would it be if this bird pronounced: To me God appears as a bird, but what he is in himself I know not. To the bird the highest nature is the bird-nature; take from him the conception of this, and you take from him the conception of the highest being. How, then could he ask whether God in himself were winged? To ask whether God is in himself what he is for me, is to ask whether God is God, is to lift oneself above one's God, to rise up against him. . . .

Thou believest in love as a divine attribute because thou thyself lovest; thou believest that God is a wise, benevolent being because thou knowest nothing better in thyself than benevolence and wisdom; and thou believest that God exists, that therefore he is a subject — whatever exists is a subject whether it be defined as substance, person, essence, or otherwise — because thou thyself existest, art thyself a subject. Thou knowest no higher human good than to love, than to be good and wise; and even so thou knowest no higher happiness than to exist, to be a subject; for the consciousness of all reality, of all bliss, is for thee bound up in the consciousness of being a subject, of existing. God is an existence, a subject to thee, for the same reason that he is to thee a wise, a blessed, a personal being. The distinction between the divine predicates and the divine subject is only this, that to thee the subject, the existence, does not appear an anthropomorphism, because the conception of it is necessarily involved in thy own existence as a subject, whereas the predicates do appear anthropomorphisms, because their necessity — the necessity that God should be conscious, wise, good, &c. — is not an immediate necessity, identical with the being of man, but is evolved by his self-consciousness, by the activity of his thought. . . .

Whatever man conceives to be true, he immediately conceives to be real (that is, to have an objective existence), because, originally, only the real is true to him — true in opposition to what is merely conceived, dreamed, imagined. The idea of being, of existence, is the original idea of truth; or, originally, man makes truth dependent on existence, subsequently, existence dependent on truth. Now God is the nature of man regarded as absolute truth, — the truth of man; but God, or, what is the same thing, religion, is as various as are the conditions under which man conceives this his nature, regards it as the highest being. These conditions, then, under which man conceives God, are to him the truth, and for that reason they are also the highest existence, or rather they are existence itself; for only the emphatic, the highest existence, is existence, and deserves this name. Therefore, God is an existent, real being, on the very same ground that he is a particular, definite being; for the qualities of God are nothing else than the essential qualities of man himself, and a particular man is what he is, has his existence, his reality, only in his particular conditions. Take away from the Greek the quality of being Greek, and you take away his existence. . . . How then can I doubt of God, who is my being? To doubt of God is to doubt of myself. Only when God is thought of abstractly, when his predicates are the result of philosophic abstraction, arises the distinction or separation between subject and predicate, existence and nature — arises the fiction that the existence or the subject is something else than the predicate, something immediate, indubitable, in distinction from the predicate, which is held to be doubtful. But this is only a fiction. A God who has abstract predicates has also an abstract existence. Existence, being, varies with varying qualities. . . .

With the emerging of man from a state of savagery and wildness to one of culture, with the distinction between what is fitting for man and what is not fitting, arises simultaneously the distinction between that which is fitting and that which is not fitting for God. God is the idea of majesty, of the highest dignity: the religious sentiment is the sentiment of supreme fitness. The later more cultured artists of Greece were the first to embody in the statues of the gods the ideas of dignity, of spiritual grandeur, of imperturbable repose and serenity. But why were these qualities in their view attributes, predicates of God? Because they were in themselves regarded by the greeks as divinities. Why did those artists exclude all disgusting and low passions? Because they perceived them to be unbecoming, unworthy, unhuman, and consequently ungodlike. The Homeric gods eat and drink; — that implies eating and drinking is a divine pleasure. Physical strength is an attribute of the Homeric gods: Zeus is the strongest of the gods. Why? Because physical strength, in and by itself, was regarded as something glorious, divine. To the ancient Germans the highest virtues were those of the warrior; therefore their supreme god was the god of war, Odin, — war, "the original or oldest law." Not the attribute of the divinity, but the divineness or deity of the attribute, is the first true Divine Being. Thus what theology and philosophy have held to be God, the Absolute, the Infinite, is not God; but that which they have held not to be God is God; namely, the attribute, the quality, whatever has reality. Hence he alone is the true atheist to whom the predicates of the Divine Being, — for example, love, wisdom, justice, — are nothing; not he to whom merely the subject of these predicates is nothing. And in no wise is the negation of the subject necessarily also a negation of the predicates considered in themselves. These have an intrinsic, independent reality; they force their recognition upon man by their very nature; they are self-evident truths to him; they prove, they attest themselves. It does not follow that goodness, justice, wisdom are chimaeras because the existence of God is a chimaera, nor truths because this is a truth. The idea of God is dependent on the idea of justice, of benevolence; a God dependent on the idea of justice, of benevolence; a God who is not benevolent, not just, not wise, is no God; but the converse does not hold. The fact is not that a quality is divine because God has it, but that God has it because it is in itself divine: because without it God would be a defective being. Justice, wisdom, in general every quality which constitutes the•divinity of God, is determined and known by itself independently, but the idea of God is determined by the qualities which have thus been previously judged to be worthy of the divine nature; only in the case in which I identify God and justice, in which I think of God immediately as the reality of the idea of justice, is the idea of God self-determined. But if God as a subject is the determined, while the quality, the predicate, is the determining, then in truth the rank of the godhead is due not to the subject, but to the predicate. . . .

God is the highest subjectivity of man abstracted from himself; hence man can do nothing of himself, all goodness comes from God. The more subjective God is, the more completely does man divest himself of his subjectivity, because God is, *per se*, his relinquished self, the possession of which he however again vindicates to himself. As the action of the arteries drives the blood into the extremities, and the action of the veins brings it back again, as life in general consists in a perpetual systole and diastole; so is it in religion. In the religious systole man propels his own nature from himself, he throws himself outward; in the religious diastole he receives the rejected nature into his heart again. God alone is the being who acts of himself, — this is the force of repulsion in religion; God is the being who acts in me, with me, through me, upon me, for me, is the principle of my salvation, of my good dispositions and actions, consequently my own good principle and nature, — this is the force of attraction in religion.

Man[2] has his highest being, his God in himself; not in himself as an individual, but in his essential nature, his species. No individual is an

2 *Ibid.*, Appendix, section 1.

adequate representation of his species, but only the human individual is conscious of the distinction between the species and the individual; in the sense of this distinction lies the root of religion. The yearning of man after something above himself is nothing else than the longing after the perfect type of his nature, the yearning to be free from himself, *i.e.*, from the limits and defects of his individuality. Individuality is the self-conditioning, the self-limitation of the species. Thus man has cognisance of nothing above himself, of nothing beyond the nature of humanity; but to the individual man this nature presents itself under the form of an individual man. Thus, for example, the child sees the nature of man *above itself* in the form of its parents, the pupil in the form of his tutor. But all feelings which man experiences towards a superior man, nay, in general, all moral feelings which man has towards man, are of a religious nature. *Man feels nothing towards God which he does not also feel towards man. Homo homini deus est.*

AUGUSTE COMTE

AUGUSTE COMTE (1798-1857), a Frenchman, father of the philosophy of Positivism, founder of Sociology, was born on Jan. 19, 1798 at Montpellier. A man of independent thought and a renegade by spirit, he became involved in a mutiny which broke up the École Polytechnique where he was being educated. Leaving school in 1816, he went to Paris where he gave instruction in mathematics for his livelihood. In the late teens of the Nineteenth Century, Comte became associated with Saint-Simon, who exercized a profound and permanent influence upon him. In 1833, he was an examiner for the École Polytechnique, an appointment which today is commonly known as director of admissions, a post he held for many years. His personal life was a stormy one which included imprisonment for refusing to serve in the French national guard, separation from his wife in 1842, a lawsuit with his publisher, and dismissal as examiner from the École Polytechnique.

Credited with coining the terms **Positivism** and **altruism,** Comte has left an unmistakable philosophical influence on posterity with his Positivism, a Phenomenalism akin to that of Hume and Kant. Comte's Religion of Humanity, the forerunner of contemporary Religious Humanism, has definitively established itself. His main works are: **Positive Polity** (1851-1854), **Positive Philosophy** (1830-1842), and **Positive Catechism** (1852).

Comte sought to found a religion of which he was chief priest, The Religion of Humanity, the forerunner of contemporary Religious Humanism. God, the Grand Being **(Grand-Être),** the creation of man, man's highest aspiration, is the object of worship and human veneration.

30

AUGUSTE COMTE

Humanism (God as Humanity)[1]

The Religion of Humanity

Love, then, is our principle; Order our basis; and Progress our end.
Such, as the preceding chapters have shown, is the essential character of
the system of life which Positivism offers for the definite acceptance of
society; a system which regulates the whole course of our private and
public existence, by bringing Feeling, Reason, and Activity into permanent harmony. In this final synthesis, all essential conditions are far more
perfectly fulfilled than in any other. Each special element of our nature
is more fully developed, and at the same time the general working of
the whole is more coherent. Greater distinctness is given to the truth that
the affective element predominates in our nature. Life in all its actions and
thoughts is brought under the control and inspiring charm of Social
Sympathy.

By the supremacy of the Heart, the Intellect, so far from being crushed,
is elevated; for all its powers are consecrated to the service of the social
instincts, with the purpose of strengthening their influence and directing
their employment. . . .

Humanity Is the Centre to Which Every Aspect of Positivism Converges

All essential phases in the evolution of society answer to corresponding
phases in the growth of the individual, whether it has proceeded spontaneously or under systematic guidance, supposing always that his development be complete. But it is not enough to prove the close connexion
which exists between all modes and degrees of human regeneration. We
have yet to find a central point round which all will naturally meet. In
this point consists the unity of Positivism as a system of life. Unless it

[1] Auguste Comte, *A General View of Positivism*, tr. J. H. Bridges (1865); original
French edition, 1848; excerpts from chapter VI, "The Religion of Humanity."

can be thus condensed, round one single principle, it will never wholly supersede the synthesis of Theology, notwithstanding its superiority in the reality and stability of its component parts, and in their homogeneity and coherence as a whole. There should always be a central point in the system towards which Feeling, Reason, and Activity alike converge. The proof that Positivism possesses such a central point will remove the last obstacles to its complete acceptance, as guide of private or of public life.

Such a centre we find in the great conception of Humanity, towards which every aspect of Positivism naturally converges. By it the conception of God will be entirely superseded, and a synthesis be formed, more permanent than that provisionally established by the old religions. Through it the new doctrine becomes at once accessible to men's hearts in its full extent and application. From their heart it will penetrate their minds, and thus the immediate necessity of beginning with a long and difficult course of study is avoided, though this must of course be always indispensable to its systematic teachers.

This central point of Positivism is even more moral than intellectual in character: it represents the principle of Love upon which the whole system rests. It is the peculiar characteristic of the Great Being who is here set forth, to be compounded of separable elements. Its existence depends therefore entirely upon mutual Love knitting together its various parts. The calculations of self-interest can never be substituted as a combining influence for the sympathetic instincts.

Yet the belief in Humanity, while stimulating Sympathy, at the same time enlarges the scope and vigour of the Intellect. For it requires high powers of generalization to conceive clearly of this vast organism as the result of spontaneous co-operation, abstraction made of all partial antagonism. Reason, then, has its part in this central dogma as well as Love. It enlarges and completes our conception of the Supreme Being, by revealing to us the external and internal conditions of its existence.

Lastly, our active powers are stimulated by it no less than our feelings and our reason. For since Humanity is so far more complex than any other organism, it will react more strongly and more continuously on its environment, submitting to its influence and so modifying it. Hence results Progress which is simply the development of Order, under the influence of Love.

Thus, in the conception of Humanity, the three essential aspects of Positivism, its subjective principle, its objective dogma, and its practical object, are united. Towards Humanity, who is for us the only true Great Being, we, the conscious elements of whom she is composed, shall henceforth direct every aspect of our life, individual or collective. Our thoughts will be devoted to the knowledge of Humanity, our affections to her love, our actions to her service.

Positivists then may, more truly than theological believers of whatever creed, regard life as a continuous and earnest act of worship; worship which will elevate and purify our feelings, enlarge and enlighten our thoughts, ennoble and invigorate our actions. It supplies a direct solution, so far as a solution is possible, of the great problem of the Middle Ages, the subordination of Politics to Morals. For this follows at once from the consecration now given to the principle that social sympathy should preponderate over self-love.

Thus Positivism becomes, in the true sense of the word, a Religion; the only religion which is real and complete; destined therefore to replace all imperfect and provisional systems resting on the primitive basis of theology. . . .

With the Discovery of Sociological Laws, a Synthesis on the Basis of Science Becomes Possible, Now Concentrated on the Study of Humanity

. . . By entirely renouncing wealth and worldly position, and that not as individuals merely, but as a body, the priests of Humanity will occupy a position of unparalleled dignity. For with their moral influence they will combine what since the downfall of the old theocracies has always been separated from it, the influence of superiority in art and science. Reason, Imagination, and Feeling will be brought into unison: and so united will react strongly on the imperious conditions of practical life; bringing it into close accordance with the laws of universal morality, from which it is so prone to deviate. And the influence of this new modifying power will be the greater that the synthesis on which it rests will have preceded and prepared the way for the social system of the future; whereas theology could not arrive at its central principle, until the time of its decline was approaching. All functions, then, that co-operate in the elevation of man will be regenerated by the Positive priesthood. Science, Poetry, Morality, will be devoted to the study, the praise, and the love of Humanity, in order that under their combined influence, our political action may be more unremittingly given to her service.

With such a mission, Science acquires a position of unparalleled importance, as the sole means through which we come to know the nature and conditions of this Great Being, the worship of whom should be the distinctive feature of our whole life. For this all-important knowledge, the study of Sociology would seem to suffice: but Sociology itself depends upon preliminary study, first of the outer world, in which the actions of Humanity take place; and secondly, of Man, the individual agent.

The object of Positivist worship is not like that of theological believers and absolute, isolated, incomprehensible Being, whose existence admits of no demonstration, or comparison with anything real. The evidence of the Being here set forward is spontaneous, and is shrouded in no mystery. Before we can praise, love, and serve Humanity as we ought, we must know something of the laws which govern her existence, an existence more complicated than any other of which we are cognizant.

Statical Aspects of Humanity

And by virtue of this complexity, Humanity possesses the attributes of vitality in a higher degree than any other organization; that is to say, there is at once more intimate harmony of the component elements, and more complete subordination to the external world. Immense as is the magnitude of this organism measured both in Time and Space, yet each of its parts carefully examined will show the general consensus of the whole. At the same time it is more dependent than any other upon the conditions of the outer world; in other words, upon the sum of the laws that regulate inferior phenomena. Like other vital organisms, it submits to mathematical, astronomical, physical, chemical, and biological conditions; and, in addition to these, is subject to special laws of Sociology with which lower organisms are not concerned. But as a further result of its higher complexity it reacts upon the world more powerfully; and is indeed in a true sense its chief. Scientifically defined, then, it is truly the Supreme Being: the Being who manifests to the fullest extent all the highest attributes of life.

But there is yet another feature peculiar to Humanity, and one of primary importance. That feature is, that the elements of which she is composed must always have an independent existence. In other organisms the parts have no existence when severed from the whole; but this, the greatest of all organisms, is made up of lives which can really be separated. There is, as we have seen, harmony of parts as well as independence, but the last of these conditions is as indispensable as the first. Humanity would cease to be superior to other beings were it possible for her elements to become inseparable. These two conditions are equally necessary: but the difficulty of reconciling them is so great as to account at once for the slowness with which this highest of all organisms has been developed. It must not, however, be supposed that the new Supreme Being is, like the old, merely a subjective result of our powers of abstraction. Its existence is revealed to us, on the contrary, by close investigation of objective fact. Man, indeed, as an individual, cannot properly be said to exist, except in the exaggerated abstractions of modern metaphysicians. Existence in the true sense can only be predicated of Humanity. . . .

Dynamical Aspects

Having now viewed our subject statically, we may come to its dynamical aspect; reserving more detailed discussion for the third volume of the treatise, which deals with my fundamental theory of human development. The Great Being whom we worship is not immutable any more than it is absolute. Its nature is relative; and, as such is eminently capable of growth. In a word it is the most vital of all living beings known to us. It extends and becomes more complex by the continuous successions of generations. But in its progressive changes as well as in its permanent functions, it is subject to invariable laws. And these laws considered, as we may now consider them, as a whole, form a more sublime object of contemplation than the solemn inaction of the old Supreme Being, whose existence was passive except when interrupted by acts of arbitrary and unintelligible volition. Thus it is only by Positive science that we can appreciate this highest of all destinies to which all the fatalities of individual life are subordinate. . . .

Poetic Portraiture of the New Supreme Being, and Contrast with the Old

In our religion the object of worship must be conceived distinctly, in order to be ardently loved and zealously served. Science, especially in subjects of this nature, is confined within narrow limits; it leaves inevitable deficiencies which esthetic genius must supply. And there are certain qualities in Art as opposed to Science, which specially qualify it for the representation of Humanity. For Humanity is distinguished from other forms of life by the combination of independence with co-operation, attributes which also are natural to Poetry. For while Poetry is more sympathetic than Science, its productions have far more individuality; the genius of their author is more strongly marked in them, and the debt to his predecessors and contemporaries is less apparent. Thus the synthesis on which the inauguration of the final religion depends, is one in which Art will participate more than Science, Science furnishing merely the necessary basis. Its influence will be even greater than in the times of Polytheism; for powerful as Art appeared to be in those times, it could in reality do nothing but embellish the fables to which the confused ideas of theocracy had given rise. By its aid we shall for the first time rise at last to a really human point of view, and be enabled distinctly to understand the essential attributes of the Great Being of whom we are members. The material power of Humanity and the successive phases of her physical, her intellectual, and, above all, her moral progress will each in turn be depicted. Without the difficulties of analytical study, we shall gain a clear knowledge of her nature and her conditions, by the poet's description of her future destiny, of her constant struggle against painful fatalities, which have at last become a source of happiness and greatness, of the slow growth of her infancy, of her lofty hopes now so near fulfilment. The history of universal Love, the soul by which this Great Being is animated; the history, that is, of the marvellous advance of man, individually or socially, from brutish appetite to pure unselfish sympathy, is of itself an endless theme for the poetry of the future.

Comparisons, too, may be instituted, in which the poet, without specially attacking the old religion, will indicate the superiority of the new. The attributes of the new Great Being may be forcibly illustrated, especially during the time of transition, by contrast with the inferiority of her various predecessors. All theological types are absolute, indefinite, and immutable; consequently in none of them has it been possible to combine to a satisfactory extent the attributes of goodness, wisdom, and power. Nor can we conceive of their combination, except in a Being whose existence is a matter of certainty, and who is subject to invariable laws. The gods of Polytheism were endowed with energy and sympathy, but possessed neither dignity nor morality. They were superseded by the sublime deity of Monotheism, who was sometimes represented as inert and passionless, sometimes as impenetrable and inflexible. But the new Supreme Being, having a real existence, an existence relative and modifiable, admits of being more distinctly conceived than the old; and the influence of the conception will be equally strong and far more elevating. Each one of us will recognize in it a power superior to his own, a power on which the whole destiny of his life depends, since the life of the individual is in every respect subordinate to the evolution of the race. But the knowledge of this power has not the crushing effect of the old conception of omnipotence. For every great or good man will feel that his own life is an indispensable element in the great organism. The supremacy of Humanity is but the result of individual co-operation; her power is not supreme, it is only superior to that of all beings whom we know. Our love for her is tainted by no degrading fears, yet it is always coupled with the most sincere reverence. Perfection is in no wise claimed for her; we study her natural defects with care in order to remedy them as far as possible. The love we bear to her is a feeling as noble as it is strong; it calls for no degrading expressions of adulation, but it inspires us with unremitting zeal for moral improvement. But these and other advantages of the new religion, though they can be indicated by the philosopher, need the poet to display them in their full light. The moral grandeur of man when freed from the chimeras that oppress him, was foreseen by Goethe, and still more clearly by Byron. But the work of these men was one of destruction; and their types could only embody the spirit of revolt. Poetry must rise above the negative stage in which, owing to the circumstances of the time, their genius was arrested, and must embrace in the Positive spirit the system of sociological and other laws to which human development is subject, before it can adequately portray the new Man in his relation to the new God.

HERBERT SPENCER

HERBERT SPENCER (1820-1903), English philosopher, ardent proponent of the philosophy of Evolution, was born in Derby, England, on April 27, 1820, and died on the eighth of December, 1903. Declining the generous offer of an uncle who was willing to send him to Cambridge University, Spencer became a self-taught man. He spent the years from 1837 to 1846 both studying and gainfully employed as an engineer for the newly formed London and Birmingham Railway; the years from 1848 to 1853 found him as sub-editor of the **Economist.** His long and fruitful career as author of philosophical works began at approximately this time, for in 1850 he published **Social Statics;** in 1852, **The Development Hypothesis;** in 1855, **Principles of Psychology;** in 1857, **Progress, Its Law and Cause;** in 1862, **First Principles;** in 1864, **Principles of Biology;** in 1870-1872, the two volume second edition of **Principles of Psychology;** in 1877-1896, **Principles of Sociology;** in 1879, **The Data of Ethics,** which became Part I of the two volume work, **Principles of Ethics** (1891-1893); in 1884, **Man versus the State;** in 1886, **Factors of Organic Evolution;** in 1893, **Inadequacy of Natural Selection;** in 1894, **A Rejoinder to Professor Weismann;** in 1897, **Fragments;** in 1902, **Facts and Comments;** and a two volume **Autobiography** posthumously published in 1904. The selection chosen for inclusion in the present volume is from his **First Principles** treating The Unknowable, a position known in philosophy of religion as Agnostic Realism.

Spencer, following Mansell, proclaimed the doctrine of the Inconceivability of the Nature of God, by which he sought a reconciliation of science and religion on the basis of the ultimate as unknowable. God, the Unknowable, although a proper inference from empirical fact, cannot be known, especially the particulars regarding him. God, who is the Absolute, the Unconditioned, the Unitary Being, Force, is **Unknowable,** and so termed. Philosophy has sought in vain for definite ideas respecting God, for he is by his very nature incapable of determination, due to the limitations of human knowledge in interpreting and being restricted to the bounds of phenomena. Only the manifestations of the Unknowable are available to man, not his real Being. The manner in which the Absolute manifests himself in

197

the particular sciences is evolution, the transformation of natural structures from homogeneity to a heterogeneous one, utilizing the two processes of evolution: differentiation and integration. Out of these processes, new unities arise which are superior to the original; **e.g.,** from the single cell, the higher unity of the animal organism eventually arises, eventuating in the highest goal, not man as an individual, but society.

31

HERBERT SPENCER

Agnostic Realism (God as 'The Unknowable' Source of All Being)[1]

Respecting the origin of the universe three verbally intelligible suppositions may be made. We may assert that it is self-existent; or that it is self-created; or that it is created by an external agency. Which of these suppositions is most credible it is not needful here to inquire. The proper question, into which this finally merges, is, whether any one of them is even conceivable in the true sense of the word. Let us successively test them.

When we speak of a man as self-supporting, of an apparatus as self-acting, or of a tree as self-developed, our expressions, however inexact, stand for things that can be realized in thought with tolerable completeness. Our conception of the self-development of a tree is doubtless symbolic. But though we cannot really represent in consciousness the entire series of complex changes through which the tree passes, yet we can thus represent the leading features of the series; and general experience teaches us that by long-continued observation we could gain the power to realize in thought a series of changes more fully representing the actual series; that is, we know that our symbolic conception of self-development can be expanded into something like a real conception; and that it express, however inaccurately, an actual process in nature. But when we speak of self-existence, and, helped by the above analogies, form some vague symbolic conception of it, we delude ourselves in supposing that this symbolic conception is of the same order as the others. On joining the word *self* to the word *existence,* the force of association makes us believe we have a thought like that suggested by the compound

---

[1] Herbert Spencer, *First Principles of a New System of Philosophy;* first edition, 1862; sixth edition, 1903; the above selection is from part I ("The Unknowable"), chapter II, ("Ultimate Religious Ideas"), sections 11, 12, and 31.

word self-acting. An endeavor to expand this symbolic conception, however, will undeceive us.

In the first place, it is clear that by self-existence we especially mean an existence independent of any other — not produced by any other; the assertion of self-existence is simply an indirect denial of creation. In thus excluding the idea of any antecedent cause, we necessarily exclude the idea of a beginning; for to admit the idea of a beginning — to admit that there was a time when the existence had not commenced — is to admit that its commencement was determined by something, or was caused; which is a contradiction. Self-existence, therefore, necessarily means existence without a beginning; and to form a conception of self-existence is to form a conception of existence without a beginning. Now by no mental effort can we do this. To conceive existence through infinite past-time, implies the conception of infinite past-time, which is an impossibility.

To this let us add, that even were self-existence conceivable, it would not in any sense be an explanation of the universe. No one will say that the existence of an object at the present moment is made easier to understand by the discovery that it existed an hour ago, or a day ago, or a year ago; and if its existence now is not made in the least degree more comprehensible by its existence during some previous finite period of time, then no accumulation of such finite periods, even could we extend them to an infinite period, would make it more comprehensible. Thus the atheistic theory is not only absolutely unthinkable, but, even if it were thinkable, would not be a solution. The assertion that the universe is self-existent does not really carry us a step beyond the cognition of its present existence; and so leaves us with a mere re-statement of the mystery.

The hypothesis of self-creation, which practically amounts to what is called pantheism, is similarly incapable of being represented in thought. Certain phenomena, such as the precipitation of invisible vapor into cloud, aid us in forming a symbolic conception of a self-evolved universe; and there are not wanting indications in the heavens, and on the earth, which help us to render this conception tolerably definite. But while the succession of phases through which the universe has passed in reaching its present form may perhaps be comprehended as in a sense self-determined, yet the impossibility of expanding our symbolic conception of self-creation into a real conception, remains as complete as ever. Really to conceive self-creation, is to conceive potential existence passing into actual existence by some inherent necessity; which we cannot do.

We cannot form any idea of a potential existence of the universe, as distinguished from its actual existence. If represented in thought at all, potential existence must be represented as *something*, that is as an actual existence; to suppose that it can be represented as nothing involves two absurdities — that nothing is more than a negation, and can be positively represented in thought; and that one nothing is distinguished from all other nothings by its power to develop into something. Nor is this all. We have no state of consciousness answering to the words — an inherent necessity by which potential existence became actual existence. To render them into thought, existence, having for an indefinite period remained in one form, must be conceived as passing without any external or additional impulse, into another form; and this involves the idea of a change without a cause — a thing of which no idea is possible. Thus the terms of this hypothesis do not stand for real thoughts; but merely suggest the vaguest symbols incapable of any interpretation.

Moreover, even were it true that potential existence is conceivable as a different thing from actual existence, and that the transition from the one to the other can be mentally realized as a self-determined change, we should still be no forwarder; the problem would simply be removed a step back. For whence the potential existence? This would just as much require accounting for as actual existence; and just the same difficulties would meet us. Respecting the origin of such a latent power, no other suppositions could be made than those above named — self-existence, self-creation, creation by external agency. The self-existence of a potential universe is no more conceivable than we have found the self-existence of the actual universe to be. The self-creation of such a potential universe would involve over again the difficulties here stated — would imply behind this potential universe a more remote potentiality; and so on in an infinite series, leaving us at last no forwarder than at first. While to assign as the source of this potential universe an external agency would be to introduce the notion of a potential universe for no purpose whatever.

There remains to be examined the commonly received or theistic hypothesis — creation by external agency. Alike in the rudest creeds and in the cosmogony long current among ourselves, it is assumed that the genesis of the heavens and the earth is affected somewhat after the manner in which a workman shapes a piece of furniture. And this assumption is made not by theologians only, but by the immense majority of philosophers, past and present. Equally in the writings of Plato and in those of not a few living men of science, we find it taken for granted that there is an analogy between the process of creation and the process of manufacture.

Now, in the first place, not only is this conception one that cannot by any cumulative process of thought or the fulfillment of predictions based on it be shown to answer to anything actual; and not only is it that in the absence of all evidence respecting the process of creation, we have no proof of correspondence even between this limited conception and some limited portion of the fact; but it is that the conception is not even consistent with itself — cannot be realized in thought when all its assumptions are granted. Though it is true that the proceedings of a human artificer may vaguely symbolize to us a method after which the universe might be shaped, yet they do not help us to comprehend the real mystery; namely, the origin of the material of which the universe consists. The artizan does not make the iron, wood or stone he uses, but merely fashions and combines them. If we suppose suns and planets and satellites, and all they contain to have been similarly formed by a "Great Artificer," we suppose merely that certain pre-existing elements were thus put into their present arrangement. But whence the pre-existing elements? The comparison helps us not in the least to understand that; and unless it helps us to understand that it is worthless. The production of matter out of nothing is the real mystery, which neither this simile nor any other enables us to conceive; and a simile which does not enable us to conceive this may just as well be dispensed with.

Still more manifest does the insufficiency of this theory of creation become when we turn from material objects to that which contains them — when, instead of matter, we contemplate space. Did there exist nothing but an immeasurable void, explanation would be needed as much as now. There would still arise the question — how came it so? If the theory of creation by external agency were an adequate one, it would supply an answer; and its answer would be — space was made in the same manner that matter was made. But the impossibility of conceiving this is so manifest that no one dares to assert it. For if space was created, it must have been previously non-existent. The non-existence of space cannot, however, by any mental effort be imagined. It is one of the most familiar truths that the idea of space, as surrounding us on all sides, is not for a moment to be got rid of — not only are we compelled to think of space as now everywhere present, but we are unable to conceive its absence either in the past or the future. And if the non-existence of space is absolutely inconceivable, then, necessarily, its creation is absolutely inconceivable.

Lastly, even supposing that the genesis of the universe could really be represented in thought as the result of an external agency, the mystery would be as great as ever; for there would still arise the question — how came there to be an external agency? To account for this only the same three hypotheses are possible — self-existence, self-creation, and creation by external agency. Of these the last is useless; it commits us to an infinite series of such agencies, and even then leaves us where we were. By the second we are practically involved in the same predicament; since, as already shown, self-creation implies an infinite series of potential existences. We are obliged, therefore, to fall back upon the first, which is the one commonly accepted and commonly supposed to be satisfactory. Those who cannot conceive a self-existent universe, and who therefore assume a creator as a source of the universe, take for granted that they can conceive a self-existent creator. The mystery which they recognize in this great fact surrounding them on every side, they transfer to an alleged source of this great fact; and then suppose that they have solved the mystery. But they delude themselves. As was proved at the outset of the argument, self-existence is rigorously inconceivable; and this holds true whatever be the nature of the object of which it is predicated. Whoever agrees that the atheistic hypothesis is untenable because it involves the impossible idea of self-existence, must perforce admit that the theistic hypothesis is untenable if it contains the same impossible idea.

Thus these three different suppositions respecting the origin of things, verbally intelligible though they are, and severally seeming to their respective adherents quite rational, turn out, when critically examined, to be literally unthinkable. It is not a question of probability, or credibility, but of conceivability. Experiment proves that the elements of these hypotheses cannot even be put together in consciousness; and we can entertain them only as we entertain such pseudo-ideas as a square fluid and a moral substance — only by abstaining from the endeavor to render them into actual thoughts. Or, reverting to our original mode of statement, we may say that they severally involve symbolic conceptions of the illegitimate and illusive kind. Differing so widely as they seem to do, the atheistic, the pantheistic, and the theistic hypotheses contain the same ultimate element. It is impossible to avoid making the assumption of self-existence somewhere; and whether that assumption be made nakedly, or under complicated disguises, it is equally vicious, equally unthinkable. Be it a fragment of matter, or some fancied potential form of matter, or some more remote and still less imaginable cause, our conception of its self-existence can be formed only by joining with it the notion of unlimited duration through past time. And as unlimited duration is inconceivable, all those formal ideas into which it enters are inconceivable; and, indeed, if such an expression is allowable, are the more inconceivable in proportion as the other elements of the ideas are indefinite. So that, in fact, impossible as it is to think of the actual universe as self-existing, we do but multiply impossibilities of thought by every attempt we make to explain its existence.

If from the origin of the universe we turn to its nature, the like insurmountable difficulties rise up before us on all sides — or, rather the same difficulties under new aspects. We find ourselves on the one hand obliged to make certain assumptions which cannot be represented in thought.

When we inquire what is the meaning of the various effects produced upon our senses — when we ask how there come to be in our consciousness impressions of sounds, of color, of tastes, and of those various attributes which we ascribe to bodies, we are compelled to regard them as the effects of some cause. We may stop short in the belief that this cause is what we call matter. Or we may conclude, as some do, that matter is only a certain mode of manifestation of spirit; which is, therefore, the true cause. Or, regarding matter and spirit as proximate agencies, we may attribute all the changes wrought in our consciousness to immediate divine power. But be the cause we assign what it may, we are obliged to suppose *some* cause. And we are not only obliged to suppose some cause, but also a first cause. The matter, or spirit, or whatever we assume to be the agent producing on us these various impressions, must either be the first cause of them or not. If it is the first cause the conclusion is reached. If it is not the first cause, then by implication there must be a cause behind it, which thus becomes the real cause of the effect. Manifestly, however complicated the assumptions, the same conclusion must inevitably be reached. We cannot think at all about the impressions which the external world produces on us, without thinking of them as caused; and we cannot carry out an inquiry concerning their causation without inevitably committing ourselves to the hypothesis of a first cause.

But now if we go a step farther and ask what is the nature of this cause, we are driven by an inexorable logic to certain further conclusions. Is the first cause finite or infinite? If we say finite we involve ourselves in a dilemma. To think of the first cause as finite is to think of it as limited. To think of it as limited necessarily implies a conception of something beyond its limits; it is absolutely impossible to conceive a thing as bounded without conceiving a region surrounding its boundaries. What now must we say of this region? If the first cause is limited, and there consequently lies something outside of it, this something must have no first cause — must be uncaused. But if we admit that there can be something uncaused there is no reason to assume a cause for anything. If, beyond that finite region over which the first cause extends, there lies a region which we are compelled to regard as infinite, over which it does not extend — if we admit that there is an infinite uncaused surrounding the finite caused — we tacitly abandon the hypothesis of causation altogether. Thus it is impossible to consider the first cause as finite. And if it cannot be finite it must be infinite.

Another inference concerning the first cause is equally unavoidable. It must be independent. If it is dependent it cannot be the first cause; for that must be the first cause on which it depends. It is not enough to say that it is partially independent; since this implies some necessity which determines its partial dependence, and this necessity, be it what it may, must be a higher cause, or the true first cause, which is a contradiction. But to think of the first cause as totally independent, is to think of it as that which exists in the absence of all other existence; seeing that if the presence of any other existence is necessary, it must be partially dependent on that other existence, and so cannot be the first cause. Not only, however, must the first cause be a form of being which has no necessary relation to any other form of being, but it can have no necessary relation within itself. There can be nothing in it which determines change, and yet nothing which prevents change. For if it contains something which imposes such necessities or restraints, this something must be a cause higher than the first cause, which is absurd. Thus the first cause must be in every sense perfect, complete, total; including within itself all power and transcending all law. Or, to use the established word, it must be absolute.

Here, then, respecting the nature of the universe, we seem committed to certain unavoidable conclusions. The objects and actions surrounding us, not less than the phenomenon of our own consciousness, compel us to ask a cause; in our search for a cause we discover no restingplace until we arrive at the hypothesis of a first cause; and we have no alternative but to regard this first cause as infinite and absolute. These are inferences forced upon us by arguments from which there appears no escape. . . .

. . . . .

. . . May we not affirm that a sincere recognition of the truth that our own and all other existence is a mystery absolutely beyond our comprehension, contains more of true religion than all the dogmatic theology ever written?

Meanwhile let us recognize whatever of permanent good there is in these persistent attempts to frame conceptions of that which cannot be conceived. From the beginning it has been only through the successive failures of such conceptions to satisfy the mind, that higher and higher ones have been gradually reached; and doubtless, the conceptions now current are indispensable as transitional modes of thought. Even more than this may be willingly conceded. It is possible, nay probable, that under their most abstract forms, ideas of this order will always continue to occupy the background of our consciousness. Very likely there will ever remain a need to give shape to that indefinite sense of an Ultimate Existence, which forms the basis of our intelligence. We shall always be under the necessity of contemplating it as *some* mode of being; that is, of representing it to ourselves in *some* form of thought, however vague. And we shall not err in doing this so long as we treat every notion we thus frame as merely a symbol. Perhaps the constant formation of such symbols and constant rejection of them as inadequate, may be hereafter, as it has hitherto been, a means of discipline. Perpetually to construct ideas requiring the utmost stretch of our faculties, and perpetually to find that such ideas must be abandoned as futile imaginations, may realize to us more fully than any other course, the greatness of that which we vainly strive to grasp. By continually seeking to know and being continually thrown back with a deepened conviction of the impossibility of knowing, we may keep alive the consciousness that it is alike our highest wisdom and our highest duty to regard that through which all things exist as The Unknowable.

32

JOSIAH ROYCE

Pantheism (God as the Whole of Reality)[1]

. . . Now we seem to look upon a truth that satisfies indeed no selfish longings of ours, no whims of theological tradition, no demands of our personal narrow lives. We shall not learn in this way who is first in the kingdom of heaven, nor how the dead are raised, nor any answer to any other special demand of any set of men. We learn, however, this at least: *All truth is known to One Thought, and that Infinite.* What does that imply? Let us see.

Our argument is somewhat near to the thought that partially satisfied St. Augustine when he found it in his Plato. That there should be a truth at all implies, we have seen,[2] that there should be an Infinite Truth, known to an Infinite Thought; or, in other words, that all is for thought, and without thought is nothing that is. We also are a part of this infinite thought. We know not yet more of the nature of this thought, save that it must be eternal, all-embracing, and One. What then shall we be able further to say about it?

. . . Man, as lover, demands success in love, and the course of the world may thwart him; as toiler, he demands for himself personal immortality, and the course of the world may care naught for his individual life . . . . He will take comfort in the assurance that an Infinite Reason is above all and through all, embracing everything, judging everything, infallible, perfect. To this Thought he may look up, saying: "Thou All-Knowing One seest us, what we are, and how we strive. Thou knowest our frame, and rememberest that we are as dust. In thy perfection is our Ideal. That thou art, is enough for our moral comfort. That thou knowest our evil and our good, that gives us our support in our little striving for

[1] Josiah Royce, *The Religious Aspect of Philosophy* (Boston: Houghton Mifflin and Co., 1885); excerpts from chapter XII, "The Religious Insight" (section I, "Religious Aspect of Philosophical Idealism," and section II, "The Doctrine of the Absolute Thought as Perfect."

[2] See the chapter on Royce in part I, "Theism."

the good. Not worthless would we be in thy sight; not of the vile, the base, the devilish party in the warfare of this world. Thou that judgest shalt say that we, even in our poor individual lives, are better that naught. Thou shalt know that in our weakness and blindness, in our pain and sorrow, in our little days, in our dark world, ignorant as to the future, confused with many doubts, beset with endless temptations, full of dread, of hesitation, of sloth, we yet sought, such as we were, to be in our own fashion like thee; to know the truth as thou knowest it, to be full of higher life as thou art full, to be above strife as thou art above it, to be of one Spirit as thou art One, to be perfect as thou art perfect. This thou shalt see in us, and this record shall be eternal like our knowledge. In thee what we vaguely aim to conceive is clear light. In thee the peace that we strive to find is experienced. And when we try to do right; we know that thou seest both our striving and our successes and our failures. And herein we have comfort. We perish, but thou endurest. Ours is not thy eternity. But in thy eternity we would be remembered, not as blots on the face of this part of thy infinite reality, but as healthy leaves that flourished for a time on the branches of the eternal tree of life, and that have fallen, though not into forgetfulness. For to thee nothing is forgotten."

This thought, of the Judge that never ceases to think of us and of all things, never changes, never mistakes, and that knows the Good simply because that God is an element of the Truth — perhaps this can sustain us when all else fails. Nothing but this may be certain; but this, if it be not all that some people have sought, may be a help to us. This Religion may have no such hot little fires on its altars as we at first longed for; but then it is a very old objection to the stars to say that they bake us no bread, and only glitter up there in the dark to be looked at. Yet even the stars are worth something to us.

But if we leave these limitations of our view, and pass to its positive religious value, our first sense is one of joy and freedom to find that our long sought ideal of a perfect unity of life is here attained. Let us look away for a moment from our finite existence, with its doubts and its problems, to the conception of that infinite life. In that life is all truth, fully present in the unity of one eternal moment. The world is no mass of separate facts, stuck one to another in an external way, but, for the infinite, each fact is what it is only by reason of its place in the infinite unity. The world of life is then what we desired it to be, an organic total; and the individual selves are drops in this ocean of the absolute truth.

Thus then, seen in the light of this our result, the human tasks that we sketched in our ethical discussion find their place in the objective world. Now, and in fact for the first time, we can see what we were really trying to accomplish through our ideal. We were trying in a practical way to realize what we now perceive to be the fullness of the life of God. So that the one highest activity, in which all human activities were to join, is known to us now as the *progressive realization by men of the eternal life of an Infinite Spirit.* So whereas we formerly had to say to men: Devote yourselves to art, to science, to state, or to any like work that does tend to organize your lives into one life, we may now substitute one absolute expression for all those accidental expressions, and may say: *Devote yourselves to losing your lives in the divine life.* For all these special aims that we have mentioned are but means of accomplishing the knowledge of the fullness of the truth. And Truth is God.

Now this precept is no barren abstraction. It means to take hold of every act of life, however humble and simple. "Where art thou, O man?" our ideal says to us. "Art thou not in God? To whom dost thou speak? With whom dost thou walk? What life is this in whose midst thou livest? What are all these things that thou seemest to touch? Whose is all this beauty that thou enjoyest in art, this unity that thou seekest to produce in the state, this truth that thou pursues in thy thought? All this is in God and of God. Thou hast never seen, or heard, or touched, or handled, or loved anything but God. Know this truth, and thy life must be transformed to thee in all its significance. Serve the whole God, not the irrationally separate part that thy delusions have made thee suppose to be an independent thing. Live out thy life in its full meaning; for behold it is God's life."

So, as it seems, the best that we could have wished from the purely moral side is attained. The Divine Thought it is that actually accomplishes what we imperfectly sought to attain, when we defined for ourselves Duty. In the Divine Thought is perfectly and finally realized the Moral Insight and the Universal Will of our ethical discussion. And this insight and will are not realized as by some Power, that then should set about to accomplish their fulfillment externally. But in the infinite, where all is eternally complete, the insight is both present and fulfilled; the universal will gets what it seeks. There is no lack there, nor hesitation, nor striving, nor doubt, nor weariness; but all is eternally perfect triumph.

Now this, though it sounds mystical enough to our untrained common sense, is no mere poetry of thought. It is the direct philosophical outcome of what we have found by a purely logical process. The driest thought, the simplest fragment of rationality, involves this absolute, infinite, and perfect thought. And this it involves because it involves the possibility of error, and because, as separate from the infinite, this possibility of error in a single thought becomes unintelligible and contradictory. We did all that we could to escape this conclusion. We wandered in the thickets of confusion and contradiction, until there was no chance of finding there a further pathway. And then we turned to see, and behold, God was in this place, though we had known it not. The genuine God that we thus found was no incomplete, struggling God, whom we might pity in his conflict with evil, but the all-embracing thought, in which the truth is eternally finished. And this God it is that we now see as the complete realization of our own ideal, as of all worthy ideals.

For consider if you will this element in our conception of this Thought. Can this infinite know itself as imperfect, or as not possessing some object that it knows to be good? This is impossible, and doubly so. Not only does the conception of an Infinite, in which and for which are all things, wholly exclude the possibility of any good thing beyond the Infinite itself, but also in still another way does the same truth appear. . . .

The world then, as a whole, is and must be absolutely good, since the infinite thought must know what is desirable, and knowing it, must have present in itself the true objects of desire. The existence of any amount of pain or of other evil, of crime or baseness in the world as we see it, is, thus viewed, no evidence against the absolute goodness of things, rather a guaranty thereof. For all evil viewed externally is just an evidence to us finite beings that there exists something desirable, which we have not, and which we just now cannot get. However stubborn this evil is for us, that has naught to do with the perfection of the Infinite. For the infinite did not make this evil, but the evil, *together with the making of it*, which indeed was also in its separateness evil, — all this is a phenomenon for the infinite thought, which, in knowing this evil, merely knows the absolute desirableness of that which it also possesses, namely, the absolutely good.

. . . For the Infinite then the question, "Is there anything better than what exists?" must be nonsense. For him the actual and the possible fall together in one truth; and this one truth cannot be evil . . . .

· · · · ·

. . . No[2] one is known save by God, and to him all alike are known. To be sure, to know this is the same as understanding rightly, that thou art in truth what thou art. All truth is truth because it is known by a conscious Thought: therefore whatsoever thou art, whether it is consciously or unconsciously existent in thee, is known to the all-seeing Universal Consciousness. But commonplace as this seems to the philosopher, is it not more than a mere commonplace to thee, if thou lovest genuine righteousness? For is it not something to feel that thy life is, all of it, in God

[2] *Ibid.*, section VI.

and for God? No one else knows thee. Alone thou wanderest in a dead world, save for this Presence . . . .

The Divine Thought. There is the opinion of thee to which thou canst look up. To be sure it is revealed to thee only in thy consciousness of what righteousness is and of what truth is. Nowhere else hast thou a guide that can do more for thee than to help to quicken thy insight. But, then, thy religious comfort is to be, not that the moral law is thundered down from mountain-tops as if some vast town-crier were talking, but that when thou seekest to do right, the Infinite all-seeing One knows and approves thee. If thou lovest righteousness for its own sake, then this will comfort thee. . . .

EDWARD GLEASON SPAULDING

EDWARD GLEASON SPAULDING (1873-1940) was born in Burlington, Vermont on August 6, 1873, and died in Princeton, New Jersey on Jan. 31, 1940, after spending most of his professional career at Princeton University as Professor of Philosophy. After receiving his B.S. degree from the University of Vermont in 1894, he went to Columbia University where he was granted the A.M. in 1896. The pursuit of doctoral studies took him to Germany where in 1900 he was awarded the Ph.D. from the University of Bonn. His Alma Mater, the University of Vermont, honored him with an LL.D. degree in 1921. His post-doctoral career began at the College of the City of New York where from 1900 to 1905 he was an instructor, and advanced to Assistant Professor of Philosophy from 1905 to 1914. In 1914, Princeton University appointed him Professor of Philosophy, and here he remained for the rest of his academic career, except for an interruption for service in World War I.

Among his publications are: **The New Rationalism** (1918), the source used in the present text as the best expression characterizing Impersonal Idealism; **What Am I?** (1928), **A World of Chance** (1936). He also co-authored **The New Realism** (1912) and **Roads to Knowledge** (1932).

The thesis of Spaulding's **A World of Chance** is the world is indeterministic owing to its contingent nature. Contingency is chance, and chance is probability. By indeterminism, objective indeterminism, is meant the absence of necessity, either causal or logical necessity, and the presence of chance or contingency. Objective indeterminism in nature is located in the subatomic realm, hence coinciding with the principle of the Indeterminacy of Matter found in the field of physics. Chance or contingency (which is the same thing) precludes the presence of either necessity or impossibility, that is to say, Nature alone knows the "deal of the cards."

The metaphysical position, as the above paragraph purports, does not eliminate the existence of God, for Spaulding believes in God as the system of Ideal Values, namely, **Impersonal Idealism.** Thus God is the entire network of Ideal Values: Justice, Truth, Beauty, Love, etc., yet God is not personal, a conscious mind, but rather Impersonal Ideals, or still better, Nonpersonal Ideals. These Impersonal Ideals possess Being, though lacking in personal or conscious Being. Unlike Humanists who assert that God is man's aspiration, this school of thought predicates objective existence to God (Ideals).

33

EDWARD GLEASON SPAULDING

Impersonal Idealism (God as the System of Ideal Values)[1]

. . . God is the totality of values, both existent and subsistent, and of those agencies and efficiencies with which these values are identical. He is also at once the multiplicity of these entities and the unity of their organization *in that* they are related. This means that God *is* justice and truth and beauty, both as these are "above" our world and as they are *in* it, and that He is thus both transcendent and immanent. Accordingly, if God is personality, He is also more than personality even as the moral situation among men is more than personality. He is love and affection and goodness, respect and reverence, as these *exist* among and in men, but He is these also as they subsist by themselves, *and act efficiently* upon men. In brief, God is Value, the active, "living" principle of the conservation of values and of their efficiency.

Yet God is not all. There *are* values, but *not all* is value. For there are also *"non-value"* entities. But, also, if the universe is that totality of all entities which are facts in some sense, *there* is not only the realm of non-values, such as numbers, space and time, electrons, atoms, masses, molecules, and the like, but there is also the realm of falsity and error, and, especially, of *evil and ugliness*, that is directly opposed to the true, the good, and the beautiful. This problem of evil is *not* an easy one, and hardly any solution of it will meet with wide acceptance. Only a brief analysis of it can be made at this juncture.

· · · · ·

. . . It is to the acceptance, not of the mere seemingness of evil and ugliness, but of their *actuality*, that the great majority of *good* men direct their practical activities for human betterment. Indeed, if *the fighting of evil* were good *merely because of the fight*, and not because of the evil, then would the fight be *self-defeating*. Practically and actually, however, men fight evil, not for the sake of the fight, but because evil is evil, and because they wish to eliminate it and replace it with good. Not the fight, therefore, not the evil, but the *fighting evil* is good, and this is so, because evil is evil and good is good.

We must conclude, that evil is an entity that retains its own peculiar character, and that is *not* transformable into, nor reducible to, *positive values*. It is an immediate and self-sufficient entity that, although it is opposed to, is not in the least *dependent* upon good, although, of course, it is related to good, which is quite possible, since relatedness does not imply dependence, as we have repeatedly discovered.

The general character of our solution of *the theological problem*, as this is based on our solution of the problem of goods and of evils, is sufficiently indicated in these considerations. It is a solution that supports a *theistic*, and not a pantheistic position, and that holds to the *irreducible factuality* of evil and of "powers for evil," as well as of good and of "powers for good."

God is "above" the world of existents, in that He *is* Justice and Goodness and Beauty and Truth as these subsist eternally in a non-temporal and non-spatial realm. Ths is transcendent Theism. But He is *in* the world even as concrete particular existences conform in a greater or less degree to these ideals. Above the world in this sense, God is *supernatural* yet this does not mean that He in any sense contradicts nature. For God and nature are each a different universe of discourse, a different realm. But there is also evil, both in a subsistent realm and in existents, and this can neither be argued out of its actuality nor reduced to anything else.

The religious consciousness may accordingly be described as the persistent *conviction* that there *are* these two *powers*, and that each is efficient in the realm of human motives and acts, deeds and accomplishments. Respect and reverence and love for values and worths and for all that either *is* these or that "makes for" them, form part of the religious consciousness. But another part also is the *hatred* and *detestation* of all that is evil and ugly and false, and the desire and *will to fight these*. Such a consciousness is, however, clearly opposed to the passive and inactive philosophical position that evil is but *a means to an end*, or that it is mere *appearance*, so that "God's in His heaven, all's right with the world," but it is, rather, the active, militant attitude of hatred and of combativeness. The passive position is blighting, but *the active* is full of life. Yet evil does not therewith become good—as a means to stimulating the effort for its own annihilation. For it is not the evil, but *the hatred of evil* that is the stimulus. Freedom, too, is given for the fight. For that level of existence at which there is the love of good and the hatred of evil, is one that is the result of a creative process in which new "things" appear that, *as new,* are *free to follow their own nature.*

Such a scheme of life in one neither of resplendent optimism nor of enervating pessimism. Evil is a reality, and deserves only to be fought. But the means are given to do this. For there is a Power for good that works not only side by side with man, but also *in him and through him, flowering in that freedom which is given to his reason to get at truth, to his emotions* to love the beautiful, the good, and the true, and detest the ugly, the evil, and the false, and *to his will and manhood to engage in the struggle.*

SAMUEL ALEXANDER

SAMUEL ALEXANDER (1859-1938), British Neorealist and Emergent Evolutionist, was born in Sidney Australia, and educated at Wesley College, Melbourne, The University of Melbourne, and Baliol College, Oxford. In 1888, for his **Moral Order and Progress** (1889), he was awarded the Green Moral Philosophy Prize. Prior to undertaking the study of experimental psychology in Germany under the tutelege of Hugo Munsterberg in 1890-1891, he was elected to a fellowship at Oxford, the first Jew to be accorded this honor at Oxbridge. Following his studies in Germany, he was appointed Professor of Philosophy at Owens College, Manchester in 1893, a post he held until his retirement in 1924, though he continued to live in Manchester until his death, Sept. 13, 1938.

In addition to the prize winning book mentioned, Alexander wrote: **Beauty and Other Forms of Value** (1933), **Philosophical and Literary Pieces** (posthumously published in 1939 under the editorship of John Laird), and his influential classic, the Gifford Lectures for 1916 to 1918, **Space, Time, and Deity** (1920), selections from which appear in the present text. Alexander is best known for his philosophical contributions to the Theory of Evolution, his concept of Space-Time, and that of a **nisus** toward Deity, which is developed in the present work.

S. Alexander, a Naturalist, believes, as do all Naturalists, that nature is an eternal cosmic process, a creative one, not a mere conglomeration of atoms, but a process capable of producing new properties which prior to their appearance were impossible of prediction. Alexander distinguishes between God and Deity: whereas God is the universe as possessing Deity, Deity is that particular point which is just beyond the present level of evolution, the new emergent level which is to be — the new emergent reality which the evolutionary process anticipates. For humans, life possessing minds, there is a **nisus** toward Deity, an urge toward a still higher quality. Alexander's Religious Naturalism differs from Humanism by regarding the supermind or superman to come as Deity, not man; man is Deity only for the stage beneath him, namely, physical organisms. A further distinction is that God is viewed objectively as nature as a whole, not subjectively as man's highest aspiration as in Humanism.

34

SAMUEL ALEXANDER

Religious Naturalism (God as the Tendency of Nature to Support or Produce Values)[1]

Deity the Next Higher Empirical Quality than Mind

Within the all-embracing stuff of Space-Time, the universe exhibits an emergence in Time of successive levels of finite existences, each with its characteristic empirical quality. The highest of these empirical qualities known to us is mind or consciousness. Deity is the next higher empirical quality to the highest we know; and, as shall presently be observed, at any level of existence there is a next higher empirical quality which stands towards the lower quality as deity stands towards mind. Let us for the moment neglect this wider implication and confine our attention to ourselves. There is an empirical quality which is to succeed the distinctive empirical quality of our level; and that new empirical quality is deity. If Time were as some have thought a mere form of sense or understanding under which the mind envisages things, this conception would be meaningless and impossible. But Time is an element in the stuff of which the universe and all its parts are made, and has no special relation to mind, which is but the last complexity of Time that is known to us in finite existence. Bare Time in our hypothesis, whose verification has been in progress through each stage of the two preceding Books and will be completed by the conception of God, — bare Time is the soul of its Space, or performs towards it the office of soul to its equivalent body or brain; and this elementary mind which is Time becomes in the course of time so complicated and refined in its internal grouping that there arise finite beings whose soul is materiality, or colour, or life, or in the end what is familiar as mind. Now since Time is the principle of growth and Time is infinite, the internal development of the world, which

---

[1] S. Alexander, *Space, Time, and Deity* (London: Macmillan and Co., Ltd., 1920, 2 vols.); excerpts from bk. IV, ch. 1, "Deity and God." Reprinted by permission.

before was described in its simplest terms as the redistribution of moments of Time among points of Space, cannot be regarded as ceasing with the emergence of those finite configurations of space-time which carry the empirical quality of mind. We have to think upon the lines already traced by experience of the emergence of higher qualities, also empirical. There is a nisus in Space-Time, which, as it has borne its creatures forward through matter and life to mind, will bear them forward to some higher level of existence. There is nothing in mind which requires us to stop and say this is the highest empirical quality which Time can produce from now throughout the infinite Time to come. It is only the last empirical quality which we who are minds happen to know. Time itself compels us to think of a later birth of Time. For this reason it was legitimate for us to follow up the series of empirical qualities and imagine finite beings which we called angels, who would enjoy their own angelic being but would contemplate minds as minds themselves cannot do, in the same way as mind contemplates life and lower levels of existence. This device was adopted half-playfully as a pictorial embodiment of the conception forced upon us by the fact that there is this series of levels of existence. It was used illustratively to point the distinction of enjoyment and contemplation. But we now can see that it is a serious conception. For the angelic quality the possession of which enables such beings to contemplate minds is this next higher empirical quality of deity and our supposed angels are finite beings with this quality. We shall have to ask how such finite deities are related to the infinite God, for they themselves are finite gods.

Deity is thus the next higher empirical quality to mind, which the universe is engaged in bringing to birth. That the universe is pregnant with such a quality we are speculatively assured. What that quality is we cannot know; for we can neither enjoy nor still less contemplate it. Our human altars still are raised to the unknown God. If we could know what deity is, how it feels to be divine, we should first have to have become as gods. What we know of it is but its relation to the other empirical qualities which precede it in time. Its nature we cannot penetrate. We can represent it to ourselves only by analogy. It is fitly described in this analogical manner as the colour of the universe. For colour, we have seen, is a new quality which emerges in material things in attendance on motions of a certain sort. Deity in its turn is a quality which attends upon, or more strictly is equivalent to, previous or lower existences of the order of mind which itself rests on a still lower basis of qualities, and emerges when certain complexities and refinements of arrangement have been reached. Once more I am leaning for help upon Meredith, in whose *Hymn to Colour,* colour takes for a moment the place of what elsewhere he calls Earth: a soul of things which is their last perfection; whose relation to our soul is that of bridegroom to bride. He figures the relation of our soul to colour under the metaphor of love; but as I read the poem, deity as the next higher empirical quality is not different from colour as he conceives it; save only that for him the spirit of the world is timeless, whereas for us deity is like all other empirical qualities a birth of Time and exists in Time, and timelessness is for us a non-entity, and merely a device for contrasting God's infinite deity with the relative imperfection of the finite things we know. . . .

·   ·   ·   ·   ·

God as Universe Possessing Deity [2]

In the religious emotion we have the direct experience of something higher than ourselves which we call God, which is not presented through the ways of sense but through this emotion. The emotion is our going out or endeavour or striving towards this object. Speculation enables us to say wherein the divine quality consists, and that it is an empirical quality the next in the series which the very nature of Time compels us to postulate, though we cannot tell what it is like. But besides assuring us of the place of the divine quality in the world, speculation has also to ask wherein this quality resides. What is the being which possesses deity? Our answer is to be a philosophical one; we are not concerned with the various forms which the conception of God has assumed in earlier or later religions. Ours is the modester (and let me add far less arduous) inquiry what conception of God is required if we think of the universe as Space-Time engendering within itself in the course of time the series of empirical qualities of which deity is the one next ahead of mind. God is the whole world as possessing the quality of deity. Of such a being the whole world is the 'body' and deity is the 'mind.' But this possessor of deity is not actual but ideal. As an actual existent, God is the infinite world with its nisus towards deity, or, to adapt a phrase of Leibniz, as big or in travail with deity.

Since Space-Time is already a whole and one, why, it may be urged, should we seek to go beyond it? Why not identify God with Space-Time? Now, no one could worship Space-Time. It may excite speculative or mathematical enthusiasm and fill our minds with intellectual admiration, but it lights no spark of religious emotion. Worship is not the response which Space-Time evokes in us, but intuition. Even Kant's starry heavens are material systems, and he added the moral law to them in describing the sources of our reverence. In one way this consideration is irrelevent; for if philosophy were forced to this conclusion that God is nothing but

2 *Ibid.*

Space-Time, we should needs be content. But a philosophy which left one portion of human experience suspended without attachment to the world of truth is gravely open to suspicion; and its failure to make the religious emotion speculatively intelligible betrays a speculative weakness. For the religious emotion is one part of experience, and an empirical philosophy must include in one form or another the whole of experience. The speculative failure of the answer is patent. It neglects the development within Space-Time of the series of empirical qualities in their increasing grades of perfection. The universe, though it can be expressed without remainder in terms of Space and Time, is not merely spatio-temporal. It exhibits materiality and life and mind. It compels us to forecast the next empirical quality or deity. On the one hand we have the totality of the world, which in the end is spatio-temporal; on the other the quality of deity engendered, or rather being engendered, within that whole. These two features are united in the conception of the whole world as expressing itself in the character of deity, and it is this and not bare Space-Time which for speculation is the ideal conception of God.

Belief in God, though an act of experience, is not an act of sight, for neither deity nor even the world as tending to deity is revealed to sense, but of speculative and religious faith. A word will be said later to compare the faith we have in God with the faith we have in the minds of other persons than ourselves. Any attempt, therefore, to conceive God in more definite manner must involve a large element of speculative or reflective imagination. Even the description of God as the whole universe, as possessing deity, or as in travail with deity, is full of figurative language. If we are to make our conception less abstract we must try to represent to ourselves some individual in whom deity is related to its basis in the lower levels of empirical quality as far down as the purely spatio-temporal; and a being of this kind is, as we shall see, rather an ideal of thought than something which can be realised in fact in the form of an individual. What we have to do is to be careful to conceive the ideal in conformity with the plan of what we know of things from experience.

· · · · ·

God as Actual [3]

We are now led to a qualification of the greatest importance. The picture which has been drawn of the infinite God is a concession to our figurative or mythological tendency and to the habit of the religious consciousness to embody its conception of God in an individual shape. Its sole value lies in its indication of the relation that must be understood

[3] *Ibid.*

upon the lines traced by experience to subsist between deity and mind. This is adequate for finite gods, supposing the stage of deity to have been reached. But the infinite God is purely ideal or conceptual. The individual so sketched is not asserted to exist; the sketch merely gives body and shape, by a sort of anticipation, to the actual infinite God whom, on the basis of experience, speculation declares to exist. As actual, God does not possess the quality of deity but is the universe as tending to that quality. This nisus in the universe, though not present to sense, is yet present to reflection upon experience. Only in this sense of straining towards deity can there be an infinite actual God. For, again following the lines of experience, we can see that if the quality of deity were actually attained in the empirical development of the world in Time, we should have not one infinite being possessing deity but many (at least potentially many) finite ones. Beyond these finite gods or angels there would be in turn a new empirical quality looming into view, which for them would be deity — that is, would be for them what deity is for us. Just as when mind emerges it is the distinctive quality of many finite individuals with minds, so when deity actually emerges it would be the distinctive quality of many finite individuals. If the possessor of deity were an existent individual he must be finite and not infinite. Thus there is no actual infinite being with the quality of deity; but there is an actual infinite, the whole universe, with a nisus to deity; and this is the God of the religious consciousness, though that consciousness habitually forecasts the divinity of its object as actually realised in an individual form.

BORDEN PARKER BOWNE

BORDEN PARKER BOWNE (1847-1910) was born in Leonardsville, New Jersey, and trained at New York University, Paris, Halle, and Göttingen, where he came under the influence of Erdmann, Ulrici, and Lotze. Other influential thinkers, not contemporary with him but having a part in the shaping of Bowne's philosophy, were Berkeley and Kant.

On his return to the United States, he pursued the field of journalism, occupying in 1875 a position on the editorial staff of the New York **Independent.** The following year he accepted an appointment at Boston University as Professor of Philosophy; the year 1888 found him Dean of the Graduate School of that institution, a position he held until his death in 1910.

Bowne found himself a permanent place in philosophy when he became a founder of the philosophy of Personalism (a form of Lotzean Idealism) termed by him Kantian Berkeleianism, Transcendental Empiricism, as well as Personalism. His principal works are: **The Principles of Ethics** (1892), **The Theory of Thought and Knowledge** (1897), **Metaphysics** (1882, 1898), **Theism** (1902), **Personalism** (1908), **Studies in Christianity** (1909), **Kant and Spencer** (1912, posthumously). Bowne was a militant Personalist and Theist, hence it is most appropriate that the selection chosen to represent the personal concept of God, Theism, should be taken from his **Theism** (1902).

Personalism, the philosophy which holds the key to reality to be personality, interprets all reality in terms of personality. Persons alone comprise ultimate reality and are of infinite intrinsic value. The world and its values are basically personal, as is the World Ground — God, and his major creation, man. Values exist in and for persons solely. Beyond personality, there is no reality. Chief characteristics of personality are: will, intelligence, purpose and values.

35

BORDEN PARKER BOWNE

Theism (God as Personal)[1]

... It was pointed out that thought demands some things, forbids some things, and permits some things. The first class must be accepted, for it consists of the laws and categories of reason and their implications. The second class must be rejected, as it violates the nature of reason. The third class belongs to the great realm of probability and practical life. In this realm we reach conclusions, not by logical demonstration, but by a weighing of probabilities, or a consideration of practical needs, or by a taking for granted in the interest of ideal tendencies. Our fundamental practical beliefs are not speculative deductions from formal premises, but formulations of life itself; and they depend for their evidence mainly on the energy of the life they formulate. In this realm belief, or assent, involves an element of volition. Abstract logic leaves us in uncertainty; and the living self with all its furniture of interest and instinctive tendency and concrete experience comes in to overturn the speculative equilibrium and precipitate the conclusion.

We have abundantly seen that theistic faith has its root in all of these realms, and cannot dispense with any of them. Each contributes something of value. The speculative intellect necessarily stops short of the religious idea of God, but it gives us some fundamental elements of the conception. It is, too, of the highest service in outlining the general form which the theistic conception must take in order to be consistent with itself and the laws of thought. Here speculation performs the invaluable negative service of warding off a multitude of misconceptions, especially of a pantheistic type, which have been morally as pernicious in history as they are speculatively absurd. But a mind with only cognitive interests would find no occasion to consider more than the metaphysical attributes of God. The demand to consider God as having ethical

[1] Borden P. Bowne, *Theism* (1887, 1902); excerpts from the chapter entitled: "Conclusion."

and aesthetic attributes arises not from the pure intellect, but from the moral and aesthetic nature. Here the understanding has only the negative function of maintaining consistency and preventing collision with the laws of thought. The positive content of these attributes cannot be learned from logic, and the faith in their objective reality must at last rest on our immediate conviction that the universe is no more the abode of the true than it is of the beautiful and the good. Indeed, the true itself, except as truth of fact, is a purely ideal element, and derives all its significance from its connection with the beautiful and the good. For truth of fact has only a utilitarian value, apart from the nature of the fact that is true. If the universe were only a set of facts, — such as, Water boils at 100° C., — it would have nothing in it to awaken wonder, enthusiasm, and reverence; and "cosmic emotion" would be quite as much out of place as religious sentiment. Such a universe would not be worth knowing; and scientific interest beyond its practical bearing would soon vanish along with religion.

Logically considered, our entire system of fundamental belief rests upon a fallacy of the form known as the illicit process; in other words, our conclusions are too large for the premises. A set of ideals arise in the mind under the stimulus of experience, but not as transcripts of experience. These ideals implicitly determine our mental procedure, and they do it all the more surely because we are generally unconscious of them. Our so-called proofs consist, not in deducing them from experience, but in illustrating them by experience. The facts which make against the ideal are set aside as problems not yet understood. In this way we maintain our conception of a rational universe, or of a God of perfect wisdom and goodness. We illustrate by picked facts, and this passes for proof. Of course it is not proof, but only an illustration of preexisting conceptions. For one who has not the conceptions and the interests expressed in them, the argument is worthless.

Logic, then, is in its full right in pointing out the non-demonstrative character of these arguments, but it is miserably narrow when it fails to see that these undemonstrated ideals are still the real foundation of our mental life. Without implicit faith in them no step can be taken in any field. The mind as a whole, then, is in its full right when, so long as these ideals are not positively disproved, it accepts them on its own warrant and works them out into the rich and ever-growing conquests of our modern life. By the side of this great faith and its great results the formal objections of formal logic sink into an almost despicable impertinence.

Of all these ideals that rule our life theism is the sum and source. The cognitive ideal of the universe, as a manifestation of the Supreme

Reason, leads to theism. The moral ideal of the universe, as a manifestation of the Supreme Righteousness, leads to theism. The practical ideal
of a "far-off divine event to which the whole creation moves" leads to
theism. In short, while theism is demonstrated by nothing, it is implicit
in everything. It cannot be proved without begging the question, or
denied without ending in absurdity.

But so far as logic goes atheism is no better off. Rigor and vigor
methods, we have seen, are fatal to all concrete thinking. To assume the
general truth and fairness of things may be a venture beyond knowledge,
but to assume their essential untruth and unfairness is equally so. The
assumption that sense knowledge is the only real knowledge, which has
always been the mainstay of atheism, is not only not proved, but is
demonstrably false in the sense in which it is commonly taken. The
undeniable things, as we have seen, are not the mechanical factors of
atheistic thinking, but the coexistence of persons, the common law of
intelligence, and the common order of experience. And the task of
philosophy is to interpret these facts, for the satisfaction of our total
nature. As soon as this is seen, the impossibility of atheism becomes
manifest. It makes a great many flourishes about "reason," "science,"
"progress," and the like, in melancholy ignorance of the fact that it has
made all these impossible. On the one hand, there is a complete ignorance of all the implications of valid knowing, and on the other a ludicrous identification of itself with science. Its theory of knowledge is picked
up ready-made among the crudities of spontaneous thought, and when
the self-destructive implications of atheism are pointed out, instead of
justifying itself from its own premises, it falls back on thoughtless common sense, which forthwith rejects the implications. Of course the question is not whether the implications be true or false, but whether they
be implications. This point is happily ignored, and the defense is complete. Its crude realism is found to be equally obnoxious to criticism.
Its mechanical realities, instead of being the substantial facts of existence,
are found to be only hypostatized abstractions that have no existence
apart from intelligence. Its interpretations furnish no insight. It must
proclaim our entire nature misleading. The universe that has evolved
the human mind as the "correspondence of inner relations to outer
relations" has produced a strange non-correspondence here. The all-illu-
minating formula, It is because it must be, sheds only a feeble light. The
conception of blind power working for apparent ends, of non-intelligence
producing intelligence, of unconsciousness producing consciousness, of
necessity producing ideas of freedom and duty, — this conception is not a
transparent one. But all this the atheist steadfastly believes, and professes to be supremely logical and rational meanwhile.

Considering atheistic procedure as a whole, an ill-conditioned mind might lose patience with it; but there is no occasion for warmth, for according to the theory itself, logical thought is not possible. Thoughts come and go, not according to any inherent rationality, but as produced by necessity. This probably contains the explanation of some of the extraordinary logic of atheistic treatises. Any hiatus between premises and conclusion is due to necessity. Any strange backwardness in drawing a manifest conclusion has the same cause. All lapses into sentiment just when logic is called for are equally necessary. Even the mistakes of theism and the hardness and uncircumcision of the critical heart have an equally solid foundation. A great authority, speaking of the advanced thinker, says, "He, like every other man, may properly consider himself as one of the myriad agencies through whom works the Unknown Cause; and when the Unknown Cause produces in him a certain belief he is thereby authorized to profess and act out that belief." With this conclusion the limits of mental self-respect are transcended, and the theory breaks up in a melancholy farce. The theist may take some comfort, however, in remembering that his faith is no homemade fancy of his own, but a genuine product of the Unknown Cause, and he is thereby authorized to profess and act it out.

No more need be said about atheism. As soon as its implications are understood, it disappears of itself. It is a kind of intellectual parasite and flourishes on the confusion and oversights of theism rather than through any force of its own. These superficialties and oversights of theism have been the chief source of atheistic doubt. This fact leads us to gather up some points which should be borne in mind in recommending theism.

1. Our fundamental practical beliefs are formulations of life rather than speculative deductions; and their evidence must be found mainly in the energy of the life that produces them, and in their harmony with life and one another. The function of the understanding with regard to them is regulative rather than constitutive. It formulates and systematizes them; it cannot demonstrate or deduce them. Deduction of the rigor and vigor type is impossible and absurd in our human conditions. Thus the problem of our deepest beliefs is seen to be one of life and experience and history, rather than of academic reflection alone.

2. We should note the complete emptiness of all mechanical or impersonal explanation. The necessary logical equivalence of cause and effect in such cases makes progress impossible and reduces explanation to tautology. The only explanation that escapes this futility consists in exhibiting the facts as the work of intelligence. Hence in explaining the world the alternative is theism or nothing.

3. A further specification of this fact is that all philosophizing on the

impersonal plane must lose itself in tautology or the infinite regress, and in either case comes to naught. For by the law of the sufficient reason and the logical equivalence of cause and effect, we are shut up to endless repetition of the facts with which we start without any possibility of transcending them. Free intelligence is the only solution of this contradiction.

4. The previous difficulty was logical. Metaphysics further claims that there can be no philosophizing on the impersonal plane, because all the categories of the understanding, when impersonally taken, are only forms of thought without contents. They can be realized and made intelligible only when viewed as forms of living experience. As abstract principles they vanish. Hence in cosmic thinking, the alternative is theism or positivism. Mechanical naturalism is a pure illusion.

5. Not every theory of things is compatible with the validity of knowledge. All necessitarian theories of whatever kind inevitably break down on the problem of error, and establish the truth of opposing views as well as their own. The result is the overthrow of all knowledge and science. The alternative is freedom in the world-ground and in the finite knower. This point is especially to be borne in mind, because it is so generally undreamed of. At present in the uninstructed goodness of our hearts, we show the largest hospitality toward all theories without ever dreaming of inquiring into their bearings upon the problem of knowledge. If any critic points out that a given theory destroys reason and thus violates the conditions of all thinking, such is our good nature that we conclude the consequences of the theory must be aberrations of the critic. The self-destructive theory is thus enabled to reserve all its strength for attack, and falls back on common sense to defend it from itself. This solemn folly will continue until it is recognized that the problem of knowledge is a real one, and one which cannot be finally settled by the crude assumptions of spontaneous thought.

6. Any tenable theory of knowledge must bring the world of things within the sphere of thought; and this can be done only by rejecting the extramental things of crude realism and irreligious naturalism altogether, and making the world the incarnation of the thought of a Supreme Intelligence immanent in it. But this Intelligence is not to be viewed as an abstract logical mechanism or function of categories, but as a Living Will, a synthesis at once of knowledge and power.

7. We must regard the division of labor between science and speculation. The former traces the uniformities of order in experience, the latter deals with their meaning and causation. Both inquiries are necessary to the full satisfaction of the mind and the complete mastery of experi-

ence; and they cannot conflict except through confusion. Theism is content to affirm a divine causality in the world, and leaves it to science to discover the modes of its operation.

When these points are duly regarded, atheism will appear in its crudity and baselessness; and science and religion will be seen to have their common source and justification in theism.

EDGAR SHEFFIELD BRIGHTMAN

EDGAR SHEFFIELD BRIGHTMAN (1884-1953), born in Holbrook, Massachusetts, trained at Brown and Boston Universities in this country and at Berlin and Marburg abroad. Brightman's educational career began in 1906 at Brown University where he taught Greek as well as philosophy; from 1912 to 1915, he was at Nebraska Wesleyan University, and from 1915 to 1919 at Wesleyan University. His long and successful career at Boston University began in 1919, continuing to his death on Feb. 25, 1953. His memorial service was comprised of excerpts from his own writings.

Although Brightman is known to the philosophical world as a staunch defender of Personalism, his most influential contribution has been to empirical Personalism in the form of a temporal **finite** God whose will is restricted by the nonrational Given, hence the appellation of his system as **Theistic Finitism.** His principal writings are: **Sources of the Hexateuch** (1918), **Introduction to Philosophy** (1925, 1951), **Religious Values** (1925), **Philosophy of Ideals** (1928), **Moral Laws** (1933), **Philosophy of Religion** (1940), **Nature and Values** (1945), **Person and Reality** (1958, posthumously).

Brightman asserts that God's will is limited by two classes of experience, both eternal and unified within his own personality: (1) the rational, and (2) the nonrational **Given.** God, a temporal Being, one who exists not outside of time, but within it at all times, is the Controller of the Given, **i.e.,** the nonrational nature of God which composes phenomena — the stuff out of which God made the world, a portion of his nature, his activity. Out of his nonrational nature, a good God by his intelligence created this world which he is striving to perfect with the cooperation of man (meliorism replaces optimism). God is not perfect in the sense of being complete (Aristotelian), but he is inexhaustible perfectibility.

36

EDGAR SHEFFIELD BRIGHTMAN

Theistic Finitism (God as Limited)[1]

A theistic finitist is one who holds that the eternal will of God faces given conditions which that will did not create, whether those conditions are ultimately within the personality of God or external to it. If those conditions are external to the divine personality, the position is a kind of dualism (or dualistic personalism); if they are all within divine personality, then the position is a variety of idealistic personalism. All theistic finitists agree that there is something in the universe not created by God and not a result of voluntary divine self-limitation, which God finds as either obstacle or instrument to his will.

(1) The hypothesis of a finite God *does not need to derive any of its basic evidence from our ignorance.* All that it asserts is based on an interpretation of actual experience. (2) *The surd evils are not ascribed to the will of God,* although idealistic personalists assert that the surds are to be found within God's experience of himself as an eternal person. (3) Finitism maintains *the eternal distinction between what is good and what is evil.* (4) Finitism is *an inspiring challenge to eternal coöperative moral endeavor* — a coöperation between God and man. (5) Finally, *finitism is empirical.* It is based on the truly empirical motive of giving a complete and a rational account of all of the experiences of man. It resists attempts to explain the known by the unknown; starting from the known, it explores the unknown. . . .

. . . . .

. . . God is personal consciousness of eternal duration; his consciousness is an eternally active will, which eternally finds and controls The Given within every moment of his eternal experience. The Given consists of the eternal, uncreated laws of reason and also of equally eternal and

[1] Edgar S. Brightman, *A Philosophy of Religion* © 1940, By permission of Prentice-Hall, Inc., Englewood Cliffs, New Jersey. Excerpts from chapter 10, sections 3, 5, and 6.

uncreated processes of nonrational consciousness which exhibit all the
ultimate qualities of sense objects (*qualia*), disorderly impulses and desires, such experiences as pain and suffering, the forms of space and
time, and whatever in God is the source of surd evil. The common characteristic of all that is "given" (in the technical sense) is, first, that it
is eternal within the experience of God and hence had no other origin
than God's eternal being; and, secondly, that it is not a product of will
or created activity. For The Given to be in consciousness at all means
that it must be process; but unwilled, nonvoluntary consciousness is distinguishable from voluntary consciousness, both in God and in man.
God's finiteness thus does not mean that he began or will end; nor does
it mean he is limited by anything external to himself. Strictly we should
speak of a God whose will is finite rather than a finite God; for even the
finite God is absolute in the sense of being the ultimate source of all
creation.

God's will, then, is in a definite sense finite. But we have called him
"finite-infinite." Although the power of his will is limited by The Given,
arguments for the objectivity of ideals give ground for the postulate
that his will for goodness and love is unlimited; likewise he is infinite in
time and space, by his unbegun and unending duration and by his inclusion of all nature within his experience; such a God must also be unlimited in his knowledge of all that is, although human freedom and
the nature of The Given probably limit his knowledge of the precise
details of the future.

The further predicate of "Controller of The Given" needs explanation.
God's will is eternally seeking new forms of embodiment of the good.
God may be compared to a creative artist eternally painting new pictures,
composing new dramas and new symphonies. In this process, God, finding The Given as an inevitable ingredient, seeks to impose ever new combinations of given rational form on the given nonrational content. Thus
The Given is, on the one hand, God's instrument for the expression of
his aesthetic and moral purposes, and, on the other, an obstacle to their
complete and perfect expression. God's control of The Given means that
he never allows The Given to run wild, that he always subjects it to law
and uses it, as far as possible, as an instrument for realizing the ideal
good. Yet the divine control does not mean complete determination; for
in some situations The Given, with its purposeless processes, constitutes
so great an obstacle to divine willing that the utmost endeavors of God
lead to a blind alley and temporary defeat. At this point, God's control
means that no defeat or frustration is final; that the will of God, partially
thwarted by obstacles in the chaotic Given, finds new avenues of advance, and forever moves on in the cosmic creation of new values.

The view may by clarified by comparing and contrasting it with Plato's conception of a finite God. According to Demo's sound analysis, which rests on the *Philebus* and the *Timaeus* as the definitive formulation of the Platonic philosophy, the creative factors in the universe for Plato are: God (the Demiurge or cosmic Artisan), the Pattern (the eternal ideal, corresponding to the Ideas in the earlier dialogues), and the Receptacle (the primordial chaos of space, discordant and disorderly motion). The actual world is caused by union of the forms (or Pattern) with the Receptacle. The motive of creation is the Good, the principle of value.

It is easy to see that the Pattern corresponds to what we have called the formal aspect of The Given, while the Receptacle is the content aspect of The Given. But there is an essential difference between Plato's view and that which has been developed in this chapter. Plato is a dualist or pluralist. The Receptacle (certainly) and the Pattern (probably) are external to God. The relations among them, and their ontological status, are therefore obscure. Much of this obscurity and unrelatedness is removed by our hypothesis which enlarges the idea of God so that Pattern and Receptacle are both included in God.

The Pattern becomes the system of conscious rational and necessary laws to which divine thinking conforms; the Receptacle becomes the spatial aspect of the stream of divine consciousness. The relatedness of these factors is established by their presence within one personality which controls and directs them all by its will to the Good. When we transform Plato's inspired and illuminating, but obscure, dualism into a personalism, his dualism is transcended through a monism of purpose and personal identity; and yet the pluralistic phase is retained by the analysis into will and Given as well as by the concept of a society of interacting selves and persons.

This personalized Platonism, which may also be called organic pluralism, owes much to Hegelian influences. The dialectic of thesis and antithesis, the principle of negativity, and the union of finite and infinite have been fructifying contributions. A rather remarkable parallel is found in Yoga analysis into rajas, sattva, and tamas, which mean energy, intelligence, and materiality, and correspond closely to will, reason, and content.

· · · · ·

Along with the notion of a finite God goes a revised notion of perfection. Etymologically the word perfection means completion; divine perfection would thus mean ideal completion. For a theistic absolutist who denies the reality of time and who acknowledges nothing given in God which his will did not determine (save the laws of reason, which his will approves or "ratifies"), it is quite possible to conceive of God as timelessly completed ideality, perfection in the literal sense. Yet such "perfection" is as far above human comprehension as it is above concrete imagination; and it is so remote from the facts of experience as to be incoherent (although doubtless consistent) with them.

If the universal human longing for perfection is to be coherently fulfilled it cannot be by the traditional conception of a timelessly perfected, completed God. When, however, we substitute for perfection the ideal of inexhaustible perfectibility, we have a concept applicable to both God and man and adequate to man's religious need. Not optimism but meliorism; not completeness, but ever new tasks in accordance with the eternal principles of the Good; not timeless perfection, but inexhaustible perfectibility in everlasting time — these are the perspectives which open for the cosmos and for every enduring person in it if the empirical evidence for a finite God has guided us toward truth. The wearisomeness sometimes ascribed to this perspective does not exist for anyone to whom the variety of the values of life and the joys of creation and communication, even amidst pain and struggle, are profoundly real. For the Buddhist, perfection may be the cessation of all desire; but for him who values personality, cooperation with the unshakable purposes of the Eternal Person and joint responsibility for the creation of new forms of control of The Given elevate life to its loftiest ideal plane.

JULIAN HUXLEY

JULIAN SORELL HUXLEY (1887-   ) received his education at Eton and Balliol College, Oxford University. A Fellow of the Royal Society and holder of the D.Sc. degree, he enjoyed a long and successful career, the highlights of which are: Lecturer in Zoology, Balliol College from 1910 to 1912, the Research Associate and Assistant Professor until 1916; after which he left for the U.S.A. and Italy, returning to Oxford from 1919 to 1925; from 1926 to 1929, he was Professor of Physiology in the Royal Institution, from 1935 to 1942 secretary of the Zoological Society of London, and from 1944 on the editorial board of the New Naturalist. From 1946 to 1948, he assumed the post of Director General of UNESCO, and was the Biological Editor of the 14th edition of the **Encyclopaedia Britannica.**

Among his many publications are: **The Individual in the Animal Kingdom** (1911), **Essays of a Biologist** (1923), **The Stream of Life** (1926), **Religion without Revelation** (1927), **The Science of Life** (1929, with H. G. and G. P. Wells), **What I Dare Think?** (1931), **An Introduction to Science** (1931-1935, 4 vols. with E. Andrade), **Scientific Research and Social Needs** (1934), **If I Were Dictator** (1934), **We Europeans** (1935, with A. C. Haddon), **The Living Thoughts of Darwin** (1939), **The Uniqueness of Man** (1941), **Democracy Marches** (1941), **Evolution, the Modern Synthesis** (1942), **Evolutionary Ethics** (1943), **On Living in a Revolution** (1944), **Man in the Modern World** (1947), **Evolution in Action** (1952), **New Bottles for New Wine** (1957).

37

JULIAN HUXLEY

Evolutionary Humanism (God as Human Hypotheses Accounting for Phenomena)[1]

Let me try to outline this new vision as briefly as possible. On the basis of our present understanding, all reality is in a perfectly valid sense one universal process of evolution. The single process occurs in three phases — first, the inorganic or cosmic, operating by physical and to a limited extent chemical interaction, and leading to the production of such organizations of matter as nebulae, stars, and solar systems; in our galaxy this phase has been going on for at least six billion years. In the rare places where matter has become self-reproducing, the inorganic has been succeeded by the organic or biological phase; this operates primarily by the ordering agency we call natural selection, and leads to the production of increasingly varied insects, cuttlefish, and vertebrates, and to the emergence of mind and increasingly higher organizations of awareness. On our planet this has been operating for rather under three billion years.

Finally, in what must be the extremely rare places (we only know for certain of one) where, to put it epigrammatically, mind has become self-reproducing through man's capacity to transmit experience and its products cumulatively, we have the human or psycho-social phase. This operates by the self-perpetuating but self-varying and (within limits) self-correcting process of cumulative learning and cumulative transmission, and leads to the evolution of increasingly varied and increasingly higher psycho-social products, such as religions, scientific concepts, labour-saving machinery, legal systems, and works of art.

Our pre-human ancestors arrived at the threshold of the critical stem to this phase around a million years ago; but they became fully human, and psycho-social evolution began to work really effectively, only within

[1] Julian Huxley, "The New Divinity," *The Twentieth Century*, CLXX, 1011, (1961), 10-18. Reprinted by permission.

the last few tens of millennia. During that short span of evolutionary time, man has not changed genetically in any significant way, and his evolution has been predominantly cultural, manifested in the evolution of his social systems, his ideas, and his technological and artistic creations.

The new vision enlarges our future as much as our past. Advance in biological evolution took place through a succession of so-called dominant types — in the last four hundred million years from jawless, limbless vertebrates to fish, then through amphibians to reptiles, from reptiles to mammals, and finally to man. Each new dominant type is in some important way biologically more efficient than the last, so that when it breaks through to evolutionary success it multiplies and spreads at the expense of its predecessors.

Man is the latest dominant type to arise in the evolution of this earth. There is no possibility of his dominant position in evolution being challenged by any existing type of creature, whether rat or ape or insect. All that could happen to man (if he does not blow himself up with nuclear bombs or convert himself into a cancer of his planet by over-multiplication) is that he could transform himself as a whole species into something new. He has nearly three billion years of evolution behind him, from his first pre-cellular beginnings: barring accidents, he has at least as much time before him to pursue his evolutionary course.

Yeats implied, or indeed affirmed, that if the Christian God were rejected, a Savage God would take his place. This certainly could happen, but it need not happen, and we can be pretty sure that in the long run it will not happen.

The new framework of ideas on which any new dominant religion will be based is at once evolutionary and humanist. For evolutionary humanism, gods are creations of man, not vice versa. Gods begin as hypotheses serving to account for certain phenomena of outer nature and inner experience: they develop into more unified theories, which purport to explain the phenomena and make them comprehensible; and they end up being hypostatized as supernatural personal beings capable of influencing the phenomena. As theology develops, the range of phenomena accounted for by the god-hypothesis is extended to cover the entire universe, and the gods become merged in God.

However, with the development of human science and learning, this universal or absolute God becomes removed further and further back from phenomena and any control of them. As interpreted by the more desperately "liberal" brands of Christianity today, he appears to the humanist as little more than the smile of a cosmic Cheshire cat, but one which is irreversibly disappearing.

But though I believe that gods and God in any meaningful non-Pickwickian sense are destined to disappear, the stuff of divinity out of which they have grown and developed remains and will provide much of the raw material from which any new religions will be fashioned. This religious raw material consists in those aspects of nature and elements in experience which are usually described as divine. The term divine did not originally imply the existence of gods: on the contrary, gods were constructed to interpret man's experiences of this quality in phenomena.

Some events and some phenomena of outer nature transcend ordinary explanation and ordinary experience. They inspire awe and seem mysterious, explicable only in terms of something beyond or above ordinary nature — "super-natural" power, a "super-human" element at work in the universe.

Such magical, mysterious, awe-inspiring, divinity-suggesting facts have included wholly outer phenomena like volcanic erruptions, thunder, and hurricanes; biological phenomena such as sex and reproduction, birth, disease, and death; and also phenomena of man's inner life such as intoxication, possession, speaking with tongues, inspiration, insanity, and mystic vision.

With the growth of knowledge most of these phenomena have ceased to be mysterious so far as rational or scientific inexplicability is concerned. But there remains the fundamental mystery of existence, and in particular the existence of mind. Our knowledge of physics and chemistry, physiology and neurology does not account for the basic fact of subjective experience, though it helps us to understand its workings. The stark fact of mind sticks in the throat of pure rationalism and reductionist materialism.

However, it remains true that many phenomena are charged with a magic quality of transcendent and even compulsive power, and introduce us to a realm beyond ordinary experience. Such events and such experiences merit a special designation. For want of a better, I use the term divine, though this quality of divinity is not truly *super*natural but *trans*natural — it grows out of ordinary nature, but transcends it. The divine is what man finds worthy of adoration, that which compels his worship: and during history it evolves like everything else.

Much of every religion is aimed at the discovery and safeguarding of divinity, and seeks contact and communion with what is regarded as divine. A humanist-based religion must redefine divinity, strip the divine of the theistic qualities which man has anthropomorphically projected into it, search for its habitations in every aspect of existence, elicit it, and establish fruitful contact with its manifestations. Divinity is the chief raw material out of which gods have been fashioned. Today we must melt down the gods and refashion the material into new and effective agencies, enabling man to exist freely and fully on the spiritual level as well as on the material level.

The character of all religions depends primarily on the pattern of its supporting framework of ideas, its theology in an extended sense; and this in its turn depends on the extent and organization of human knowledge at the time. I feel sure that the world will see the birth of a new religion based on what I have called evolutionary humanism. Just how it will develop and flower no one knows — but some of its underlying beliefs are beginning to emerge and in any case it is clear that a humanism of this sort can provide powerful religious, moral, and practical motivation for life.

Its beliefs are not based on revelation in the supernatural sense, but on the revelations that science and learning have given us about man and the universe. A humanist believes with full assurance that man is not alien to nature, but a part of nature, albeit a unique one. He is made of the same matter and works by the same energy as the rest of the universe. He is not only a product of the universal process of evolution, but capable of affecting the process which has produced him, and of affecting it either for good or ill. His true destiny is to guide the future course of evolution on earth towards greater fulfilment, so as to realize more and higher potentialities. And this can only be done by intelligently cooperating with outer nature, not by senselessly exploiting and wasting its resources; and by intelligently guiding his own nature, not by senselessly succumbing to his conflicting instincts and moods — reproductive, acquisitive, despairing, idealistic, or aggressive.

Evolution is essentially creative. It is constantly generating improved, more varied, and higher types. During the time of man's evolution from some pre-cellular submicroscopic speck to the dominant type of terrestrial organism, the evolutionary process has realized almost inconceivable potentialities — of adaptability and power, awareness and emotion, intelligence and love. During his own evolution, man has realized farther and equally inconceivable potentialities. Some are good and grandeur, in the shape of comprehensive scientific theories, soul-compelling religions, glorious buildings, fantastic machines, undying works of art, inspiring moral codes. But he has also realized equally inconceivable potentialities of horror and evil — torture by the Inquisition, Hitler's gas chambers for Jews, the ruthlessness of Genghiz Khan, war after war, the horror of the atomic bomb, and the incredible stupidity of the nuclear deterrent stalemate.

A humanist religion will have the task of redefining the categories of good and evil in terms of fulfilment and of desirable or undesirable realizations of potentiality, and setting up new targets for its morality to aim at. In this process of transvaluation, to borrow Nietzsche's phrase, a humanist religion will certainly do something new — it will assign a high religious value to the increase of scientifically based knowledge; for it is on knowledge and its applications that anything which can properly be called human advance or progress depends. It will also assign a high value to the creative imagination and the works of art and beauty and significance which it produces; for it is they which are the highest expressions of the spirit of man.

As regards the individual, it will, like the Ancient Greeks, stress excellence. But as complementary to this, it will go further than the Greek principle of moderation — *maden agan:* nothing too much — and will make psychological integration and total wholeness an essential aim, and in some sense of the equivalent of the state of salvation in Christian terminology. Finally, it can give the individual much-needed protection against the tyrannies of society, much-needed support against the pressures of authoritarianism and conformism, by proclaiming the vital truth that in realizing his own potentialities and in developing his own personality, the individual is making his own unique contribution to the universal process of evolutionary fulfilment.

Integration implies the resolution of dichotomies and conflicts, through their incorporation in a unified, balanced, dynamic pattern, well equipped with feedback mechanisms. In Marxism, the individual is presented in opposition to society. In humanism, the individual and society are seen as inevitably interrelated; integration here implies making the interrelation more profound and more harmonious. In the evolutionary humanist view, the dichotomy between heredity and environment support each other and act synergistically so as to secure a more complete development.

Humanism also differs from all supernaturalist religions in centering its long-term aims not on the next world but on this. One of its fundamental tenets is that this world and life in it can be improved, and that it is our duty to try to improve it, socially, culturally, and politically. The humanist goal must therefore be, not technocracy, nor theocracy, nor the monolithic and authoritarian state, nor the welfare state, nor the consumption economy, but the fulfilment society. By this I mean a society organized in such a way as to give the greatest number of people the fullest opportunities of realizing their potentialities — of achievement and enjoyment, morality and community. It will do so by providing opportunities for education, for adventure and achievement, for cooperating in worthwhile projects, for meditation and withdrawal, for self-development and unselfish action.

Above all, a humanist religion will uphold the ideal of quality against the assaults of mere quantity, of richness and variety against drabness and monotony, and of active, open, and continuous development, personal, social, and evolutionary, as against static self-complacency or unreal millenary fanaticism.

But I must end. I hope I have succeeded in showing that the religious spirit must soon break through from its old frameworks to a new system of expression, and that an evolutionary humanism will inevitably provide the pattern of ideas and beliefs at its core.

JOHN DEWEY

JOHN DEWEY (1859-1952), Dean of American Philosophers, was born in Burlington, Vermont, on October 20, 1859 and died in New York City on June 1, 1952. His higher education began in the town of his birth, where he graduated from the University of Vermont in 1879; graduate studies, leading to his terminal degree in 1884, were undertaken at Johns Hopkins University. Although the major portion of his career was spent at Columbia University, beginning in 1904 and retiring in 1930 with the title of Professor Emeritus, he taught prior to this appointment at the University of Minnesota during the school year 1888-1889, at the University of Michigan from 1889 to 1894, and at the University of Chicago from 1889 to his appointment at Columbia.

Initial fame was accorded him while at the University of Chicago where he functioned in the capacity of Director of the School of Education. Here, he introduced his **new pedagogy,** functionalism, instrumentalism, and the experimental school of philosophy. His fame gained international proportions, and his work carried him to Peking, Turkey, and Mexico. He is regarded as the most influential of American philosophers, particularly in the fields of education and social thought.

Listed among his many publications are **Leibnitz's New Essays Concerning Human Understanding** (1888), **The Influence of Darwin on Philosophy** (1910), **Democracy and Education** (1916), **Reconstruction in Philosophy** (1920), **Experience and Nature** (1925), **Ethics** (1908, with Tufts), **School and Society** (1915), **Human Nature and Conduct** (1927), **The Quest for Certainty** (1929, Gifford Lectures), **How We Think** (1910), **Essays in Experimental Logic** (1916), **Creative Intelligence** (1917), **Art as Experience** (1934), **A Common Faith** (1935), **Logic, The Theory of Inquiry** (1938), **Freedom and Culture** (1939), **Education Today** (1940), **Problems of Men** (1946).

38

JOHN DEWEY

Religious Humanism (God as Man's Highest Social Experiences)[1]

The aims and ideals that move us are generated through imagination. But they are not made out of imaginary stuff. They are made out of the hard stuff of the world of physical and social experience. The locomotive did not exist before Stevenson, nor the telegraph before the time of Morse. But the conditions for their existence were there in physical material and energies and in human capacity. Imagination seized hold upon the idea of rearrangement of existing things that would evolve new objects. The same thing is true of a painter, a musician, a poet, a philanthropist, a moral prophet. The new vision does not arise out of nothing, but emerges through seeing, in terms of possibilities, that is, of imagination, old things in new relations serving a new end which the new end aids in creating.

Moreover the process of creation is experimental and continuous. The artist, scientific man, or good citizen, depends upon what others have done before him and are doing around him. The sense of new values that become ends to be realized arises first in dim and uncertain form. As the values are dwelt upon and carried forward in action they grow in definiteness and coherence. Interaction between aim and existent conditions improves and tests the idea; and conditions are at the same time modified. Ideals change as they are applied in existent conditions. The process endures and advances with the life of humanity. What one person and one group accomplish becomes the standing ground and starting point of those who succeed them. When the vital factors in this natural process are generally acknowledged in emotion, thought and action, the process will be both accelerated and purified through elimination of that irrelevant element that culminates in the idea of the supernatural.

[1] John Dewey, *A Common Faith* (New Haven: Yale University Press, 1934), 49-54. Reprinted by permission.

When the vital factors attain the religious force that has been drafted into supernatural religions, the resulting reinforcement will be incalculable.

These considerations may be applied to the idea of God, or, to avoid misleading conceptions, to the idea of the divine. This idea is, as I have said, one of ideal possibilities unified through imaginative realization and projection. But this idea of God, or of the divine, is also connected with all the natural forces and conditions — including man and human association — that promote the growth of the ideal and that further its realization. We are in the presence neither of ideals completely embodied in existence nor yet of ideals that are mere rootless ideals, fantasies, utopias. For there are forces in nature and society that generate and support the ideals. They are further unified by the action that gives them coherence and solidity. It is this *active* relation between ideal and actual to which I would give the name "God." I would not insist that the name *must* be given. There are those who hold that the associations of the term with the supernatural are so numerous and close that any use of the word "God" is sure to give rise to misconception and be taken as a concession to traditional ideas.

They may be correct in this view. But the facts to which I have referred are there, and they need to be brought out with all possible clearness and force. There exist concretely and experimentally goods — the values of art in all its forms, of knowledge, of effort and of rest after striving, of education and fellowship, of friendship and love, of growth in mind and body. These goods are there and yet they are relatively embryonic. Many persons are shut out from generous participation in them; there are forces at work that threaten and sap existent goods as well as prevent their expansion. A clear and intense conception of a union of ideal ends with actual conditions is capable of arousing steady emotion. It may be fed by every experience, no matter what its material.

In a distracted age, the need for such an idea is urgent. It can unify interests and energies now dispersed; it can direct action and generate the heat of emotion and the light of intelligence. Whether one gives the name "God" to this union, operative in thought and action, is a matter for individual decision. But the *function* of such a working union of the ideal and actual seems to me to be identical with the force that has in fact been attached to the conception of God in all the religions that have a spiritual content; and a clear idea of that function seems to me urgently needed at the present time.

The sense of this union may, with some persons, be furthered by mystical experiences, using the term "mystical" in its broadest sense,

That result depends largely upon temperament. But there is a marked difference between the union associated with mysticism and the union which I had in mind. There is nothing mystical about the latter; it is natural and moral. Nor is there anything mystical about the perception or consciousness of such union. Imagination of ideal ends pertinent to actual conditions represents the fruition of a disciplined mind. There is, indeed, even danger that resort to mystical experiences will be an escape, and that its result will be the passive feeling that the union of actual and ideal is already accomplished. But in fact this union is active and practical; it is a *uniting*, not something given.

One reason why personally I think it fitting to use the word "God" to denote that uniting of the ideal and actual which has been spoken of, lies in the fact that aggressive atheism seems to me to have something in common with traditional supernaturalism. I do not mean merely that the former is mainly so negative that it fails to give positive direction to thought, though that fact is pertinent. What I have in mind especially is the exclusive preoccupation of both militant atheism and supernaturalism with man in isolation. For in spite of supernaturalism's reference to something beyond nature, it conceives of this earth as the moral center of the universe and of man as the apex of the whole scheme of things. It regards the drama of sin and redemption enacted within the isolated and lonely soul of man as the one thing of ultimate importance. Apart from man, nature is held either accursed or negligible. Militant atheism is also affected by lack of natural peity. The ties binding man to nature that poets have always celebrated are passed over lightly. The attitude taken is often that of man living in an indifferent and hostile world and issuing blasts of defiance. A religious attitude, however, needs the sense of a connection of man, in the way of both dependence and support, with the enveloping world that the imagination feels is a universe. Use of the words "God" or "divine" to convey the union of actual with ideal may protect man from a sense of isolation and from consequent despair or defiance.

In any case, whatever the name, the meaning is selective. For it involves no miscellaneous worship of everything in general. It selects those factors in existence that generate and support our idea of good as an end to be striven for. It excludes a multitude of forces that at any given time are irrelevant to this function. Nature produces whatever gives reinforcement and direction but also what occasions discord and confusion. The "divine" is thus a term of human choice and aspiration. A humanistic religion, if it excludes our relation to nature, is pale and thin, as it is presumptuous, when it takes humanity as an object of worship. Matthew Arnold's conception of a "power not ourselves" is too narrow in its reference to operative and sustaining conditions. While it is selective, it is too narrow in its basis of selection — righteousness. The conception thus needs to be widened in two ways. The powers that generate and support the good as experienced and as ideal, work *within* as well as without. There seems to be a reminiscence of an external Jehovah in Arnold's statement. And the powers work to enforce other values and ideals than righteousness. Arnold's sense of an opposition between Hellenism and Hebraism resulted in exclusion of beauty, truth, and friendship from the list of the consequences toward which powers work within and without.

Part Five: THE SOUL

Its Nature and Freedom

ST. AUGUSTINE

ST. AURELIUS AUGUSTINE (354-430), born in Tagaste, North Africa, was Bishop of Hippo in proconsular Africa from 396 to his death in 430. In his early life he was influenced by the philosophy of Cicero and Manicheanism, then was for a brief period of time a Skeptic, after which he became a Neo-Platonist with strong strains of influence from Plotinus' teaching and method.

Augustine, a most prolific and influential writer, has, with the exception of Aquinas, dominated the thought of the Roman Catholic world, and through Martin Luther, an Augustinian monk, decisively influenced the Protestant branch of Christian philosophy and theology.

Augustine wrote a number of influential philosophical works, his greatest being **The City of God,** from which has been excerpted material pertaining to the soul, its freedom and the cause of evil within it; **The Enchiridion,** which has become a classic in secular as well as religious ethics, has provided us with material treating the source or origin of evil. A selected number of other of his writings are: **Confessions, On the Immortality of the Soul, On Grace and Free Will, On the Morals of the Catholic Church, Concerning the Nature of Good, On the Predestination of the Saints, On Nature and Grace, On the Trinity, On the Profit of Believing, Soliloquies, On the Spirit and the Letter, Concerning the Teacher, On the Grace of Christ and on Original Sin.**

St. Augustine contends that the existence of God is established a posteriori based on (1) the contingent character of the world, (2) its orderliness, (3) the testimony of consciousness, and (4) universal consent. Augustine's preferred proof for God's existence "rests on the interpretation of the characters of necessity and immutability of our ideas, and of the primordial judgments which are the basis of our knowledge and of our conduct: the object of these ideas can be necessary and immutable only because it participates in the divine essence; our judgments on truth, goodness and beauty which is related to them as a norm. Hence God exists." [1] The exist-

[1] Maurice de Wulf, **History of Mediaeval Philosophy,** tr. Ernest C. Messenger (New York: Dover Publications, Inc., 1952), vol. 1, 88.

ence of God follows necessarily from the fact of reality and of rational thought.

The world is ultimately and initially good since it is the creation of a good God; the presence of evil in the universe is attributable to the perversion of nature by man; corruption of natural good then is the essence of evil. Viewing it from another standpoint, evil is the absence of good. Man's supreme good is God, Supreme Goodness, and man's ultimate objective ("Thou hast made us for thyself, O Lord; and our hearts are restless until they find their rest in thee"); when man's soul is united with that of Deity, supreme happiness ensues.

Human will, both psychologically and morally free, assumes primacy over knowledge, and must be kept pure in order that the soul may be holy. The human soul, a spiritual substance, owns the intellectual as its chief characteristic quality. The soul's immortality is grounded in its spirituality, that is, the extent to which it participates in eternal and immutable truths. The soul both utilizes and governs the physical body. It has triune manifestations: (1) memory, the reservoir of thought life; (2) understanding, the intellectual life; and (3) will, the moral life.

39

ST. AUGUSTINE

Divine Foreknowledge and Freedom of the Will[1]

CHAPTER IX

Of God's Foreknowledge and Man's Freedom

Against those men Tully thinks he cannot hold argument, unless he overthrow divination, and therefore he labours to prove that there is no prescience, nor foreknowledge of things to come, either in God or man; there is directly no such matter. Thus denies he God's foreknowledge, and idly seeks to subvert the radiant lustre of true prophecies, by propounding certain ambiguous and fallible oracles, whose truth notwithstanding he does not confute. But these conjectures of the mathematicians he lays flat, for indeed they are of the kind to destroy themselves. But for all that, their opinion is more tolerable, that ascribe a fate unto the stars, than his, that rejects all foreknowledge of things to come. For to acknowledge a God, and yet deny that, is monstrous madness: which he observing, went about to prove even that which 'the fool hath said in his heart; there is no God.' Not, however, in his own person, for he saw the danger of malice too well; and therefore when making Cotta dispute against the Stoics upon this theme, in his books *De Natura Deorum*, he seems more willing to hold with Lucilius Balbus, that defended the Stoics, that with Cotta, that argued against the divine essence. But in his books *De Divinatione*, he directly opposes the foreknowledge of things, of himself and in his own person; all which it seems he did lest he should yield unto fate, and so lose the freedom of election: for he supposed that in yielding to this foreknowledge, fate would follow necessarily thereupon, without any denial. But howsoever the philosophers wind themselves in webs of disputations, we, as we confess the great and true God, so do we acknowl-

---

[1] St. Augustine, *The City of God*, tr. John Healey (1610, revised 1620, spelling modernized, 1890; original Latin text of *De Civitate Dei*, 413-416); excerpts from book 5.

TITLE PAGE

INDEX

CALL NO.	NOS. PER VOL.	VOLS. PER YEAR	FREQUENCY
	BOUND		
	PREPARED	IN BINDERY	

DEMCO

YEAR	SER.	VOL.	JAN	FEB	MAR	APR	MAY	JUN	JUL	AUG	SEP	OCT	NOV	DEC	T.P.	I.	CLAIMED
		1															
		2															
		3															
		4															
		5															
		1															
		2															
		3															
		4															
		5															
		1															
		2															
		3															
		4															
		5															

INC.   JAN | FEB | MAR | APR | MAY | JUN | JUL | AUG | SEP | OCT | NOV | DEC   BIND edge His high will, power, and foreknowledge. Nor let us fear that we do not perform all our actions by our own will, because He, whose foreknowledge cannot err, knew before that we should do thus or thus: which Tully feared, and therefore denied foreknowledge; and the Stoics, that held not all things to be done by necessity, thought that they were done by fate. What then did Tully fear in this prescience, that he framed such detestable arguments against it? Verily this, that if all events were known before they came to pass, they should come to pass according to that foreknowledge. And if they come so to pass, then God knows the certain order of things beforehand, and consequently the certain order of the causes; and if He know a certain order of causes in all events, then are all events disposed by fate: which if it be so, we have nothing left in our power, nothing in our will: 'which granted,' says he, 'the whole course of humanity is overturned: law, correction, praise, disgrace, exhortation, prohibition, all are to no end: nor is there any justice in punishing the bad and rewarding the good.' For avoiding of which inconveniences (so absurd and so pernicious) he utterly rejects this foreknowledge of things, and draws the religious mind into this strait, that either there must be somewhat in the power of our will, or else that there is a foreknowledge of things to come; but that the granting of the one is the subversion of the other: choosing the foreknowledge, we must lose the freedom of election, and choosing this we must deny the other. Now this learned and devout man, of the two makes choice of freedom of election: and to confirm it, denies the foreknowledge utterly, and so instead of making men free, makes them blasphemous. But the religious mind chooses them both, confesses and confirms them both. 'How,' says he? 'For granting this foreknowledge, there follow so many consequences that they quite subvert all power of our will: and holding this free will, by the same degree of reasoning we ascend, till we find there is no prescience of future things at all; for these are the steps in our argument. If there be any freedom of the will, all things do not follow destiny: if all things follow not destiny, then is there no set order in the causes of things: now if there be no set order in the causes of all things, then is there no set order of the things themselves in God's foreknowledge, since they come from their causes. If there be not a set order of all things in God's foreknowledge, then all things fall not out according to the said knowledge. Now if all things fall not out as He had His foreknowledge of them, then is there in God no foreknowledge of things to come.' To these sacrilegious and wicked opposers, thus we reply: God doth both know all things ere they come to pass, and we do all things willingly, which we do not feel ourselves and know ourselves directly enforced to. We hold not that all things, but rather that nothing follows fate: and

whereas fate is wont to be taken for a position of the stars in nativities
and conceptions, we hold this a vain and frivolous assumption: we neither
deny an order of causes wherein the will of God is all in all, neither
do we call it by the name of fate, unless fate be derived of *fari,* 'to speak,'
for we cannot deny that the scripture says: 'God spake once, these two
things I have heard, that power belongeth unto God, and to Thee, O
Lord, mercy, for Thou wilt reward every man according to his works.'
For whereas He says: 'God spake once,' it is meant that He spoke un-
moveably and unchangeably, that all things should fall out as He spoke,
and meant to have them. In this respect we may derive fate from *fari,*
'to speak,' but we must needs say withal that it is used in another sense
than we should have men to think upon. But it does not follow that
nothing should be left free to our will, because God knows the certain
and set order of all events. For our very wills are in that order of causes,
which God knows so surely and hath in His prescience; human wills
being the cause of human actions: so that He that keeps a knowledge of
the causes of all things, cannot leave men's wills out of that knowledge,
knowing them to be the causes of their actions. For Tully's own words:
'Nothing comes to pass without an efficient cause,' is sufficient alone to
sway down this matter quite against himself: for what avails the subse-
quence: 'Nothing is without cause, but every cause is not fated, because
there are causes of chance, nature, and will'? It is sufficient that nothing
is done but by precedent cause. For those causes that are casual, giving
origin to the name of fortune, we deny not: we say they are secret, and
ascribe them either to the will of the true God, or of any other spirit.
The natural causes we do never divide from His will, who is nature's
Creator: but the voluntary causes, God, angels, men, and divers other
creatures have often in their will and power; if we may call that power
a will by which the brute beasts avoid their own hurt and desire their
good by nature's instinct. That there is a will in angels, I do absolutely
affirm; be they good whom we call God's angels, or evil whom we call
the devil's angels, fiends, or devils themselves. Do men good and bad
have all their wills: and hereby it is apparent that the efficient causes of
all effects are voluntary causes and nothing but the decrees of that nature,
which is 'the spirit of life.' For air or wind is called a spirit; but because
it is a body, it is not the spirit of life. But the spirit of life that quickens
all things in the Creator of all bodies and all created spirits: this is God,
'a Spirit from eternity, uncreated': in His will there is that height of
power which assists the wills of the good spirits, judges the bad, disposes
of all, giving power to whom He pleases, and holding it from whom He
wills. For as He is a Creator of all natures, so is He of all powers: but
not the giver of all wills; for wicked wills are not of Him, being against

that nature which is of Him. So the bodies are all subject unto diverse wills: some to our own wills (that is, the wills rather of men than of beasts), some to the angels, but all to the will of God: unto whom all wills are subject, because they have no power but what He gives them. The cause then that makes all, and is not made itself, is God. The other causes do both effect and are effected: such are all created spirits, chiefly the reasonable ones. The corporal causes, which are rather effects than otherwise, are not to be counted as efficient causes, because they came but to do that which the will of the spirit within them doth enjoin them: how then can that set order of causes in God's foreknowledge deprive our wills of power, seeing our wills bear such a sway amongst the very causes themselves? But let Cicero wrangle, and his fellows, that say this order is fated, or rather fate itself; which we abhor, because of the word's being chiefly used in a false sense: but whereas he denies that God knows assuredly the set order of those causes, we detest his assertion, endeavours under a false person in his books *De Natura Deorum*, or if he do acknowledge Him, yet in denying Him this foreknowledge he says but as the fool said in his heart, 'There is no God'; for if God lack the prescience of all future events He is not God. And therefore our wills are of as much power as God would have them, and knew before that they should be; and the power that they have is theirs free, to do what they shall do truly and freely: because He foreknew that they should have this power, and do these acts, whose foreknowledge cannot be deceived. Wherefore if I wish to use the word fate in anything, I would rather say that it belonged to the weaker, and that will belonged to the higher who has the other in his power, rather than grant that our liberty of will were taken away by that set order which the Stoics (after a peculiar phrase of their own) call fate.

CHAPTER X

Whether Necessity Has Any Dominion over the Will of Man

Nor need we fear that necessity which the Stoics were so afraid of, that in their distinctions of causes, they put some under necessity and some not under it; and in those that they did not subject unto it they put our wills also, lest they should lose their freedom by being subject to necessity. But if that be necessity in us which is not in our power, but will be done, do what we can against it, as the necessity of death; then is it plain that our wills are subject to no such necessity, use we them howsoever, well or badly: for we do many things which we could not do against our wills. And first of all to will itself: if we will a thing, there is our will; if we will not, it is not. For we cannot will against our wills. Now is necessity be defined to be 'that whereby such a thing must needs fall out thus, or thus,' I see no reason we should fear that it could hinder the freedom of our wills in anything. For we neither subject God's being nor His prescience unto necessity, when we say God must needs live eternally, and God must needs foreknow all things; no more than His honour is diminished in saying He cannot err, He cannot die, He cannot do this. Why? Because His power were less, if He could do it, than now it is in that He cannot. Justly is He called almighty, yet may He not die nor err. He is almighty because He can do all that is in His will, not because He can suffer what is not His will; which if He could He were not almighty. So that He cannot do some things, because He can do all things. So when we say that if we will anything, we must of necessity will it with a freedom of will, that is true; and we do not put our will under any such necessity as deprives it of the freedom. So that our wills are ours, willing what we will; and if we will it not, neither do they will it: and if any man suffer anything by the will of another against his own will, his will has its own power still, and his sufferance comes rather from the power of God than from his own will: for if he willed that it should be otherwise, and yet could not have it so, his will must needs be hindered by a greater power: yet his will should be free still, and not in any other's power but his that willed it, though he could not have his will performed: wherefore whatsoever a man suffers against his will, he ought not to attribute it unto the wills of angels, men, or any other created spirits, but even to His who gave their wills this power. So then, our wills are not useless, because God foresees what will be in them: He that foresaw it whatever it be, foresaw somewhat: and if He did foreknow somewhat, then by His foreknowledge there is something in our wills. Wherefore we are neither compelled to leave our freedom of will by retaining God's foreknowledge, nor by holding our wills freedom to deny God's foreknowledge. God forbid that we should. We believe and affirm them both constantly and truly, the latter as a part of our good faith, the former as a rule for our good life: and badly does he live that believes not aright of God. So God forbid that to be free we should deny His foreknowledge, by whose help we either are or shall be free. Therefore law, correction, praise, disgrace, exhortation, and prohibition are not in vain: because He foreknew that there should be such. They have that power which He foreknew they should have; and prayers are powerful to attain those things which He foreknows that He will give to such as pray for them. Good deeds has He predestinated to reward, and evil to punishment. Nor does man sin because God foreknew that he would sin: nay it is doubtless he that sins, when he does sin, because God, whose knowledge cannot be mistaken, foresaw that neither fate nor fortune, nor anything else, but the man himself would sin, who if he had not been willing, he had not sinned: but whether he should be unwilling to sin or no, that also did God foreknow.

JOHN CALVIN

JOHN CALVIN (1509-1564) of Noyon, Picardy, trained in theology and law, opened his career with a flair for literature by publishing **de Clementia,** a commentary of Seneca, in 1532. Leaving France in 1536, owing to the stigma of his new theology, he arrived at Geneva, where the Reformation was already under way. Exiled from Geneva in 1538, he went to Strassburg, until 1541, when he returned to Geneva, remaining there for the duration of his life.

His classic work, **The Institutes of the Christian Religion** (1536), provides the source from which the material in the present work is taken. His influence in the philosophical and theological world has been so completely decisive that the doctrine of Predestinarianism is often referred to by his own name, **Calvinism.**

Calvinism is the doctrine that man's will is corrupt due to the Fall of man in Adam, whose sin all mankind inherits as biological heirs of the first man. Man's prime duty, the fulfillment of the will of God, is no longer possible as a result of man's Fall in Adam. Hence, each man is rightfully damned, deserving only his just desert, eternal punishment, but God out of his good grace elects to save some persons by redeeming whom he will. Only those predestined to salvation are capable of performing the will of God, and this is done at God's direction, yet the lives of all others are precluded to a predestined end, a destiny over which no one, but God, has control. Those predestined to be numbered among the elect, alone are capable of performing God's will; a sign that one is numbered among the elect is indicated in moral or regenerate behavior.

40

JOHN CALVIN

Predestinarianism (Fatalism)[1]

Through the Fall and Revolt of Adam, the Whole Human Race Made Accursed and Degenerate. Of Original Sin.

Self-knowledge consists in this, *first*, When reflecting on what God gave us at our creation, and still continues graciously to give, we perceive how great the excellence of our nature would have been had its integrity remained, and, at the same time, remember that we have nothing of our own, but depend entirely on God, from whom we hold at pleasure whatever he has seen it meet to bestow; *secondly*, When viewing our miserable condition since Adam's fall, all confidence and boasting are overthrown, we blush for shame, and feel truly humble. For as God at first formed us in his own image, that he might elevate our minds to the pursuit of virtue, and the contemplation of eternal life, so to prevent us from heartlessly burying those noble qualities which distinguish us from the lower animals, it is of importance to know that we endued with reason and intelligence, in order that we might cultivate a holy and honourable life, and regard a blessed immortality as our destined aim. At the same time, it is impossible to think of our primeval dignity without being immediately reminded of the sad spectacle of our ignominy and corruption, ever since we fell from our original in the person of our first parent. In this way, we feel dissatisfied with ourselves, and become truly humble, while we are inflamed with new desires to seek after God, in whom each may regain those good qualities of which all are found to be utterly destitute....

As Adam's spiritual life would have consisted in remaining united and bound to his Maker, so estrangement from him was the death of his soul. Nor is it strange that he who perverted the whole order of nature in heaven and earth deteriorated his race by his revolt....

[1] John Calvin, *Institutes of the Christian Religion*, tr. Henry Beveridge (1845, 1895); excerpts from volume I, book 2, chapters 1-4.

We thus see that the impurity of parents is transmitted to their children, so that all, without exception, are originally depraved. The commencement of this depravity will not be found until we ascend to the first parent of all as the fountain head. We must, therefore, hold it for certain that, in regard to human nature, Adam was not merely a progenitor, but, as it were, a root, and that accordingly, by his corruption, the whole human race was deservedly vitiated. . . .

To the understanding of this subject, there is no necessity for an anxious discussion (which in no small degree perplexed the ancient doctors) as to whether the soul of the child comes by transmission from the soul of the parent. It should be enough for us to know that Adam was made the depository of the endowments which God was pleased to bestow on human nature, and that, therefore, when he lost what he had received, he lost not only for himself but for us all. Why feel any anxiety about the transmission of the soul, when we know that the qualities which Adam lost he received for us not less than for himself, that they were not gifts to a single man, but attributes of the whole human race? There is nothing absurd, therefore, in the view, that when he was divested, his nature was left naked and destitute, that he having been defiled by sin, the pollution extends to all his seed. Thus, from a corrupt root corrupt branches proceeding, transmit their corruption to the saplings which sprang from them. The children being vitiated in their parent, conveyed the taint to the grandchildren; in other words, corruption commencing in Adam, is, by perpetual descent, conveyed from those preceding to those coming after them. . . .

Original sin, then, may be defined a hereditary corruption and depravity of our nature, extending to all parts of the soul, which first makes us obnoxious to the wrath of God, and then produces in us works which in Scripture are termed works of the flesh. . . .

I only wish briefly to observe, that the whole man, from the crown of the head to the sole of the foot, is so deluged, as it were, that no part remains exempt from sin, and, therefore, everything which proceeds from him is imputed as sin. Thus Paul says, that all carnal thoughts and affections are enmity against God, and consequently death (Rom. viii. 7).

Let us have done, then, with those who dare to inscribe the name of God on their vices, because we say that men are born vicious. The divine workmanship, which they ought to look for in the nature of Adam, when still entire and uncorrupted, they absurdly expect to find in their depravity. The blame for our ruin rests with our own carnality, not with God, its only cause being our degeneracy from our original condition. And let no one here clamour that God might have provided better for our safety by preventing Adam's fall. This objection, which, from the daring presumption implied in it, is odious to every pious mind, relates to the mystery of predestination, which will afterwards be considered in its own place.... Meanwhile, let us remember that our ruin is attributable to our own depravity, that we may not insinuate a charge against God himself, the Author of Nature. It is true that nature has received a mortal wound, but there is a great difference between a wound inflicted from without, and one inherent in our first condition. It is plain that this wound was inflicted by sin; and, therefore, we have no ground of complaint except against ourselves....

Man Now Deprived of Freedom of Will, and Miserably Enslaved

Having seen that the dominion of sin, ever since the first man was brought under it, not only extends to the whole race, but has complete possession of every soul, it now remains to consider more closely, whether, from the period of being thus enslaved, we have been deprived of all liberty; and if any portion still remains, how far its power extends. In order to facilitate the answer to this question, it may be proper in passing to point out the course which our inquiry ought to take. The best method of avoiding error is to consider the dangers which beset us on either side. Man being devoid of all uprightness, immediately takes occasion from the fact to indulge in sloth, and having no ability in himself for the study of righteousness, treats the whole subject as if he had no concern in it. On the other hand, man cannot arrogate anything, however minute, to himself, without robbing God of his honour, and through rash confidence subjecting himself to a fall. To keep free of both of these rocks, our proper course will be, first, to show that man has no remaining good in himself, and is beset on every side by the most miserable destitution; and then teach him to aspire to the goodness of which he is devoid, and the liberty of which he has been deprived: thus giving him a stronger stimulus to exertion than he could have if he imagined himself possessed of the highest virtue....

Everything Proceeding from the Corrupt Nature of Man Damnable

... [Man] thunders not against certain individuals, but against the whole posterity of Adam — not against the depraved manners of any single age, but the perpetual corruption of nature. His object in the passage is not merely to upbraid men in order that they may repent, but to teach that all are overwhelmed with inevitable calamity, and can be delivered from it only by the mercy of God. As this could not be proved without previously proving the overthrow and destruction of nature, he produced those passages to show that its ruin is complete.

Let it be a fixed point, then, that men are such as is here described, not only vicious custom, but by depravity of nature....

When the will is enchained as the slave of sin, it cannot make a movement towards goodness, far less steadily pursue it. Every such movement is the first step in that conversion to God, which in Scripture is entirely ascribed to divine grace.... Nevertheless, there remains a will which both inclines and hastens on with the strongest affection towards sin; man, when placed under this bondage, being deprived not of will, but of soundness of will. Bernard says not improperly, that all of us have a will; but to will well is proficiency, to will ill is defect. Thus simply to will is the part of man, to will ill, the part of corrupt nature, to will well the part of grace. Moreover, when I say that the will, deprived of liberty, is led or dragged by necessity to evil, it is strange that any should deem the expression harsh, seeing there is no absurdity in it, and it is not at variance with pious use. It does, however, offend those who know not how to distinguish between necessity and compulsion. Were any one to ask them, Is not God necessarily good, is not the devil necessarily wicked, what answer would they give? The goodness of God is so connected with his Godhead, that it is not more necessary to be God than to be good; whereas, the devil, by his fall, was so estranged from goodness, that he can do nothing but evil.... Man, since he was corrupted by the fall, sins not forced or unwilling, but voluntarily, by a most forward bias of the mind; not by violent compulsion, or external force, but by the movement of his own passion; and yet is the depravity of his nature, that he cannot move and act except in the direction of evil. If this is true, the thing not obscurely expressed is, that he is under a necessity of sinning....

It is certainly easy to prove that the commencement of good is only with God, and that none but the elect have a will inclined to good. But the cause of election must be sought out of man; and hence it follows that a right will is derived not from man himself, but from the same good pleasure by which we were chosen before the creation of the world. Another argument much akin to this may be added. The beginning of right will and action being of faith, we must see whence faith itself is. But since Scripture proclaims throughout that it is the free gift of God, it follows, that when men, who are with their whole soul naturally prone to evil, begin to have a good will, it is owing to mere grace....

How God Works in the Hearts of Men

That man is so enslaved by the yoke of sin, that he cannot of his own nature aim at good either in wish or actual pursuit, has, I think, been sufficiently proved. Moreover, a distinction has been drawn between

compulsion and necessity, making it clear that man, though he sins necessarily, nevertheless sins voluntarily. But since, from his being brought into bondage to the devil, it would seem that he is actuated more by the devil's will than his own, it is necessary, first, to explain what the agency of each is, and then solve the question, Whether in bad actions anything is to be attributed to God, Scripture intimating that there is some way in which he interferes? Augustine (in Psalm xxxi and xxxiii.) compares the human will to a horse preparing to start, and God and the devil the riders. "If God mounts, he, like a temperate and skilful rider, guides it calmly, urges it when too slow, reins it in when too fast, curbs its forwardness and over-action, checks its bad temper, and keeps it on the proper course; but if the devil has seized the saddle, like an ignorant and rash rider, he hurries it over broken ground, drives it into ditches, dashes it over precipices, spurs it into obstinacy or fury." With this simile, since a better does not occur, we shall for the present be contented. When it is said, then, that the will of the natural man is subject to the power of the devil, and is actuated by him, the meaning is, not that the will, while reluctant and resisting, is forced to submit (as masters oblige unwilling slaves to execute their orders), but that, fascinated by the impostures of Satan, it necessarily yields to his guidance, and does him homage. Those whom the Lord favours, not with the direction of his Spirit, he, by a righteous judgment, consigns to the agency of Satan. . . .

Satan is properly said to act in the reprobate, over whom he exercises his sway, which is that of wickedness. God also is said to act in his own way; because even Satan, when he is the instrument of divine wrath, is completely under the command of God, who turns him as he will in the execution of his first judgments. I say nothing here of the universal agency of God, which, as it sustains all the creatures, also gives them all their power of acting. I am now speaking only of that special agency which is apparent in every act. We thus see that there is no inconsistency in attributing the same act to God, to Satan, and to man, while, from the difference in the end and mode of action, the spotless righteousness of God shines forth at the same time that the iniquity of Satan and of man is manifested in all its deformity. . . .

The ministry of Satan is employed to instigate the reprobate, whenever the Lord, in the course of his providence, has any purpose to accomplish in them. . . .

In those actions which in themselves are neither good nor bad, and concern the corporeal rather than the spiritual life, the liberty which man possesses, although we have above touched upon it, . . . has not yet been explained. Some have conceded a free choice to man in such actions; more, I suppose, because they were unwilling to debate a matter of no great moment, than because they wished positively to assert what they were prepared to concede. While I admit that those who hold that man has no ability in himself to do righteousness, hold what is most necessary to be known for salvation, I think it ought not to be overlooked that we owe it to the special grace of God, whenever, on the one hand, we choose what is for our advantage, and whenever with heart and soul we shun what would otherwise do us harm. And the interference of Divine Providence goes to the extent not only of making events turn out as was foreseen to be expedient, but of giving the wills of men the same direction. If we look at the administration of human affairs with the eye of sense, we will have no doubt that, so far, they are placed at man's disposal; but if we lend an ear to the many passages of Scripture which proclaim that even in these matters the minds of men are ruled by God, they will compel us to place human choice in subordination to his special influence. . . .

Whenever God is pleased to make way for his providence, he even in external matters so turns and bends the wills of men, that whatever the freedom of their choice may be, it is still subject to the disposal of God. That your mind depends more on the agency of God than the freedom of your own choice, daily experience teaches. Your judgment often fails, and in matters of not great difficulty, your courage flags; at other times, in matters of the greatest obscurity, the mode of explicating them at once suggests itself, while in matters of moment and danger, your mind rises superior to every difficulty. . . .

Let the reader here remember, that the power of the human will is not to be estimated by the event, as some unskilful persons are absurdly wont to do. They think it an elegant and ingenious proof of the bondage of the human will, that even the greatest monarchs are sometimes thwarted in their wishes. But the ability of which we speak must be considered as within the man, not measured by outward success. In discussing the subject of free will, the question is not, whether external obstacles will permit a man to execute what he has internally resolved, but whether, in any matter whatever, he has a free power of judging and of willing. If men possess both of these, Attilus Regulus, shut up in a barrel studded with sharp nails, will have a will no less free than Augustus Caesar ruling with imperial sway over a large portion of the globe.

41

ST. AUGUSTINE

The Source of Human Evil[1]

CHAPTER I

Of the Nature of Good and Evil Angels

. . . It seems requisite to speak of the congruity and suitability of the society of men with angels and to show that there are not four, but rather two societies of men and angels similar in quality, and combined together, the one consisting of both good angels and good men, and the other of evil. That the contrariety of desires between the good and evil angels arose from their diverse natures and beginnings, we may on no account believe, God having been alike good in both their creations, and in all things beside them. But this diversity arises from their wills, some of them persisting in God their common good, and in His truth, love, and eternity; while others, delighting more in their own power, as though it were from themselves, fell from that common all-blessing good to dote upon their own, and taking pride for eternity, vain deceit for firm truth, and factious envy for perfect love, became proud, deceitful, and envious. The cause of their beatitude was their adherence unto God; so must their misery's cause be the direct contrary, namely, their not adhering unto God. Wherefore if when we are asked why they are blessed, and we answer well: 'Because they stuck fast unto God,' and being asked why these are wretched, we answer well: 'Because they stuck not unto God': then is there no beatitude for any reasonable or understanding creature to attain but in God. So then though all creatures cannot be blessed (for beasts, trees, stones, etc., are incapable hereof), yet those that are, are not so of themselves, being created of nothing, but have their blessedness from the Creator. Attaining Him they are happy, losing Him unhappy. But He Himself is good only of Himself, and therefore

[1] St. Augustine, *The City of God*, tr. John Healey (1610, rev. 1620, spelling modernized, 1890; original *De Civitate Dei*, 413-426); excerpts from book 12.

cannot lose His good, because He cannot lose Himself. Therefore the one true blessed God we say is the only immutable good; and those things He made are good also because they are from Him, but they are mutable because they were made of nothing. Wherefore though they be not the chief goods, God being above them, yet are they great, in being able to adhere unto the chief good and so be happy, without which adherence they cannot be wretched. Nor are other parts of the creation better in that they cannot be wretched: for we cannot say our other members are better than our eyes in that they cannot be blind. But even as sensitive nature in the worst plight is better than the insensible stone, so is the reasonable (albeit miserable) above the brutish, that cannot therefore be miserable. This being so, then this nature (created in such excellence, that though it be mutable, yet by inherence with God, that unchangeable good, it may become blessed; which cannot satisfy its own need without blessedness, nor has any means to attain this blessedness but God) truly commits a great error and enormity in not adhering unto Him. And all sin is against nature and hurtful thereunto. Wherefore that creature which adheres not unto God differs not in nature from that which adheres unto God, but in vice; and yet in that vice is the nature itself laudable still. For the vice being justly blamed commends the nature; the true dispraise of vice being that it disgraceth an honest nature. And therefore as, when we call blindness a fault of the eyes, we show that sight belongs to the eye, and in calling the fault of the ears deafness, that hearing belongs to the ear; so likewise, when we say it was the angels' fault not to adhere unto God, we show that that adherence belonged to their natures. And how great a praise it is to continue in this adherence, enjoying and living in so great a good without death, error, or trouble, who can sufficiently declare or imagine? Wherefore since it was the evil angels' fault not to adhere unto God (all vice being against nature), it is manifest that God created their nature good, since it is hurt only by their departure from Him.

· · · · ·

CHAPTER III

Of God's Enemies Not by Nature, but Will, Which Hurting Them, Hurts Their Good Nature; Because There Is No Vice but Hurts Nature

The scripture calls them God's enemies, because they oppose His sovereignty not by nature but will, having no power to hurt Him, but themselves. Their will to resist, not their power to hurt, makes them His foes, for He is unchangeable and wholly incorruptible: wherefore the vice that makes them oppose God is their own hurt, and in no way

God's; solely because it corrupts their good nature. It is not their nature but their vice that is contrary to God; evil only being contrary to good. And who denies that God is the best good? So then vice is contrary unto God, as evil is unto good. The nature also which it corrupts is good, and therefore opposed by it: but while it stands against God only as evil against good, against this nature it stands as evil and hurt also; for evil cannot hurt God, but corruptible natures only, which are good by the testimony of the hurt that evil does them, for if they were not good, vice could not hurt them: for what does it in hurting them but abolish their integrity, lustre, virtue, safety, and whatever vice can diminish or root out of a good nature? And if this good be not therein, vice takes it not away, and therefore hurts not: for it cannot be both a vice, and hurtless; when we gather that though vice cannot hurt that unchangeable good, yet it can hurt nothing but good; because it only exists where it hurts. And so we may say that vice cannot be in the highest good, nor can it be but in some good. Good therefore may exist alone, but so cannot evil: because the natures that an evil will has corrupted, though in so far as they be polluted they are evil, yet in so far as they are natures they are good. And when this vicious nature is punished, there is this good besides the goodness of its nature, that it is not unpunished. For this is just, and what is just is beyond question good, and no man is punished for the faults of his nature, but of his will; for that vice that has grown from a custom into a habit and seems natural, had its origin from corruption of will. For now we are speaking of the vices of that nature, wherein is a soul capable of the intellectual light, whereby we discern between just and unjust.

• • • • •

CHAPTER V

That the Creator Has Deserved Praise in Every Form and Kind of Nature

Wherefore all natures are good, because they have their form, kind, and a certain harmony withal in themselves. And when they are in their true posture of nature, they preserve their essence in the full manner as they received it. And that, whose essence is not eternal, follows the laws of the Creator that sways it, and changes into better, or worse, tending (by God's disposition) still to that end which the order of the universe requires, so that that corruption which brings all mortal natures into dissolution can only dissolve that which was, that it may become afterwards that which it was before, or that which it should be. Which being so, then God, the highest being, who made all things that are not Himself (no creature being fit for equality with Him, being made of nothing, and consequently not being able to have been but by Him), is not to be found fault with because offence is taken at the creatures' faults, but to be honoured upon the due consideration of the perfection of all natures.

CHAPTER VI

The Cause of the Good Angels' Bliss, and the Evil Ones' Misery

The true cause therefore of the good angels' bliss is their adherence to that most high essence, and the just cause of the bad angels' misery is their departure from that high essence, to turn back upon themselves, that were not such. Which vice, what is it else but pride? 'For pride is the root of all sin.' These would not therefore stick unto Him their strength, and having power to be more perfect by adherence to this highest good, they preferred themselves that were His inferiors before Him. This was the first fall, misery, and vice of their nature, which though it were not created to have the highest being, yet might it have beatitude by fruition of the highest being; but which falling from Him becomes not indeed nothing, but yet less than it was, and consequently miserable. Seek the cause of this evil will, and you shall find just none. For what can cause the will's evil, the will being sole cause of all evil? The evil will therefore cause evil works, but nothing causes the evil will. If there be such a cause, then either it has a will or none. If it have, it is either a good one or a bad; if good, what fool will say that a good will is cause of an evil will? It should be if it caused sin; but this were extreme absurdity to affirm. But if it have an evil will, then I ask what cause this evil will in it. And to limit my questions, I ask the cause of the first evil will. For that which another evil will has caused is not the first evil will, but that which none has caused: for still that which causes is before the thing caused. If I be answered, that nothing caused it, but it was from the beginning, I ask then whether it were in any nature. If it were in none, it had no being; if it were in any, it corrupted it, hurt it, and deprived it of all good; and therefore this advice could not be in an evil nature, but in a good, where it might do hurt: for if it could not hurt, it was no vice, and therefore no bad will; and if it did hurt, it was by privation of good, or diminishing of it. Therefore a bad will could not be from eternity in that wherein a good nature had been before, which the evil will destroyed by hurt. Well, if it were not eternal, who made it? It must be answered, something that had no evil will. What was this — inferior, superior, or equal unto it? If it were the superior, it was better. Why then had it not a will, nay, a better will?

This may also be said if it were equal: for two good wills never make one another bad. It remains, then, that some inferior thing that had no will was cause of that vicious will in the angels. Aye, but all things below them, even to the lowest earth, being natural, are also good, and have the goodness of form and kind in all order. How then can a good thing produce an evil will? How can good be cause of evil? For the will turning from the superior to the inferior, becomes bad, not because the thing whereunto it turns is bad, but because the turning is bad and perverse. No inferior thing then depraves the will, but the will depraves itself by following inferior things inordinately. For if two men like in body and mind should behold one beauteous personage, and the one of them be stirred with a lustful desire towards it, and the other's thoughts stand chaste, what shall we think was cause of the evil will in the one and not in the other? Not the seen beauty, for it transformed not the will in both, and yet both saw it alike. Not the flesh of the beholder's face. For if so, why not the flesh of the other? Nor the mind, for we presupposed them both alike in body and mind. Shall we say the devil secretly suggested it unto one of them, as though he consented not to it in his own proper will.

This consent, therefore — the cause of this assent of the will to vicious desire — is what we seek. For, to take away one difficulty from the question, if both were tempted, and the one yielded, and the other did not, why was this, but because the one would continue chaste, and the other would not? Whence then was this secret fall but from the individual will, where there was such parity in body and mind, a like sight and a like temptation? So then he that desires to know the cause of the vicious will in the one of them, if he mark it well, shall find nothing. For if we say that he caused it, what was he ere his will became vicious but a creature of a good nature, the work of God, that unchangeable good? Wherefore he that says that he that consented to this lustful desire which the other withstood (both being before alike in body and soul, and beholding the beautiful object alike) was cause of his own evil will, whereas he was good before this vice of will; let him ask why he cause this — whether from his nature, or because his will was made of nothing; and he shall find that his evil will arose not from his nature, but from nothing: for if we shall make his nature the effecter of his vicious will, what shall we do but affirm that good is the efficient cause of evil? But how can it be that nature (good though it be mutable), before it have a vicious will, should do viciously, namely in making the will vicious?

CHAPTER VII

That We Ought Not to Seek Out the Cause of the Vicious Will

Let none therefore seek the efficient cause of an evil will; for it is not efficient by deficient, nor is there effect but defect, namely falling from that highest essence unto lower, this is to have an evil will. The causes whereof (being not efficient but deficient) if one endeavour to seek, it is as if he should seek to see the darkness, or to hear silence. We know them both, this by the ear, and that by the eye, but not by any forms of theirs, but privation of forms. Let none then seek to know that of me which I know not myself, unless he will learn not to know what he must know that he cannot know: for the things that we know by privation and not by form, are rather (if you can follow me) known by not knowing, and in knowing them, are still unknown. For the body's eye coursing over bodily objects sees no darkness, save when it ceases to see. And so it belongs to the ear and to no other sense to know silence, which notwithstanding is not known save by not hearing. So our intellect contemplates the intelligible forms, but where they fail it learns by not learning. For 'who can understand his faults?' This I know, that God's nature can never fail anywhere or in any way: but all things that are made of nothing may decay. And yet in so far as these things achieve good results they have efficient causes; but in that they fail, and fall off, and do evil, they have deficient causes. And what do they then but vanity?

CHAPTER VIII

Of the Perverse Love, Whereby the Soul Goes from the Unchangeable To the Changeable Good

I know besides that wherein the vicious will is resident, therein is that done, which, if the will would not, should not be done: and therefore the punishment falls justly upon those acts which are wills and not necessities. It is not the thing to which we fall, but our fall that is evil: that is, we fall to no evil natures, but against nature's order, from the highest to the lower. Herein is evil. Covetousness is no vice in the gold, but in him that perversely leaves justice to love gold, whereas justice ought always to be preferred before riches. Nor is lust the fault of sweet beauteous bodies, but the soul's that runs perversely to bodily delights, neglecting temperance, which scorns all company with those, and prepares us unto far more excellent and spiritual pleasures. Vain-glory is not a vice proper to human praise, but the soul's that perversely desires praise of men, not respecting the conscience's testimony. Nor is pride his vice that gives the power, but the soul's perversely loving that power, contemning the justice of the Most Mighty. So then, he that perversely desires a good of nature, though he attain it, is evil himself in the enjoyment of this good, and wretched, being deprived of a better.

42

RENÉ DESCARTES

The Classic Cogito[1]

All that I have, up to this moment, accepted as possessed of the highest truth and certainty, I received either from or through the senses. I observed, however, that these sometimes misled us; and it is the part of prudence not to place absolute confidence in that by which we have even once been deceived.

But it may be said, perhaps, that, although the senses occasionally mislead us respecting minute objects, and such as are so far removed from us as to be beyond the reach of close observation, there are yet many other of their informations (presentations), of the truth of which it is manifestly impossible to doubt; as for example, that I am in this place, seated by the fire, clothed in a winter dressing-gown, that I hold in my hands this piece of paper, with other intimations of the same nature. But how could I deny that I possess these hands and this body, and withal escape being classed with persons in a state of insanity, whose brains are so disordered and clouded by dark bilious vapours as to cause them pertinaciously to assert that they are monarchs when they are in the greatest poverty; or clothed [in gold] and purple when destitute of any covering; or that their head is made of clay, their body of glass, or that they are gourds? I should certainly be not less insane than they were I to regulate my procedure according to examples so extravagant.

Though this be true, I must nevertheless here consider that I am a man, and that, consequently, I am in the habit of sleeping, and representing to myself in dreams those same things, or even sometimes others less probable, which the insane think are presented to them in their waking moments. How often have I dreamt that I was in these familiar circumstances — that I was dressed, and occupied this place by the fire, when I was lying undressed in bed? . . . and in amazement I almost persuade myself that I am now dreaming. . . .

[1] René Descartes, *Meditations on the First Philosophy*, tr. John Veitch (1853), original French, 1641; excerpts from Meditations I and II.

The Meditation of yesterday has filled my mind with so many doubts, that it is no longer in my power to forget them. Nor do I see, meanwhile, any principle on which they can be resolved; and just as if I had fallen all of a sudden into very deep water, I am so greatly disconcerted as to be unable either to plant my feet firmly on the bottom or sustain myself by swimming on the surface. I will, nevertheless, make an effort, and try anew the same path on which I had entered yesterday, that is, proceed by casting aside all that admits of the slightest doubt, not less than if I had discovered it to be absolutely false; and I will continue always in this track until I shall find something that is certain, or at least, if I can do nothing more, until I shall know with certainty that there is nothing certain. Archimedes, that he might transport the entire glove from the place it occupied to another, demanded only a point that was firm and immovable; so also, I shall be entitled to entertain the highest expectations, if I am fortunate enough to discover only one thing that is certain and indubitable.

I suppose, accordingly, that all the things which I see are false (fictitious); I believe that none of those objects which my fallacious memory represents ever existed; I suppose that I possess no senses; I believe that body, figure, extension, motion, and place are merely fictions of my mind. What is there, then, that can be esteemed true? Perhaps this only, that there is absolutely nothing certain.

But how do I know that there is not something different altogether from the objects I have now enumerated, of which it is impossible to entertain the slightest doubt? Is there not a God, or some being, by whatever name I may designate him, who causes these thoughts to arise in my mind? But why suppose such a being, for it may be I myself am capable of producing them? Am I, then, at least not something? But I before denied that I possessed senses or a body; I hesitate, however, for what follows from that? Am I so dependent on the body and the senses that without these I cannot exist? But I had the persuasion that there was absolutely nothing in the world, that there was no sky and no earth, neither minds nor bodies; was I not, therefore, at the same time, persuaded that I did not exist? Far from it; I assuredly existed, since I was persuaded. But there is I know not what being, who is possessed at once of the highest power and the deepest cunning, who is constantly employing all his ingenuity in deceiving me. Doubtless, then, I exist, since I am deceived; and, let him deceive me as he may, he can never bring it about that I am nothing, so long as I shall be conscious that I am something. So that it must, in fine, be maintained, all things being maturely and carefully considered, that this proposition (*pronunciatum*) I am, I exist, is necessarily true each time it is expressed by me, or conceived in my mind.

JONATHAN EDWARDS

JONATHAN EDWARDS (1703-1758), early American philosopher and theologian, was born in East Windsor, Conn. on Oct. 5, 1703. A precocious childhood found him writing a treatise on **The Nature of the Soul** when he was but ten years of age; at twelve, he composed another on **The Habits of Spiders.** Entering Yale University at 13, he mastered Locke's **Essays Concerning the Human Understanding** at 14, and graduated from Yale as valedictorian at 17. He continued at Yale for a couple of years of graduate study, then for another two, tutored at the same institution.

The major portion of his career was spent as a Congregational minister at Northampton, Mass., where at the age of 47, he was dismissed; in 1750, he went to an Indian mission in Stockbridge where most of his treatises were written; in 1758, he became President of Princeton University (then called the College of New Jersey), where on March 22, 1758 as the result of a smallpox epidemic which swept the state of New Jersey, he died.

Edwards lived in a day dominated by Calvinism, a philosophy of which he became the recognized champion in America. The Calvinist doctrine of Predestination, he treats in what is regarded his **magnum opus, The Freedom of the Will,** the source which provides the selection in the present book. Other writings of his are: **Sinners in the Hands of an Angry God, The Nature of True Virtue, Doctrine of Original Sin Defended, The Justice of God in the Damnation of Sinners, The Future Punishment of the Wicked Unavoidable and Intolerable, Dissertation concerning the End for Which God Created the World.**

Edwards, the Calvinist, emphasized the doctrine of Election, the belief that a person is predestined to enter eternal bliss in heaven or eternal damnation in hell — exercise of will proves ineffectual in salvation, only God's free grace suffices in the effectual salvation of one's soul. Man is void of will, consequently cannot choose to save himself — whatever good a man does is directed by God as his emissary or channel. The impotency of human will is due to the Fall of Adam (doctrine of the Total Depravity of Man), who although originally good, is now corrupt, and whose sin mankind inherits.

43

JONATHAN EDWARDS

Calvinism (Fatalism)[1]

Concerning the Nature of the Will

. . . The Will (without any metaphysical refining) is plainly, that by
which the mind chooses any thing. The faculty of the Will is that faculty
or power or principle of mind by which it is capable of choosing; an
act of the Will is the same as an act of choosing or choice.

If any think it is a more perfect definition of the Will, to say, that it is
that by which the soul either chooses or refuses; I am content with it:
though I think that it is enough to say, it is that by which the soul
chooses: for in every act of Will whatsoever, the mind chooses one thing
rather than another; it chooses something rather than the contrary,
or rather than the want or non-existence of that thing. So in every act
of refusal, the mind chooses the absence of the thing refused; the positive and the negative are set before the mind for its choice, and it chooses
the negative; and the mind's making its choice in that case is properly
the act of the Will; the Will's determining between the two is a voluntary determining; but that is the same thing as making a choice. So that
whatever names we call the act of the Will by, choosing, refusing,
approving, disapproving, liking, disliking, embracing, rejecting, determining, directing, commanding, forbidding, inclining or being averse, a
being pleased or displeased with; all may be reduced to this of choosing.
For the soul to act voluntarily, is evermore to act electively. . . .

Concerning the Determination of the Will

By *determining the Will*, if the phrase be used with any meaning,
must be intended, causing that the act of the Will or choice should be
thus, and not otherwise: and the Will is said to be determined, when, in
consequence of some action or influence, its choice is directed to, and

---

[1] Jonathan Edwards, *Freedom of the Will.*

fixed upon a particular object. As when we speak of the determination of motion, we mean causing the motion of the body to be such a way, or in such a direction, rather than another.

To talk of the determination of the Will, supposes an effect, which must have a cause. If the Will be determined, there is a determiner. This must be supposed to be intended even by them that say, the Will determines itself. If it be so, the Will is both determiner and determined; it is a cause that acts and produces effects upon itself, and is the object of its own influence and action.

With respect to that grand inquiry, What determines the Will? it would be very tedious and unnecessary at present to enumerate and examine all the various opinions which have been advanced concerning this matter; nor is it needful that I should enter into a particular disquisition of all points debated in disputes on that question, whether the Will always follows the last dictate of the understanding. It is sufficient to my present purpose to say, it is that motive, which, as it stands in the view of the mind, is the strongest, that determines the Will.

Whether Any Event Whatsoever, and Volition in Particular, Can Come to Pass without a Cause of Its Existence

. . . When I speak of connection of Causes and Effects, I have respect to moral Causes, as well as those that are called natural in distinction from them. Moral Causes may be Causes in as proper a sense, as any causes whatsoever; may have as real an influence, and may as truly be the ground and reason of an Event's coming to pass.

Therefore I sometimes use the word *Cause*, in this inquiry, to signify any antecedent, either natural or moral, positive or negative, on which an Event, either a thing, or the manner and circumstance of a thing, so depends, that it is the ground and reason, either in whole, or in part, why it is, rather than not; or why it is as it is, rather than otherwise; or in other words, any antecedent with which a consequent Event is so connected, that it truly belongs to the reason why the proposition which affirms that Event, is true; whether it has any positive influence or not. And in agreebleness to this, I sometimes use the word Effect for the consequence of another thing, which is perhaps rather an occasion than a Cause, most properly speaking.

I am the most careful thus to explain my meaning, that I may cut off occasion, from any that might seek occasion to cavil and object against some things which I may say concerning the dependence of all things which come to pass, on some Cause, and their connection with their Cause.

Having thus explained what I mean by Cause, I assert that nothing ever comes to pass without a Cause. What is self-existent must be from eternity, and must be unchangeable; but as to all things that begin to be, they are not self-existent, and therefore must have some foundation of their existence without themselves; that whatsoever begins to be which before was not, must have a Cause why it then begins to exist, seems to be the first dictate of the common and natural sense which God hath implanted in the minds of all mankind, and the main foundation of all our reasonings about the existence of things, past, present, or to come. . . .

If this grand principle of common sense be taken away, all arguing from effects to Causes ceaseth, and so all knowledge of any existence, besides what we have by the most direct and immediate intuition. Particularly all our proof of the being of God ceases: we argue His being from our own being and the being of other things, which we are sensible once were not, but have begun to be; and from the being of the world, with all its constituent parts, and the manner of their existence; all which we see plainly are not necessary in their own nature, and so not self-existent, and therefore must have a Cause. But if things, not in themselves necessary, may begin to be without a Cause, all this arguing is vain. . . .

But if once this grand principle of common sense be given up, that what is not necessary in itself, must have a Cause; and we begin to maintain, that things may come into existence, and begin to be, which heretofore have not been, of themselves without any Cause; all our means of ascending in our arguing from the creature to the Creator, and all our evidence of the Being of God, is cut off at one blow. In this case, we cannot prove that there is a God, either from the Being of the world, and the creatures in it, or from the manner of their being, their order, beauty and use. For if things may come into existence without any Cause at all, then they doubtless may without any Cause answerable to the effect. Our minds do alike naturally suppose and determine both these things; namely, that what begins to be has a Cause, and also that it has a Cause proportionable and agreeable to the effect. The same principle which leads us to determine, that there cannot be any thing coming to pass without a Cause, leads us to determine that there cannot be more in the effect than in the Cause. . . .

.   .   .   .   .

If any should imagine, there is something in the sort of Event that renders possible for it to come into existence without a Cause, and should say, that the free acts of the Will are existences of an exceeding different nature from other things; by reason of which they may come into existence without any previous ground or reason of it, though other things cannot; if they make this objection in good earnest, it would be an evidence of their strangely forgetting themselves; for they would be giving an account of some ground of the existence of a thing, when at the same time they would maintain there is no ground of its existence. Therefore I would observe, that the particular nature of existence, be it ever so diverse from others, can lay no foundation for that thing's coming into existence without a Cause; because to suppose this, would be to suppose the particular nature of existence to be a thing prior to the existence; and so a thing which makes way for existence, with such a circumstance, namely, without a cause or reason of existence. But that which in any respect makes way for a thing's coming into being, or for any manner or circumstance of its first existence, must be prior to the existence. The distinguished nature of the effect, which is something belonging to the effect, cannot have influence backward, to act before it is. The peculiar nature of that thing called volition, can do nothing, can have no influence, while it is not. And afterwards it is too late for its influence; for then the thing has made sure of existence already, without its help.

So that it is indeed as repugnant to reason, to suppose that an act of the Will should come into existence without a Cause, as to suppose the human soul, or an angel, or the globe of the earth, or the whole universe, should come into existence without a Cause. And if once we allow, that such a sort of effect as a Volition may come to pass without a Cause, how do we know but that many other sorts of effects may do so too? It is not the particular kind of effect that makes the absurdity of supposing it has been without a Cause, but something which is common to all things that ever begin to be, viz., that they are not self-existent, or necessary in the nature of things. . . .

Conclusion

. . . It is easy to see, how the decision of most of the points in controversy, between *Calvinist* and *Arminians,* depends on the determination of this grand article concerning *the freedom of the Will, requisite to moral agency;* and that by clearing and establishing the *Calvinistic* doctrine in this point, the chief arguments are obviated, by which *Arminian* doctrines in general are supported, and the contrary doctrines demonstratively confirmed. Hereby it becomes manifest, that God's moral government over mankind, his treating them as moral agents, making them the objects of his commands, counsels, calls, warnings, expostulations, promises, threatenings, rewards and punishments, is not inconsistent with a *determining disposal* of all events, of every kind, throughout the universe, in his *providence;* either by positive efficiency, or permission. Indeed, such an *universal, determining Providence* infers some kind of necessity of all events, such a necessity as implies an infallible, previous fixedness of the futurity of the event; but no other necessity of moral events, or volitions of intelligent agents, is needful in order to this, than *moral necessity;* which does as much ascertain the futurity of the event, as any other necessity. But, as has been demonstrated, such a necessity is not at all repugnant to moral agency, and a reasonable use of commands, calls, rewards, punishments, &c. Yea, not only are objections of this kind against the doctrine of an universal *determining Providence,* removed by what has been said, but the truth of such a doctrine is demonstrated.

As it has been demonstrated, that the futurity of all future events is established by previous necessity, either natural or moral; so it is manifest that the Sovereign Creator and Disposer of the world has ordered this necessity, by ordering his own conduct, either in designedly acting or forbearing to act. For, as the being of the world is from God, so the circumstances in which it had its being at first, both negative and positive, must be ordered by him, in one of these ways; and all the necessary consequences of these circumstances, must be ordered by him. And God's active and positive interpositions, after the world was created, and the consequence of these interpositions, also every instance of his forbearing to interpose, and the sure consequences of this forbearance, must all be determined according to his pleasure. And therefore every event, which is the consequence of any thing whatsoever, or that is connected with any foregoing thing or circumstance, either positive or negative, as the ground or reason of its existence, must be ordered of God; either by a designed efficiency and interposition, or a designed forbearing to operate or interpose. But, as has been proved, all events whatsoever are necessarily connected with something foregoing, either positive or negative, which is the ground of their existence: it follows, therefore, that the whole series of events is thus connected with something in the state of things, either positive or negative, which is original in the series; i.e. something which is connected with nothing preceding that, but God's own immediate conduct, either his acting or forbearing to act. From whence it follows, that as God designedly orders his own conduct, and its connected consequences, it must necessarily be, that he designedly orders all things.

44

IMMANUEL KANT

The Autonomy of Will[1]

The Idea of Freedom as the Key to the Autonomy of the Will

The *will* is the causality of living beings in so far as they are rational. *Freedom* is that causality in so far as it can be regarded as efficient without being *determined* to activity by any cause other than itself. Natural *necessity* is the property of all nonrational beings to be determined to activity by some cause external to themselves.

The definition of freedom just given is *negative*, and therefore it does not tell us what freedom is in itself; but it prepares the way for a *positive* conception of a more specific and more fruitful character. The conception of causality carries with it the conception of determination by law (*Gesetz*), for the effect is conceived as determined (*gesetzt*) by the cause. Hence freedom must not be regarded as lawless (*gesetzlos*), but simply as independent of laws of nature. A free cause does conform to unchangeable laws, but these laws are peculiar to itself; and, indeed, apart from law a free will has no meaning whatever. A necessary law of nature, as we have seen, implies the heteronomy of efficient causes; for no effect is possible at all, unless its cause is itself determined to activity by something else. What, therefore, can freedom possibly be but autonomy, that is, the property of the will to be a law to itself? Now, to say that the will in all its actions is a law to itself, is simply to say that its principle is, to act from no other maxim than that the object of which is itself as a universal law. But this is just the formula of the categorical imperative and the principle of morality. Hence a free will is the same thing as a will that conforms to moral laws.

If, then, we start from the presupposition of freedom of the will, we can derive morality and the principle of morality simply from an analysis

[1] Immanuel Kant, *The Fundamental Principles of the Metaphysics of Ethics,* tr. John Watson (1901); original German Edition, *Grundlegung zur Metaphysik der Sitten,* Riga, 1785; 2. Aufl. 1787.

of the conception of freedom. Yet the principle of morality, namely, that an absolutely good will is a will the maxim of which can always be taken as itself a universal law, is a synthetic proposition. For by no possibility can we derive this property of the maxim from an analysis of the conception of an absolutely good will. The transition from the conception of freedom to the conception of morality can be made only if there is a third proposition which connects the other two in a synthetic unity. The *positive* conception of freedom yields this third proposition, and not the conception of nature, in which a thing is related causally only to something else.

Freedom Is a Property of All Rational Beings

It cannot in any way be proved that the will of man is free, unless it can be shown that the will of all rational beings is free. For morality is a law for us only in so far as we are rational beings, and therefore it must apply to all rational beings. But morality is possible only for a free being, and hence it must be proved that freedom also belongs to the will of all rational beings. Now I say that a being who cannot act *except under the idea of freedom,* must for that very reason be regarded as free so far as his actions are concerned. In other words, even if it cannot be proved by speculative reason that his will is free, all the laws that are inseparably bound up with freedom must be viewed by him as laws of his will. And I say, further, that we must necessarily attribute to every rational being that has a will the idea of freedom, because every such being always acts under that idea. A rational being we must conceive as having a reason that is practical, that is, a reason that has causality with regard to its objects. Now, it is impossible to conceive of a reason which should be consciously biased in its judgments by some influence from without, for the subject would in that case regard its judgments as determined, not by reason, but by a natural impulse. Reason must therefore regard itself as the author of its principles of action, and as independent of all external influences. Hence, as practical reason, or as the will of a ration being, it must be regarded by itself as free. The will of a rational being, in other words, can be his own will only if he acts under the idea of freedom, and therefore this idea must in the practical sphere be ascribed to all rational beings.

JOHN McTAGGART ELLIS McTAGGART

JOHN McTAGGART ELLIS McTAGGART (1866-1925), British Neo-Hegelian, Pluralistic Idealist, taught that ultimate reality is an Absolute composed of a society of eternal finite selves. His principal works are: **Studies in the Hegelian Dialectic** (1896), **Studies in Hegelian Cosmology** (1901), **Some Dogmas of Religion** (1906), **Human Immortality and Pre-Existence** (1915), **The Nature of Existence** (1921).

Although McTaggart is a Personalist, asserting that the Absolute is a system of immortal selves, and despite his ardent belief in immortality, he is, nevertheless, an Atheist. The metaphysically real, ultimate reality, is spiritual, an interrelated structure of selves, persons whose prime bond is love. Since the nature of all reality is spiritual, the existence of a spiritual afterlife is creditable.

45

JOHN McTAGGART ELLIS McTAGGART

Free Will[1]

1. The question whether a man is free in his actions is ambiguous. We may distinguish four senses in which it may be taken. In the first place, we may say that a man is free to do anything which nothing but his own nature prevents him from doing. In this sense I am not free to draw a triangle with two right angles, since this would be impossible whatever my nature might be. Nor am I, in this sense, free to save a man's life if I am tied at a distance from him by a chain which I cannot break. For I should be equally unable to do it, whatever my nature might be. It is true that I could do it, if my body was sufficiently strong to break the chain. But a man's body is not generally held to be part of himself in such a sense as to make its characteristics part of his nature. Any one who made no distinction between a man and his body would, I suppose, hold that I was free, in this sense of freedom, to break the chain.

But if I do not save a man's life because I mistake the nature of his illness, or because it is too much trouble, then I am acting freely. For if my nature were such as to give me greater discernment, or such as to make me think more of human life and less of my own trouble, I should have saved him. And I should still, in this sense of freedom, be held to be acting freely, however certain it was that my action was absolutely determined by the character with which I was born, combined with the circumstances of my life. I was not determined from without to be unable to save the life, and internal determination does not, in this sense of freedom, prevent me from acting freely.

2. Freedom, when the word is used in this sense, may be called freedom of self-determination. The use has some importance from a metaphysical point of view, but in ordinary life it is not often employed. Much more common is the second use of the word, according to which

---

[1] John McTaggart Ellis McTaggart, *Some Dogmas of Religion* (London: Edward Arnold, 1906), 140-146.

a man is free to do anything which nothing but his own will prevents him from doing. So far as a man is free in this sense he can direct his life as he chooses. We may call this, then, freedom of self-direction.

When the word is used in this sense, I should not be called free to save a man when I fail to do so because I mistake the character of his illness. This mistake comes from my nature, but not from my will. I may make it in spite of willing not to make it. But if I do not save his life because it would be too much trouble, I am acting freely in not saving it. I abstain from saving it because I choose to avoid trouble rather than save a life. If my choice — that is to say, my will — had been different, I should have saved him.

Here, as with the freedom of self-determination, I should not be held less free because my choice was absolutely determined by my character and my past history. I am free because I act as I choose, whether the choice is completely determined or not.

3. In the third place a man is said to act freely when he acts according to the ultimate ideal of his nature. The implication here seems to be that freedom is essentially the absence of such limitation as is felt to thwart and constrain the being who is limited, and that no person can be completely free from such constraint except by attaining the ultimate ideal of his nature. Thus it is often said that only the wise or the good are free, although it would be admitted that folly or wickedness might issue from the character of some men by the same inevitable determination which produced in others wisdom and virtue.

This use is extended by analogy to beings which are not believed to feel constraint. Thus we say of a tree that it grows freely when it grows to its normal size in the ground, and that it does not grow freely when it is stunted by being planted in a pot. And yet it is equally the nature of the tree to be stunted in the one case as not to be stunted in the other. The unstunted growth is called free because it is looked on as the ideal.

Virtue is certainly part of the ideal of man. And therefore virtuous action will be called free, in this sense, when wicked action is not. So, also, will a reasonable action as against a foolish action. For this there is also another ground. We often regard reason and conscience as more truly parts of our nature than desires or passions, which we speak of as though they were forces acting on us from outside. When I act according to a passion it is said to master me. When reason or conscience prevents me from doing so, I am said to master my passion. Thus virtuous and reasonable action will appear, by the suggestion of such phrases, as more truly self-determined than other action.

Freedom in this sense may be called freedom of self-realization. It has considerable importance in philosophy, but we shall not have much concern with it in the present chapter.

4. Freedom, finally, is used in a fourth sense, which is the one which mainly concerns us here. In this sense a man is free in any action, if his choice of that action is not completely determined. The supporters of this view do not, I conceive, maintain that a man can ever act without a motive, nor do they consider that the existence of a motive is incompatible with freedom. But if the motive completely determined the act — either because there was no other motive, or because it was determined to be more effective than any other — then the act would not be freely done. It is essential for freedom that there should be motives prompting to different courses, between which the agent chooses. And it is essential that this choice should not be determined. We may call this freedom of indetermination. My object in this chapter is to consider whether it exists.

Freedom of indetermination is commonly spoken of as Free Will. This seems to be justified. If freedom were defined otherwise, the proper question might be 'Am I free to act?' not 'Am I free to will?' But, if freedom is to imply the absence of complete determination, it can only be the will that is free. The voluntary act is completely determined — in so far as it is not determined by outside circumstances it is determined by the volition on which it follows. No indeterminist would deny this. It is only the volition which is undetermined, and only the volition which is free. When an indeterminist says, for example, that a man has freely committed a murder, he means that he was free in willing to do it. Indeed, in so far as the will did not completely determine the act, as when a bullet meant for a tiger kills a man, the indeterminist would deny that the shooter had acted freely in killing the man.

5. The law of Causality asserts that every event is determined by previous events in such a way that, if the previous events are as they are, it is impossible that the subsequent event should not be as it is. If this was the only general principle valid as to causality, however, we should not be able to accept as valid any of the laws of science which deal with causation. For these are all general laws, which assert that whatever has a particular quality produces an effect with a particular quality. Thus it is said that all alcohol, taken in large quantities, produces intoxication. But claret differs from whisky, and the effects produced by drinking them are not completely alike, nor are the effects exactly the same with all men. In order to have any warrant for such generalizations we need the additional principle that for a quality, B, in an effect, there is always a quality A in the cause, of such a nature that every other cause which has the quality A produces an effect having the quality B. In other

words, the knowledge that exactly similar causes will produce exactly similar effects has no practical utility, since we could never know two causes to be exactly similar, even if it were possible that they should be so. What is required is the knowledge that partially similar causes will produce partially similar effects.

I do not propose to consider whether Causality and the Uniformity of Nature are valid of events other than volitions. To deny that they had any validity at all would involve almost complete scepticism, since no expectation of any future event would have the least justification, and all arguments for the existence of anything not perceived at the moment would be absolutely baseless. The indeterminist does not, as a rule, deny that all events except volitions must be completely determined by previous events. Indeed, all his arguments as to the goodness or badness of particular volitions imply that such volitions will result in consequences which will inevitably follow from them, unless interfered with by fresh volitions. He only maintains that volitions are not subject to the law of Causality in so far as to be themselves completely determined. It is this view which I propose to discuss in this chapter.

Some persons, no doubt, are indeterminists as to the will, because they reject the law of Causality altogether, and are indeterminists as to everything. But this position has not sufficient influence on religious thought in general to be of importance for our present purpose.

Determinists, on the other hand, maintain that our volitions are as completely determined as all other events. From this it is generally, and I think correctly, held to follow that it would be ideally possible to deduce the whole of the future course of events from the present state of reality — though, of course, a mind enormously more powerful than ours would be required to do it.

6. We have now to consider the arguments advanced by indeterminists in favour of their contention that volitions are not completely determined. These arguments may be brought under five heads. Firstly, it may be asserted that I have an immediate certainty of the proposition that my will is free. Secondly, that each volition is accompanied by a feeling of freedom in volition, and that this cannot be accounted for except on the supposition that the will is free. Thirdly, that with those volitions which are recognized by us morally right or wrong is connected a judgment of moral obligation, which cannot be accounted for except on the supposition that the will is free. Fourthly, that the freedom of the will must be true, because its falsity would make all choice absurd. Fifthly, that it must be true, because of the disastrous consequences which would follow if it were not true. . . .

CARL GUSTAV JUNG

CARL GUSTAV JUNG (1875-1961), the son of a philologist and minister, was born in Kesswyl, Switzerland, on July 26, 1875 and died in Küsnacht, Switzerland, on June 6, 1961. His educational training was in medicine which he acquired at the University of Basle. Subsequently, owing to his appointment as assistant in the celebrated Burghölzli Hospital in Zurich, he cultivated the association of the famed Bleuler and Janet. From 1900 to 1909, he was active in the psychiatric clinic at the University of Zurich, and from 1905 to 1913, a Lecturer in Psychology at that institution. His association with Freud was initiated through correspondence as early as 1906, eventuating in his becoming the first president of the International Psychoanalytical Association in 1910, but lasted only until 1914 when Jung terminated his association with both Freud and the society by creating his own school of Analytical Psychology.

Jungian Analytical Psychology is one of the few schools which stands resolute on the theory that the human soul exists as an empirically verified reality. The selection chosen characteristic of this Jungian contention is from his **Modern Man in Search of a Soul** (1933). Of his voluminous works, the following (in addition to the one mentioned) are the more influential: **Analytical Psychology** (1916), **Collected Papers on Analytical Psychology** (1917), **Studies in Word Association** (1918), **Psychology of the Unconscious** (1925), **Contributions to Analytical Psychology** (1928), **Psychological Types** (1933), **Psychology and Religion** (1938), **The Integration of Personality** (1939), **Essays on a Science of Mythology** (1949), **Psychological Reflections** (1953), **Answer to Job** (1954), **The Interpretation of Nature and the Psyche** (1956), **The Undiscovered Self** (1958), **Psyche and Symbol** (1958).

Unlike his colleagues of the Psychoanalytical School, Jung believes in a "psychology with a soul." This conclusion he maintains is obligatory on the psychologist due to unmistakable data obtained from clinical treatment, aetiology, and symptoms of neuroses. A neurosis is an ailment which, although purely psychic in cause and nature, produces symptoms which are physical, that is to say, physical ailments caused by psychic factors and cured psychically or spiritually. Psychosomatic ailments indicate a psyche, a soul. To deny this fact is to ignore data in clinical psychotherapy.

46

CARL GUSTAV JUNG

Psychological Science Discovers a Soul[1]

Investigation, however, has established beyond a doubt that the crux of the psycho-neuroses is to be found in the psychic factor; that this is the essential cause of the pathological state, and must therefore be recognized in its own right along with other admitted pathogenic factors such as inheritance, disposition, bacterial infection, and so forth. All attempts to explain the psychic factor in terms of more elementary physical factors were doomed to failure. There was more promise in the attempt to delimit the psychic factor by the concept of the drive or instinct — a concept taken over from biology. It is well known that instincts are observable physiological urges which are traceable to the functioning of the glands, and that, as experience shows, they condition or influence psychic processes. What could seem more plausible, therefore, than to seek the specific cause of the psycho-neuroses, not in the mystical notion of the "soul," but in a disturbance of the impulses which might possibly be curable in the last resort by medicinal treatment of the glands? As a matter of fact, this is Freud's standpoint when establishing his well-known theory which explains the neuroses in terms of disturbances of the sexual impulse. Adler likewise resorts to the concept of the drive, and explains the neuroses in terms of disturbances of the urge to power. We must admit, indeed, that this concept is further removed from physiology, and is of a more psychic nature than that of the sexual drive.

The concept of instinct is anything but well defined in the scientific sense. It applies to a biological manifestation of great complexity, and is not much more than a notion of quite indefinite content standing for an unknown quantity. I do not wish to enter here upon a critical discussion of the concept of instinct. Instead I will consider the possibility that the psychic factor is just a combination of instincts which for their

[1] From *Modern Man in Search of a Soul* by Carl G. Jung. Reprinted by permission of Harcourt, Brace & World, Inc.

part may again be reduced to the functioning of the glands. We may even discuss the possibility that everything that is usually called psychic is embraced in the sum-total of instincts, and that the psyche itself is therefore only an instinct or a conglomerate of instincts, being in the last analysis nothing but the functioning of the glands. A psycho-neurosis would thus be a glandular disease. This statement, however, has not been proved, and no glandular extract that will cure a neurosis has as yet been found. On the other hand, we have been taught by all too many mistakes that organic medicine fails completely in the treatment of neuroses, while psychic methods cure them. These psychic methods are just as effective as we might suppose the glandular extracts would be. So far, then, as our present experience goes, neuroses are to be influenced or cured by considering them, not from the side of their irreducible elements, the glandular secretions, but from that of psychic activity, which must be taken as a reality. For example, a suitable explanation or a comforting word to the patient may have something like a healing effect which may even influence the glandular secretions. The doctor's words, to be sure, are "only" vibrations in the air, yet they constitute a particular set of vibrations corresponding to a particular psychic state in the doctor. The words are effective only in so far as they convey a meaning or have significance. It is their meaning which is effective. But "meaning" is something mental or spiritual. Call it a fiction if you like. None the less it enables us to influence the course of the disease in a far more effective way than with chemical preparations. We can even influence the biochemical processes of the body by it. Whether the fiction rises in me spontaneously, or reaches me from without by way of human speech, it can make me ill or cure me. Nothing is surely more intangible and unreal than fictions, illusions and opinions; yet nothing is more effective in the psychic and even the psychophysical realm.

It was by recognizing these facts that science discovered the psyche, and we are now in honour bound to admit its reality. It has been shown that the drive, or instinct, is a condition of psychic activity, while at the same time the psychic processes seem to condition the instincts.

It is no reproach to the Freudian and Adlerian theories that they are based upon the drives; the only trouble is that they are one-sided. The kind of psychology they represent leaves out the psyche, and is suited to people who believe that they have no spiritual needs or aspirations. In this matter both the doctor and the patient deceive themselves. Although the theories of Freud and Adler come much nearer to getting at the bottom of the neuroses than does any earlier approach to the question from the side of medicine, they still fail, because of their exclusive concern with the drives, to satisfy the deeper spiritual needs of the patient. They are still bound by the premises of nineteenth-century science, and they are too self-evident — they give too little value to fictional and imaginative processes. In a word, they do not give meaning enough to life. And it is only the meaningful that sets us free.

Everyday reasonableness, sound human judgments, and science as a compendium of common sense, certainly help us over a good part of the road; yet they do not go beyond that frontier of human life which surrounds the commonplace and matter-of-fact, the merely average and normal. They afford, after all, no answer to the question of spiritual suffering and its innermost meaning. A psycho-neurosis must be understood as the suffering of a human being who has not discovered what life means for him. But all creativeness in the realm of the spirit as well as every psychic advance of man arises from a state of mental suffering, and it is spiritual stagnation, psychic sterility, which causes this state.

The doctor who realizes this truth sees a territory opened before him which he approaches with the greatest hesitation. He is now confronted with the necessity of conveying to his patient the healing fiction, the meaning that quickens — for it is this that the patient longs for, over and above all that reason and science can give him. The patient is looking for something that will take possession of him and give meaning and form to the confusion of his neurotic mind.

Is the doctor equal to this task? To begin with, he will probably hand over his patient to the clergyman or the philosopher, or abandon him to that perplexity which is the special note of our day. As a doctor he is not required to have a finished outlook on life, and his professional conscience does not demand it of him. But what will he do when he sees only too clearly why his patient is ill; when he sees that it arises from his having no love, but only sexuality; no faith, because he is afraid to grope in the dark; no hope, because he is disillusioned by the world and by life; and no understanding, because he has failed to read the meaning of his own existence?

Part Six: IMMORTALITY

The Survival of the Soul

JOSEPH BUTLER

JOSEPH BUTLER (1692-1752), an Anglican Divine, Bishop of Durham, England, was born on May 18, 1692 at Wantage, Berkshire. His training was at Oriel College, Oxford, after which he was appointed Preacher at Rolls Chapel, a post he occupied until 1726, and where he delivered the sermons which found him a permanent place in the field of ethics as a Classical Intuitionist. The addresses were published under the title, **Fifteen Sermons Preached at the Rolls Chapel** (1726).

In 1736, he was made prebendary of Rochester, and later the same year clerk of the closet to the queen; it was during this tenure that he published his classic, **The Analogy of Religion** (1736), from which the present text has excerpted his famous argument for immortality by analogy. Butler, a Deist and life-time bachelor, died on June 16, 1752 at Bath; his interment was at Bristol Cathedral, where Southy wrote his epitaph.

Confident that natural law and revelation operate harmoniously together, Butler is of the belief that a synthesis of conscience and self-interest combine compatibly to establish grounds of moral responsibility.

His **Analogy of Religion** is deemed by him sufficient proof to establish belief in immortality. Essentially, it depicts various analogies in nature, such as the caterpillar changing into a butterfly, as proof that at death it is possible for the human body to assume a new one, thereby surviving to a future life.

48

JOSEPH BUTLER

The Argument from Analogy[1]

Let us consider what the analogy of nature, and the several changes which we have undergone and those which we know we may undergo without being destroyed, suggest as to the effect which death may or may not have upon us; and whether it be not from thence probable that we may survive this change and exist in a future state of life and perception.

I. From our being born into the present world in the helpless imperfect state of infancy and having arrived from then to mature age, we find it to be a general law of nature in our own species that the same creatures, the same individuals, should exist in degrees of life and perception, with capacities of action, enjoyment and suffering in one period of their being greatly different from those appointed them in another period of it. And in other creatures the same law holds. For the difference of their capacities and states of life at their birth (to go no higher) and in maturity — the change of worms into flies and the vast enlargement of their locomotive powers by such change; and birds and insects bursting the shell, their habitation, and by this means entering into a new world, furnished with new accommodations for them, and finding a new sphere of action assigned them: these are instances of this general law of nature. Thus all the various and wonderful transformations of animals are to be taken into consideration here. But the states of life in which we ourselves existed formerly, in the womb and in our infancy, are almost as different from our present, in mature age, as it is possible to conceive any two states or degrees of life can be. Therefore, that we are to exist hereafter in a state as different (suppose) from our present as this is from our former is but according to the analogy of nature — according to a natural order or appointments of the very same kind as what we have already experienced.

[1] Joseph Butler, *Analogy of Religion* (1736); excerpts from part I, ch. 1.

II. We know we are endued with capacities of action, of happiness and misery, for we are conscious of acting, of enjoying pleasure and suffering pain. Now, that we have these powers and capacities before death is a presumption that we shall retain them through and after death, indeed a probability of it sufficient to act upon, unless there be some positive reason to think that death is the destruction of those living powers — because there is in every case a probability that all things will continue as we experience they are, in all respects except those in which we have some reason to think they will be altered. This is that kind of presumption or probability from analogy, expressed in the very word *continuance,* which seems our only natural reason for believing the course of the world will continue tomorrow as it has done so far as our experience or knowledge of history can carry us back. Nay, it seems our only reason for believing that any one substance now existing will continue to exist a moment longer — the self-existent substance only excepted. Thus, if men were assured that the unknown event, death, was not the destruction of our faculties of perception and of action, there would be no apprehension that any other power or event unconnected with this of death would destroy their faculties just at the instant of each creature's death — and therefore no doubt that they would remain after it; which shows the high probability that our living powers will continue after death, unless there be some ground to think that death is their destruction. For if it would be in a manner certain that we should survive death, provided it were certain that death would not be our destruction, it must be highly probable that we shall survive it if there be no ground to think death will be our destruction.

Now though I think it must be acknowledged that prior to the natural and moral proofs of a future life commonly insisted upon, there would arise a general confused suspicion that in the great shock and alteration which we shall undergo by death we (that is, our living powers) might be wholly destroyed; yet even prior to these proofs there is really no particular distinct ground or reason for this apprehension at all, so far as I can find. If there be, it must arise either from *the reason of the thing* or from *the analogy of Nature.*

But we cannot argue from *the reason of the thing* that death is the destruction of living agents, because we know not at all what death is in itself, but only some of its effects, such as the dissolution of flesh, skin and bones. And these effects do in no wise appear to imply the destruction of a living agent. And besides, as we are greatly in the dark upon what the exercise of our living powers depends, so we are wholly ignorant what the powers themselves depend upon — the powers themselves as distinguished not only from their actual exercise but also from the present capacity of exercising them, and as opposed to their destruction: for sleep or . . . a swoon shows us not only that these powers exist when they are not exercised but shows also that they exist when there is no present capacity of exercising them, or that the capacities of exercising them for the present, as well as the actual exercise of them, may be suspended and yet the powers themselves remain undestroyed. Since then, we know not at all upon what the existence of our living powers depends, this shows farther there can no probability be collected from the reason of the thing that death will be their destruction; because their existence may depend upon something in no degree affected by death — upon something quite out of the reach of this king of terrors — so that there is nothing more certain than that *the reason of the thing* shows us no connection between death and the destruction of living agents. Nor can we find anything throughout the whole *analogy of Nature* to afford us even the slightest presumption that animals ever lose their living powers, much less, if it were possible, that they lose them by death; for we have no faculties wherewith to trace any beyond or through it, so as to see what becomes of them. This event removes them from our view. It destroys the *perceptible* proof which we had before their death of their being possessed of living powers, but does not appear to afford the least reason to believe that they are then, or by that event, deprived of them.

And our knowing that they were possessed of these powers, up to the very period to which we have faculties capable of tracing them, is itself a probability of their retaining them beyond it. And this is confirmed, and a sensible credibility is given to it, by observing the very great and astonishing changes which we have experienced; so great that our existence in another state of life, of perception and of action will be but according to a method of providential conduct the like to which has been already exercised even with regard to ourselves according to a course of nature the like to which we have already gone through.

However, as one cannot but be greatly sensible how difficult it is to silence imagination enough to make the voice of reason even distinctly heard in this case, as we are accustomed from our youth up to indulge that forward delusive faculty ever obtruding beyond its sphere — of some assistance indeed to apprehension, but the author of all error, as we plainly lose ourselves in gross and crude conceptions of things, taking for granted that we are acquainted with what, indeed, we are wholly ignorant of — it may be proper to consider the imaginary presumptions that death will be our destruction arising from these kinds of early and lasting prejudices, and to show how little they can really amount to, even though we cannot wholly divest ourselves of them. And:

I. All presumption of death's being the destruction of living beings must go upon supposition that they are compounded and so dissoluble; but since consciousness is a single and indivisible power it should seem that the subject in which it resides must be so too. For were the motion of any particle of matter absolutely one and indivisible so that it should imply a contradiction to suppose part of this motion to exist and part not to exist — that is, part of this matter to move and part to be at rest — then its power of motion would be indivisible and so also would the subject in which the power inheres, namely the particle of matter; for if this could be divided into two, one part might be moved and the other at rest, which is contrary to the supposition. In like manner it has been argued, and, for anything appearing to the contrary, justly, that since the perception or consciousness which we have of our own existence is indivisible, so as that it is a contradiction to suppose one part of it should be here and the other there, the perceptive power or the power of consciousness is indivisible too, and consequently the subject in which it resides, that is, the conscious being. Now upon supposition that the living agent each man calls himself is thus a single being, which there is at least no more difficulty in conceiving than in conceiving it to be a compound, and of which there is the proof now mentioned, it follows that our organized bodies are no more ourselves or part of ourselves than any other matter around us. And it is as easy to conceive how matter, which is no part of ourselves, may be appropriated to us in the manner which our present bodies are, as how we can receive impressions from and have power over any matter. It is as easy to conceive that we may exist out of bodies as in them; that we might have animated bodies of any other organs and senses wholly different from these now given us and that we may hereafter animate these same or new bodies variously modified and organized; as to conceive how we can animate such bodies as our present. And lastly, the dissolution of all these several organized bodies, supposing ourselves to have successively animated them, would have no more conceivable tendency to destroy the living beings, ourselves, or deprive us of living faculties, the faculties of perception and action, than the dissolution of any foreign matter, which we are capable of receiving impressions from and making use of for the common occasions of life.

49

JOHN STUART MILL

The Possibility of Immortality[1]

The indications of immortality may be considered in two divisions: those which are independent of any theory respecting the Creator and his intentions, and those which depend upon an antecedent belief on that subject.

Of the former class of arguments speculative men have in different ages put forward a considerable variety, of which those in the *Phaedon* of Plato are an example; but they are for the most part such as have no adherents and need not be seriously refuted now. They are generally founded upon preconceived theories as to the nature of the thinking principle in man, considered as distinct and separable from the body, and on other preconceived theories respecting death. As, for example, that death or dissolution is always a separation of parts; and the soul being without parts, being simple and indivisible, is not susceptible of this separation. Curiously enough, one of the interlocutors in the *Phaedon* anticipates the answer by which an objector of the present day would meet this argument: namely, that thought and consciousness, though mentally distinguishable from the body, may not be a substance separable from it, but a result of it; standing in a relation to it (the illustration is Plato's) like that of a tune to the musical instrument on which it is played, and that the arguments used to prove that the soul does not die with the body would equally prove that the soul does not die with the instrument but survives its destruction and continues to exist apart. In fact, those moderns who dispute the evidences of the immortality of the soul do not, in general, believe the soul to be a substance *per se*, but regard it as the name of a bundle of attributes — the attributes of feeling, thinking, reasoning, believing, willing etc.; and these attributes they regard as a consequence of the bodily organization, which therefore,

[1] John Stuart Mill, *Three Essays on Religion* (1875, 4th ed.); from the essay *Theism,* the section entitled: "Immortality."

they argue, it is as unreasonable to suppose surviving when that organization is dispersed as to suppose the color or odor of a rose surviving when the rose itself has perished. Those, therefore, who would deduce the immortality of the soul from its own nature have first to prove that the attributes in question are not attributes of the body but of a separate substance. Now what is the verdict of science on this point? It is not perfectly conclusive either way. In the first place, it does not prove, experimentally, that any mode of organization has the power of producing feeling or thought. To make that proof good it would be necessary that we should be able to produce an organism, and try whether it would feel; which we cannot do; organisms cannot by any human means be produced, they can only be developed out of a previous organism for its immediate antecedent or accompaniment; that the specific variations and especially the different degrees of complication of the nervous and cerebral organization correspond to differences in the development of the mental faculties; and though we have no evidence, except negative, that the mental consciousness ceases forever when the functions of the brain are at an end, we do know that diseases of the brain disturb the mental functions and that decay or weakness of the brain enfeebles them. We have therefore sufficient evidence that cerebral action is, if not the cause, at least, in our present state of existence, a condition *sine qua non* of mental operations; and that assuming the mind to be a distinct substance, its separation from the body would not be, as some have vainly flattered themselves, a liberation from trammels and restoration of freedom, but would simply put a stop to its functions and remand it to unconsciousness unless and until some other set of conditions supervenes, capable of recalling it into activity, but of the existence of which experience does not give us the smallest indication.

At the same time it is of importance to remark that these considerations only amount to defect of evidence; they afford no positive argument against immortality. We must beware of giving *a priori* validity to the conclusions of an *a posteriori* philosophy. The root of all *a priori* thinking is the tendency to transfer to outward things a strong association between the corresponding ideas in our own minds; and the thinkers who most sincerely attempt to limit their beliefs by experience, and honestly believe that they do so, are not always sufficiently on their guard against this mistake. There are thinkers who regard it as a truth of reason that miracles are impossible; and in like manner there are others who, because the phenomena of life and consciousness are associated in their minds by undeviating experience with the action of material organs, think it an absurdity *per se* to imagine it possible that those phenomena can exist under any other conditions. But they should remember that the uniform coexistence of one fact with another does not make the one fact a part of the other, or the same with it. The relation of thought to a material brain is no metaphysical necessity, but simply a constant coexistence within the limits of observation. And when analyzed to the bottom on the principles of the associative psychology, the brain just as much as the mental functions is, like matter itself, merely a set of human sensations either actual or inferred as possible, namely, those which the anatomist has when he opens the skull, and impressions which we suppose we should receive of molecular or some other movements when the cerebral action was going on if there were no bony envelope and our senses or our instruments were sufficiently delicate. Experience furnishes us with no example of any series of states of consciousness without this group of contingent sensations attached to it; but it is as easy to imagine such a series of states without, as with, this accompaniment, and we know of no reason in the nature of things against the possibility of its being thus disjoined. We may suppose that the same thoughts, emotions, volitions, and even sensations which we have here may persist or recommence somewhere else under other conditions, just as we may suppose that other thoughts and sensations may exist under other conditions in other parts of the universe. And in entertaining this supposition we need not be embarrassed by any metaphysical difficulties about a thinking substance. Substance is but a general name for the perdurability of attributes: wherever there is a series of thoughts connected together by memories, that constitutes a thinking substance. This absolute distinction in thought and separability in representation of our states of consciousness from the set of conditions with which they are united only by constancy of concomitance is equivalent in a practical point of view to the old distinction of the two substances — matter and mind.

There is, therefore, in science no evidence against the immortality of the soul but that negative evidence which consists in the absence of evidence in its favor. And even the negative evidence is not so strong as negative evidence often is. In the case of witchcraft, for instance, the fact that there is no proof which will stand examination of its having ever existed is as conclusive as the most positive evidence of its nonexistence would be; for it exists, if it does exist, on this earth, where if it had existed the evidence of fact would certainly have been available to prove it. But it is not so as to the soul's existence after death. That it does not remain on earth and go about visibly or interfere in the events of life is proved by the same weight of evidence which disproves witchcraft. But that it does not exist elsewhere, there is absolutely no proof. A very faint, if any, presumption is all that is afforded by its disappearance from the surface of this planet.

Some may think that there is an additional and very strong presumption against the immortality of the thinking and conscious principle from the analysis of all the other objects of nature. All things in nature perish, the most beautiful and perfect being, as philosophers and poets alike complain, the most perishable. A flower of the most exquisite form and coloring grows up from a root, comes to perfection in weeks or months, and lasts only a few hours or days. Why should it be otherwise with man? Why indeed? But why, also, should it *not* be otherwise? Feeling and thought are not merely different from what we call inanimate matter, but are at the opposite pole of existence, and analogical inference has little or no validity from the one to the other. Feeling and thought are much more real than anything else; they are the only things which we directly know to be real, all things else being merely the unknown conditions on which these, in our present state of existence or in some other, depend. All matter apart from the feelings of sentient beings has but a hypothetical and unsubstantial existence; it is a mere assumption to account for our sensations; itself we do not perceive, we are not conscious of it, but only of the sensations which we are said to receive from it: in reality it is a mere name for our expectation of sensations or for our belief that we can have certain sensations when certain other sensations give indication of them. Because these contingent possibilities of sensation sooner or later come to an end and give place to others, is it implied in this, that the series of our feelings must itself be broken off? This would not be to reason from one kind of substantive reality to another, but to draw from something which has no reality except in reference to something else, conclusions applicable to that which is the only substantive reality. Mind (or whatever name we give to what is implied in consciousness of a continued series of feelings) is in a philosophical point of view the only reality of which we have any evidence, and no analogy can be recognized or comparison made between it and other realities because there are no other known realities to compare it with. That is quite consistent with its being perishable; but the question whether it is so or not is *res integra,* untouched by any of the results of human knowledge and experience. The case is one of those very rare cases in which there is really a total absence of evidence on either side, and in which the absence of evidence for the affirmative does not, as in so many cases it does, create a strong presumption in favor of the negative.

The belief, however, in human immortality, in the minds of mankind generally, is probably not grounded on any scientific arguments either physical or metaphysical, but on foundations with most minds much stronger, namely, on one hand, the disagreeableness of giving up existence (to those at least to whom it has hitherto been pleasant), and on the other hand, the general traditions of mankind. The natural tendency of belief to follow these two inducements — our own wishes and the general assent of other people — has been in this instance reinforced by the utmost exertion of the power of public and private teaching; rulers and instructors having at all times, with the view of giving greater effect to their mandates, whether from selfish or from public motives, encouraged to the utmost of their power the belief that there is a life after death in which pleasures and sufferings far greater than on earth depend on our doing or leaving undone while alive what we are commanded to do in the name of the unseen powers. As causes of belief these various circumstances are most powerful. As rational grounds of it they carry no weight at all.

That what is called the consoling nature of an opinion — that is, the pleasure we should have in believing it to be true — can be a ground for believing it, is a doctrine irrational in itself and which would sanction half the mischievous illusions recorded in history or which mislead individual life. It is sometimes, in the case now under consideration, wrapped up in a quasi-scientific language. We are told that the desire of immortality is one of our instincts, and that there is no instinct which has not corresponding to it a real object fitted to satisfy it. Where there is hunger there is somewhere food, where there is a sexual feeling there is somewhere sex, where there is love there is somewhere something to be loved, and so forth: in like manner, since there is the instinctive desire of eternal life, eternal life there must be. The answer to this is patent on the very surface of the subject. It is unnecessary to go into any recondite considerations concerning instincts, or to discuss whether the desire in question is an instinct or not. Granting that wherever there is an instinct there exists something such as that instinct demands, can it be affirmed that this something exists in boundless quantity or sufficient to satisfy the infinite craving of human desires? What is called the desire of eternal life is simply the desire of life; and does there not exist that which this desire calls for? Is there not life? And is not the instinct, if it be an instinct, gratified by the possession and preservation of life? To suppose that the desire of life guarantees to us personally the reality of life through all eternity is like supposing that the desire of food assures us that we shall always have as much as we can eat through our whole lives and as much longer as we can conceive our lives to be protracted to.

The argument from tradition or the general belief of the human race, if we accept it as a guide to our own belief, must be accepted entire: if so, we are bound to believe that the souls of human beings not only survive after death but show themselves as ghosts to the living; for we find no people who have had the one belief without the other. Indeed it is probable that the former belief originated in the latter, and that primitive men would never have supposed that the soul did not die with the body if they had not fancied that it visited them after death. Nothing could be more natural than such a fancy; it is, in appearance, completely realized in dreams, which in Homer and in all ages like Homer's are supposed to be real apparitions. To dreams we have to add not merely waking hallucinations, but the delusions, however baseless, of sight and hearing, or rather the misinterpretations of those senses: sight and hearing supplying mere hints from which imagination paints a complete picture and invests it with reality. These delusions are not to be judged of by a modern standard; in early times the line between imagination and perception was by no means clearly defined; there was little or none of the knowledge we now possess of the actual course of nature, which makes us distrust or disbelieve any appearance which is at variance with known laws. In the ignorance of men as to what were the limits of nature and what was or was not compatible with it, no one thing seemed, as far as physical considerations went, to be much more improbable than another. In rejecting, therefore, as we do, and as we have the best reason to do, the tales and legends of the actual appearance of disembodied spirits, we take from under the general belief of mankind in a life after death what in all probability was its chief ground and support and deprive it of even the very little value which the opinion of rude ages can ever have as evidence of truth. If it be said that this belief has maintained itself in ages which have ceased to be rude and which reject the superstitions with which it once was accompanied, the same may be said of many other opinions of rude ages, and especially on the most important and interesting subjects, because it is on those subjects that the reigning opinion whatever it may be, is the most sedulously inculcated upon all who are born into the world. This particular opinion, moreover, if it has on the whole kept its ground, has done so with a constantly increasing number of dissentients, and those especially among cultivated minds. Finally, those cultivated minds which adhere to the belief ground it, we may reasonably suppose, not on the belief of others, but on arguments and evidences; and those arguments and evidences, therefore, are what it concerns us to estimate and judge.

The preceding are a sufficient sample of the arguments for a future life which do not suppose an antecedent belief in the existence, or any theory respecting the attributes of the godhead. It remains to consider what arguments are supplied by such lights, or such grounds of conjecture, as natural theology affords on those great questions.

We have seen that these lights are but faint; that of the existence of

a Creator they afford no more than a preponderance of probability; of
his benevolence a considerably less preponderance; that there is, however, some reason to think that he cares for the pleasures of his creatures,
but by no means that this is his sole care, or that other purposes do not
often take precedence of it. His intelligence must be adequate to the
contrivance apparent in the universe, but need not be more than adequate
to them, and his power is not only proved to be infinite, but the only
real evidences in natural theology tend to show that it is limited, contrivance being a mode of overcoming difficulties, and always supposing
difficulties to be overcome.

We have now to consider what inference can legitimately be drawn
from these premises in favor of a future life. It seems to me, apart from
express revelation, none at all.

The common arguments are: the goodness of God; the improbability
that he would ordain the annihilation of his noblest and richest work
after the greater part of its few years of life had been spent in the acquisition of faculties which time is not allowed him to turn to fruit;
and the special improbability that he would have implanted in us an instinctive desire of eternal life and doomed that desire to complete disappointment.

These might be arguments in a world the constitution of which made
it possible without contradiction to hold it for the work of a Being at
once omnipotent and benevolent. But they are not arguments in a world
like that in which we live. The benevolence of the divine Being may be
perfect, but his power being subject to unknown limitations, we know
not that he could have given us what we so confidently assert that he
must have given — *could* (that is) without sacrificing something more
important. Even his benevolence, however justly inferred, is by no means
indicated as the interpretation of his whole purpose, and since we cannot tell how far other purposes may have interfered with the exercise of
his benevolence, we know not that he *would*, even if he could have
granted us eternal life. With regard to the supposed improbability of
his having given the wish without the gratification, the same answer
may be made; the scheme which either limitation of power or conflict of
purposes compelled him to adopt may have *required* that we should have
the wish although it were not destined to be gratified. One thing, however, is quite certain in respect to God's government of the world; that
he either could not, or would not, grant to us everything we wish. We
wish for life, and he has granted some life; that we wish (or some of us
wish) for a boundless extent of life and that it is not granted is no exception to the ordinary modes of his government. Many a man would like to
be a Croesus or an Augustus Caesar, but has his wishes gratified only to

the moderate extent of a pound a week or the secretaryship of his trades union. There is, therefore, no assurance whatever of a life after death on grounds of natural religion. But to anyone who feels it conducive either to his satisfaction or to his usefulness to hope for a future state as a possibility, there is no hindrance to his indulging that hope. Appearances point to the existence of a Being who has great power over us — all the power implied in the creation of the cosmos, or of its organized beings at least — and of whose goodness we have evidence though not of its being his predominant attribute; and as we do not know the limits either of his power or of his goodness, there is room to hope that both the one and the other may extend to granting us this gift provided that it would really be beneficial to us. The same ground which permits the hope warrants us in expecting that if there be a future life it will be at least as good as the present, and will not be wanting in the best feature of the present life — improvability by our own efforts. Nothing can be more opposed to every estimate we can form of probability than the common idea of the future life as a state of rewards and punishments in any other sense than that the consequences of our actions upon our own character and susceptibilities will follow us in the future as they have done in the past and present. Whatever be the probabilities *of* a future life, all the probabilities *in case of* a future life are that such as we have been made or have made ourselves before the change, such we shall enter into the life hereafter; and that the fact of death will make no sudden break in our spiritual life, nor influence our character any otherwise than as any important change in our mode of existence may always be expected to modify it. Our thinking principle has its laws which in this life are invariable, and any analogies drawn from this life must assume that the same laws will continue. To imagine that a miracle will be wrought at death by the act of God making perfect everyone whom it is his will to include among his elect, might be justified by an express revelation duty authenticated, but is utterly opposed to every presumption that can be deduced from the light of nature.

50

WILLIAM JAMES

Human Immortality[1]

Preface

So many critics have made one and the same objection to the doorway to immortality which my lecture claims to be left open by the "transmission-theory" of cerebral action, that I feel tempted, as the book is again going to press, to add a word of explanation.

If our finite personality here below, the objectors say, be due to the transmission through the brain of portions of a preëxisting larger consciousness, all that can remain after the brain expires is the larger consciousness itself as such, with which we should thenceforth be perforce reconfounded, the only means of our existence in finite personal form having ceased.

But this, the critics continue, is the pantheistic idea of immortality, survival, namely, in the soul of the world; not the Christian idea of immortality, which means survival in strictly personal form.

In showing the possibility of a mental life after the brain's death, they conclude, the lecture has thus at the same time shown the impossibility of its identity with the personal life, which is the brain's function.

Now I am myself anything but a pantheist of the monistic pattern; yet for simplicity's sake I did in the lecture speak of the "mother-sea" in terms that must have sounded pantheistic, and suggested that I thought of it myself as a unit . . . . I even added that future lecturers might prove the loss of some of our personal limitations after death not to be matter for absolute regret. The interpretation of my critics was therefore not unnatural; and I ought to have been more careful to guard against its being made.

[1] William James, *Human Immortality* (1898). The preface is from the second edition; the original was the Ingersoll Lecture.

. . . I partially guarded against it by saying that the "mother-sea" from which the finite mind is supposed to be strained by the brain, need not be conceived of in pantheistic terms exclusively. There might be, I said, many minds behind the scenes as well as one. The plain truth is that *one may conceive the mental world behind the veil in as individualistic a form as one pleases, without any detriment to the general scheme by which the brain is represented as a transmissive organ.*

If the extreme individualistic view were taken, one's finite mundane consciousness would be an extract from one's larger, truer personality, the latter having even now some sort of reality behind the scenes. And in transmitting it — to keep to our extremely mechanical metaphor, which confessedly throws no light on the actual *modus operandi* — one's brain would also leave effects upon the part remaining behind the veil; for when a thing is torn, both fragments feel the operation.

And just as (to use a very coarse figure) the stubs remain in a check-book whenever a check is used, to register the transaction, so these impressions on the transcendent self might constitute so many vouchers of the finite experiences of which the brain had been the mediator; and ultimately they might form that collection within the larger self of memories of our earthly passage, which is all that, since Locke's day, the continuance of our personal identity beyond the grave has by psychology been recognized to mean.

It is true that all this would seem to have affinities rather with pre-existence and with possible re-incarnations that with the Christian notion of immortality. But my concern in the lecture was not to discuss immortality in general. It was confined to showing it to be *not incompatible* with the brain-function theory of our present mundane consciousness. I hold that it is so compatible, and compatible moreover in fully individualized form. The reader would be in accord with everything that the text of my lecture intended to say, were he to assert that every memory and affection of his present life is to be preserved, and that he shall never in *saecula saeculorum* cease to be able to say to himself: "I am the same personal being who in old times upon the earth had those experiences."

Human Immortality

. . . In the hour that lies before us, then, I shall seek to justify my appointment by offering what seem to me two such grains of truth, two points well fitted, if I am not mistaken, to combine with anything that other lecturers may bring.

These points are both of them in the nature of replies to objections, to difficulties which our modern culture finds in the old notion of a life hereafter, — difficulties that I am sure rob the notion of much of its old power to draw belief, in the scientifically cultivated circles to which this audience belong.

The first of these difficulties is relative to the absolute dependence of our spiritual life, as we know it here, upon the brain. One hears not only physiologists, but numbers of laymen who read the popular science books and magazines, saying all about us, How can we believe in life hereafter when Science has once for all attained to proving, beyond possibility of escape, that our inner life is a function of that famous material, the so-called 'gray matter' of our cerebral convolutions? How can the function possibly persist after its organ has undergone decay?

Thus physiological psychology is what is supposed to bar the way to the old faith. And it is now as a physiological psychologist that I ask you to look at the question with me a little more closely.

It is indeed true that physiological science has come to the conclusion cited; and we must confess that in so doing she has only carried out a little farther the common belief of mankind. Every one knows that arrests of brain development occasion imbecility, that blows on the head abolish memory or consciousness, and that brain-stimulants and poisons change the quality of our ideas. The anatomists, physiologists, and pathologists have only shown this generally admitted fact of a dependence to be detailed and minute. What the laboratories and hospitals have lately been teaching us is not only that thought in general is one of the brain's functions, but that the various special forms of thinking are functions of special portions of the brain. When we are thinking of things seen, it is our occipital convolutions that are active; when of things heard, it is a certain portion of our temporal lobes; when of things to be spoken, it is one of our frontal convolutions. Professor Flechsig of Leipzig (who perhaps more than any one may claim to have made the subject his own) considers that in other special convolutions those processes of association go on, which permit the more abstract of thought, to take place. I could easily show you these regions if I had here a picture of the brain. Moreover, the diminished or exaggerated associations of what this author calls the *Körperfühlsphäre* with the other regions, accounts, according to him, for the complexion of our emotional life, and eventually decides whether one shall be a callous brute or criminal, an unbalanced sentimentalist, or a character accessible to feeling, and yet well poised. Such special opinions may have to be corrected: yet so firmly established do the main positions worked out by the anatomists, physiologist, and pathologists of the brain appear, that the youth of our medical schools are everywhere taught unhesitatingly to believe them. The assurance that observation will go on to establish them ever more and more minutely is the inspirer of all contemporary research. And almost any of our young psychologists will tell you that only a few belated scholastics, or possibly some crack-brained theosophist or psychical researcher, can be found holding back, and still talking as if mental phenomena might exist as independent variables in the world.

For the purposes of my argument, now, I wish to adopt this general doctrine as if it were established absolutely, with no possibility of restriction. During this hour I wish you also to accept it as postulate, whether you think it incontrovertibly established or not; so I beg you to agree with me to-day in subscribing to the great psycho-physiological formula: *Thought is a function of the brain.*

The question is, then, Does this doctrine logically compel us to disbelieve in immortality? Ought it to force every truly consistent thinker to sacrifice his hopes of an hereafter to what he takes to be his duty of accepting all the consequences of a scientific truth?

Most persons imbued with what one may call the puritanism of science would feel themselves bound to answer this question with a yes. If any medically or psychologically bred young scientists feel otherwise, it is probably in consequence of the incoherence of mind of which the majority of mankind happily enjoy the privilege. At one hour scientists, at another they are Christians of common men, with the will to live burning hot in their breasts; and, holding thus the two ends of the chain, they are careless of the intermediate connection. But the more radical and uncompromising disciple of science makes the sacrifice, and, sorrowfully or not, according to his temperament, submits to giving up his hopes of heaven.

This, then, is the objection to immortality; and the next thing in order for me is to try to make plain to you why I believe that it has in strict logic no deterrent power. I must show you that the fatal consequence is not coercive, as is commonly imagined; and that, even though our soul's life (as here below it is revealed to us) may be in literal strictness the function of a brain that perishes, yet it is not at all impossible, but on the contrary quite possible, that life may still continue when the brain itself is dead.

The supposed impossibility of its continuing comes from too superficial a look at the admitted fact of function dependence. The moment we inquire more closely into the notion of functional dependence, and ask ourselves, for example, how many kinds of functional dependence there may be, we immediately perceive that there is one kind at least that does not exclude a life hereafter at all. The fatal conclusion of the physiologist flows from his assuming offhand another kind of functional dependence, and treating it as the only imaginable kind.

When the physiologist who thinks that his science cut off all hope of immortality pronounces the phrase, "Thought is a function of the brain," he thinks of the matter just as he thinks when he says, "Steam is function of the tea-kettle," "Light is a function of the electric circuit," "Power is a function of the moving waterfall." In these latter cases the several material objects have the function of inwardly creating or engendering their effects, and their function must be called *productive* function. Just so, he thinks, it must be with the brain. Engendering consciousness in its interior, much as it engenders cholesterin and creatin and carbonic acid, its relation to our soul's life must also be called productive function. Of course, if such a production be the function, then when the organ perishes, since the production can no longer continue, the soul must surely die. Such a conclusion as this is indeed inevitable from that particular conception of the facts.

But in the world of physical nature productive function of this sort is not the only kind of function with which we are familiar. We have also releasing or permissive function; and we have transmissive function.

The trigger of a crossbow has a releasing function: it removes the obstacle that holds the string, and lets the bow fly back to its natural shape. So when the hammer falls upon a detonating compound. By knocking out the inner molecular obstructions, it lets the constituent gases resume their normal bulk, and so permits the explosion to take place.

In the case of a colored glass, a prism, or a refracting lens, we have transmissive function. The energy of light, no matter how produced, is by the glass sifted and limited in color, and by the lens or prism determined to a certain path and shape. Similarly, the keys of an organ have only a transmissive function. They open successively the various pipes and let the wind in the air-chest escape in various ways. The voices of the various pipes are constituted by the columns of air trembling as they emerge. But the air is not engendered in the organ. The organ proper, as distinguished from its air-chest, is only an apparatus for letting portions of it loose upon the world in these peculiarly limited shapes.

My thesis now is this: that, when we think of the law that thought is a function of the brain, we are not required to think of productive function only; *we are entitled also to consider permissive or transmissive function.* And this the ordinary psychophysiologist leaves out of his account.

Suppose, for example, that the whole universe of material things — the furniture of earth and choir of heaven — should turn out to be a mere surface-veil of phenomena, hiding and keeping back the world of genuine realities. Such a supposition is foreign neither to common sense nor to philosophy. Common sense believes in realities behind the veil even too superstitiously; and idealistic philosophy declares the whole world of natural experience, as we get it, to be but a time-mask, shattering or refracting the one infinite Thought which is the sole reality into those millions of finite streams of consciousness known to us as our private selves.

> "Life, like a dome of many-colored glass,
> Stains the white radiance of eternity."

Suppose, now, that this were really so, and suppose, moreover, that the dome, opaque enough at all times to the full super-solar blaze, could at certain times and places grow less so, and let certain beams pierce through into this sublunary world. These beams would be so many finite rays, so to speak, of consciousness, and they would vary in quantity and quality as the opacity varied in degree. Only at particular times and places would it seem that, as a matter of fact, the veil of nature can grow thin and rupturable enough for such effects to occur. But in those places gleams, however finite and unsatisfying, of the absolute life of the universe, are from time to time vouchsafed. Glows of feeling, glimpses of insight, and streams of knowledge and perception float into our finite world.

Admit now that *our brains* are such thin and half-transparent places in the veil. What will happen? Why, as the white radiance comes through the dome, with all sorts of staining and distortion imprinted on it by the glass, or as the air now comes through my glottis determined and limited in its force and quality of its vibrations by the peculiarities of those vocal chords which form its gate of egress and shape it into my personal voice, even so the genuine matter of reality, the life of souls as it is in its fullness, will break through our several brains into this world in all sorts of restricted forms, and with all the imperfections and queernesses that characterize our finite individualities here below.

According to the state in which the brain finds itself, the barrier of its obstructiveness may also be supposed to rise or fall. It sinks so low, when the brain is in full activity, that a comparative flood of spiritual energy pours over. At other times, only such occasional waves of thought as heavy sleep permits get by. And when finally a brain stops acting altogether, or decays, that special stream of consciousness which it subserved will vanish entirely from this natural world. But the sphere of being that supplied the consciousness would still be intact; and in that more real world with which, even whilst here, it was continuous, the consciousness might, in ways unknown to us, continue still.

You see that, on all these suppositions, our soul's life, as we here know it, would none the less in literal strictness be the function of the brain. The brain would be the independent variable, the mind would vary dependently on it. But such dependence on the brain for this natural life would in no wise make immortal life impossible, — it might be quite compatible with supernatural life behind the veil hereafter.

As I said, then, the fatal consequence is not coercive, the conclusion which materialism draws being due solely to its onesided way of taking the word 'function.' And, whether we care or not for immortality in itself, we ought, as mere critics doing police duty among the vagaries of mankind, to insist on the illogicality of a denial based on the flat ignoring of a palpable alternative. How much more ought we to insist, as lovers of truth, when the denial is that of such a vital hope of mankind!

In strict logic, then, the fangs of cerebralistic materialism are drawn. My words ought consequently already to exert a releasing function on your hopes. You *may* believe henceforward, whether you care to profit by the permission or not. But, as this is a very abstract argument, I think it will help its effect to say a word or two about the more concrete conditions of the case.

All abstract hypotheses sound unreal; and the abstract notion that our brains are colored lenses in the wall of nature, admitting light from the super-solar source, but at the same time tingeing and restricting it, has a thoroughly fantastic sound. What is it, you may ask, but a foolish metaphor? And how can such a function be imagined? Isn't the common materialistic notion vastly simpler? Is not consciousness really more comparable to a sort of steam, or perfume, or electricity, or nerve-glow, generated on the spot in its own peculiar vessel? Is it not more rigorously scientific to treat the brain's function as function of production?

The immediate reply is, that, if we are talking of science positively understood, function can mean nothing more than bare concomitant variation. When the brain-activities change in one way, consciousness changes in another; when the currents pour through the occipital lobes, consciousness *sees* things; when through the lower frontal region, consciousness *says* things to itself; when they stop, she goes to sleep, etc. In strict science, we can only write down the bare fact of concomitance; and all talk about either production or transmission, as the mode of taking place, is pure superadded hypothesis, and metaphysical hypothesis at that, for we can frame no more notion of details on the one alternative than on the other. Ask for any indication of exact process either of transmission or of production, and Science confesses her imagination to be bankrupt. She has, so far, not the least glimmer of a conjecture or suggestion, — not even a bad verbal metaphor or pun to offer. *Ignoramus, ignorabimus,* is what most physiologists, in the words of one of their number, will say here. The production of such a thing as consciousness in the brain, they will reply with the late Berlin professor of physiology, is the absolute world-enigma, — something so paradoxical and abnormal as to be a stumbling block to Nature, and almost a self-contradiction. Into the mode of production of steam in a tea-kettle we have conjectural insight, for the terms that change are physically homogeneous one with another, and we can easily imagine the case to consist of nothing but alternations of molecular motion. But in the production of consciousness by the brain, the terms are heterogeneous natures altogether; and as far as our understanding goes, it is as great a miracle as if we said, Thought is 'spontaneously generated,' or 'created out of nothing.'

The theory of production is therefore not a jot more simple or credible in itself than any other conceivable theory. It is only a little more popular. All that one need do, therefore, if the ordinary materialist should challenge one to explain how the brain *can* be an organ for limiting and determining to a certain form a consciousnessness elsewhere produced, is to retort with a *tu quoque,* asking him in turn to explain how it can be an organ for producing consciousness out of whole cloth. For polemic purposes, the two theories are thus exactly on a par.

But if we consider the theory of transmission in a wider way, we see that it has certain positive superiorities, quite apart from its connection with the immortality question.

Just how the process of transmission may be carried on, is indeed unimaginable; but the outer relations, so to speak, of the process, encourage our belief. Consciousness in this process does not have to be generated *de novo* in a vast number of places. It exists already, behind the scenes, coeval with the world. The transmission-theory not only avoids in this way multiplying miracles, but it puts itself in touch with general idealistic philosophy better than the production-theory does. It should always be reckoned a good thing when science and philosophy thus meet.

It puts itself also in touch with the conception of a 'threshold,' — a word with which, since Fechner wrote his book called 'Psychophysik,' the so-called 'new Psychology' has rung. Fechner imagines as the condition of consciousness a certain kind of psycho-physical movement, as he terms it. Before consciousness can come, a certain degree of activity in the movement must be reached. This requisite degree is called the 'threshold;' but the height of the threshold varies under different circumstances: it may rise or fall. When it falls, as in states of great lucidity, we grow conscious of things of which we should be unconscious at other times; when it rises, as in drowsiness, consciousness sinks in amount. This rising and lowering of a psycho-physical threshold exactly conforms to our notion of a permanent obstruction to the transmission of consciousness, which obstruction may, in our brains, grow alternately greater or less.

The transmission-theory also puts itself in touch with a whole class of experiences that are with difficulty explained by the production-theory. I refer to those obscure and exceptional phenomena reported at all times throughout human history which the 'psychical-researchers,' with Mr. Frederic Myers at their head, are doing so much to rehabilitate; such phenomena, namely, as religious conversions, providential leadings in answer to prayer, instantaneous healings, premonitions, apparitions at time of death, clairvoyant visions or impressions, and the whole range of mediumistic capacities, to say nothing of still more exceptional and incomprehensible things. If all our human thought be a function of the brain, then of course, if any of these things are facts, — and to my own mind some of them are facts, — we may not suppose that they can occur without preliminary brain-action. But the ordinary production-theory of consciousness is knit up with a peculiar notion of how brain-action *can* occur, — that notion being that all brain-action without exception, is due to a prior action, immediate or remote, of the bodily sense-organs *on* the brain. Such action makes the brain produce sensations and mental images, and out of the sensations and images the higher forms of thought and knowledge in their turn are framed. As transmissionists, we also must admit this to be the condition of all our usual thought. Sense-action is what lowers the brain-barrier. My voice and aspect, for instance, strike upon your ears and eyes; your brain thereupon becomes more pervious, and an awareness on your part of what I say and who I am slips into this world from the world behind the veil. But, in the mysterious phenomena to which I allude, it is often hard to see where the sense-organs can come in. A medium, for example, will show knowledge of his sitter's private affairs which it seems impossible he should have acquired through sight or hearing, or inference therefrom. Or you will have an apparition of some one who is now dying hundreds of miles away. On the production-theory one does not see from what sensations such odd bits of knowledge are produced. On the transmission-theory, they don't have to be 'produced,' — they exist ready-made in the transcendental world, and all that is needed is an abnormal lowering of the brain-threshold to let them through. In cases of conversion, in providential leadings, sudden mental healings, etc., it seems to the subject themselves of the experience as if a power from without, quite different from the ordinary action of the senses or of the sense-led mind, came into their life, as if the latter suddenly opened into that greater life in which it has its source. The word 'influx,' used in Swedenborgian circles, well describes this impression of new insight, or new willingness, sweeping over us like a tide. All such experiences, quite paradoxical and meaningless on the production-theory, fall very naturally into place on the other theory. We need only suppose the continuity of our consciousness with a mother sea, to allow for exceptional waves occasionally pouring over the dam. Of course the causes of these odd lowerings of the brain's threshold still remain a mystery on any terms.

Add, then, to this advantage to the transmission-theory, — an advantage which I am well aware that some of you will not rate very high, — and also add the advantage of not conflicting with a life hereafter, and I hope you will agree with me that it has many points of superiority to the more familiar theory. It is a theory which, in the history of opinion on such matters has never been wholly left out of account, though never developed at any great length. In the great orthodox philosophic tradition, the body is treated as an essential condition to the soul's life in this world of sense; but after death, it is said, the soul is set free, and becomes a purely intellectual and nonappetitive being. Kant expresses this idea in terms that come singularly close to those of our transmission-theory. The death of the body, he says, may indeed be the end of the sensational use of our mind, but only the beginning of the intellectual use. "The body," he continues, "would thus be, not the cause of our thinking, but merely a condition restrictive thereof, and, although essential to our sensuous and animal consciousness, it may be regarded as an impeder of our pure spiritual life."[2] And in a recent book of great suggestiveness and power, less well-known as yet than it deserves, — I mean 'Riddles of the Sphinx,' by Mr. F.C.S. Schiller of Oxford, late of Cornell University, — the transmission-theory is defended at some length. . . .

[2] See *Kritik der reinen Vernunft*, second edition, p. 809.

FREDERICK ROBERT TENNANT

FREDERICK ROBERT TENNANT (1866-1961), influential British philosopher and theologian, was born in Burslem, Staffs, and educated at Caius College, Cambridge University, where, in 1906, he was granted the degree of Doctor of Divinity. He was ordained to the Anglican ministry in 1891, appointed chaplain of Caius College in 1897, and rector of Hockwold in 1903. The latter position he held until 1913 when he was appointed Lecturer in Philosophy and Theology, as well as a fellow of Trinity College, Cambridge. In 1935, he became a fellow of the British Academy, while his career at Cambridge extended to 1938.

His books consist of: **The Origin and Propagation of Sin** (1902), **The Sources of the Doctrine of the Fall and Original Sin** (1903), **The Concept of Sin** (1912), **Miracle and Its Philosophical Presuppositions** (1925), **Philosophy of the Sciences** (1932), **The Nature of Belief** (1943), and his classic **Philosophical Theology** (vol. I, 1928; vol. II, 1930) from which a discussion on the problem of evil, and another on immortality, have been excerpted.

Tennant, a Theist who employs the Teleological Argument to establish the being of God, argues for the existence of Deity on the basis of regularity and interdependence found in nature, knowledge, and value. Such facts are indicative of a Creator, both personal and good, who is responsible for the existence, purposive direction, and arrangements of reality.

Although Tennant believes in the presence of real individual natural evils, when taken as a whole, nature is good. Evils are necessary in the present world, otherwise the universe could not have been created on the basis of natural law; **e.g.,** water is good because it obeys natural law with invariable regularity, but it has the evil property of drowning a person, its irradicable and essential characteristic.

Immortality is based on the moral order of the world: since nature produces moral persons who must satisfy moral demands, then life must follow after death in order for man to fulfill his moral purposes, otherwise God would be unjust and the world inexplicable. Ultimately, the moral argument for immortality is based on the goodness or righteousness of God as the conserver of value.

51

FREDERICK ROBERT TENNANT

The Moral Argument for Immortality[1]

Arguments for and against human immortality, or life after death, may be classified thus:

I. Arguments not presupposing theism.
    (1)   Empirical.
    (2)   Metaphysical — *i.e.* ontological.
    (3)   Ethical.

II. Arguments presupposing theism, to the effect that immortality is, or is not, a corollary of theism.

1. (1) The form in which the question as to human immortality is usually propounded, viz. has man an immortal soul? tacitly assumes that the man is primarily his body. And there are doubtless reasons why this assumption should be ingrained in common thought leavened with science. Matter seems, to those who have not pursued philosophical inquiries, so much better known than mind or spirit, and mind seems to be so much more dependent upon body than changes in the body are dependent upon mental activities. But while science shews the close connexion between brain and thought it does not warrant the conclusion that the soul and its activities are products of the brain, and that they must vanish when the physical organism dies. The sensation with which we are acquainted is mediated by the body; but it is not a scientifically established fact that the kind of body which we now possess is essential for the soul's life and possession of personality. And there is no scientific reason for believing that the soul shares the change and decay of material things. Their dissolution is generally describable as resolution into parts; but the soul cannot be supposed to consist of separable parts, or to be an aggregate of mind-dust. For all that physiology knows, the soul may at death enter into connexion with another kind of body, about which, how-

[1] F. R. Tennant, *Philosophical Theology* (Cambridge: The University Press, 1928), vol. II, 269-272. Reprinted by permission.

ever, it is futile to speculate. It is possible that while the body that now is determines the nature of the soul's activities, sensations, etc., as we know them, it at the same time imposes limitations upon the potentialities of the soul; and that though the death of the body may put an end to sensation it may be the beginning of a non-sensible experience, or of an experience in which another kind of *rapport* than that which constitutes sensation is substituted for it. Empirical science, therefore, cannot infer, from the fact that the present life of the self is dependent on that of the present body, the impossibility of a future life of the soul. Science here leaves room for faith.

On the other hand, psychical research cannot be said as yet to have established the soul's survival of bodily death. The proofs which have been alleged are based chiefly on facts concerning what is called cross-reference: *i.e.* two independent mediums may write fragments, both series of which are meaningless by themselves but yield sense when pieced together. But communication from a disembodied spirit is not to be taken to be the only and the certain explanation of the facts until, e.g., telepathy of the living has been shewn to be inadmissible.

(2) Metaphysical arguments for the immortality of the soul, of several kinds, were put forth by Plato. One of these was based on the fancy that knowledge is reminiscence; others rest on the mistaken notion that knowledge is pure thought about pure essences, or is eternal and implies eternal knowers. Perhaps the most influential of them is that (in the *Phaedo*) which sets out from the assertion that the essence of the soul is life, whence it is concluded that the soul is essentially living. Of course, if the soul be defined as the reified abstraction, life, so to speak of a mortal soul involves self-contradiction; but, like all *a priori* proofs, this one assumes that the definition from which the desired consequent is deductible has application to anything that is actual.

Kant brought the same charge, amongst others, against the rational psychology of his day. This, proceeding on lines laid down by Descartes, deduced a *res cogitans* from the empirically given *cogito,* identified this *res* with substance, in the most abstract sense of the term, and asserted it to be imperishable because simple or indiscerptible. Plainly this reasoning is only a linkage of abstract ideas; that the soul, the actuality of which is demanded by the facts of observable human mentality, is a substance as thus conceived, and is consequently imperishable or self-subsistent as well as indiscerptible, is a question of fact, not of ideas, and one which the forthcoming facts do not enable us to answer in the positive.

It may be observed that if the arguments based on definitions of substance, etc., were valid, they would not serve to establish personal immortality: survival of soul-substance is not necessarily continuity of personality. Yet it is immortality in the latter sense that alone is of human interest, of religious worth, and of significance for theistic theology. Some philosophers assert that memory of the previous life, or lives, is essential to personal immortality; others, deeming memory to be conditioned by the body, credit the soul with a power to retain the effects of experiences of the embodied life, *e.g.* wisdom and love, even if memory be lost. This however, is dogma concerning the unknowable. And whenever immortality is asserted on metaphysical grounds that are independent of theistic belief or exclusive of such belief, as when souls are identified with self-subsistent differentiations of The Absolute, it would seem that the limits of knowledge are transcended and that definitions of concepts are confounded with matters of fact or actualities.

(3) Moral arguments belonging to class I all rest on ethical postulates which, apart from theism, are uncertain or improbable. Thus, one of Plato's arguments assumes that the soul is made for virtue, *i.e.* for freeing itself from bodily passions, and concludes that the soul is destined to be separated from the body. Another, resembling Kant's argument which is confessed to rest upon a postulate, assumes the final harmonisation of virtue and happiness: immortality is a condition of the realisation of the highest good. But, apart from theism, there is no ground for reasonable belief as to the realisation of the highest good.

The outcome of the foregoing review of arguments which do not presuppose theism is that a future life is not impossible or inconceivable, but, on the other hand, is not demonstrable.

II. With the presupposition of theism we pass into the sphere of probability and faith. Immortality becomes a matter of more or less reasonable belief, as distinct from deductibility from assured metaphysical principles or from more or less arbitrary postulations concerning the harmonising of moral experience. It is no matter, however, of subjective or personal desires, *e.g.* for the continuance of life or love, but rather a demand for coherence in what is, as a matter of fact, a moral universe. The world would not be irrational, in the logical sense, were the present life the only life; but it is a further question whether the world would be reasonable, or rational in the teleological sense: in other words, whether theism does not imply human immortality.

Theists are not altogether agreed on this point. Those who incline toward absolute monism are sometimes disposed to disparage human personality, to regard it as unworthy of survival, and to speak of the conservation of personal values, universalised, in abstraction from the personal bearers of them. But in so far as monism is approached, theism is deserted: wherefore, strictly speaking, these views are irrelevant to the present inquiry. Some theists, however, consider that, before we can assert immortality to be an implication of theism, it is necessary to know more than is known concerning God's purpose for the world. The facts and generalisations which receive an adequate explanation in the postulate of an intelligent and ethical world-ground, it is said, do not of themselves authorise belief in the *perfect* reasonableness of the world, but only in so much of reasonableness as we actually find. It may be the divine purpose in the world to produce moral personalities; but it is a further venture of faith, and a venture which transcends reasonable belief, to assert that the divine purpose includes the perfecting of finite moral persons, or provision for the fulfilment of their aspirations toward holiness and harmony with the will of God.

At first sight this representation, that empirically established theism does not imply immortality, may seem to be more congruent with the inferences reached in this volume than is the opposite view. But, on further examination, the conclusion appears doubtful. The facts, of which theism is the interpretation, may of themselves indicate no more than that the world is a moral order to the extent of producing moral persons and the conditions of rational and moral life. But, just because moral personality is what it is, this interpretation seems to involve more than do the facts themselves. If the *raison d'être* of the world were merely to produce moralised persons and not to provide for their perduringness, the world-purpose could be described as moral, but not in the sense of seeking the highest conceivable good: a Devil might cause moral beings to emerge, in order to tantalise them. A moral order, in the latter sense, must not only produce moral beings: it must also respect moral persons and satisfy moral demands. God cannot be an ethically perfect Being and not respect the moral aspirations of the personalities which He has called into existence.

> Thou madest man, he knows not why,
> He thinks he was not made to die;
> And Thou hast made him: Thou art just.

The world, in short, cannot safely be regarded as realising a *divine* purpose unless man's life continues after death. If the world is inexplicable without God, its purpose is immoral without divine righteousness. But righteousness is not merely compensating justice. Just distribution of rewards and punishments is no function of the present dispensation. The righteousness which theism must ascribe to God consists rather in provision of adequate opportunities for the development of all that is potential in God-given personality, conservation of the valuable, and love such as precludes the mockery of scheming that a rational creature's guiding light through life shall be a Will o' the wisp.

52

JOHN McTAGGART ELLIS McTAGGART

The Refutation of Mortality[1]

60. I do not propose to offer here any arguments in support of the positive assertion that men are immortal. I believe that such arguments exist, and that, in spite of the difficulty and obscurity of the subject, they are of sufficient strength to justify a belief in our immortality. But to expound these arguments would require an elaborate and lengthy treatise of technical metaphysics, for they could only be proved by a demonstration of some ideal theory of the fundamental nature of reality. My present design is merely to consider some arguments against immortality which have been based on certain facts of ordinary observation, and on certain results of physical science. I shall endeavour to show that those arguments are invalid, and that the presumption against immortality, which they have produced in many people, should be discarded. . . .

61. What reasons are there for supposing that our existence is only temporary? I see around me bodies which behave so like my own, that I conclude that they are related to other conscious selves in the same way that my body is related to myself. But from time to time these bodies are observed to cease to behave in this way, and to become motionless, unless moved from outside. Shortly after this the body dissolves into its constituent parts. Its form and identity as a body are completely destroyed. The experience of the past leads me to the conclusion that the same thing will happen in the future to every human body now existing, including my own.

How does this affect the question of my existence? It is clear that if I am a mere effect of my body — a form of its activity — I shall cease when the body ceases. And it is also clear that, if I could not exist without this particular body, then the destruction of the body will be a sign that I have ceased to exist.

[1] John McTaggart Ellis McTaggart, *Some Dogmas of Religion* (London: Edward Arnold, 1906); excerpts from chapter 3, "Human Immortality."

But, besides death, there is another characteristic of nature which tends to make us doubt our immortality. Of all the things around us, from a pebble to a solar system, science tells us that they are transitory. Each of them arose out of something else, each of them will pass away into something else. What is a man that he should be exempt from this universal law?

Thus we have three questions to consider: (1) Is my self an activity of my body? (2) Is my present body an essential condition of the existence of my self? (3) Is there any reason to suppose that my self does not share the transitory character which I recognize in all the material objects around me? . . .

65. . . . Inquiry will, I think, show us that matter cannot be independent of spirit, that, on the contrary, matter is only an appearance to the mind which observes it, and cannot, therefore, exist independently of spirit. If this is the case we cannot be entitled to consider the self as the activity of its body. . . .

66. What reason can be given for a belief in the existence of matter? I conceive that such a belief can only be defended on the ground that it is a legitimate inference from our sensations.

This view has been contested, but I believe that the objection to it rests on a misunderstanding. It has been said, and with perfect truth, that my belief in the existence of matter does not *arise* as an inference from my sensations. I do not first become aware of my sensations and then infer the existence of an orange. On the contrary, I am aware of the existence of the orange first. If I am studying psychology or am doubtful of the validity of my knowledge I may then consider the sensations of sight, touch, and so on, connected with my knowledge of the object. But in most cases I never do consider the sensations at all. And there are young children who are quite aware of the existence of a material world, but who have never realized that they have sensations. . . .

Since disbelief in the existence of matter is neither impossible nor contradictory, the question becomes inevitable — what is the justification of the belief? And it becomes more pressing, because in many cases our judgements as to the existence of matter are admitted to be wrong. In the first place, the quite unreflective consciousness has no more doubt that the world of matter is coloured than it has that the world of matter is extended. But either this or the more reflective judgements of science and the modern world must be wrong here, since they disagree. Again, if a man, who sees a cloak hanging up by moonlight, believes that he sees before him the body of a dead friend, it is obvious that he has completely mistaken the character of the matter before him. And if our judgements as to what the external object is are so often wrong, we have little justification for assuming without inquiry that our judgement that there is an external object is ever right.

There is a stronger case than this. For in dreams we do not only make wrong judgements as to the nature of matter, but as to the existence of matter. If a believer in the existence of matter dreams that he sees a roc's egg, he no more doubts, during his dream, that the roc's egg exists as independent matter, than he doubts, during waking life, that his table exists as independent matter. And yet, on waking, he will admit that in his dream he was neither observing a roc's egg nor any other really existing matter which he mistook for a roc's egg. Not only was his dream-belief 'this is a roc's egg' mistaken, but his dream-belief 'this is independently existing matter,' was also mistaken. And if this is mistaken, it is mere credulity to trust his belief in the table's existence without examination. For that belief is no stronger and no more evident than the other had been previously.

67. On what can we base a justification of the belief in the independent existence of matter? Nothing is available except the sensations. . . .

68. It is evident that the sensations are not themselves the matter in question. A sensation is not matter, and it cannot exist apart from the self to whom it belongs. It can have no independent existence. But the sensations, since they begin to exist, must have causes. Now it cannot be said to be obviously impossible that all the causes of my sensations should lie within my own nature. It is certain that they do not lie within that part of my own nature of which I am conscious, for I am not conscious of producing my sensations . . . . I am prepared to admit — what seems to me by far the more probable view — that all my sensations have causes which are not myself. Such causes must in each case be merely part-causes. I am unquestionably *one* of the causes of my own sensations, for, if I did not exist, my sensations also would not exist.

It may thus be admitted that my sensations make it, at any rate, highly probable that some reality exists, which is not myself or anything within myself, but exists independently of me. But we have not got to the matter. A reality which exists independently of me need not be matter — it might, for example, be another spirit. We do not call anything matter unless it possesses the primary qualities of matter given above. These qualities correspond to certain sensations, or elements in sensations, and the presence of the sensation in me is held to prove the existence of the corresponding quality in the material object.

69. But is this legitimate? The independent reality has been admitted to be the part-cause of the sensations, but that does not prove that it is like them. Causes do not necessarily resemble their effects. Happiness in

A does not resemble the misery which it may cause to the envious *B*. An angry man does not resemble a slammed door. A ray of sunshine does not resemble a faded water-colour.

70.   And, on this very theory, the external causes of all mental events do not resemble those events. When I see a sphere of red-hot iron I have sensations of form, sensations of colour, and (if I am near enough) a feeling of pain. Now the ordinary theory of matter makes the matter the cause of the sensations of colour and of the feeling of pain, as much as of the sensations of form. Yet it denies that the matter is red or painful. . . .

71.   . . . Of course the independent existence and ultimate nature of matter is a question for metaphysics and not for science. And therefore a metaphysical theory that matter possesses the secondary qualities as well as the primary cannot be upset by the fact that science, working from its own more superficial point of view, finds it convenient to treat matter as possessing only the primary qualities. If science keeps to its own sphere, it cannot clash with any metaphysical theory. If attempts are made to treat its results as if they were metaphysical truths, they have no claim to validity in this sphere, and a metaphysical theory is none the worse for being incompatible with these misapplications.

But the theory that matter exists depended very largely for its plausibility on the illegitimate support which it obtained by taking science as if it were metaphysics; and if it loses this support, as it must in the suggested new form, it loses, indeed, no real strength, but much of what caused people to believe it. As has been already said, the fact that physical science treats matter as independent of spirit, and that physical science forms a vast system, coherent, accepted, and, from its own standpoint, irrefutable, has done much to strengthen the belief that matter, at least, must be real, and that, if one of the two must be explained away by the other, it is spirit which must go, and matter which must stay. The inference is quite illegitimate, since nothing in physical science touches, or can touch, the question of the independent existence of matter. But it is an inference which is frequently made. And when the theory of the independent existence of matter defines the nature of that matter in a manner completely different from the definitions of physical science, it will no longer be able to gain apparent support in this way.

72.   Nor does the amended theory, while less inconsistent than the original form, altogether avoid inconsistency. The red-hot sphere of iron is now admitted not only to be a sphere, independent of any observer, but to be red, independent of any observer. But the pain still remains. It is not asserted that the iron is painful, although it cause me pain. Now the pain is a result produced in the observer which is quite as real as the sensations of form and colour, and quite as independent of the observer's

will. It is likewise just as uniform. The iron will not give me the sensations except under certain conditions. (I shall not see it to be red, for example, if I am blind, or have my eyes shut.) And, under certain conditions, quite as definite, it will inevitably give me the feeling of pain. Yet nothing resembling the mental effect is attributed to the cause in this case. Why should a difference be made between this case and the others? . . .

76.   . . . It might be supposed that the theory I have been advocating was a form of agnosticism. Agnosticism holds that we can know nothing but phenomena. Beneath these phenomena lies a reality on which they are based, but of this reality, agnosticism declares, we can only know of the external causes of our sensations that they do cause the sensations, have we not in effect taken up the agnostic theory that the reality on which phenomena depend is unknowable?

But this is not the case. Agnosticism says that we can know nothing whatever of the reality behind the phenomena. And, in saying this, it contradicts itself. For it asserts that such a reality exists, and that it stands in certain relations to the phenomena. Thus we do know something about it, and it is therefore not the case that we can know nothing about it.

But the theory which I have put forward does not say that we can know nothing about the causes of sensations. It only says that we do not know that they are like the sensation they cause. . . . We might, for example, be led to the conclusion that all substance was spirit. . . .

77.   And we have thus, I think, proved our original contention that the self cannot be one of the activities of its own body. If the self were, as such a theory would require it to be, merely a way in which matter behaved under certain circumstances, it would be possible to explain the self satisfactorily in terms of matter. And it would be possible that a state of things should exist in which those circumstances, which determine the activity of matter to take the form of spirit, occurred nowhere in the universe, which would then be a universe of matter without any consciousness. But so far is this from being the case that we can, as we now see, only explain matter in terms of a conscious self, and to talk of matter existing without consciousness is absurd. Matter is so far from being the sole reality, of which the self is only an activity, that, taken by itself, it is not a reality at all. The only things which have, in any sense, the qualities attributed to matter, are the sensations experienced by selves. In place of an independent reality we find events in men's minds which are real, indeed, but not an independent reality. Matter is simply our illegitimate inference from these events.

This may be put in another way. If my self is one of the activities of my body, then, since my body is only events in the life of some conscious being, my self must also be events in the life of some conscious being. It is clearly absurd to suppose that I am an activity of my body, as my body is known to myself, for then I should be events in my own life. . . .

78. The bearing of this discussion of the question of our immortality is that it disproves a hypothesis which would render immortality incredible. If the self was an activity of the body, it would be impossible that it should continue to exist when the body had ceased to exist. We might as well suppose, in that case, that the digestion survived the body as that the self did. But the body, as we have now seen, only exists for the selves which observe it, and we cannot, therefore, reduce any self to be an activity of its own body. . . .

If the self is an independent reality, it is a non-material reality. And, granted the independent existence of matter, more unity would be gained by denying the independent reality of spirit. But without independently existing matter the case is changed. No increased unity is gained by making the self a mere activity of something else, unless that something else is already known to exist and to be of a non-spiritual nature. Independently existing matter would, of course, be of a non-spiritual nature. But, when we have rejected this, I have no reason to believe that the reality outside myself is non-spiritual, and so I should gain no increased unity for the universe by denying the independent reality of myself.

And, again, if the self is an activity of its body, it must be a temporary activity, since the body is only a temporary combination of matter. But if the self were an activity of some non-material reality outside itself, there would be nothing to disprove the permanence of the state of things which produces the self — though, of course, there would equally be nothing which proves that permanence.

79. We must now pass on to our second question. My self cannot be a form of the activity of my body. But it is still possible that the nature of my self makes the possession of my present body essential to it. Granted that the body could not exist except for knowledge, it may be that the knowledge of my body, by myself or other selves, is a necessary condition of the existence of my self. In that case it would be an inevitable inference that when my body dissolves, and ceases to be known as a body at all, my self must have ceased also. If A, whenever it exists, is necessarily accompanied by B, then the cessation of B is a sure sign of the cessation of A.

What evidence is there in favour of such a view? In the first place, while we have plenty of experience of selves who possess bodies, we have no indubitable experience of selves who exist without bodies, or after their bodies have ceased to exist. Beside this, the existence of a self seems to involve the experience of sensations. Without them, the self would have no material for thought, will, or feeling, and it is only in these that the self exists. Now there seems good reason to suppose that sensations never occur in our minds at present without some corresponding modifications of the body. This is certainly the case with normal sensations. And, even if the evidence for clairvoyance and thought-transference were beyond dispute, it could never prove the possibility of sensation without bodily accompaniments. . . .

80.　But, after all, these considerations would, at the most, go to show that *some* body was necessary to my self, and not that its present body was necessary. Have we, after the results already reached, any reason to suppose that the death of the body must indicate anything more than that the self had transferred its manifestations to a new body, and had, therefore, passed from the knowledge of the survivors, who had only known it through the old body? The apparent improbability of this lies, I think, simply in our instinctive recurrence to the theory that the self is an activity of the body. In that case, no doubt, it would be impossible that it should be successively connected with two bodies. But that theory we have seen to be untenable. The most that a body can be is an essential accompaniment of the self. And then the supposition that the self has another body would fit the facts quite as well as the supposition that the self has ceased to exist.

There seems no reason why such a change should not be instantaneous. But even if it were not so, no additional difficulty would be created. If a body is essential to the action of a self, the self would be in a state of suspended animation in the interval between its possession of its two bodies — a state which we might almost call one of temporary non-existence. But this is nothing more than what happens, as far as we can observe, in every case of dreamless sleep. During such a sleep the self, so far as we know, is unconscious — as unconscious as it could be without a body. Yet this does not prevent its being the same man who went to sleep and who woke up again. Why should the difficulty be greater in a change of bodies?

81.　And then, have we any reason, after all, to suppose that a body is essential to a self? It seems to me that the facts only support a very different proposition — namely, that, *while a self has a body*, that body is essentially connected with the self's mental life.

For example, no self can be conceived as conscious unless it has sufficient data for its mental activity. This material is only given, as far as our observations can go, in the form of sensations, and sensations again, as far as our observations can go, seem invariably connected with changes in a body. But it does not follow, because a self which has a body cannot get its data except in connexion with that body, that it would be impossible for a self without a body to get data in some other way. It may be just the existence of the body which makes these other ways impossible at present. If a man is shut up in a house, the transparency of the windows is an essential condition of his seeing the sky. But it would not be prudent to infer that, if he walked out of the house, he could not see the sky because there was no longer any glass through which he might see it.

With regard to the connexion of the brain with thought, the chief evidence for it appears to be that diseases or mutilations of the brain affect the course of thought. But this does not prove that, even while a man has a brain, his thoughts are directly connected with it. Many things are capable of disturbing thought, which are not essential to its existence. For example, a sufficiently severe attack of toothache may render all consecutive abstract thought impossible. But if the tooth was extracted, I should still be able to think. And, in the same way, the fact that an abnormal state of the brain may affect our thoughts does not prove that the normal states of the brain are necessary for thought.

Even if the brain is essential to thought while we have bodies, it would not follow that when we ceased to have brains we could not think without them. The same argument applies here as with the organs of sense. It might be that the present inability of the self to think except in connexion with the body was a limitation which was imposed by the presence of the body, and which vanished with it. . . .

83.   We now come to the third question. Is there any reason to suppose that my self does not share the transitory character which I recognize in all the material objects around me?

What exactly is this transitory character? When science says that a material object — a planet, or a human body — ceases to exist, what does it mean? It does not mean that anything is annihilated. It means that units, which were combined in a certain way, are now combined otherwise. The form has changed. But everything which was there before is there now.

We need not inquire whether this distinction between an unchanging matter and a changing form can have more than a rough approximate correctness. It is sufficient to note that the analogy of science — whatever weight may be attached to it — does not give us reason to suppose anything to be transitory except combinations.

84.   Is the self a combination? It certainly resembles a combination in one respect, for it is differentiated and contains a plurality. We can have different sensations at the same moment, and sensations, thoughts, and desires can exist simultaneously. But it does not follow from this that a self is a combination. For if a whole is a combination it is built

up of parts which could exist without being combined in that way, while the combination could not exist without them. If the bricks of a wall, for instance, were destroyed, the wall would be destroyed too. But the wall might be destroyed by being taken to pieces, and the bricks would remain unchanged.

Do the parts of the self stand in this relation to it? Could my thoughts, my volitions, my emotions, exist isolated, or in new combinations, when my self had ceased to exist? It seems clear to me — the point is too ultimate for discussion — that they cannot. It is inconceivable that a thought, a sensation, a volition, or an emotion should exist outside of a self. And it is inconceivable that the same thought, sensation, volition, or emotion which was once part of my mind could ever be part of somebody else's. The self, we must say, is complex, but not a compound. It has parts, but it is not built up out of them. For, while it depends upon them, they depend just as much on it.

The self, therefore, cannot cease by the separation of its parts. For its parts only exist as united in it, and therefore could not separate from it. If it did cease to exist, it could only be by annihilation. It is not only that the form would have changed, but that the form and content alike would have perished.

Now there is no analogy in science to suggest the probability of this. For science treats nothing as perishable except combinations. This, indeed, does not give us any safe analogy for the persistence of the self. In the first place, there is reason to doubt the absolute validity of the distinction betwen content and form, which science finds it convenient to make. And in the second place, the difference between a self and matter is too great for an analogy from one to the other to be very conclusive. But at any rate science gives no analogy against us.

A. SETH PRINGLE-PATTISON

ANDREW SETH PRINGLE-PATTISON (1856-1931) was a Scottish phi-losopher, born in Edinburgh, and trained in its institutions. On completion of his studies at Edinburgh High School, he entered the University of Edinburgh. His name initially was Andrew Seth, but in 1898 he added to it Pringle-Pattison, after he had succeeded to the Haining estate. The major aspect of his career began in 1880, when he was appointed Assistant Professor of Logic and Metaphysics at the University of Edinburgh, but in 1883 he was offered a professorship in logic and philosophy at the found-ing of the University College of Cardiff. In 1887 to 1891, he went to St. Andrews as Professor of Philosophy, and from 1891 to 1919 he accepted a similar appointment at the University of Edinburgh. He was Hibbert Lec-turer for the year 1921, and Gifford Lecturer for the succeeding two years, as well as for the 1912-1913 season.

His major works comprise the Gifford Lectures for 1912 and 1913, **The Idea of God in the Light of Recent Philosophy** (1913), and **The Idea of Immortality** (1922), the Gifford Lectures for the academic year 1921-1922. Other philosophical writings of his are: **The Development from Kant to Hegel** (1882), and **Man's Place in the Cosmos** (1897, rev. ed. 1902).

53

A. SETH PRINGLE-PATTISON

The Idea of Immortality[1]

Religion is thus, as Hegel has finely said, 'the realm where all the riddles of the world are solved, all the contradictions of probing thought are unveiled, and all pangs of feeling cease, the region of eternal truth, of eternal rest. The whole complexity of human relations, activities, enjoyments, everything that man values and esteems, wherein he seeks his happiness, his glory, his pride — all find their final centre in religion, in the thought, the consciousness, the feeling of God. . . . God is known in religion. Religion just means being occupied with this object. In this occupation the spirit casts off all its finitude; in it it finds its satisfaction and perfect freedom. All nations accordingly have looked upon this religious consciousnes as their true dignity, as the Sunday of their lives; every care and anxiety, this "bank and shoal of time" itself, vanishes in this aether, in the immediate feeling of devotion or of hope.' . . .

It is, then, on the possibility of such experiences as we have been considering that any valid theory of immortality must be based. Their reality is beyond dispute, whether reached in the apprehension of Truth, through Beauty, or through Goodness. By whatever gate a man may enter, the eternal foundations of the world are there discovered to him, and he knows that in his hold on these realities lies all that is worth striving for, all that is of value in his life. The being of these realities and his own relation to them 'stand sure' beyond the risks of time and change, even the change which we call death. He who has tasted eternal life is not wont to be troubled in heart about the question of his personal survival; for such survival would mean nothing to him, if he were separated from the object in which he has found his true life. His immortality

[1] A. Seth-Pringle Pattison, *The Idea of Immortality* (Oxford: The Clarendon Press, 1922), 146-147, and Lecture X (excerpts). Reprinted by permission.

lies for him in his union with the eternal object on which his affections are set, and he seeks no other assurance.

. . . . .

. . . Truth, Beauty, Goodness have no reality as self-existent abstractions; they have no meaning apart from conscious experience. They carry us therefore to a primal Mind in whose experience they are eternally realized. God himself is at once the supreme Reality and, as Dante calls him, the supreme Value — *il primo, il summo Valore*. And the highest conception we can form of perfect personality is Love, not in any shallow sentimental sense, but the self-giving Love which expends itself for others, and lives in all their joys and sorrows. Such love, then, the principle of our argument bids us take as the ultimate value of which the universe is the manifestation. It bids us conceive the inmost being of God not solely as the realization of eternal Truth and the enjoyment of perfect Beauty, but pre-eminently as the exercise and fruition of his nature as Love. And if so, the value of the finite world to the Spirit of the universe must lie, above all else, if one may so speak with modesty and reverence, in the spirits to whom he has given the capacity to make themselves in his own image. The spirits themselves must be the values to God, not simply the degrees of intelligence and virtue, abstractly considered, which they respectively realize. They are not made, then — we seem justified in concluding — to be broken up and cast aside and be replaced by relays of others in a continual succession.

Here again, as throughout, we are applying the idea of the divine perfection, appealing for the interpretation of the more and the less perfect to our own experience. . . .

Many voices bid us distrust a hope which, they tell us, is but the phantom offspring of our own desire . . . . Desire in itself is irresponsible; seeing only its own object, it is blind to all the larger ends which are incompatible with its demands. So long, therefore, as it remains the desire of private satisfaction, no such desire can be regarded as secure of fulfilment. The existence of the very general, if not universal, desire of immortality is sometimes adduced as itself a powerful argument for the belief that the desire will be satisfied. But so long as it remains simply a desire for personal continuance — an instinctive shrinking from death — we cannot build upon it in the way suggested. Desire, at such a level, has no lien upon the universe; unless it be purged of its original selfishness, it can be no guide to us in such a question. The familiar message of religion everywhere is renunciation, death to self, as the gateway to freedom and to the wider life which is life indeed. The desires of the religious man are, therefore, for 'the brethren' rather than for himself —

for himself only as one with them, a member of what Royce called 'the blessed community'; and in a large sense the object of their corporate desire may be said to be an increasing knowledge of God and of his will. At such a standpoint, the belief in immortality is not based by the religious man on any personal claim for himself or even for others; it seems rather, as our argument has suggested, to be an inference from the character of God.

. . . 'Too good to be true'; is a saying often on our lips; and the mood it expresses is on the whole a prudent one, when it is a case of worldly goods and prospects. But, as some one has said, 'too good *not* to be true' is the more fitting expression, where it is a question of the ultimate ideals and hopes which have been the nursing-fathers and nursing-mothers of mankind. For serious philosophical reflection nothing can be more foolish than the common talk which tries to set these down as the baseless dreams of subjective fancy — as if man were self-created, and as if he developed his ideals in the internal vacancy of his individual mind. Man can no more rise spiritually above himself in his own strength than he can raise himself from the ground by tugging at his own shoulder-straps. We did not make ourselves, and we do not weave our ideals out of nothing. They are all derived; they point to their source in a real Perfection, in which is united all that, and more than, it hath entered into the heart of man to conceive. The essential meaning of the old ontological argument, I have argued elsewhere, is that the best we think, or can think, must *be*.

'A strange mystery it is', says Mr. Bertrand Russell, 'that Nature, omnipotent but blind, in the revolutions of her secular hurryings through the abysses of space, has brought forth at last a child, subject still to her power, but gifted with sight, with knowledge of good and evil, with the capacity of judging all the works of his unthinking Mother.' And he proceeds to explain how God is the 'creation of our own conscience', 'created by our own love of the good', and to tell us that it is for man to 'worship at the shrine that his own hands have built', although well aware that the Deity within has no being in the actual world. A strange mystery indeed! The mystery rather is that Mr. Russell should apparently never have brought his philosophical reflection to bear upon the sheer incredibility of the supposition — the idea of a complete absence of relation between the world of fact and the world of values, the world of fact or reality consisting solely of 'the blind empire of matter', and the world of values being a world of phantoms produced by autosuggestion in the brain of one of the casual products of this 'omnipotent matter' as it 'rolls on in its relentless way'. If we refuse to entertain so extravagant a hypothesis, we shall not be reduced to building our soul's habitation, as Mr. Russell advises us, 'on the firm foundation of unyielding despair'. We shall believe that here, as elsewhere, nothing comes from nothing — that whatever elements of goodness exist in us must have their source in the Power that brought us into being, and that the ideals of unattained perfection to which we reach forward are due to the same inspiration. On this, which seems the only reasonable view, the permanent ideals which have lighted mankind on its way must be taken as our best clue to the inmost nature of the real, and even the so-called instinct of immortality will not lose its legitimate significance. For we may say without exaggeration that it is man's meditation upon death that has made him, and makes him, the human creature he is. His philosophy, his religion, his greatest poetry, all have their roots in the fact of death and in his refusal to accept it as final. The central and beneficent function of death in human experience has been finely expressed by Hawthorne: 'What a blessing to mortals,' he wrote,' what a kindness of Providence, that life is made so uncertain, that Death is thrown in among the possibilities of our being. For without it, how would it be possible to be heroic, how we should plod along in commonplace for ever! . . . God gave the whole world to man, and if he is left alone with it, it will make a clod of him at last; but to remedy that, God gave man a grave, and it redeems all, and makes an immortal spirit of him in the end.'

It does not follow, however, that we are to think of personal immortality as an inherent possession of every human soul, or talismanic gift conferred indiscriminately on every being born in human shape. We talk very loosely of 'souls' and 'persons', as if these were static entities, magically called into being, and complete from the outset. But it is manifestly a question of degree: *how much* personality, how much of a coherent soul has the experience of life developed within the animal creature? For personality or selfhood is not anything that can be conferred by another, it is emphatically something that must be won before there can be any question of its conservation. What is given is simply the opportunity. A true self comes into being as the result of continuous effort, and the same effort is needed to hold it together and ensure its maintenance; for the danger of disintegration is always present. . . .

> A man, for aye removed
> From the developed brute; a god though in the germ.[2]

To identify reason with the computative understanding, and to limit the field of its operation to the economic struggle, is gratuitously and unwarrantably to impoverish the meaning of the word. Art and science, morality and religion, all have their roots in reason, and these are to us the character of our common humanity. The perception of beauty — the

---

[2] Browning, 'Rabbi ben Ezra'.

whole range of aesthetic emotion and artistic practice, from the cave man onwards — is quite useless for the preservation of the individual or of the species. Scientific truth man certainly be applied as serviceable knowledge; but the pursuit of truth for truth's sake, which is the inspiration of science, is unaffected by such material inducements. Bacon's philosophy predisposed him to emphasize the practical function of knowledge, the inventions to which it gives rise for the development of the 'regnum hominis' and 'the relief of man's estate'; yet he tells us that 'without doubt the contemplation of things as they are, without superstition or imposture, without error or confusion, is in itself a nobler thing than the whole harvest of inventions'.[3] 'God hath framed the mind of man as a mirror or glass, capable of the image of the universal world, and joyful to receive the impression thereof, as the eye joyeth to receive light.'[4] Truth, Beauty, and Goodness: in view of man's admission to worlds like these it becomes the merest travesty of the facts — I would say a mere affectation — to ignore, as naturalism does, the difference in scale between such a life and that of any of his animal compeers. For the difference is not quantitave — not merely one of degree, that is to say — but qualitative and decisive. And it is just the discrepancy between human capacities and ideals and the limited opportunities of man's earthly existence that has throughout the history of the race so insistently suggested that the life we see must be only part of a large plan.

[3] *Novum Organum*, bk. I, Aphorism 129.
[4] *Advancement of Learning*, bk. I, i. 3.

DOUGLAS CLYDE MACINTOSH

DOUGLAS CLYDE MACINTOSH (1877-1948), formerly Professor of Theology and Philosophy of Religion at Yale University, was born in Toronto, Canada. Among his many writings are: **The Reaction against Metaphysics in Theology** (1911), **The Problem of Knowledge** (1915), **God in a World at War** (1918), **Theology as an Empirical Science** (1919), **The Reasonableness of Christianity** (1925), **The Pilgrimage of Faith in the World of Modern Thought** (1931), **Social Religion** (1939), **The Problem of Religious Knowledge** (1940), **Personal Religion** (1942), **Thinking about God** (1942).

Macintosh finds reasonable grounds for immortality in the presence of value in the world. It is unthinkable that a good God would destroy values by idly standing by and allowing them to perish. By the goodness of God is meant the creator and preserver of values. Since it is in human personality that values are found, and found in their highest form, for God, to terminate the existence of persons is tantamount to annihilating values. Hence, a good God with sufficient power would conserve human existence beyond bodily death.

54

DOUGLAS CLYDE MACINTOSH

The Conservation of Values[1]

Our discovery of the reasonableness of the Christian conviction that man enjoys a measure of moral freedom is but the beginning of what we may expect to find involved in moral optimism for religious belief and for the reasonableness of Christianity. Let us look further into the implications of our fundamental principle.

Moral optimism assumes man's right to an optimistic outlook on moral conditions. As a life-attitude it is moral and critical enough to recognize the unconditional imperative of the moral law, and at the same time normal and healthy-minded enough to rest assured that he whose life is consecrated to the moral ideal, to the discovery and performance of his duty, has a right to be nobly unconcerned as to what may happen to himself. What it logically involves is the faith that no absolute and final disaster can happen to man through purely external or physical events; that, even when outside forces have done their worst, no ultimate and irremediable evil, no final loss of spiritual values, can have befallen the will that was steadfastly devoted to the realization of the true ideal.

If we turn to human experience for confirmation of this conviction, we are confronted at once with the universal fact of physical death. Sooner or later each individual dies and disappears; only the race remains. Is this consistent with moral optimism? The ultimate conservation of all absolute, that is, spiritual, values, in spite of physical death, is obviously involved in the morally optimistic faith upon which we have taken our stand; for only under such conditions would the moral will be justified in facing any possible physical event with equanimity.

But the adequate conservation of spiritual values necessarily involves the conservation of persons. If all genuine spiritual values are to be conserved without final loss, the death of the body cannot mean the end of personal existence. There are spiritual values, moral and social values particularly, but other values also, which are inseparably bound up with the existence of the individuals in and for whom they exist. Since the human individual is a free agent, as we have seen, he is able creatively to produce spiritual values. This means that, given every new opportunity for activity, he would be of infinite value as a possible means of creating such values. In other words, by virtue of his moral personality, man is of potentially infinite value as a means. Thus we find reflective support for love's intuitive certainty of the infinite value of the individual as an end. There is a cynical proverb to the effect that love is blind, and this may be true of some kinds of love. But all noble and true loves are glimpses into the infinite worth of the personal individual as such, and he who does not know from experience what true love is, is blind. Feeling has cognitive value, and, generally speaking, the true worth of personality is not discovered apart from love.

There is nothing more fundamental or essential in Christianity than this appreciation of the infinite value of the human individual, and it is in this essentially Christian insight that we find the true answer to latter-day speculations about a merely conditional immortality. Wherever a divine all-seeing love would find absolute values, actual or potential, there is something the conservation of which divine love imperatively demands. If personalities in whom such absolute values exist are allowed to sink into nothingness, then faith in the conservation of absolute values is mistaken, and moral optimism is an illusory dream.

We are aware that some high-minded persons would turn attention away from the individual to the race, urging that while the individual unit may cease to exist, the race will persist; that values produced by the individual will be conserved in the race. Now this is true enough of some of the spiritual values produced by the individual, but it is not true of all. In character and friendship are moral and social values which are inseparable bound up with the existence of the individual. Spiritual personality is of value as an end, and not merely as a means. We can view with composure the final disappearance of merely relative and instrumental values; but spiritual personality is of absolute value as an end. And spiritual personality is always individual, even when it is also social. Wherefore the moral optimism which affirms the conservation of all spiritual values cannot be satisfied with the persistence of the race alone. Besides, in spite of the speculations of some thinkers, it remains doubtful whether without the immortality of the individual there can be an immortality for the race. If, then, at last upon the physically embodied race inhabiting this gradually cooling planet the "slow, sure doom" shall fall, without personal immortality all values of and for human personality, social as well as individual, will be as if they never had been, and moral optimism will have been all along a delusion and a lie.

Just what will be invoved in the undiminished conservation of spiritual personality, with its absolute values, we may not be able to surmise, except in a general way. But there must of necessity be included not only continued existence of intelligence, with experience, selective memory, and thought, but moral activity with the development of character, and social relations, with the conservation of all true friendship and love. All this, with the vision beatific, moral optimism must postulate and the conservation of absolute values include. And with this, essential Christianity is in full accord. Apart from figurative and merely negative descriptions of the ideal future life, our Christian scriptures contain statements in terms of relationship to Christ which may be regarded as expressions of a more general truth. "To be with Christ" — this stands for ideal social relations. "We shall be like Him" — this means progressive realization of ideal character. "His servants shall serve Him" — taken with the words of the parable of judgment, "Inasmuch as ye have done it unto one of the least of these my brethren, ye have done it unto Me," can only mean ideal human activity along lines of social service. All of this is essentially Christian and all is logically involved in moral optimism, so that if the attitude we have so designated is reasonable and true, the same may be said of this vital and essentially Christian hope.

It will be seen that from the point of view of moral optimism the question as to whether the individual desires a future life is comparatively unimportant. Whether we desire immortality or not, the conservation of every person whose will is actually or even potentially moral is as imperative as the value of every such person is absolute. We may not want to live again; but as it is our duty to act morally whether we want to or not, so it is our duty to want to live again to do in a future existence whatever good it may then be possible for us to accomplish. The desire to live forever is not a selfish or unworthy desire, if the extension of existence is not desired for unworthily selfish purposes. If to live is in itself better than not to live, to continue to live is similarly better than not to continue to live. It could never be right to refuse or not to desire further opportunity to develop and express the good will, and any adequate appreciation of the moral ideal with its categorical imperative must be accompanied by desire amounting to an absolute demand for opportunity progressively to realize that ideal.

We have seen that belief in human immortality is logically involved in moral optimism. We have also seen that moral optimism is normal and necessary for spiritual ends so that, finding it as far as we went into the matter, we have continued to regard it as a reasonable fundamental faith. With equal cogency we conclude that belief in immortality is reasonable also. But it is always true that the more general hypothesis is tested in the tests applied to the propositions logically deduced from it, and we may raise the further question whether belief in a future life, together with the moral optimism of which it is one expression, is still theoretically permissible when we come to look further into the facts of nature and human life. It is admitted that with the morally discerning and those who have known friendship dearer than life itself, the demand for immortality is too imperious for the hope to be given up for anything short of its refutation by indubitable facts of experience. But the question remains whether, in the light of modern science, such refutation may not be forthcoming.

It must be admitted that it is the opinion of some scientists that human consciousness depends upon the brain in such a way that without that organ the conscious existence of the individual would be impossible; but this is not the teaching of science itself. As William James, William McDougall, and other eminent psychologists have said, and as every psychologist who has not needlessly sold out to materialism knows, there are no known facts concerning the relation of consciousness to the brain which require us to believe that the physical organ is indispensably necessary for conscious survival. Consciousness is instrumental to the body, without doubt; but increasingly the inverse relationship tends to establish itself. More and more as development proceeds in the individual and in the race, brain and body come to be instrumental to mind, whose interests reach out far beyond the bodily organism and its physical environment. It is not necessarily an unreasonable interpretation of the facts, therefore, when mind is regarded as destined for a position of ultimate independence with reference to the present physical body. That normal faith of the healthy mind and moral will which we have called moral optimism, leading necessarily, as it does, to belief in human immortality, cannot be dismissed as forbidden by the facts. We who are still in the body have not yet verified the future life directly. The time for that will come when this earthly physical life is over. Whether we shall ever in this life verify the other life indirectly, through completely demonstrated communication from the departed, may well be doubted. When fraud, hallucination, and mere chance coincidence have been eliminated from the phenomena to which spiritists appeal, it seems always possible to regard the facts as due to subconscious activities of the medium and others present, and to telepathy between living persons. However, it may be remarked in passing that if mind in its relation to body is independent enough to make telepathy under certain conditions a fact, it seems not unreasonable to think that mind may be independent enough to continue to exist and act when set free from the body at death.

A more assured argument for the possibility of immortality is found in the fact of human freedom, already sufficiently established as morally certain. Human freedom being granted in the sense in which we have defined the term, it follows that mind or the self acts in an originative manner in and through the brain; and if the mind is independent enough to act thus creatively in and through the brain, it may conceivably be independent enough to act independently of this particular organism altogether. If mind is an agent and not a mere phenomenon, it may conceivably find or be furnished with another instrument when the one it is now using becomes no longer serviceable. In spite, then, of anything the pessimistic or doubting critic can show by appeal to reason or experience, belief in the undiminished survival of human personality is theoretically permissible and, in view of its foundation in moral optimism, presumably true. Considering, then, the central place the belief occupies in the Christian religious faith, we are in a position to claim, at this point also, further confirmation of essential Christianity as reasonable and so presumably true.

Before leaving the subject, however, one very important thing remains to be said. If we ask the secret of the persistence of belief in immortality in the absence of any absolute empirical demonstration of the truth of the doctrine, the answer is that, after an appreciation of the worth of human personality, the chief factor in the belief has been the idea of God, that is, of a Power great enough and good enough to conserve the human individual in spite of bodily death. If we can be adequately assured, through experience or argument, of the existence of such a Being, we can at the same time be reassured of the truth of immortality. If we can be assured that the Supreme Being in the universe loves man with an everlasting love, we can be assured that man is intended for everlasting life.

Part Seven: EVIL

The Problem of Its Origin

55

ST. AUGUSTINE

Evil as the Privation of Good[1]

CHAPTER X

The Supremely Good Creator Made All Things Good

By the Trinity, thus supremely and equally and unchangeably good, all things were created; and these are not supremely and equally and unchangeably good, but yet they are good, even taken separately. Taken as a whole, however, they are very good, because their *ensemble* constitutes the universe in all its wonderful order and beauty.

CHAPTER XI

What Is Called Evil in the Universe Is but the Absence of Good

And in the universe, even that which is called evil, when it is regulated and put in its own place, only enhances our admiration of the good; for we enjoy and value the good more when we compare it with the evil. For the Almighty God, who, as even the heathen acknowledge, has supreme power over all things, being Himself supremely good, would never permit the existence of anything evil among His works, if He were not so omnipotent and good that He can bring good even out of evil. For what is that which we call evil but the absence of good? In the bodies of animals, disease and wounds mean nothing but the absence of health; for when a cure is effected, that does not mean that the evils which were present — namely, the diseases and wounds — go away from the body and dwell elsewhere: they altogether cease to exist; for the wound or disease is not a substance, but a defect in the fleshly substance — the flesh itself being a substance, and therefore something good, of which those evils — that is, privations of the good which we call health — are accidents. Just in the same way, what are called vices in the soul are

[1] From St. Augustine, *The Enchiridion on Faith, Hope, and Love*, tr. J. F. Shaw (1892).

nothing but privations of natural good. And when they are cured, they are not transferred elsewhere: when they cease to exist in the healthy soul, they cannot exist anywhere else.

CHAPTER XII

All Beings Were Made Good, but Not Being Made Perfectly Good, Are Liable to Corruption

All things that exist, therefore, seeing that the Creator of them all is supremely good, are themselves good. But because they are not, like their Creator, supremely and unchangeably good, their good may be diminished and increased. But for good to be diminished is an evil, although, however much it may be diminished, it is necessary, if the being is to continue, that some good should remain to constitute the being. For however small or of whatever kind the being may be, the good which makes it a being cannot be destroyed without destroying the being itself. An uncorrupted nature is justly held in esteem. But if, still further, it be incorruptible, it is undoubtedly considered of still higher value. When it is corrupted, however, its corruption is an evil, because it is deprived of some sort of good. For if it be deprived of no good, it receives no injury; but it does receive injury, therefore it is deprived of good. Therefore, so long as a being is in process of corruption, there is in it some good of which it is being deprived; and if a part of the being should remain which cannot be corrupted, this will certainly be an incorruptible being, and accordingly the process of corruption will result in the manifestation of this great good. But if it do not cease to be corrupted, neither can it cease to possess good of which corruption may deprive it. But if it should be thoroughly and completely consumed by corruption, there will then be no good left, because there will be no being. Wherefore corruption can consume the good only by consuming the being. Every being, therefore, is a good; a great good, if it can not be corrupted; a little good, if it can: but in any case, only the foolish or ignorant will deny that it is a good. And if it be wholly consumed by corruption, then the corruption itself must cease to exist, as there is no being left in which it can dwell.

CHAPTER XIII

There Can Be No Evil Where There Is No Good; and an Evil Man Is an Evil Good

Accordingly, there is nothing of what we call evil, if there be nothing good. But a good which is wholly without evil is a perfect good. A good, on the other hand, which contains evil is a faulty or imperfect good; and there can be no evil where there is no good. From all this we arrive at the curious result: that since every being, so far as it is a being, is good, when we say that a faulty being is an evil being, we just seem to say that what is good is evil, and that nothing but what is good can be evil, seeing that every being is good, and that no evil can exist except in a being. Nothing then, can be evil except something which is good. And although this, when stated, seems to be a contradiction, yet the strictness of reasoning leaves us no escape from the conclusion. We must, however, beware of incurring the prophetic condemnation: "Woe unto them that call evil good, and good evil: that put darkness for light, and light for darkness: that put bitter for sweet, and sweet for bitter." [2] And yet our Lord says: "An evil man out the evil treasure of his heart bringeth forth that which is evil." [3] Now, what is an evil man but an evil being? for a man is a being. Now, if a man is a good thing because he is a being, what is an evil man but an evil good? Yet, when we accurately distinguish these two things, we find that it is not because he is a man that he is evil, or because he is wicked that he is good; but that he is good because he is a man, and an evil because he is wicked. Whoever, then, says, "To be a man is an evil," or, "To be wicked is a good," falls under the prophetic denunciation: "Woe unto them that call evil good and good evil!" For he condemns the work of God, which is the man, and praises the defect of man, which is the wickedness. Therefore every being, even if it be a defective one, in so far as it is a being is good, and in so far as it is defective is evil.

CHAPTER XIV

Good and Evil Are an Exception to the Rule that Contrary Attributes Cannot Be Predicated of the Same Subject. Evil Springs Up in What Is Good, and Cannot Exist Except in What Is Good

Accordingly, in the case of these contraries which we call good and evil, the rule of the logicians, that two contraries cannot be predicated at the same time of the same thing, does not hold. No weather is at the same time dark and bright: no food or drink is at the same time sweet and bitter: no body is at the same time and in the same place black and white: none is at the same time and in the same place deformed and beautiful. And this rule is found to hold in regard to many, indeed nearly all, contraries, that they cannot exist at the same time in any one thing. But although no one can doubt that good and evil are contraries, not only can they exist at the same time, but evil cannot exist without good, or in

[2] Isaiah 5:20.
[3] Luke 6:45.

anything that is not good. Good, however, can exist without evil. For a man or an angel can exist without being wicked; but nothing can be wicked except a man or an angel: and so far as he is a man or an angel, he is good; so far as he is wicked, he is an evil. And these two contraries are so far co-existent, that if good did not exist in what is evil, neither could evil exist; because corruption could not have either a place to dwell in, or a source to spring from, if there were nothing that could be corrupted; and nothing can be corrupted except what is good, for corruption is nothing else but the destruction of good. From what is good, then, evils arose, and except in what is good they do not exist; nor was there any other source from which any evil nature could arise. For if there were then, in so far as this was a being, it was certainly a good: and a being which was incorruptible would be a great good; and even one which was corruptible must be to some extent a good, for only by corrupting what was good in it could corruption do it harm.

GOTTFRIED WILHELM LEIBNIZ

GOTTFRIED WILHELM LEIBNIZ (1646-1716), a Continental Rationalist, was born in Leipzig, in July 1646 and died on the fourteenth of November, 1716. Since his father died when Leibniz was a boy of only seven, from 1652, he educated himself by private reading, and at the age of fifteen, he entered the University of Leipzig. The institution refused him his doctorate owing to his youth, but Altorf, the university town of Nuremberg, not only conferred upon him the degree of Doctor of Laws in 1666, but offered him a professor's chair for his brilliant doctoral dissertation. Declining the offer, at the age of only 21, and with several notable essays to his credit, he entered into the service of the Archbishop Elector of Mainz, the Archchancellor of the Empire. His official responsibilities carried him to Paris, where he became associated with Arnauld, Malebranche, and the profound thought of France's greatest philosopher, Descartes. From France, he went to Holland, there to become well acquainted with Spinoza and his philosophy. On the death of the Elector of Mainz in 1673, Leibniz accepted an appointment as court-librarian at Hanover, a post he kept to the close of his life.

Some scholars consider Leibniz the most "universal scientific genius of modern times;" he is credited with discovering the infinitesimal calculus (with Isaac Newton), symbolic logic, and with siring the philosophy of Panpsychism. His chief philosophical works are: **Theodicy** (1710), **The Monadology** (1714), and **The Principles of Nature and Grace** (1714).

Leibniz believes that the present world is the "best of all possible worlds," that is, taking into account the necessary make-up of the universe, its ingredients such as intelligence, morality, finitude, will, matter, etc., the world around us is the best that can possibly be constructed under existing conditions. Evil, therefore, is a necessary element; to eradicate it would entail reducing man to the state of animal existence, consequently diminishing the glory and achievement of God. Thus, to rebel against evil is to object to being a man.

56

GOTTFRIED WILHELM LEIBNIZ

The Best of All Possible Worlds[1]

Abridgement of the Argument Reduced to Syllogistic Form

Some intelligent persons have desired that this supplement be made [to the Theodicy], and I have the more readily yielded to their wishes as in this way I have an opportunity again to remove certain difficulties and to make some observations which were not sufficiently emphasized in the work itself.

I. *Objection.* Whoever does not choose the best is lacking in power, or in knowledge, or in goodness.

God did not choose the best in creating this world.

Therefore, God has been lacking in power, or in knowledge, or in goodness.

Answer. I deny the minor, that is, the second premise of this syllogism; and our opponent proves it by this

Prosyllogism. Whoever makes things in which there is evil, which could have been made without any evil, or the making of which could have been omitted, does not choose the best.

God has made a world in which there is evil; a world, I say, which could have been made without any evil, or the making of which could have been omitted altogether.

Therefore, God has not chosen the best.

Answer. I grant the minor of the prosyllogism; for it must be confessed that there is evil in this world which God has made, and that it was possible to make a world without evil, or even not to create a world at all, for its creation has depended on the free will of God; but I deny the major, that is, the first of the two premises of the prosyllogism, and I might content myself with simply demanding its proof; but in order to make the matter clearer, I have wished to justify this denial by showing

[1] Gottfried Wilhelm Leibniz, *The Theodicy,* in *The Philosophical Works of Leibniz,* tr. George Martin Duncan, (1890); 1710 is the date of the original *Theodicy.*

that the best plan is not always that which seeks to avoid evil, since it may happen that *the evil is accompanied by a greater good*. For example, a general of an army will prefer a great victory with a slight wound to a condition without wound and without victory. We have proved this more fully in the large work by making it clear, by instances taken from mathematics and elsewhere, that an imperfection in the part may be required for a greater perfection in the whole. In this I have followed the opinion of St. Augustine, who has said a hundred times, that God has permitted evil in order to bring about good, that is, a greater good; and that of Thomas Aquinas (in libr. II. sent. dist. 32, qu. I, art. 1), that the permitting of evil tends to the good of the universe. I have shown that the ancients called Adam's fall *felix culpa*, a happy sin, because it had been retrieved with immense advantage by the incarnation of the Son of God, who has given to the universe something nobler than anything that ever would have been among creatures except for it. For the sake of a clearer understanding, I have added, following many good authors, that it was in accordance with order and the general good that God allowed to certain creatures the opportunity of exercising their liberty, even when he foresaw that they would turn to evil, but which he could so well rectify; because it was not fitting that, in order to hinder sin, God should always act in an extraordinary manner. To overthrow this objection, therefore, it is sufficient to show that a world with evil might be better than a world without evil; but I have gone even farther, in the work, and have even proved that this universe must be in reality better than every other possible universe.

II.   *Objection.*   If there is more evil than good in intelligent creatures, then there is more evil than good in the whole work of God.

Now, there is more evil than good in intelligent creatures.

Therefore, there is more evil than good in the whole work of God.

Answer, I deny the major and the minor of this conditional syllogism. As to the major, I do not admit it at all, because this pretended deduction from a part to the whole, from intelligent creatures to all creatures, supposes tacitly and without proof that creatures destitute of reason cannot enter into comparison nor into account with those which possess it. But why may it not be that the surplus of good in the non-intelligent creatures which fill the world, compensates for, and even incomparably surpasses, the surplus of evil in the rational creatures? It is true that the value of the latter is greater; but, in compensation, the others are beyond comparison the more numerous, and it may be that the proportion of number and quantity surpasses that of value and of quality.

As to the minor, that is no more to be admitted; that is, it is not at all to be admitted that there is more evil than good in the intelligent creatures. There is no need even of granting that there is more evil than good in the human race, because it is possible, and in fact very probable, that the glory and the perfection of the blessed are incomparably greater than the misery and the imperfection of the damned, and that here the excellence of the total good in the smaller number exceeds the total evil in the greater number. The blessed approach the Divinity, by means of a Divine Mediator, as near as may suit these creatures, and make such progress in good as is impossible for the damned to make in evil, approach as nearly as they may to the nature of demons. God is infinite, and the devil is limited; the good may and does go to infinity, while evil has its bounds. It is therefore possible, and is credible, that in the comparison of the blessed and the damned, the contrary of that which I have said might happen in the comparison of intelligent and non-intelligent creatures, takes place; namely, it is possible that in the comparison of the happy and the unhappy, the proportion of degree exceeds that of number, and that in the comparison of intelligent and non-intelligent creatures, the proportion of number is greater than that of value. I have the right to suppose that a thing is possible so long as its impossibility is not proved; and indeed that which I have here advanced is more than a supposition.

But in the second place, if I should admit that there is more evil than good in the human race, I have still good grounds for not admitting that there is more evil than good in all intelligent creatures. For there is an inconceivable number of genii, and perhaps of other rational creatures. And an opponent could not prove that in all the City of God, composed as well of genii as of rational animals without number and of an infinity of kinds, evil exceeds good. And although in order to answer an objection, there is no need of proving that a thing is, when its mere possibility suffices; yet, in this work, I have not omitted to show that it is a consequence of the supreme perfection of the Sovereign of the universe, that the kingdom of God is the most perfect of all possible states of governments, and that consequently the little evil there is, is required for the consummation of the immense good which is found there.

III.   *Objection.*   If it is always impossible not to sin, it is always unjust to punish.

Now, it is always impossible not to sin; or, in other words, every sin is necessary.

Therefore, it is always unjust to punish.

The minor of this is proved thus:

1.   *Prosyllogism.*   All that is predetermined is necessary.

Every event is predetermined.

Therefore, every event (and consequently sin also) is necessary.

Again this second minor is proved thus:

2. *Prosyllogism.* That which is future, that which is foreseen, that which is involved in the causes, is predetermined.

Every event is such.

Therefore, every event is predetermined.

Answer. I admit in a certain sense the conclusion of the second prosyllogism, which is the minor of the first; but I shall deny the major of the first prosyllogism, namely, that every thing predetermined is necessary; understanding by the *necessity* of sinning, for example, or by the impossibility of not sinning, or of not performing any action, the necessity with which we are here concerned, that is, that which is essential and absolute, and which destroys the morality of an action and the justice of punishments. For if anyone understood another necessity or impossibility, namely, a necessity which should be only moral, or which was only hypothetical (as will be explained shortly); it is clear that I should deny the major of the objection itself. I might content myself with this answer and demand the proof of the proposition denied; but I have again desired to explain my procedure in this work, in order to better elucidate the matter and to throw more light on the whole subject, by explaining the necessity which ought to be rejected and the determination which must take place. That *necessity* which is contrary to morality and which ought to be rejected, and which would render punishment unjust, is an insurmountable necessity which would make all opposition useless, even if we should wish with all our heart to avoid the necessary action, and should make all possible efforts to that end. Now, it is manifest that this is not applicable to voluntary actions, because we would not perform them if we did not choose to. Also their prevision and predetermination are not absolute, but presuppose the will: if it is certain that we shall perform them, it is not less certain that we shall choose to perform them. These voluntary actions and their consequences will not take place no matter what we do or whether we wish them or not; but, *through* that which we shall do and through that which we shall wish to do, which leads to them. And this is involved in prevision and in predetermination, and even constitutes their ground. And the necessity of such an event is called conditional or hypothetical, or the necessity of consequences, because it supposes the will, and the other *requisites;* whereas the necessity which destroys the morality and renders punishment unjust and reward useless, exists in things which will be whatever we may do or whatever we may wish to do, and, in a word, is in that which is essential; and this is what is called an absolute necessity. Thus it is to no purpose, as regards what is absolutely necessary, to make prohibitions or commands, to propose penalties or prizes, to praise or to blame; it will be none the less. On the other hand, in voluntary actions and in that which depends upon them, precepts armed with power to punish and to recompense are very often of use and are included in the order of causes which make an action exist. And it is for this reason that not only cares and labors but also prayers are useful; God having had these prayers in view before he regulated things and having had that consideration for them which was proper. This is why the precept which says *ora et labora* (pray and work), holds altogether good; and not only those who (under the vain pretext of the necessity of events) pretend that the care which business demands may be neglected, but also those who reason against prayer, fall into what the ancients even then called the *lazy sophism*. Thus the predetermination of events by causes is just what contributes to morality instead of destroying it, and causes incline the will, without compelling it. This is why the *determination* in question is not a necessitation — it is certain (to him who knows all) that the effect will follow this inclination; but this effect does not follow by a necessary consequence, that is, one the contrary of which implies contradiction. It is also by an internal inclination such as this that the will is determined, without there being any necessity. Suppose that one has the greatest passion in the world (a great thirst, for example), you will admit to me that the soul can find some reason for resisting it, if it were only that of showing its power. Thus, although one may never be in a perfect indifference of equilibrium and there may be always a preponderance of inclination for the side taken, it, nevertheless, never renders the resolution taken absolutely necessary.

IV. *Objection.* Whoever can prevent the sin of another and does not do so, but rather contributes to it although he is well informed of it, is accessory to it.

God can prevent the sin of intelligent creatures; but he does not do so, and rather contributes to it by his concurrence and by the opportunities which he brings about, although he has a perfect knowledge of it.

Hence, etc.

Answer. I deny the major of this syllogism. For it is possible that one could prevent sin, but ought not, because he could not do it without himself committing a sin, or (when God is in question) without performing an unreasonable action. Examples have been given and the application to God himself has been made. It is possible also that we contribute to evil and that sometimes we even open the road to it, in doing things which we are obliged to do; and, when we do our duty or (in speaking of God) when, after thorough consideration, we do that which reason demands, we are not responsible for the results, even when we foresee them. We do not desire these evils; but we are willing to permit them for the sake of a greater good which we cannot reasonably help preferring to other considerations. And this is a *consequent* will, which results from *antecedent* wills by which we will the good. I know that some persons, in speaking of the antecedent and consequent will of God, have understood by the *antecedent* that which wills that all men should be saved; and by the *consequent*, that which wills, in consequence of persistent sin, that some should be damned. But these are merely illustrations of a more general idea, and by his consequent or final and decreeing will (that which is always followed by its effect), he wills to permit them to sin, this permission being the result of superior reasons. And we have the right to say in general that the antecedent will of God tends to the production of good and the prevention of evil, each taken in itself and as if alone (*particulariter et secundum quid*, Thom. I, qu. 19, art. 6), according to the measure of the degree of each good and of each evil; but that the divine consequent or final or total will tends toward the production of as many goods as may be put together, the combination of which becomes in this way determined, and includes also the permission of some evils and the exclusion of some goods, as the best possible plan for the universe demands. Arminius, in his *Anti-perkinsus*, has very well explained that the will of God may be called consequent, not only in relation to the action of the creature considered beforehand in the divine understanding, but also in relation to other anterior divine acts of will. But this consideration of the passage cited from Thomas Aquinas, and that from Scotus (I. dist. 46, qu. XI), is enough to show that they make this distinction as I have done here. Nevertheless, if anyone objects to this use of terms let him substitute *deliberating* will, in place of antecedent, and *final* or decreeing will, in place of consequent. For I do not wish to dispute over words.

V. *Objection.* Whoever produces all that is real in a thing, is its cause.

God produces all that is real in sin.

Hence, God is the cause of sin.

Answer. I might content myself with denying the major or the minor, since the term *real* admits of interpretations which would render these propositions false. But in order to explain more clearly, I will make a distinction. *Real* signifies either that which is positive only, or, it includes also privative beings: in the first case, I deny the major and admit the minor; in the second case, I do the contrary. I might have limited myself to this, but I have chosen to proceed still farther and give the reason for this distinction. I have been very glad therefore to draw attention to the fact that every reality purely positive or absolute is a perfection; and that imperfection comes from limitation, that is, from the privative: for to limit is to refuse progress, or the greatest possible progress. Now

God is the cause of all perfections and consequently of all realities considered as purely positive. But limitations or privations result from the original imperfection of creatures, which limits their receptivity. And it is with them as with a loaded vessel, which the river causes to move more or less slowly according to the weight which it carries: thus its speed depends upon the river, but the retardation which limits this speed comes from the load. Thus in the *Theodicy*, we have shown how the creature, in causing sin, is a defective cause; how errors and evil inclinations are born of privation; and how privation is accidentally efficient; and I have justified the opinion of St. Augustine (lib. I. as Simpl. qu. 2) who explains, for example, how God makes the soul obdurate, not by giving it something evil, but because the effect of his good impression is limited by the soul's resistance and by the circumstances which contribute to this resistance, so that he does not give it all the good which would overcome its evil. *Nec* (inquit) *ab illo erogatur aliquid quo homo fit deterior, sed tantum quo fit melior non erogatur.* But if God had wished to do more, he would have had to make either other natures for creatures or other miracles to change their natures, things which the best plan could not admit. It is as if the current of the river must be more rapid than its fall admitted or that the boats should be loaded more lightly, if it were necessary to make them move more quickly. And the original limitation or imperfection of creatures requires that even the best plan of the universe could not receive more good, and could not be exempt from certain evils, which, however, are to result in a greater good. There are certain disorders in the parts which marvelously enhance the beauty of the whole; just as certain dissonances, when properly used, render harmony more beautiful. But this depends on what has already been said in answer to the first objection.

VI. *Objection.* Whoever punishes those who have done as well as it was in their power to do, is unjust.

God does so.

Hence, etc.

Answer. I deny the minor of this argument. And I believe that God always gives sufficient aid and grace to those who have a good will, that is, to those who do not reject this grace by new sin. Thus I do not admit the damnation of infants who have died without baptism or outside of the church; nor the damnation of adults who have acted according to the light which God has given them. And I believe that if *any one has followed the light which has been given him,* he will undoubtedly receive greater light when he has need of it, as the late M. Hulseman, a profound and celebrated theologian at Leipsig, has somewhere remarked; and if such a man has failed to receive it during his lifetime he will at least receive it when at the point of death.

VII. *Objection.* Whoever gives only to some, and not to all, the means which produces in them effectively a good will and salutary final faith, has not sufficient goodness.

God does this.

Hence, etc.

Answer. I deny the major of this. It is true that God could overcome the greatest resistance of the human heart; and does it, too, sometimes, either by internal grace, or by external circumstances which have a great effect on souls; but he does not always do this. Whence comes this distinction? it may be asked, and why does his goodness seem limited? It is because, as I have already said in answering the first objection, it would not have been in order always to act in an extraordinary manner, and to reverse the connection of things. The reasons of this connection, by means of which one is placed in more favorable circumstances than another, are hidden in the depths of the wisdom of God: they depend upon the universal harmony. The best plan of the universe, which God could not fail to choose, made it so. We judge from the event itself; since God has made it, it was not possible to do better. Far from being true that this conduct is contrary to goodness, it is supreme goodness which led him to it. This objection with its solution might have been drawn from what was said in regard to the first objection; but it seemed useful to touch upon it separately.

VIII. *Objection.* Whoever cannot fail to choose the best, is not free.

God cannot fail to choose the best.

Hence, God is not free.

Answer. I deny the major of the argument; it is rather true liberty, and the most perfect, to be able to use one's free will for the best, and to always exercise this power, without ever being turned aside either by external force or by internal passions, the first of which causes slavery of the body, the second, slavery of the soul. There is nothing less servile, and nothing more in accordance with the highest degree of freedom, than to be always led toward the good, and always by one's own inclination, without any constraint and without any displeasure. And to object therefore that God had need of external things, is only a sophism. He created them freely; but having proposed to himself an end, which is to exercise his goodness, wisdom has determined him to choose the means best fitted to attain this end. To call this a *need*, is to take that term in an unusual sense which frees it from all imperfection, just as when we speak of the wrath of God.

Seneca has somewhere said that God commanded but once but that he obeys always, because he obeys laws which he willed to prescribe to himself: *semel jussit, semper paret.* But he might better have said that God always commands and that he is always obeyed; for in willing, he always follows the inclination of his own nature, and all other things always follow his will. And as this will is always the same, it cannot be said that he obeys only that will which he formerly had. Nevertheless, although his will is always infallible and always tends toward the best, the evil, or the lesser good, which he rejects, does not cease to be possible in itself; otherwise the necessity of the good would be geometrical (so to speak), or metaphysical, and altogether absolute; the contingency of things would be destroyed, and there would be no choice. But this sort of necessity, which does not destroy the possibility of the contrary, has this name only by analogy; it becomes effective, not by the pure essence of things, but by that which is outside of them, above them, namely, by the will of God. This necessity is called moral, because, to the sage, *necessity* and *what ought to be* are equivalent things; and when it always has its effect, as it really has in the perfect sage, that is, in God, it may be said that it is a happy necessity. The nearer creatures approach to it, the nearer they approach to perfect happiness. Also this kind of necessity is not that which we try to avoid and which destroys morality, rewards and praise. For that which it brings, does not happen whatever we may do or will, but because we will it so. And a will to which it is natural to choose well, merits praise so much the more; also it carries its reward with it, which is sovereign happiness. And as this constitution of the divine nature gives entire satisfaction to him who possesses it, it is also the best and the most desirable for the creatures who are all dependent on God. If the will of God did not have for a rule the principle of the best, it would either tend toward evil, which would be the worst; or it would be in some way indifferent to good and to evil, and would be guided by chance: but a will which would allow itself always to act by chance, would not be worth more for the government of the universe that the fortuitous concourse of atoms, without there being any divinity therein. And even if God should abandon himself to chance only in some cases and in a certain way (as he would do, if he did not always work entirely for the best and if he were capable of preferring a lesser good to a greater, that is, an evil to a good, since that which prevents a greater good is an evil), he would be imperfect, as well as the object of his choice; he would not merit entire confidence; he would act without reason in such a case, and the government of the universe would be like certain games, equally divided between reason and chance. All this proves that this objection which is made against the choice of the best, perverts the notions of the free and of the necessary, and represents to us the best even as evil: which is either malicious or ridiculous.

57

JOSIAH ROYCE

Evil as an Illusion[1]

. . . We have been talking of the infinite goodness; but after all, what shall we still say of that finite "partial evil" of life? We seem to have somehow proved *a priori* that it must be "universal good." For, as we have said, in the Infinite Life of our ideal there can be no imperfection. This, we have said, is the demonstration that we missed all through our study of the world of the Powers. Since we approached that world from without, and never felt the pulse of its heart's blood, we had nothing but doubt after doubt when we contemplated the evil that seemed to be in it. Our efforts to explain evil seemed hollow and worthless. There might be some deeper truth involved in these efforts; but we knew it not. Well, are we right in declaring that we have altogether overcome our difficulty now? Apparently we are as far as ever from seeing *how* the partial evil can be the universal good; we only show, from the conception of the infinite itself, *that* the partial evil must be the universal good. God must see how; and we know this because we know of God. More than this we seem to be unable to suggest.

But will this do? Have we not forgotten one terrible consequence of our doctrine? The partial evil in universal good, is it? There is no evil? All apparent imperfection is an illusion of our partial view? So then *where is the chance to be in a free way and of our own choice better than we otherwise in truth should be?* Is not the arm that is raised to strike down wickedness paralyzed by the very thought that was to give it divine strength? This evil that I fight herein this finite world is a delusion. So then, why fight it? If I do good works, the world is infinitely good and perfect. If I seem to do evil works, the world is in truth no worse. Seeming good is not better than seeming evil, for if it were, then

[1] Josiah Royce, *The Religious Aspect of Philosophy* (Boston: Houghton Mifflin and Co., 1885), 449-459; from section III "The Problem of Evil" of chapter XII, "The Religious Insight."

the seeming evil would be a real defect in God, in whose life is everything. If I have never loved aught but God, even so I have never hated
aught but God. It is all alike. God does not need just me. Or rather I may
say, in so far as he needs me to complete his infinite truth, he already
has me from all eternity. I have nothing to do with the business, save
to contemplate in dizzy indolence the whirling misty masses of seeming
evil, and to say with a sort of amused reverence that they look very ill
and opaque to me, but that of course God sees through them clearly
enough somehow. The mist is in truth crystalline water, and he has so
quick a sense as to look beyond the drops as easily as if they were in the
calm unity of a mountain lake. And so, my religion is simply a contemplation of God's wisdom, but otherwise an idle amusement.

So says the man who sees only this superficial view of our doctrine. In
so far as, standing once more outside of some evil thing, we say: "That
thing yonder looks bad, but God must see it to be good," we do indeed
remain indolent, and our religion simply means a sort of stoical indifference to the apparent distinction of good and evil. This is in fact the
proper practical attitude of even the most earnest man in the presence of
evil that he cannot understand and cannot affect. In such matters we
must indeed be content with the passive knowledge. Death and the unavoidable pains of life, the downfall of cherished plans, all the cruelty of
fate, we must learn to look at as things to us opaque, but to God, who
knows them fully, somehow clear and rational. So regarding them, we
must aim to get to the stage of stoical indifference about them. They
are to us the accidents of existence. We have no business to murmur
about them, since we see that God, experiencing them, somehow must
experience the mass elements in an absolutely perfect life. For God we
regard not as the mysterious power who made them, and who then may
have been limited to the use of imperfect means, but as the absolute
thought that knows them; so that, however inexplicable they must now
be to us, they are in themselves nothing that God vainly wishes to have
otherwise, but they are organically joined with the rest of the glorious
Whole.

Such is indeed the only present word for us finite minds about many
of the shadows of seeming evil that we have to behold in the world of the
apparently external facts. Such however is *not* the last word for us about
the only evil that has any immediate moral significance, namely, the evil
that we see, not as an external, shadowy mist, but as a present fact, experienced in us. Here it is that the objector just mentioned seems really
formidable to us. But just here it is that we find the answer to him. For
in the world of our own acts we have a wondrous experience. We realize
evil, we fight it, and, at the same time, we realize our fragment of the perfect divine life in the moment itself of struggling with the evil. And in

this wondrous experience lies the whole solution of the ancient problem of the existence of moral evil. For instance, I find in myself a selfish impulse, trying to destroy the moral insight. Now of this evil impulse I do not say, looking at it objectively: "It is somehow a part of the universal good;" but, in the moment of moral action I *make* it, even in the very moment of its sinfulness, a part of my good consciousness, *in overcoming it.* The moral insight condemns the evil that it experiences; *and in condemning and conquering this evil it forms and is, together with the evil, the organic total that constitutes the good will.* Only through this inner victory over the evil that is experienced as a conquered tendency does the good will have its being. Now since the perfect life of God must have the absolutely good will, therefore it also must be conscious of such a victory. Thus the solution of our difficulty begins to appear. And thus we reap a new religious fruit from our ethical doctrine, to whose main principles we must once more here refer the reader.

When I experience the victory of the moral insight over the bad will, I experience in one indivisible moment both the partial evil of the selfish impulse (which in itself as a separate fact would be wholly bad) and the universal good of the moral victory, which has its existence only in the overwhelming of the evil. So, in the good act, I experience the good as my evil lost in goodness, as a rebellion against the good conquered in the moment of its birth, as a peace that arises in the midst of this triumphant conflict, as a satisfaction that lives in this restless activity of inner warfare. This child of inner strife is the good, and the only moral good, we know.

What I here have present in me when I do a good act is an element of God's life. *I here directly experience how the partial moral evil is universal good;* for so it is a relatively universal good in me when, overcoming myself, I choose the universal will. The bad impulse is still in me, but is defeated. In the choice against evil is the very life of goodness, which would be a pale, stupid abstraction otherwise. Even so, to take another view, in the overcoming of our separateness as individuals lies, as we saw in the previous book, our sense of the worth of the universal life. And what we here experience in the single moment of time, and in the narrowness of our finite lives, God must experience, and eternally. In our single good acts we have thus the specimen of the eternal realization of goodness.

But now how simple becomes the answer to that terrible suggestion of a moment since! "If I want to do evil, I cannot," said the objector; "for God the perfect one includes me with the rest, and so cannot in his perfection be hurt by me. Let me do what I will, my act can only seem bad, and cannot be bad. All evil is illusion, hence there is no moral difference in action possible."

"Right indeed," we answer, "but also wrong, because half the truth. The half kills, the whole gives life. Why canst thou not do any absolute evil? Because thy evil intent, which, in its separateness, *would be* unmixed evil, thy selfish will, thy struggle against the moral insight, this evil will of thine is no lonesome fact in the world, but is an element in the organic life of God. *In him thy evil impulse forms part of a total good will, as the evil impulse of the good man forms an element in his realization of goodness.* In God thy separateness is destroyed, and with it thy sin as evil. For good will to be in himself, namely, the organic total whose truth is the *discovery of the evil.* Therefore is God's life perfect, because it includes not only the knowledge of thy finite wicked will, but the insight into its truth as a moment in the real universal will.

If then thou wert good, thou wouldst be good by including the evil impulse in a realization of its evil, and in an acceptance of the higher insight. If thou art evil, then in thyself, as separate being, thou art condemned, and just because thy separate evil is condemned, therefore is the total life of God, that includes these with thy condemnation and with the triumph over thee, good.

This is the ground for the solution of the problem. To go more into detail: Evil is for us of two classes: the external seeming evil, such as death, pain, or weakness of character; and internal evil, namely the bad will itself. Because we know so little, therefore we can never tell whether those externally seen seeming evils are blessings in disguise, or expressions of some wicked diabolical will-power at work about us. Somehow then, we never know exactly how, these seeming great evils must be in God universal good. But with regard to the only evil that we know as an inward experience, and so as a certain reality, namely, the Evil Will, we know both the existence of that, and its true relation to universal goodness, because and only because we experience both of them first and through the moral insight, and then in the good act. Goodness having its very life in the insight and in its exercise, has as its elements the evil impulse *and* its correction. The evil will as such may either be conquered in our personal experience, and then we are ourselves good; or it may be conquered both in our thought considered as a separate thought, but in the total thought to which ours is so related, as our single evil and good thoughts are related to the whole of us. The wicked man is no example of God's delight in wickedness, just as the evil impulse that is an element in the good man's goodness, and a very real element too, is no proof that the good man delights in evil. As the evil impulse is to the good man, so is the evil will of the wicked man to the life of God, in which he is an element. And just because the evil will is the only evil that we are sure of, this explanation is enough.

Thus the distinction between good and evil remains as clear as ever. Our difficulty about the matter is removed, not by any barren external theodicy, such as were the forms of guess-work that we criticised in a previous chapter, but by a plain reflection on the moral experience itself. Goodness as a moral experience is for us the overcoming of experienced evil; and in the eternal life of God the realization of goodness must have the same sort of organic relation to evil as it has in us. Goodness is not mere innocence, but realized insight. To the wicked man we say: God is good because in thinking thee he damns thy evil impulse and overwhelms it in a higher thought of which thou art a part. And in so far as thy will is truly evil, thou art in God just as the evil is in the good man; thou art known only to be condemned and overcome. That is thy blessed mission; and this mission of evil such as thine is indeed an eternal one. So that both things are true. The world is wholly good, and thou, such as thou individually art, mayest be damnably evil if so thou desirest.

We do not say then that evil must exist to set the good off by way of external contrast. That view we long since justly rejected. We say only that the evil will is a conquered element *in* the good will, and is as such necessary to goodness. Our conception of the absolute unity of God's life, and that conception alone, enables us to apply this thought here. No form of dualistic Theism has any chance to apply this, the only satisfactory theodicy. If God were conceived as external to his creatures, as a power that made them beyond himself, the hopeless problems and the unworthy subterfuges of the older theodicies would come back to torment us. As it is, the solution of the problem of evil is given us in the directest and yet in the most unexpected way. . . .

Evil therefore, as a supposed real fact, *separate* from goodness, and a totally independent entity, is and must be an illusion. . . . Moral experience has taught us how we are to explain the existence of the only partial evil that we clearly know to be even a partial evil, namely, the evil will. The explanation is that the good act has its existence and life *in the transcending of experienced present evil.* This evil must not be an external evil, beyond the good will, but must be experienced in the same indivisible moment in which it is transcended. That this wondrous union is possible, we simply find as fact in the moral experience. No genuine moral goodness is possible save in the midst of such inner warfare. The absence of the evil impulse leaves naught but innocence or instinct, morally insipid and colorless. Goodness is this organism of struggling elements. Now, as we declare, in the infinite and united thought of God this unity of goodness is eternally present. God's life is this infinite rest, *not apart from but in the endless strife,* as in substance Heraclitus so well and originally taught.

58

JOHN FISKE

The Evolutionist's Contribution to the Problem[1]

The most highly refined and scientific form of anthromorphic theism is that which we are accustomed to associate with Paley and the authors of Bridgewater treatises. It is not peculiar to Christianity, since it has been held by pagans and unbelievers as firmly as by the devoutest members of the church. The argument from design is as old as Sokrates, and was relied on by Voltaire and the English deists of the eighteenth century no less than by Dr. Chalmers and Sir Charles Bell. Upon this theory the universe is supposed to have been created by a Being possessed of intelligence and volition essentially similar to the intelligence and volition of Man. This Being is actuated by a desire for the good of his creatures, and in pursuance thereof entertains purposes and adapts means to ends with consummate ingenuity. The process by which the world was created was analogous to manufacture, as being the work of an intelligent artist operating upon unintelligent materials objectively existing. It is in accordance with this theory that books on natural theology, as well as those text-books of science which deem it edifying to introduce theological reflections where they have no proper place, are fond of speaking of the "Divine Architect" or the "Great Designer."

This theory, which is still commonly held, was in high favour during the earlier part of the present century. In view of the great and sudden advances which physical knowledge was making, it seemed well worth while to consecrate science to the service of theology; and at the same time, in emphasizing the argument from design, theology adopted the methods of science. The attempt to discover evidences of beneficent purpose in the structure of the eye and ear, in the distribution of plants and animals over the earth's surface, in the shapes of the planetary orbits and the inclinations of their axes, or in any other of the innumerable arrange-

[1] John Fiske, *The Idea of God as Affected by Modern Knowledge* (1885), selections from chapter 9.

ments of nature, was an attempt at true induction; and high praise is due to the able men who have devoted their energies to reinforcing the argument. By far the greater part of the evidence was naturally drawn from the organic world, which began to be comprehensively studied in the mutual relations of all its parts in the time of Lamarck and Cuvier. The organic world is full of unspeakably beautiful and wonderful adaptations between organisms and their environments, as well as between the various parts of the same organism. The unmistakable end of these adaptations is the welfare of the animal or plant; they conduce to length and completeness of life, to the permanence and prosperity of the species. For some time, therefore, the arguments of natural theology seemed to be victorious along the whole line. . . .

In its best days, however, there was a serious weakness in the argument from design, which was ably pointed out by Mr. Mill, in an essay wherein he accords much more weight to the general argument than could now by any possibility be granted it. Its fault was the familiar logical weakness of proving too much. The very success of the argument in showing the world to have been the work of an intelligent Designer made it impossible to suppose that Creator to be at once omnipotent and absolutely benevolent. For nothing can be clearer than that Nature is full of cruelty and maladaptation. In every part of the animal world we find implements of torture surpassing in devilish ingenuity anything that was ever seen in the dungeons of the Inquisition. We are introduced to a scene of incessant and universal strife, of which it is not apparent on the surface that the outcome is the good or the happiness of anything that is sentient. In pre-Darwinian times, before we had gone below the surface, no such outcome was discernible. Often, indeed, we find the higher life wantonly sacrificed to the lower, as instanced by the myriads of parasites apparently created for no other purpose than to prey upon creatures better than themselves. Such considerations bring up, with renewed emphasis, the everlasting problem of the origin of evil. If the Creator of such a world is omnipotent he cannot be actuated solely by a desire for the welfare of his creatures, but must have other ends in view to which this is in some measure subordinated. Or if he is absolutely benevolent, then he cannot be omnipotent, but there is something in the nature of things which sets limits to his creative power. This dilemma is as old as human thinking, and it still remains a stumbling-block in the way of any theory of the universe that can possibly be devised. But it is an obstacle especially formidable to any kind of anthropomorphic theism. For the only avenue of escape is the assumption of an inscrutable mystery which would contain the solution of the problem if the human intellect could only penetrate so far; and the more closely we invite a comparison between divine and human methods of working, the more do we close up that only outlet.

The practical solution oftenest adopted has been that which sacrifices the Creator's omnipotence in favour of his benevolence. In the noblest of the purely Aryan religions — that of which the sacred literature is contained in the Zendavesta — the evil spirit Ahriman exists independently of the will of the good Ormuzd, and is accountable for all the sin in the world, but in the fulness of time he is to be bound in chains and shorn of his power for mischief. This theory has passed into Christendom in the form of Manichaeism; but its essential features have been adopted by orthodox Christianity, which at the same time has tried to grasp the other horn of the dilemma and save the omnipotence of the Deity by paying him what Mr. Mill calls the doubtful compliment of making him the creator of the devil. By this device the essential polytheism of the conception is thinly veiled. The confusion of thought has been persistently blinded by the popular mind; but among the profoundest thinkers of the Aryan race there have been two who have explicitly adopted the solution which limits the Creator's power. One of these was Plato, who held that God's perfect goodness has been partially thwarted by the intractableness of the materials he has had to work with. This theory was carried to extremes by those Gnostics who believed that God's work consisted in redeeming a world originally created by the devil, and in orthodox Christianity it gave rise to the Augustinian doctrine of total depravity, and the "philosophy of the plan of salvation" founded thereon. The other great thinker who adopted a similar solution was Leibnitz. In his famous theory of optimism the world is by no means represented as perfect; it is only the best of all possible worlds, the best the Creator could make out of the materials at hand. In recent times Mr. Mill shows a marked preference for this view, and one of the foremost religious teachers now living, Dr. Martineau, falls into a parallel line of thinking in his suggestion that the primary qualities of matter constitute a "datum objective to God," who, "in shaping the orbits out of immensity, and determining seasons out of eternity, could but follow the laws of curvature, measure, and proportion."

But indeed it is not necessary to refer to the problem of evil in order to show that the argument from design cannot prove the existence of an omnipotent and benevolent Designer. It is not omnipotence that contrives and plans and adapts means to ends. These are the methods of finite intelligence; they imply the overcoming of obstacles; and to ascribe them to omnipotence is to combine words that severally possess meanings into a phrase that has no meaning. "God said, Let there be light: and there was light." In this noble description of creative omnipotence one would search in vain for any hint of contrivance. The most the argument from design could legitimately hope to accomplish was to make it seem probable that the universe was wrought into its present shape by an intelligent and benevolent Being immeasurably superior to Man, but far from infinite in power and resources. Such an argument hardly rises to the level of true theism.

59

FREDERICK ROBERT TENNANT

The Necessity of Evil[1]

The problem of evil has thus far been discussed with almost exclusive reference to evil of the moral kind. And the solution that has been presented consists in shewing the tenability of the belief that in our developing world all things work together, as a whole, for the highest conceivable good. The possibility of moral evil and the actuality of its consequences are inevitable concomitants of the 'best possible' evolutionary world. It is not maintained that everything is good, or that "whatever is, is right", or that partial evil is not evil because it is a condition of universal good. Nor is it implied that every particular evil is directly essential to the emergence of some particular good, or that it has its necessary place, like a dissonance in music, in the harmony of the world-process. When it is asserted that all things work together for good, by 'all things' is not meant each and every single thing, but the sum of things regarded as one whole or complex, the universe as a coherent order.

It is by adhering to this general view that the theist can best face the problem presented by the existence of that form of evil for which human freedom is not necessarily, and generally not at all, responsible: the physical evil, or the pain and suffering occasioned by the course of Nature in sentient beings. Indeed any other position than that which has just been summarised seems obviously inadequate as a basis for the explanation of the forthcomingness of physical ills. In order to reconcile the suffering inflicted by the material world upon mankind and other sentient creatures with the goodness and power of the Creator it is both superfluous and insufficient to seek to shew that in every particular case pain is essential to some special end, or that in each single instance suffering may fulfil some particular providential purpose. To attempt a theodicy on these lines is as hopeless as it would be to-day to develop a teleological argu-

[1] F. R. Tennant, *Philosophical Theology* (Cambridge: The University Press, 1928), Vol. II, 197-204. Reprinted by permission.

ment from particular instances of adaptedness, after the manner of Paley. But, as there is a wider teleology than Paley's so is there a wider theodicy than that which consists in pleading that human and animal pain are sometimes prophylactic — a warning against danger, or that human suffering is sometimes punitive or purgatorial, and thus subservient to benign ends. These assertions are undoubtedly true, and there is no need to belittle their import. But by themselves they will not carry us far towards a theodicy. They but touch the fringe of the problem: or, to change the metaphor, they do not go to the root of the matter. It is useless, again, to minimise the pain of the sentient world, or even to reduce our possibly extravagant and unscientific estimate of its intensity, except for the purpose of arguing that, in spite of pain, animal life is probably happy on the whole: otherwise a single pang of useless or superfluous pain is enough to raise our problem. It involves faulty psychology to assert that pain is the necessary background to pleasure; for a lesser pleasure would seem to yield a sufficient contrast to render the enjoyment of intenser pleasure possible. And if pain be sometimes stimulating, educational, preventitive, or remedial, as well as sometimes stunting, crushing, and provocative of moral evil, this fact is only significant for an estimation of the worth-whileness of sentient life. The knife may be nesessary to cure the disease, but why the necessity of the disease? The escape from mortal danger may require the painful warning, but why the mortal danger? Or, speaking generally, what are we to make of the remoter evil which renders the nearer evil necessary or salutary? The real problem obviously lies further back than these particular and partial solutions reach. It must be shewn that pain is either a necessary by-product of an order of things requisite for the emergence of the higher goods, or an essential instrument to organic evolution, or both. Short of this, we cannot refute the charge that the world is a clumsy arrangement or an imperfectly adjusted mechanism.

It can be argued, however, that the former of the foregoing alternatives is applicable in the case of human suffering, while the latter of them can be invoked to meet especially the case of animal pain. The suffering of the lower animals is not merely an accidental superfluity emerging out of the evolutionary process, but is essentially instrumental to organic progress. It renders unnecessary a large amount of inheritance of specialised structure and function, and so prevents the suppression of plasticity; and, as the 'sensitive edge' turned towards danger, or as prophylactic, it is of value for organic progressiveness. Although evil, it is also good for something. Much of human suffering, and many of the outrages of this present life upon our rational prudences and our most sacred affections, on the other hand, seem to be good for nothing, or to be non-essential for the realisation of goodness. If a man already has it in him to meet pain with fortitude and patience, he is not necessarily one whit the better man after actually enduring excruciating tortures; and if an all-powerful being 'appointed' him such tortures, merely in order that his fortitude might pass from potentiality to actuality, such a being would be but a superbrute. However, it be can argued that the forthcoming-ness of our suffering is inevitably incidental to a moral order in a de-veloping world. It issues ultimately out of what is inappropriately called metaphysical evil, or is a necessary outcome of a determinate cosmos of the particular kind that can sustain rational and moral life. The problem which it raises will therefore be solved if it can be maintained that no suffering such as we experience is superfluous to the cosmos as a coherent system and a moral order, however excessive pain often may be as a means to the accomplishment of specific ends such as are attainable by discipline and chastening.

It cannot be too strongly insisted that a world which is to be a moral order must be a physical order characterised by law or regularity. The routine of Nature may be differently described by the spiritualist, the dualist, etc.; but the diversity of these ultimate explanations of law does not affect the present problem. The theist is only concerned to invoke the fact that law-abidingness, on the scale which science is able to assert its subsistence in Nature as already *naturata*, is an essential condition of the world being a theatre of moral life. Without such regularity in physical phenomena there could be no probability to guide us: no pre-diction, no prudence, no accumulation of ordered experience, no pursuit of premeditated ends, no formation of habit, no possibility of character or of culture. Our intellectual faculties could not have developed. And, had they been innate, they would have wasted themselves, as Comte ob-served, in wild extravagances and sunk rapidly into incurable sloth; while our nobler feelings would have been unable to prevent the ascendancy of the lower instincts, and our active powers would have abandoned them-selves to purposeless agitation. All this is obvious; but it has often been ignored in discussion of the problem of physical evil. Nevertheless, Na-ture's regularity is the key to this problem. Once let it be admitted that, in order to be a theatre for moral life, the world must be largely char-acterised by uniformity or constancy, and most significant consequences will be seen to follow. It becomes idle to complain, as some writers have done, that the orderliness of the world is too dear at the cost of the suffer-ing and hardship which it entails, and might more or less be dispensed with for the benefit of the sentient and rational beings which people the world. As Hume admitted, if the "conducting of the world by general laws" were superseded by particular volitions, no man could employ his reason in the conduct of his life. And without rationality, morality is impossible: so, if the moral status of man be the goal of the evolutionary process, the reign of law is a *sine quâ non*. It is a condition of the forth-comingness of the highest good, in spite of that fact that it is not an unmixed good but a source of suffering. We cannot have the advantages of a determinate order of things without its logically or its causally necessary disadvantages. Nor can we be evaluating subjects without capacity to feel. The disadvantages, viz. particular ills, need not be regarded, however, as directly willed by God as ends in themselves or as particular means, among other equally possible but painless means, to particular ends. To make use of an ancient distinction, we may say that God wills them consequently, not antecedently. That is to say, they are not desired as such, or in themselves, but are only willed because the moral order, which is willed absolutely or antecedently by God, cannot be had without them. Now to will a moral order is to will the best possible world; and it also involves adoption of what we necessarily, if somewhat anthropomorphically, must call a determinate world-plan. Such a determinate method of procedure to realise a definite end in an evolutionary world, however, rules out once and for all any other possible goals and methods. As Dr. Martineau has put it, the cosmical equation being defined, only such results as are compatible with the values of its roots can be worked out, and these must be worked out. All determination is negation. If two consequences follow from a system of propositions, or two physical properties are involved in a configuration of particles, we cannot have the one without the other, though the one may be pleasing or beneficial to man and the other may be painful, or in its immediate effects hurtful. And such a result by no means implies lack of benevolence or of power on the part of the Creator, so long as power does not include inconsistency or inderterminateness. It simply bespeaks the inexorableness of logic, the compatibility of things, and the self-consistency of the Supreme Being. That painful events occur in the causal chain is a fact; but, that there could be a determinate evolutionary world of unalloyed comfort, yet adapted by its law-abidingness to the development of rationality and morality, is a proposition the burden of proving which must be allotted to the opponent of theism. One can only add that, in so far as experience in this world enables us to judge, such proof seems impossible. To illustrate what is here meant: if water is to have the various properties in virtue of which it plays its beneficial part in the economy of the physical world and the life of mankind, it cannot at the same time lack its obnoxious capacity to drown us. The specific gravity of water is as much a necessary outcome of its ultimate constitution as its freezing-point, or its thirst-quenching and cleansing functions. There cannot be assigned to any substance an arbitrarily selected group of qualities, from which all that ever may prove unfortunate to any sentient organism can be eliminated, especially if one organism's meat is to be another's poison, and yet the world, of which that substance forms a part, be a calculable cosmos. Mere determinateness and fixity of nature involve such and such concatenations of qualities, and rule out others. Thus physical ills follow with the same necessity as physical goods from the determinate 'world-plan' which secures that the world be a suitable stage for intelligent and ethical life.

And if this be so, the disadvantages which accrue from the determinateness and regularity of the physical world cannot be regarded either as absolute or as superfluous evils. They are not absolute evils because they are parts of an order which subserves the highest good in providing opportunity for moral development. And they are not superfluous ills because they are the necessary outcome of that order. They are collateral effects of what, in itself or as a whole, is good because instrumental to the highest good. They are not good, when good is hedonically defined; but they are good for good, when good is otherwise defined, rather than good for nothing.

As in the case of moral evil, so also in the case of physical evil, appeal has sometimes been made from necessary linkages and conditionings to a supposed possibility of their being over-ridden by divine omnipotence. And as it was found absurd to suppose that God could make developing beings at the same time morally free and temptationless, so it involves absurdity to suppose that the world could be a moral order without being a physical cosmos. To save mankind from the painful consequences which flow from a determinate world-order, such as the earthquake and the pestilence, would involve renunciation of a world-order, and therefore of a moral order, and the substitution of a chaos of incalculable miracle. Doubtless some directive agency, or the introduction of new streams of causation into the course of Nature, is conceivable without subversion of such regularity as is requisite for human prudence and without the stultification of our science. But the general suspension of painful events, requisite on the vast scale presupposed in the elimination of physical ills, would abolish order and convert a cosmos into an unintelligible chaos in which anything might succeed upon anything. We should have to "renounce reason" if we would thus be "saved from tears", as Martineau says.

Physical evil, then, must necessarily be. And the goodness of God is vindicated if there be no reason to believe that the world-process involves more misery than Nature's uniformity entails. It is not incumbent on the theist to prove that particular evils are never greater than we judge to be necessary for the production of particular salutary effects: that difficult task confronts only the particular kind of theism which is concerned to dispense with proximate causes and a more or less autonomous world, and regards God as the sole and immediate cause of every natural event, and of every incident in a personal life. According to the theodicy which has here been sketched, it is not necessary to suppose that every specific form of suffering that man undergoes — e.g. the agony of tetanus or of cancer — is antecedently willed by God as a means to some particular end. It can be admitted that excruciating pains are more severe than they need be for evoking virtues such as patience and fortitude, and that to assign them to God's antecedent will would be to attribute devilishness to the Deity. Moreover, the fact that some human beings are born as abortions, as imbecile or insane, seems to be inexplicable on the view that every form of suffering is a particular providence, or an antecedently willed dispensation for educating and spiritually perfecting the person on whom the affliction falls; while to suppose that suffering is inflicted on one person for the spiritual edification of another is again to conceive of God as immoral. But the hardest fact of all for human equanimity, in presence of physical and mental evil, is that the apportionment of suffering among individuals is entirely irreconcilable by us with any divine plan of adjustment of particular afflictions to the particular needs, circumstances, and stages of moral development, of individual sufferers. Even more distressing to human thought than the goading intensity of some kinds of pain is the seemingly chaotic distribution of human ills. If we could trace the utility of particular sufferings with their varying degrees of endurableness, or discern any adaptation of pain to the person's sensibility, moral state, and need of awakening or chastening, then philosophy might be able to agree with the simpleminded piety which assigns a special purpose to every instance of suffering, and finds therein the visitation or appointment of an all-wise and all-good God. But the wind is not tempered to the shorn lamb; the fieriest trials often overtake those who least need torments to inspire fear, to evoke repentance, or to perfect patience, and also those who, through no fault of their own, lack the mature religious faith and moral experience by which alone they could understand how affliction may be endured for their souls' good. "All things come alike to all: there is one event to the righteous and to the wicked" — to those who may be enabled, and to those who are unable, to profit by severe trial.

Disastrous as these facts are to the extremer forms of the doctrine of divine immanence in Nature, they are compatible with theism such as allows to the created world somewhat of delegated autonomy. According to the wider theodicy which has here been presented, the human afflictions arising from our relations with the physical world are not willed as such by God at all, or for any purpose. They are rather inevitable, if incidental, accompaniments or by-products of the world-order which, as a whole, and by means of its uniformity, is a pre-requisite of the actualisation of the highest good that we can conceive a world as embodying. The world is none the less God's world for its callousness to man; but its autonomy, not the particular incidence of each single ill, is what the religious should attribute to His "appointment".

Further, man himself does not deem his suffering to be an excessive price to pay for the dignity of his ethical status, once he recognises physical evil to be inevitable in a moral world. He is then not compelled to see in his suffering self a mere means either to the perfecting of the race, or to the realisation of a divine purpose, or to the manifestation of the 'glory' of God. And this is an important consideration for any theodicy. For man is an end for himself, whatever else he may be. *My* ills can only be justified to *me* if the remoter advantage of there being ills at all be *mine*: not humanity's, or even God's alone. But in that the remoter advantage is the enjoyment of rational and ethical dignity, the individual man can acquiesce in God's purpose for the world: God's ideal may be his also. It is the assurance that God is fulfilling us individually as well as Himself, and fulfilling us for ourselves as well as for Himself, that makes human life in this bitter-sweet world endurable by the sensitively and delicately minded, the tender-hearted, believer. It is because a being of the earth, yet so God-like as man, could not be moulded into the image of God *save from within himself*, as a person or a free agent, that man can account the payment of the sometimes exorbitant price of the chance of learning love inevitable.

Part Eight: MIRACLES

Their Nature and the Question of
Their Validity

60

ST. THOMAS AQUINAS

The Miraculous[1]

Whether God Can Do Anything Outside the Established Order of Nature?

. . . From each cause there results a certain order to its effects, since every cause is a principle; and so, according to the multiplicity of causes, there results a multiplicity of orders, subject one to the other, just as cause is subject to cause. Hence, a higher cause is not subject to a cause of a lower order, but conversely. An example of this may be seen in human affairs. On the father of a family depends the order of the household; which order is contained in the order of the city; which order again depends on the ruler of the city; while this last order depends on that of the king by whom the whole kingdom is ordered.

If, therefore, we consider the order of things according as it depends on the first cause, God cannot do anything against this order; for, if He did so, He would act against His foreknowledge, or His will, or His goodness. But if we consider the order of things according as it depends on any secondary cause, thus God can do something outside such order. For He is not subject to the order of secondary causes, but, on the contrary, this order is subject to Him, as proceeding from Him, not by a natural necessity, but by the choice of His own will; for He could have created another order of things. Therefore God can do something outside this order created by Him, when He chooses, — for instance, by producing the effects of secondary causes without them, or by producing certain effects to which secondary causes do not extend. So Augustine says: *God acts against the wonted course of nature, but by no means does He act against the supreme law; because He does not act against Himself.*

. . . In natural things something may happen outside this natural order, in two ways. It may happen by the action of an agent which did not

---

[1] St. Thomas Aquinas, *The Summa Theologica*, from the *Basic Writings of Saint Thomas Aquinas*, tr. by Lawrence Shapcote, edited and annotated by Anton C. Pegis (London: Burns & Oates, Ltd., and New York: Random House, Inc., 1945), Q. 105, Art. 6-7. Reprinted by permission.

give them their natural inclination, as, for example, when a man moves a heavy body upwards, which does not owe to him its natural inclination to move downwards. Now this would be against nature. It may also happen by the action of the agent on whom the natural inclination depends, and this is not against nature, as is clear in the ebb and flow of the tide, which is not against nature, although it is against the natural movement of water, which is moved downward; for it is owing to the influence of a heavenly body, on which the natural inclination of lower bodies depends. Therefore since the order of nature is given to things by God, if He does anything outside this order, it is not against nature. Hence Augustine says: *That is natural to each thing which is caused by Him from Whom is all limit, number and order in nature* . . .

. . . God fixed a certain order of things in such a way that at the same time He reserved to Himself whatever He intended to do otherwise than by a particular cause. So when He acts outside this order, He does not change.

Whether Whatever God Does Outside the Natural Order Is Miraculous?

. . . The term *miracle* is derived from admiration, which arises when an effect is manifest, whereas its cause is hidden; as when a man sees an eclipse without knowing its cause, as the Philosopher says in the beginning of his *Metaphysics.*[2] Now the cause of a manifest effect may be known to one, but unknown to others. Hence a thing is wonderful to one man, and not at all to others; as an eclipse is to a rustic, but not to an astronomer. Now a miracle is so called as being full of wonder, in other words, as having a cause absolutely hidden from all. This cause is God. Therefore those things which God does outside the cause which we know are called miracles.

. . . Creation, and the justification of the unrighteous, though done by God alone, are not, properly speaking, miracles, because they are not of a nature to proceed from any other cause; so they do not occur outside the order of nature, since they do not belong to the capacity of nature.

. . . An arduous thing is called a miracle, not because of the excellence of the thing wherein it is done, but because it surpasses the ability of nature. So, too, a thing is called unusual not because it does not often happen, but because it is outside the usual natural course of things. Furthermore, a thing is said to be above the ability of nature, not only by reason of the substance of the thing done, but also because of the manner and order in which it is done. Again, a miracle is said to go beyond the hope *of nature*, not above the hope *of grace*, which hope comes from faith, whereby we believe in the future resurrection. . . .

2 Aristotle, *Metaph.*, I, 2 (982b 16).

BENEDICT SPINOZA

BENEDICT SPINOZA (1632-1677), a Jewish philosopher, reasoning that he could be equally as blessed in Latin as in Hebrew, changed his name from Baruch (Hebrew for **blessed**) to the Latin, Benedict, as a result of his excommunication in 1656 from the Jewish Synagogue. He was born in Amsterdam on Nov. 24, 1632, and died 44 short years later in The Hague on Feb. 21, 1677. Spinoza's parents were crypto-Jews (Jews converted to Christianity by force during the Spanish Inquisition, yet in spirit remaining Jews), who fled Portugal for Holland where the Union of Utrecht decreed freedom of religion. The young Benedict was trained by Rabbis in Hebrew School where he came under the tutelege of Saul Morteira and Manasseh ben Israel, the most eminent scholars of the Jewish community. In 1670, Spinoza lived at Rijnsburg, the neighboring country near Amsterdam and Leyden; the years after 1670 to his death, he lived in The Hague. Refusing the chair of philosophy at Heidelberg in 1673 because he cherished absolute freedom of thought in his pursuit of philosophical truth, he earned his living by grinding lenses and offering private instruction as a tutor.

Only two works were published during Spinoza's lifetime: **Renati des Cartes Principiorum Philosophiae** (1663), and the celebrated **Tractatus Theologico-Politicus** (1670), from which has been excerpted the passage pertaining to miracles for use in the present text. His other works were published the year of his death, 1677; among which are: **Ethics, On the Improvement of the Understanding,** and **Political Treatise.**

Spinoza, a Pantheist, conceived God to be the totality of reality; all is God, and God is all. Ultimate reality, a single Substance or which is the same, God, possesses an infinite number of attributes, of which two only are known: mind and matter. Mind and matter are two aspects of the same reality, consequently when one of the two is affected the other is concomitantly affected also (the doctrine of Psychophysical Parallelism). God's existence is proved by definition, since for the Pantheist, whatever exists is God; to deny God is to deny the existence of any and all reality. As God exists by necessity, so does immortality, since Substance or God (of which human individuals comprise a part) is indestructible and eternal.

As for miracles, such things cannot exist for they run counter to the rational order of the universe. They are repugnant to God who behaves rationally; they are characteristic more of a devil than God; they substantiate Atheism, not God's existence.

61

BENEDICT SPINOZA

Criticism of Miracles[1]

As men are accustomed to call Divine the knowledge which transcends human understanding, so also do they style Divine, or the work of God, anything of which the cause is not generally known: for the masses think that the power and providence of God are most clearly displayed by events that are extraordinary and contrary to the conception they have formed of nature, especially if such events bring them any profit or convenience: they think that the clearest possible proof of God's existence is afforded when nature, as they suppose, breaks her accustomed order, and consequently they believe that those who explain or endeavour to understand phenomena or miracles through their natural causes are doing away with God and His providence. They suppose, forsooth, that God is inactive so long as nature works in her accustomed order, and *vice versâ*, that the power of nature and natural causes are idle so long as God is acting: thus they imagine two powers distinct one from the other, the power of God and the power of nature, though the latter is in a sense determined by God, or (as most people believe now) created by Him. What they mean by either, and what they understand by God and nature they do not know, except that they imagine the power of God to be like that of some royal potentate, and nature's power to consist in force and energy.

The masses then style unusual phenomenon "miracles," and partly from piety, partly for the sake of opposing the students of science, prefer to remain in ignorance of natural causes, and only to hear of those things which they know least, and consequently admire most. In fact, the common people can only adore God, and refer all things to His power by removing natural causes, and conceiving things happening out of their due

[1] Benedict Spinoza, *Theologico-Political Treatise,* tr. R. H. M. Elwes (1883); excerpts from ch. VI, "Of Miracles."

course, and only admires the power of God when the power of nature
is conceived of as in subjection to it.

This idea seems to have taken its rise among the early Jews who saw
the Gentiles round them worshipping visible gods such as the sun, the
moon, the earth, water, air, &c., and in order to inspire the conviction
that such divinities were weak and inconstant, or changeable, told how
they themselves were under the sway of an invisible God, and narrated
their miracles, trying further to show that the God whom they worshipped arranged the whole of nature for their sole benefit: this idea was
so pleasing to humanity that men go on to this day imagining miracles, so
that they may believe themselves God's favourites, and the final cause for
which God created and directs all things.

What pretension will not people in their folly advance! They have no
single sound idea concerning either God or nature, they confound God's
decrees with human decrees, they conceive nature as so limited that they
believe man to be its chief part! I have spent enough space in setting
forth these common ideas and prejudices concerning nature and miracles,
but in order to afford a regular demonstration I will show —

I.   That nature cannot be contravened, but that she preserves a fixed
and immutable order, and at the same time I will explain what is meant
by a miracle.

II.   That God's nature and existence, and consequently His providence cannot be known from miracles, but that they can all be much
better perceived from the fixed and immutable order of nature.

III.   That by the decrees and volitions, and consequently the providence of God, Scripture (as I will prove by Scriptural examples) means
nothing but nature's order following necessarily from her eternal laws.

IV.   Lastly, I will treat of the method of interpreting Scriptural
miracles, and the chief points to be noted concerning the narratives of
them.

. . . Our first point is easily proved from what we showed in Chap. IV.
about Divine law — namely, that all that God wishes or determines involves eternal necessity and truth, for we demonstrated that God's understanding is identical with His will, and that it is the same thing to say
that God wills a thing, as to say that He understands it; hence, as it
follows necessarily from the Divine nature and perfection that God understands a thing as it is, it follows no less necessarily that He wills it as
it is. Now, as nothing is necessarily true save only by Divine decree, it is
plain that the universal laws of nature are decrees of God following from
the necessity and perfection of the Divine nature. Hence, any event happening in nature which contravened nature's universal laws, would necessarily also contravene the Divine decree, nature, and understanding; or if

anyone asserted that God acts in contravention to the laws of nature, he *ipso facto*, would be compelled to assert that God acted against His own nature — an evident absurdity. One might easily show from the same premises that the power and efficiency of nature are in themselves the Divine power and efficiency, and that the Divine power is the very essence of God, but this I gladly pass over for the present.

Nothing, then, comes to pass in nature[2] in contravention to her universal laws, nay, everything agrees with them and follows from them, for whatsoever comes to pass, comes to pass by the will and eternal decree of God; that is, as we have just pointed out, whatever comes to pass, comes to pass according to laws and rules which involve eternal necessity and truth; nature, therefore, always observes laws and rules which involve eternal necessity and truth, although they may not all be known to us, and therefore she keeps a fixed and immutable order. Nor is there any sound reason for limiting the power and efficacy of nature, and asserting that her laws are fit for certain purposes, but not for all; for as the efficacy and power of nature, are the very efficacy and power of God, and as the laws and rules of nature are the decrees of God, it is in every way to be believed that the power of nature is infinite, and that her laws are broad enough to embrace everything conceived by the Divine intellect; the only alternative is to assert that God has created nature so weak, and has ordained for her laws so barren, that He is repeatedly compelled to come afresh to her aid if He wishes that she should be preserved, and that things should happen as He desires: a conclusion, in my opinion, very far removed from reason. Further, as nothing happens in nature which does not follow from her laws, and as her laws embrace everything conceived by the Divine intellect, and lastly, as nature preserves a fixed and immutable order; it most clearly follows that miracles are only intelligible as in relation to human opinions, and merely mean events of which the natural cause cannot be explained by a reference to any ordinary occurrence, either by us, or at any rate, by the writer and narrator of the miracle.

We may, in fact, say that a miracle is an event of which the causes cannot be explained by the natural reason through a reference to ascertained workings of nature; but since miracles were wrought according to the understanding of the masses, who are wholly ignorant of the workings of nature, it is certain that the ancients took for a miracle whatever they could not explain by the method adopted by the unlearned in such cases, namely, an appeal to the memory, a recalling of something similar, which is ordinarily regarded without wonder; for most people think they

---

[2] N.B. I do not mean here by "nature," merely matter and its modifications, but infinite other things besides matter.

sufficiently understand a thing when they have ceased to wonder at it. The ancients, then, and indeed most men up to the present day, had no other criterion for a miracle; hence we cannot doubt that many things are narrated in Scripture as miracles of which the causes could easily be explained by reference to ascertained workings of nature. . . .

It is now time to pass on to the second point, and show that we cannot gain an understanding of God's essence, existence, or providence by means of miracles, but that these truths are much better perceived through the fixed and immutable order of nature.

I thus proceed with the demonstration. As God's existence is not self-evident, it must necessarily be inferred from ideas so firmly and incontrovertibly true, that no power can be postulated or conceived sufficient to impugn them. They ought certainly so to appear to us when we infer from them God's existence, if we wish to place our conclusion beyond the reach of doubt; for if we could conceive that such ideas could be impugned by any power whatsoever, we should doubt of their truth, we should doubt of our conclusion, namely, of God's existence, and should never be able to be certain of anything. Further we know that nothing either agrees with or is contrary to these primary ideas; wherefore if we would conceive that anything could be done in nature by any power whatsoever which would be contrary to the laws of nature, it would be contrary to our primary ideas, and we should have either to reject it as absurd, or else to cast doubt (as just shown) on our primary ideas, and consequently on the existence of God, and on everything howsoever perceived. Therefore miracles, in the sense of events contrary to the laws of nature, so far from demonstrating to us the existence of God, would, on the contrary, lead us to doubt it, where otherwise, we might have been absolutely certain of it, as knowing that nature follows a fixed and immutable order.

Let us take miracle as meaning that which cannot be explained through natural causes. This may be interpreted in two senses: either as that which has natural causes, but cannot be examined by the human intellect; or as that which has no cause save God and God's will. But as all things which come to pass through natural causes, come to pass also solely through the will and power of God, it comes to this, that a miracle, whether it has natural causes or not, is a result which cannot be explained by its cause, that is a phenomenon which surpasses human understanding; but from such a phenomenon, and certainly from a result surpassing our understanding, we can gain no knowledge. For whatsoever we understand clearly and distinctly should be plain to us either in itself or by means of something else clearly and distinctly understood; wherefore from a miracle or a phenomenon which we cannot understand, we can gain no knowledge of God's essence, or existence, or indeed any-thing about God or nature; whereas when we know that all things are ordained and ratified by God, that the operations of nature follow from the essence of God, and that the laws of nature are eternal decrees and volitions of God, we must perforce conclude that our knowledge of God and of God's will increases in proportion to our knowledge and clear understanding of nature, as we see how she depends on her primal cause, and how she works according to eternal law. Wherefore so far as our un-derstanding goes, those phenomena which we clearly and distinctly un-derstand have much better right to be called works of God, and to be referred to the will of God than those about which we are entirely igno-rant, although they appeal powerfully to the imagination, and compel men's admiration.

It is only phenomena that we clearly and distinctly understand, which heighten our knowledge of God, and most clearly indicate His will and decree. Plainly, they are but triflers who, when they cannot explain a thing, run back to the will of God; this is, truly, a ridiculous way of ex-pressing ignorance. Again, even supposing that some conclusion could be drawn from miracles, we could not possibly infer from them the exist-ence of God: for a miracle being an event under limitations is the expres-sion of a fixed and limited power; therefore we could not possibly infer from an effect of this kind the existence of a cause whose power is infi-nite, but at the utmost only of a cause whose power is greater than that of the said effect. I say at the utmost, for a phenomenon may be the re-sult of many concurrent causes, and its power may be less than the power of the sum of such causes, but far greater than that of any one of them taken individually. On the other hand, the laws of nature, as we have shown, extend over infinity, and are conceived by us as, after a fashion, eternal, and nature works in accordance with them in a fixed and immu-table order; therefore, such laws indicate to us in a certain degree the infinity, the eternity, and the immutability of God.

We may conclude, then, that we cannot gain knowledge of the ex-istence and providence of God by means of miracles, but that we can far better infer them from the fixed and immutable order of nature. By miracle, I here mean an event which surpasses, or is thought to surpass, human comprehension: for in so far as it is supposed to destroy or inter-rupt the order of nature or her laws, it not only can give us no knowl-edge of God, but, contrariwise, takes away that which we naturally have, and makes us doubt of God and everything else.

Neither do I recognize any difference between an event against the laws of nature and an event beyond the laws of nature (that is, according to some, an event which does not contravene nature, though she is inadequate to produce or effect it) — for a miracle is wrought in, and not beyond nature, though it may be said in itself to be above nature, and, therefore, must necessarily interrupt the order of nature, which otherwise we conceive of as fixed and unchangeable, according to God's decrees. If, therefore, anything should come to pass in nature which does not follow from her laws, it would also be in contravention to the order which God has established in nature for ever through universal natural laws: it would, therefore, be in contravention to God's nature and laws, and consequently, belief in it would throw doubt upon everything, and lead to Atheism.

I think I have now sufficiently established my second point, so that we can again conclude that a miracle, whether in contravention to, or beyond, nature, is a mere absurdity; and, therefore, that what is meant in Scripture by a miracle can only be a work of nature, which surpasses, or is believed to surpass, human comprehension. . . .

I now go on to my *third* point, and show from Scripture that the decree and mandates of God, and consequently His providence, are merely the order of nature — that is, when Scripture describes an event as accomplished by God or God's will, we must understand merely that it was in accordance with the law and order of nature, not, as most people believe, that nature had for a season ceased to act, or that her order was temporarily interrupted. But Scripture does not directly teach matters unconnected with its doctrine, wherefore it has no care to explain things by their natural causes, nor to expound matters merely speculative. Wherefore our conclusion must be gathered by inference from those Scriptural narratives which happen to be written more at length and circumstantially than usual. . . .

The circumstances of the miracles clearly show, I maintain, that natural causes were needed. For instance, in order to infect the Egyptians with blains, it was necessary that Moses should scatter ashes in the air (Exod. ix. 10); the locusts also came upon the land of Egypt by a command of God in accordance with nature, namely, by an east wind blowing for a whole day and night; and they departed by a very strong west wind (Exod. x. 14, 19). By a similar Divine mandate the sea opened a way for the Jews (Exod. xiv. 21), namely, by an east wind which blew very strongly all night. . . .

Again, in John's Gospel (chap. ix) certain acts are mentioned as performed by Christ preparatory to healing the blind man, and there are numerous other instances showing that something further than the absolute fiat of God is required for working a miracle.

Wherefore we may believe that, although the circumstances attending miracles are not related always or in full detail, yet a miracle was never performed without them. . . .

There remain some points concerning the interpretation of miracles to be noted, or rather to be recapitulated, for most of them have been already stated. These I proceed to discuss in the fourth division of my subject, and I am led to do so lest anyone should, by wrongly interpreting a miracle, rashly suspect that he has found something in Scripture contrary to human reason.

It is very rare for men to relate an event simply as it happened, without adding any element of their own judgment. When they see or hear anything new, they are, unless strictly on their guard, so occupied with their own preconceived opinions that they perceive something quite different from the plain facts seen or heard, especially if such facts surpass the comprehension of the beholder or hearer, and, most of all, if he is interested in their happening in a given way. . . .

Lastly, in order to understand, in the case of miracles what actually took place, we ought to be familiar with Jewish phrases and metaphors; anyone who did not make sufficient allowance for these, would be continually seeing miracles in Scripture where nothing of the kind is intended by the writer; he would thus miss the knowledge not only of what actually happened, but also of the mind of the writers of the sacred text. . . .

The conclusion, then, that is most plainly put before us is, that miracles were natural occurrences, and must therefore be so explained as to appear neither new (in the words of Solomon) nor contrary to nature, but, as far as possible, in complete agreement with ordinary events. This can easily be done by anyone, now that I have set forth the rules drawn from Scripture. Nevertheless, though I maintain that Scripture teaches this doctrine, I do not assert that it teaches it as a truth necessary to salvation, but only that the prophets were in agreement with ourselves on the point; therefore everyone is free to think on the subject as he likes, according as he thinks it best for himself, and most likely to conduce to the worship of God and to single-hearted religion . . .

DAVID HUME

DAVID HUME (1711-1776), born in Edinburgh, Scotland on April 26, 1711, is considered by some authorities to be Britain's greatest philosopher. His education was given at home until his matriculation at the University of Edinburgh in 1723. His many attempts to acquire a professorship failed, and he had to be satisfied serving in the capacity of tutor in 1744, and as librarian in 1751, as far as the academic life was concerned. During other periods, he was secretary to Gen. James St. Clair, and secretary to the embassy (though without enjoying that title), but most of the time, he wrote.

His work of genius, the **Treatise on Human Nature** (1739) "fell dead born from the press," he writes, owing to its difficult and clumsy style; accordingly, he was induced to rewrite it. Its revision appeared in several volumes under the following titles: **An Enquiry concerning Human Understanding** (1748), **A Dissertation on the Passions** (1751), **An Enquiry concerning the Principles of Morals** (1751), **Essays, Moral, Political, and Literary** (1741). Other of his writings are: **The Natural History of Religion** (1755), **Autobiography** (1777), and **Dialogues concerning Natural Religion** (1779, posthumously).

Hume's position in philosophy has reached magnitudinal proportions; not only is he one of the greatest of English philosophers, but some contemporary Logical Positivists regard him as the founder of, or at least the individual whose philosophy inspired, Neopositivism.

Hume placed no credence in miracles. Although he was not, strictly speaking, an Atheist since he accepted the argument of God's existence from design (the Argument from Analogy), he did not believe that the proof of God could be demonstrated in the sense that scientific facts are. But miracles, he repudiated on the grounds that: (1) They are singularly extraordinary. (2) The questionability of witnesses, since individuals testifying to miracles lived in former periods and could not be cross-examined. (3) Some witnesses are of questionable integrity, or untrained and unreliable in reporting pertinent data regarding miracles.

(4) No miracle has been attested to by a sufficient number of reliable witnesses. (5) Persons are psychologically predisposed to gullibility in matters so appealing and desirable as miracles. (6) The fact that miracles abound in nations and peoples who are ignorant and barbarous serves to raise doubts as to their validity. (7) The miracles of peoples of differing nations and religions contradict one another.

62

DAVID HUME

Of Miracles[1]

Part I

There is, in Dr. Tillotson's writings, an argument against the *real presence,* which is as concise, and elegant, and strong as any argument can possibly be supposed against a doctrine, so little worthy of a serious refutation. It is acknowledged on all hands, says that learned prelate, that the authority, either of the scripture or of tradition, is founded merely in the testimony of the apostles, who were eye-witnesses to those miracles of our Saviour, by which he proved his divine mission. Our evidence, then, for the truth of the *Christian* religion is less than the evidence for the truth of our senses; because, even in the first authors of our religion, it was no greater; and it is evident it must diminish in passing from them to their disciples; nor can anyone rest such confidence in their testimony, as in the immediate object of his senses. But a weaker evidence can never destroy a stronger; and therefore, were the doctrine of the real presence ever so clearly revealed in scripture, it were directly contrary to the rules of just reasoning to give our assent to it. It contradicts sense, though both the scripture and tradition, on which it is supposed to be built, carry not such evidence with them as sense; when they are considered merely as external evidences, and are not brought home to everyone's breast, by the immediate operation of the Holy Spirit.

Nothing is so convenient as a decisive argument of this kind, which must at least *silence* the most arrogant bigotry and superstition, and free us from their impertinent solicitations. I flatter myself, that I have discovered an argument of a like nature, which, if just, will, with the wise and learned, be an everlasting check to all kinds of superstition delusion, and consequently, will be useful as long as the world endures. For so

[1] David Hume, *An Enquiry concerning Human Understanding* (1748), section X, parts 1 and 2, (excerpts).

394

extraordinary events.

long, I presume, will the accounts of miracles and prodigies be found in all history, sacred and profane.

Though experience be our only guide in reasoning concerning matters of fact; it must be acknowledged, that this guide is not altogether infallible, but in some cases is apt to lead us into errors. One, who in our climate, should expect better weather in any week of June than in one of December, would reason justly, and comformably to experience; but it is certain, that he may happen, in the event, to find himself mistaken. However, we may observe, that, in such a case, he would have no cause to complain of experience; because it commonly informs us beforehand of the uncertainty, by that contrariety of events, which we may learn from a diligent observation. All effects follow not with like certainty from their supposed causes. Some events are found, in all countries and all ages, to have been constantly conjoined together. Others are found to have been more variable, and sometimes to disappoint our expectations; so that, in our reasonings concerning matter of fact, there are all imaginable degrees of assurance, from the highest certainty to the lowest species of moral evidence.

A wise man, therefore, proportions his belief to the evidence. In such conclusions as are founded on an infallible experience, he expects the events with the last degree of assurance, and regards his past experience as full *proof* of the future existence of that event. In other cases, he proceeds with more caution; he weighs the opposite experiments; he considers which side is supported by the greater number of experiments; to that side he inclines, with doubt and hesitation; and when at last he fixes his judgment, the evidence exceeds not what we properly call *probability*. All probability, then, supposes an opposition of experiments and observations, where the one side is found to overbalance the other, and to produce a degree of evidence, proportioned to the superiority. A hundred instances or experiments on one side, and fifty on another, afford a double expectation of any event; though a hundred uniform experiments, with only one that is contradictory, reasonably begets a pretty strong degree of assurance. In all cases, we must balance the opposite experiments, where they are opposite, and deduct the smaller number from the greater, in order to know the exact force of the superior evidence.

To apply these principles to a particular instance; we may observe, that there is no species of reasoning more common, more useful, and even necessary to human life, than that which is derived from the testimony of men, and the reports of eye-witnesses and spectators. This species of reasoning, perhaps, one may deny to be founded on the relation of cause and effect. I shall not dispute about a word. It will be sufficient to observe that our assurance in any argument of this kind is derived from no other principle than our observation of the veracity of human testimony, and of the usual conformity of facts to the reports of witnesses. It being a general maxim, that no objects have any discoverable connection together, and that all the inferences, which we can draw from one to another, are founded merely on our experience of their constant and regular conjunction; it is evident, that we ought not to make an exception to this maxim in favor of human testimony, whose connection with any event seems, in itself, as little necessary as any other. Were not the memory tenacious to a certain degree; had not men commonly an inclination to truth and a principle of probity, were they not sensible to shame, when detected in a falsehood: were not these, I say, discovered by *experience* to be qualities, inherent in human nature, we should never repose the least confidence in human testimony. A man delirious, or noted for falsehood and villainy, has no manner of authority with us.

And as the evidence, derived from witnesses and human testimony, is founded on past experience, so it varies with the experience, and is regarded either as *proof* or a *probability*, according as the conjunction between any particular kind of report and any kind of object has been found to be constant or variable. There are a number of circumstances to be taken into consideration in all judgments of this kind; and the ultimate standard, by which we determine all disputes, that may arise concerning them, is always derived from experience and observation. Where this experience is not entirely uniform on any side, it is attended with an unavoidable contrariety in our judgments, and with the same opposition and mutual destruction of argument as in every other kind of evidence. We frequently hesitate concerning the reports of others. We balance the opposite circumstances, which cause any doubt or uncertainty; and when we discover a superiority on one side, we incline to it; but still with a diminution of assurance, in proportion to the force of its antagonist.

This contrariety of evidence, in the present case, may be derived from several different causes; from the opposition of contrary testimony; from the character or number of the witnesses; from the manner of their delivering their testimony; or from the union of all these circumstances. We entertain a suspicion concerning any matter of fact, when the witnesses contradict each other; when they are but few, or of a doubtful character; when they have an interest in what they affirm; when they deliver their testimony with hesitation, or on the contrary, with too violent asseverations. There are many other particulars of the same kind, which may diminish or destroy the force of any argument, derived from human testimony.

how the force of argument may diminish testimony.

Suppose, for instance, that the fact, which the testimony endeavors to establish, partakes of the extraordinary and marvellous; in the case, the evidence, resulting from the testimony, admits of a diminution, greater or less, in proportion as the fact is more or less unusual. The reason why we place any credit in witnesses and historians, is not derived from any *connection*, which we perceive *a priori*, between testimony and reality, but because we are accustomed to find a conformity between them. But when the fact attested is such a one as has seldom fallen under our observation, here is a contest of two opposite experiences; of which the one destroys the other, as far as its force goes, and the superior can only operate on the mind by the force, which remains. The very same principle of experience, which gives us a certain degree of assurance in the testimony of witnesses, gives us also, in this case, another degree of assurance against the fact, which they endeavour to establish; from which contradiction there necessarily arises a counterpoise, and mutual destruction of belief and authority.

I should not believe such a story were it told me by Cato, was a proverbial saying in Rome, even during the lifetime of that philosophical patriot. The incredibility of a fact, it was allowed, might invalidate so great an authority.

The Indian prince, who refused to believe the first relations concerning the effects of frost, reasoned justly; and it naturally required very strong testimony to engage his assent to fact, that arose from a state of nature, with which he was unacquainted, and which bore so little analogy to those events, of which he had had constant and uniform experience. Though they were not contrary to his experience, they were not conformable to it.

But in order to increase the probability against the testimony of witnesses, let us suppose, that the fact, which they affirm, instead of being only marvellous, is really miraculous; and suppose also, that the testimony considered apart and in itself, amounts to an entire proof; in that case, there is proof against proof, of which the strongest must prevail, but still with a diminution of its force, in proportion to that of its antagonist.

A miracle is a violation of the laws of nature; and as a firm and unalterable experience has established these laws, the proof against a miracle, from the very nature of the fact, is as entire as any argument from experience can possibly be imagined. Why is it more than probable, that all men must die; that lead cannot, of itself, remain suspended in the air; that fire consumes wood, and is extinguished by water; unless it be, that these events are found agreeable to the laws of nature, and there is required a violation of these laws, or in other words, a miracle to prevent them? Nothing is esteemed a miracle, if it ever happen in the common course of nature. It is no miracle that a man, seemingly in good health, should die on a sudden: because such a kind of death, though more unusual than any other, has yet been frequently observed to happen. But it is a miracle, that a dead man should come to life; because that has never been observed in any age or country. There must, therefore, be a uniform experience against every miraculous event, otherwise the event would not merit that appellation. And as a uniform experience amounts to a proof, there is here a direct and full *proof*, from the nature of the fact, against the existence of any miracle; nor can such a proof be destroyed, or the miracle rendered credible, but by an opposite proof, which is superior.

The plain consequence is (and it is a general maxim worthy of our attention), 'That no testimony is sufficient to establish a miracle, unless the testimony be of such a kind, that its falsehood would be more miraculous, than the fact, which it endeavors to establish; and even in that case there is a mutual destruction of arguments, and the superior only gives us an assurance suitable to that degree of force, which remains, after deducting the inferior.' When anyone tells me, that he saw a dead man restored to life, I immediately consider with myself, whether it be more probable, that this person should either deceive or be deceived, or that the fact, which he relates, should really have happened. I weigh the one miracle against the other; and according to the superiority, which I discover, I pronounce my decision, and always reject the greater miracle. If the falsehood of his testimony would be more miraculous, than the event which he relates; then, and not till then, can he pretend to command my belief or opinion.

Part II

In the foregoing reasoning we have supposed, that the testimony, upon which a miracle is founded, may possibly amount to an entire proof, and that the falsehood of that testimony would be a real prodigy. But it is easy to show, that we have been a great deal too liberal in our concession, and that there never was a miraculous event established on so full an evidence.

For *first*, there is not to be found, in all history, any miracle attested by a sufficient number of men, of such unquestioned good sense, education, and learning, as to secure us against all delusion in themselves; of such undoubted integrity, as to place them beyond all suspicion of any design to deceive others; of such credit and reputation in the eyes of mankind, as to have a great deal to lose in case of their being detected in any falsehood; and at the same time, attesting facts performed in such a

[handwritten at top: almost say "why can't all be assumed of miracles" — all would then have to ~~experience~~]

public manner and in so celebrated a part of the world, as to render the detection unavoidable: all which circumstances are requisite to give us a full assurance in the testimony of men.

Secondly. We may observe in human nature a principle which, if strictly examined, will be found to diminish extremely the assurance, which we might, from human testimony, have, in any kind of prodigy. The maxim, by which we commonly conduct ourselves in our reasonings, is, that the objects, of which we have no experience, resemble those, of which we have; that what we have found to be most usual is always most probable; and that where there is an opposition of arguments, we ought to give the preference to such as are founded on the greatest number of past observations. But though, in proceeding by this rule, we readily reject any fact which is unusual and incredible in an ordinary degree; yet in advancing farther, the mind observes not always the same rule; but when anything is affirmed utterly absurd and miraculous, it rather the more readily admits of such a fact, upon account of that very circumstance, which ought to destroy all its authority. The passion of *surprise* and *wonder*, arising from miracles, being an agreeable emotion, gives a sensible tendency towards the belief of those events, from which it is derived. And this goes so far, that even those who cannot enjoy this pleasure immediately, nor can believe those miraculous events, of which they are informed, yet love to partake of the satisfaction at second hand or by rebound, and place a pride and delight in exciting the admiration of others. . . .

The many instances of forged miracles, and prophecies, and supernatural events, which, in all ages, have either been detected by contrary evidence, or which detect themselves by their absurdity, prove sufficiently the strong propensity of mankind to~~believe~~ the extraordinary and the marvellous, and ought reasonably to beget a suspicion against all relations of this kind. This is our natural way of thinking, even with regard to the most common and most credible events. . . . *[handwritten margin: Some are forged, but are they all?]*

Thirdly. It forms a strong presumption against all supernatural and miraculous relations, that they are observed chiefly to abound among ignorant and barbarous nations; or if a civilized people has ever given admission to any of them, that people will be found to have received them from ignorant and barbarous ancestors, who transmitted them with that inviolable sanction and authority, which always attend received opinions. When we peruse the first histories of all nations, we are apt to imagine ourselves transported into some new world; where the whole frame of nature is disjointed, and every element performs its operations in a different manner, from what it does at present. Battles, revolutions, pestilence, famine, and death, are never the effect of those natural causes, which we experience. Prodigies, omens, oracles, judgments, quite obscure the few natural events, that are intermingled with them. But as the former grow thinner every page, in proportion as we advance nearer the enlightened ages, we soon learn, that there is nothing mysterious or supernatural in the case, but that all proceeds from the usual propensity of mankind towards the marvellous, and that, though this inclination may at intervals receive a check from sense and learning, it can never be thoroughly extirpated from human nature. . . .

I may add as a *fourth* reason, which diminishes the authority of prodigies, that there is no testimony for any, even those which have not been expressly detected, that is not opposed by an infinite number of witnesses; so that not only the miracle destroys the credit of testimony, but the testimony destroys itself. To make this the better understood, let us consider, that, in matters of religion, whatever is different is contrary; and that it is impossible the religions of ancient Rome, of Turkey, of Siam, and of China should, all of them, be established on any solid foundation. Every miracle, therefore, pretended to have been wrought in any of these religions (and all of them abound in miracles), as its direct scope is to establish the particular system to which it is attributed; so has it the same force, though more indirectly, to overthrow every other system. In destroying a rival system, it likewise destroys the credit of those miracles, on which that system was established; so that all the prodigies of different religions are to be regarded as contrary facts, and the evidences of these prodigies, whether weak or strong, as opposite to each other. According to this method of reasoning, when we believe any miracle of Mohomet or his successors, we have for our warrant the testimony of a few barbarous Arabians. And on the other hand, we are to regard the authority of Titus Livius, Plutarch, Tacitus, and, in short, of all the authors and witnesses, Grecian, Chinese, and Roman Catholic, who have related any miracle in their particular religion; I say, we are to regard their testimony in the same light as if they mentioned that Mohammedan miracle, and had in express terms contradicted it, with the same certainty as they have for the miracle they relate. This argument may appear over subtle and refined; but is not in reality different from the reasoning of a judge, who supposes, that the credit of two witnesses, maintaining a crime affirm him to have been two hundred leagues distant, at the same instant when the crime is said to have been committed.

FRIEDRICH SCHLEIERMACHER

FRIEDRICH DANIEL ERNST SCHLEIERMACHER (1768-1834), a German philosopher and theologian, was born in Breslau on Nov. 21, 1768. He was educated by the Moravians at their school at Niesky, and their seminary at Barby in 1787 where he undertook theological studies which were completed at the University of Halle. After receiving his ordination in 1794, he accepted a call as chaplain to the Charité Hospital in Berlin in 1796, remaining there until 1802. During this period he wrote a number of his major works: **On Religion** (1799), **Monologues** (1800), and **Letters from a Minister Out of Berlin,** while also contributing to the **Athenaeum.** From 1802 to 1804, he ministered in Stolp, and there wrote his **Critical View of Ethics.** In 1804, he was appointed Extraordinary Professor of Theology at Halle, and retained that post until 1807 when he left for Berlin to become pastor of Trinity Church. While in Berlin, he was elected to the Academy of Sciences, took part in the founding of the University of Berlin in 1810, and remained there as its most distinguished professor until his death on Feb. 12, 1834.

Schleiermacher's principal works are: **On Religion: Speeches to Its Cultured Despisers** (1799), **Monologues** (1800), and **Christian Ethics** (2 vols., 1821-1822). The selection used in the present text is taken from the work for which he is best known in philosophy of religion, his **Reden über Religion (Speeches on Religion).**

For Schleiermacher, God is the "identity of thought and Being." Religion is a social life or participation with the highest reality, a reality in which Being and consciousness are one and the same. In such a communion a pious feeling of absolute dependence upon God, the infinite World-Ground is experienced; an experience which is inexhaustible by thought. God transcends human knowledge and will, and it is only by mystical experiences of human vibrations, intuitions, by which man establishes a relationship with God. Knowledge is ineffectual because it is in a state of perpetual flux, a dialectical process to which we cannot

401

are the systems really rival, should these be regarded as contrary facts?

Thomas

Because of cultural variance and worldwide experience of prodigies, could it not be true but in some instances, catch up, and since God is the identity of thought and Being, he is beyond theoretical reason. Religious experience is unique and enjoys an autonomy of its own, hence theology is a special science, independent of philosophy or science for its data; furthermore, it is more than Biblical exegesis.

misunderstood or perverted in some manner. (Or just placed into the particular context of a particular culture?) This is not to say that all are true, for some persons (barbarous etc.) may misunderstand or whatever, but that it is possible they can be true is various religions and not just _one_.

63

FRIEDRICH SCHLEIERMACHER

Miracles as Events[1]

What is a miracle? What we call miracle is everywhere else called sign, indication. Our name, which means a wonder, refers purely to the mental condition of the observer. It is only in so far appropriate that a sign, especially when it is nothing besides, must be fitted to call attention to itself and to the power in it that gives it significance. Every finite thing, however, is a sign of the Infinite, and so these various expressions declare the immediate relation of a phenomenon to the Infinite and the Whole. But does that involve that every event should not have quite as immediate a relation to the finite and to nature? Miracle is simply the religious name for event. Every event, even the most natural and unusual, becomes a miracle, as soon as the religious view of it can be the dominant. To me all is miracle. In your sense the inexplicable and strange alone is miracle, in mine it is no miracle. The more religious you are, the more miracle would you see everywhere. All disputing about single events, as to whether or not they are to be called miraculous, gives me a painful impression of the poverty and wretchedness of the religious sense of the combatants. One party show it by protesting everywhere against miracle, whereby they manifest their wish not to see anything of immediate relationship to the Infinite and to the Deity. The other party display the same poverty by laying stress on this and that. A phenomenon for them must be marvellous before they will regard it as a miracle, whereby they simply announce that they are bad observers.

What is revelation? Every original and new communication of the Universe to man is a revelation, as, for example, every such moment of conscious insight as I have just referred to. Every intuition and every original feeling proceeds from revelation. As revelation lies beyond con-

[1] Friedrich Schleiermacher, *On Religion: Speeches to Its Cultured Despisers* (1806, 1821, 1831), tr. John Oman (1893); excerpts from "Second Speech — The Nature of Religion."

sciousness, demonstration is not possible, yet we are not merely to assume it generally, but each one knows best himself what is repeated and learned elsewhere, and what is original and new. If nothing original has yet been generated in you, when it does come it will be a revelation for you also, and I counsel you to weigh it well.

What is inspiration? It is simply the general expression for the feeling of true morality and freedom. But do not mistake me. It is not that marvellous and much-praised morality and freedom that accompany and embellish actions with deliberations. It is that action which springs from the heart of man, despite of, or at least, regardless of, all external occasion. In the same measure in which this action is freed from all earthly entanglement, it is felt as divine and referred to God.

What is prophecy? Every religious anticipation of the other half of a religious event, one half being given, is prophecy. It was very religious of the ancient Hebrews to measure the divineness of a prophet, neither by the difficulty of predicting, nor by the greatness of the subject, but, quite simply, by the issue, for we cannot know from one thing how complete the feeling is in everything, till we see whether the religious aspect of this one special circumstances has been rightly comprehended.

What is operation of grace? Nothing else manifestly than the common expression for revelation and inspiration, for interchange between the entrance of the world into man, through intuition and feeling, and the outgoing of man into the world, through action and culture. It includes both, in their originality and in their divine character, so that the whole life of the pious simply forms a series of operations of divine grace.

64

JOHN STUART MILL

Examination of Hume's Doctrine of Miracles[1]

It is to be remarked in the first place, that the positive evidence produced in support of an assertion which is nevertheless rejected on the score of impossibility or improbability, is never such as amounts to full proof. It is always grounded upon some approximate generalization. The fact may have been asserted by a hundred witnesses; but there are many exceptions to the universality of the generalization that what a hundred witnesses affirm is true. We may seem to ourselves to have actually seen the fact: but, that we really see what we think we see, is by no means an universal truth; our organs may have been in a morbid state, or we may have inferred something, and imagined that we perceived it. The evidence, then, in the affirmative, being never more than an approximate generalization, all will depend upon what the evidence in the negative is. If that also rests upon an approximate generalization, it is a case for comparison of probabilities. If the approximate generalizations leading to the affirmative are, when added together, less strong, or in other words, further removed from universality, than the approximate generalizations which support the negative side of the question, the proposition is said to be improbable, and is to be disbelieved, provisionally. If, however, an alleged fact be in contradiction, not to any number of approximate generalizations, but to a completed generalization grounded upon a rigorous induction, it is said to be impossible, and is to be disbelieved totally.

This last principle, simple and evident as it appears, is the doctrine which, on the occasion of an attempt to apply it to the question of the credibility of miracles, excited so violent a controversy. Hume's celebrated principle, that nothing is credible which is contradictory to experience, or at variance with laws of nature, is merely this very plain and harmless proposition, that whatever is contradictory to a complete

[1] John Stuart Mill, *A System of Logic* (1846), bk. III, ch. 25, sect. 2.

induction is incredible. That such a maxim as this should either be accounted a dangerous heresy, or mistaken for a great and recondite truth,
speaks ill for the state of philosophical speculation on such subjects.

But does not (it may be asked) the very statement of the proposition
imply a contradiction? An alleged fact, according to this theory, is not to
be believed if it contradict a complete induction. But it is essential to
the completeness of an induction that it shall not contradict any known
fact. Is it not then a *petitio principii* to say, that the fact ought to be disbelieved because the induction opposed to it is complete? How can we
have a right to declare the induction complete, while facts, supported by
credible evidence, present themselves in opposition to it?

I answer, we have that right whenever the scientific canons of induction give it to us; that is, whenever the induction *can* be complete. We
have it, for example, in a case of causation, in which there has been an
experimentum crucis. If an antecedent A, superadded to a set of antecedents in all other respects unaltered, is followed by an effect B which
did not exist before, A is, in that instance at least, the cause of B, or a
necessary part of that cause; and if A be tried again with many totally
different sets of antecedents and B still follows, then it is the whole
cause. If these observations or experiments have been repeated so often,
and by so many persons, as to exclude all supposition of error in the
observer, a law of nature is established; and so long as this law is received as such, the assertion that on any particular occasion A took place,
and yet B did not follow, *without any counteracting cause,* must be disbelieved. Such an assertion is not to be credited upon any less evidence
that what would suffice to overturn the law. The general truths, that
whatever has a beginning has a cause, and that when none but the same
causes exist, the same effects follow, rest upon the strongest inductive evidence possible; the proposition that things affirmed by even a crowd of
respectable witnesses are true, is but an approximate generalization;
and — even if we fancy we actually saw or felt the fact which is in contradiction to the law — what a human being can see is no more than a
set of appearances; from which the real nature of the phenomenon is
merely an inference, and in this inference approximate generalizations
usually have a large share. If, therefore, we make our election to hold
by the law, no quantity of evidence whatever ought to persuade us that
there has occurred anything in contradiction to it. If, indeed, the evidence produced is such that it is more likely that the set of observations
and experiments upon which the law rests should have been inaccurately
performed or incorrectly interpreted, than that the evidence in question
should be false, we may believe the evidence; but then we must abandon
the law. And since the law was received on what seemed a complete in-

duction, it can only be rejected on evidence equivalent; namely, as being inconsistent not with any number of approximate generalizations, but with some other and better established law of nature. This extreme case, of a conflict between two supposed laws of nature, has probably never actually occurred where, in the process of investigating both the laws, the true canons of scientific induction had been kept in view; but if it did occur, it must terminate in the total rejection of one of the supposed laws. It would prove that there must be a flaw in the logical process by which either one or the other was established; and if there be so, that supposed general truth is no truth at all. We cannot admit a proposition as a law of nature, and yet believe a fact in real contradiction to it. We must disbelieve the alleged fact, or believe that we were mistaken in admitting the supposed law.

But in order that any alleged fact should be contradictory to a law of causation, the allegation must be, not simply that the cause existed without being followed by the effect, for that would be no uncommon occurrence; but that this happened in the absence of any adequate counteracting cause. Now in the case of an alleged miracle, the assertion is the exact opposite of this. It is, that the effect was defeated not in the absence, but in consequence, of a counteracting cause, namely, a direct interposition of an act of the will of some being who has power over nature; and in particular of a being, whose will having originally endowed all the causes with the powers by which they produce their effects, may well be supposed able to counteract them. A miracle (as was justly remarked by Brown) is no contradiction to the law of cause and effect; it is a new effect, supposed to be produced by the introduction of a new cause. Of the adequacy of that cause, if it exist, there can be no doubt; and the only antecedent improbability which can be ascribed to the miracle, is the improbability that any such cause had existence in the case.

All, therefore, which Hume has made out, and this he must be considered to have made out, is, that no evidence can be sufficient to prove a miracle to any one who did not previously believe the existence of a being or beings with supernatural power; or who believed himself to have full proof that the character of the Being whom he recognizes, is inconsistent with his having seen fit to interfere on the occasion in question. The truth of this (however fatal to a school of theology which has recently been revived in this country, and which has the weakness to rest all the evidences of religion upon tradition and testimony) may be, and is, admitted by all defenders of revelation who have made much figure as such during the present century. It is now acknowledged by nearly all the ablest writers on the subject, that natural religion is the necessary basis of revealed; that the proofs of Christianity presuppose the being and moral attributes of God; and that it is the conformity of a religion to those attributes which determines whether credence ought to be given to its external evidences; that (as the proposition is sometimes expressed) the doctrine must prove the miracles, not the miracles the doctrine. It is hardly necessary to point out the complete accordance of these views with the opinions which (not to mention other testimonies) the New Testament itself shows to have been generally prevalent in the apostolic age; when it was believed indeed that miracles were necessary as credentials, and that whoever was sent by God must have the power of working them; but no one dreamed that such power sufficed by itself as proof of a divine mission, and St. Paul expressly warned the churches, if any one came to them working miracles, to observe what he taught, and unless he preached "Christ, and him crucified," not to listen to the teaching. There is no reason, therefore, that timid Christians should shrink from accepting the logical canon of the Grounds of Disbelief. And it is not hazarding much to predict that a school which peremptorily rejects all evidences of religion, except such as, when relied upon exclusively, the canon in question irreversibly condemns; which denies to mankind the right to judge of religious doctrine, and bids them depend on miracles as their sole guide; must, in the present state of the human mind, inevitably fail in its attempt to put itself at the head of the religious feelings and convictions of this country: by whatever learning, argumentative skill, and even, in many respects, comprehensive views of human affairs, its peculiar doctrines may be recommended to the acceptance of thinkers.

Part Nine: PRAYER

Communion with the Divine

65

GEORGE SANTAYANA

The Efficacy of Prayer[1]

Prayer Is Not Utilitarian in Essence

. . . The instinct to prayer is one of the chief avenues to the deity, and
the form prayer takes helps immensely to define the power it is addressed
to; indeed, it is in the act of praying that men formulate to themselves
what God must be, and tell him at great length what they believe and
what they expect of him. The initial forms of prayer are not so absurd as
the somewhat rationalised forms of it. Unlike sacrifice, prayer seems to
be justified by its essence and to be degraded by the transformations it
suffers in reflection, when men try to find a place for it in their cosmic
economy; for its essence is poetical, expressive, contemplative, and it
grows more and more nonsensical the more people insist on making it a
prosaic, commercial exchange of views between two interlocutors.

Prayer is a soliloquy; but being a soliloquy expressing need, and being
furthermore, like sacrifice, a desperate expedient which men fly to in
their impotence, it looks for an effect: to cry aloud, to make vows, to
contrast eloquently the given with the ideal situation, is certainly as
likely a way of bringing about a change for the better as it would be to
chastise one's self severely, or to destroy what one loves best, or to perform acts altogether trivial and arbitrary. Prayer also is magic, and as
such it is expected to do work. The answer looked for, or one which may
be accepted instead, very often ensues; and it is then that mythology begins to enter in and seeks to explain by what machinery of divine passions and purposes that answering effect was produced.

Its Supposed Efficacy Magical

Magic is in a certain sense the mother of art, art being the magic that
succeeds and can establish itself. For this very reason mere magic is

[1] George Santayana, *The Life of Reason*, vol. III, *Reason in Religion* (New York:
Charles Scribner's Sons, 1905); excerpts from chapter 3, "Magic, Sacrifice, and
Prayer."

never appealed to when art has been found, and no unsophisticated man
prays to have that done for him which he knows how to do for himself.
When his art fails, if his necessity still presses, he appeals to magic, and
he prays when he no longer can control the event, provided this event is
momentous to him. Prayer is not a substitute for word; it is a desperate
effort to work further and to be efficient beyond the range of one's powers. It is not the lazy who are most inclined to prayer; those pray most
who care most, and who, having worked hard, find it intolerable to be
defeated.

. . . . .

A Real Efficacy Would Be Mechanical

The situation would not be improved if we surrendered that mystical
optimism, and maintained that prayer might really attract superhuman
forces to our aid by giving them a signal without which they would not
have been able to reach us. If experience lent itself to such a theory there
would be nothing in it more impossible than in ordinary telepathy;
prayer would then be an art like conversation, and the exact personages
and interests would be discoverable to which we might appeal . . . .

True Uses of Prayer

What successful religion really should pass into is contemplation,
ideality, poetry, in the sense in which poetry includes all imaginative
moral life. That this is what religion looks to is very clear in prayer and
in the efficacy which prayer consistently can have. In rational prayer the
soul may be said to accomplish three things important to its welfare:
it withdraws within itself and defines its good, it accommodates itself to
destiny, and it grows like the ideal which it conceives.

It Clarifies the Ideal

If prayer springs from need it will naturally dwell on what would satisfy that necessity; sometimes, indeed, it does nothing else but articulate
and eulogise what is most wanted and prized. This object will often be
particular, and so it should be, since Socrates' prayer "for the best"
would be perfunctory and vapid indeed in a man whose life had not
been spent, like Socrates', in defining what the best was. Yet any particular good lies in a field of relations; it has associates and implications, so
that the mind dwelling on it and invoking its presence will naturally be
enticed also into its background, and will wander there, perhaps to come
upon greater goods, or upon evils which the coveted good would make
inevitable. An earnest consideration, therefore, of anything desired is
apt to enlarge and generalise aspiration till it embraces an ideal life; for
from almost any starting-point the limits and contours of mortal happiness are soon described. Prayer, inspired by a pressing need, already re-

lieves its importunity by merging it in the general need of the spirit and of mankind. It therefore calms the passions in expressing them, like all idealisation, and tends to make the will conformable with reason and justice.

It Reconciles to the Inevitable

A comprehensive ideal, however, is harder to realise than a particular one: the rain wished for may fall, the death feared may be averted, but the kingdom of heaven does not come. It is in the very essence of prayer to regard a denial as possible. There would be no sense in defining and begging for the better thing if that better thing had at any rate to be. The possibility of defeat is one of the circumstances with which meditation must square the ideal; seeing that my prayer may not be granted, what in that case should I pray for next? Now the order of nature is in many respects well known, and it is clear that all realisable ideals must not transgress certain bounds. The practical ideal, that which under the circumstances it is best to aim at and pray for, will not rebel against destiny. Conformity is an element in all religion and submission in all prayer; not because what must be is best, but because the best that may be pursued rationally lies within the possible, and can be hatched only in the general womb of being. The prayer, "Thy will be done," if it is to remain a prayer, must not be degraded from its original meaning, which was that an unfulfilled ideal should be fulfilled; it expressed aspiration after the best, not willingness to be satisfied with anything. Yet the inevitable must be accepted, and it is easier to change the human will than the laws of nature. To wean the mind from extravagant desires and teach it to find excellence in what life affords, when life is made as worthy as possible, is a part of wisdom and religion. Prayer, by confronting the ideal with experience and fate tends to render that ideal humble, practical, and efficacious.

It Fosters Spiritual Life by Conceiving It in Its Perfection

A sense for human limitations, however, has its foil in the ideal of deity, which is nothing but the ideal of man freed from those limitations which a humble and wise man accepts for himself, but which a spiritual man never ceases to feel as limitations. Man, for instance, is mortal, and his whole animal and social economy is built on that fact, so that his practical ideal must start on that basis, and make the best of it; but immortality is essentially better, and the eternal is in many ways constantly present to a noble mind; the gods therefore are immortal, and to speak their language in prayer is to learn to see all things as they do and as reason must, under the form of eternity. The gods are furthermore no respecters of persons; they are just, for it is man's ideal to be so. Prayer, since it addresses deity, will in the end blush to be selfish and partial; the majesty of the divine mind envisaged and consulted will tend to pass into the human mind. . . .

Discipline and Contemplation Are Their Own Reward

Prayer, in fine, though it accomplishes nothing material, constitutes something spiritual. It will not bring rain, but until rain comes it may cultivate hope and resignation and may prepare the heart for any issue, opening up a vista in which human prosperity will appear in its conditioned existence and conditional value. A candle wasting itself before an image will prevent no misfortune, but it may bear witness to some silent hope or relieve some sorrow by expressing it; it may soften a little the bitter sense of impotence which would consume a mind aware of physical dependence but not of spiritual dominion. Worship, supplication, reliance on the gods, express both these things in an appropriate parable. Physical impotence is expressed by man's appeal for help; moral dominion by belief in God's omnipotence. This belief may afterwards seem to be contradicted by events. It would be so in truth if God's omnipotence stood for a material magical control of events by the values they were to generate. But the believer knows in his heart, in spite of the confused explanations he may give of his feelings, that a material efficacy is not the test of his faith. His faith will survive any outward disappointment. In fact, it will grow by that discipline and not become truly religious until it ceases to be a foolish expectation of improbable things and rises on stepping-stones of its material disappointments into a spiritual peace. What would sacrifice be but a risky investment if it did not redeem us from the love of those things which it asks us to surrender? What would be the miserable fruit of an appeal to God which, after bringing us face to face with him, left us still immersed in what we could have enjoyed without him? The real use and excuse for magic is this, that by enticing us, in the service of natural lusts, into a region above natural instrumentalities, it accustoms us to that rarer atmosphere, so that we may learn to breathe it for its own sake. By the time we discover the mechanical futility of religion we may have begun to blush at the thought of using religion mechanically; for what should be the end of life if friendship with the gods is a means only? When thaumaturgy is discredited, the childish desire to work miracles may itself have passed away. Before we weary of the attempt to hide and piece out our mortality, our concomitant immortality may have dawned upon us. While we are waiting for the command to take up our bed and walk we may hear a voice saying: Thy sins are forgiven thee.

WILLIAM ERNEST HOCKING

WILLIAM ERNEST HOCKING (1873-   ), born in Cleveland, Ohio on August 10, 1873, was educated at Harvard University, the University of Göttingen, Berlin, and Heidelberg. He received his A.B. in 1901, his A.M. in 1902, and his Ph.D. in 1904. In addition to those degrees mentioned, he has been awarded nine honorary doctorates from universities in this country and abroad. He began his career at Andover Theological Seminary in 1906 as Instructor of Philosophy; the school year of 1907-1908 was spent at the University of California as Assistant Professor of Philosophy; and from 1908 to 1913, he taught at Yale, where he achieved the rank of full Professor of Philosophy. His long Harvard career in philosophy began in 1914, and when he retired in 1943, he was honored by being appointed Professor Emeritus.

The pericope on **prayer** in the present text is from his classic **The Meaning of God in Human Experience** (1912); other works of his are: **Human Nature and Its Remaking** (1918), **Morale and Its Enemies** (1918), **Man and the State** (1926), **Spirit of World Politics** (1928), **Types of Philosophy** (1929), **Thoughts on Death and Life** (1937), **Living Religions and a World Faith** (1940), **Recent Trends in American Philosophy** (1941), **Lasting Elements of Individualism** (1937), **The Coming World Civilization** (1956), **Meaning of Immortality in Human Experience** (1957), **Strength of Men and Nations** (1959).

66

WILLIAM ERNEST HOCKING

Prayer: Its Meaning and Answer[1]

But of all these objects, God is the only one always accessible to direct pursuit; the only one admitting such a conscious, voluntary cult as worship is. Our pleasures are so many discoveries; friendships, appreciations, loves generally, happen to men as by good chance: once they have dawned upon us, we may pursue them as vigorously as we will, but the appreciations themselves cannot be directly sought. It is only such vision of God as one at any time that enables him to recognize the pleasant, the beautiful, in things and persons: the only net that can be spread for the loving of men and things is the consciousness of the absolute. So far as these other objects retain their value, that is to say, their idea, we may turn to them; but their salt has a tendency to lose its savor, and cannot be salted again by its own kind. This is the root of our trouble. We know always that life is worth living; we know, too, that we have in us somewhere the power of appreciating it; we know that nothing is common or unclean, and nothing hopeless: only — we cannot see it so. We have lost our primitive joy in primitive things; we have lost our freshness of impression. It is no longer true that "the scent of a flower, the flight of sea-gulls round a cliff, the cornfield in the sun, stir us to strange and cosmic delights." And it is worse than useless, so we find, to try with might and main to *feel* in these things what we have once felt. Nothing is more common than this trying, and nothing more fatal. Yet the thing is there. There are great funds of enthusiasm and literal love of men and things in us, if we could but reach them. There is a love of life, if we can discern its true nature, which is at bottom a love of God: it is that mystic thread which "in the ground of the soul" is never broken. If we can regain that, all the rest will follow. And only by regaining that can we

[1] William Ernest Hocking, *The Meaning of God in Human Experience* (New Haven: Yale University Press, 1912), 435-439. Reprinted by permission.

416

surely recover the rest. It is for this reason that we must add to all the other means for keeping or recovering our spiritual integrity, prayer. And what, in this present day of grace, does prayer mean?

It means, in the first place, that we maintain our discontent, returning again and again to the demand that our existence shall find itself justified in our own eyes. The first practical principle of religion is to hold without weakening the right of every individual life to know its own worth. We must not let reality go, this reality which has produced us, until it satisfies us: it must yield us the idea which unites what we most deeply desire with *what is*. This is the prayer of Jacob; and in a fundamental sense it is the first prayer of every human being. We are right in wishing to see first and be loyal afterward.

It means, in the second place, that we understand clearly to what self this right belongs, and cultivate that self. This right to see does not belong to our complex and strident personality which goes about, thinking by omnipotent effort to earn its happiness and its certainty. It belongs only to that in us which is simple and sincere. The sincere is that which is moved by necessity not by effort (no feeling is sincere which is made by will): the genuine will is that will which goes forth from effortless attention, that is to say, from love — and that is to say, from sight. We have the right to see first and be loyal afterward only because *unless we see we cannot be loyal,* nor in any sense sincere or moral. No determination to be a lover of life, no resolve to fight down desire or grief or regret or aversion, no attempt to transform one's own nature, can succeed by dint of the effortful will alone. But sight does its own transforming: sight turns the energy of our own desires into the work of their own re-making. It is thus an effortless self, and therewith a necessary will, that we have to seek. And for the same reason, it is a simple self, not involved in our artificial distinctions.

To be able to command this simple and sincere self is the critical condition of religious insight. Hence (thirdly) we in this day must still follow, in some fashion significant for ourselves, the negative path of all the mystics. We require the sight which cannot come through trying to see; we must try, then, to put ourselves consciously where sight must follow. We must deliberately review and reject, from time to time, whatever is falsely artificial and self-assertive in our outgoing purposes; we must track, as far as we can, the points of our own partiality. We must, even in this modern world of ours, know how to shake off the prepossessions of our theoretic wills; to regard all ambitions and duties for the time as non-existent; to reduce all reality to the primitive terms of self, universe, and the present moment (wherein everything begins from the beginning.) In this stark, original selfhood, detached from action and

from the warping of the interests of action, we view all that active career
as in drama, as the life of another, in the light of what we can then and
there muster of the whole. Its loves and hates rise up before us in a more
universal frame. We must recall especially whatever is still to us of effortless value, whatever we do still sincerely enjoy and love, and we must
pray for the vision of the whole of which these various goods are fragments, and upon which they depend as their absolute. I use the word
'pray,' because, in the end, there is no other word which conveys that
attitude of will in which effort is so combined with noneffort, and self-
assertion with consciousness of absolute dependence. Nor do I know
why this word should be translated into anything more scholastic. The
insight we require is both a right and a gift, the justest gift in all experience; we dare not be too proud to comply with its evident conditions. We
must know that in doing these things, we are already using a degree of
mystic insight: we are relying upon an attachment to the whole which is
too deep in us to be lost or overcome; we are striving to 'enter into ourselves,' to recognize this attachment for what it is, the love of the God
of that alienated world. This is prayer.

And the answer to prayer is whatever of simplicity, of naturalness, of
original appreciation, is brought into our view of things by this act of
obedience of the mind to its absolute object. In proportion as our prayer
is honest, we shall find ourselves less thinking, and more seeing; and we
can turn again to meet experience with so much better poise and understanding. How full, how instantaneous, how overwhelming may be the
vision of the deity of the world and the worth of one's own part in it, no
one can say: certainly it is beyond the province of philosophy to prescribe. Neither can it be told when or through what apparent accidents
the deeper insights of our experience may occur. Philosophy can only
point out the fundamental law of religious life, the right to see first and
be loyal afterward; and interpret in its own abstract language the conditions of that vision.

FRIEDRICH HEILER

FRIEDRICH HEILER (1892-   ), was born in Munich, Germany, received his doctorate from the University of Munich, and taught the history of religions there until 1920 when he was appointed Professor of the History of Religions in the University of Marburg. A Roman Catholic who became a Lutheran, he championed the cause of Christian unity. His book, **Prayer: A Study in the History and Psychology of Religion** (1918, 1923), from which the present selection has been taken, is without peer. Other works of his are: **Buddhistische Versenkung** (1918, 1922), **Katholizismus** (1923), **Sadhu Sundar Singh** (1923-1925), **Mystik in den Upanishaden** (1925), **Christlicher Glaube und indisches Geistesleben** (1926), **Evangelische Katholizitaet** (1926), **Spirit of Worship** (1926), **Mission des Christentums in Indien** (1931), **Im Ringen um die Kirche** (1931), **Urkirche und Ostkirche** (1937), **Altkirchliche Autonomie und paepslicher Zentralismus** (1941), **Alfred Loisy** (1947), **Mysterium caritatis, Predigten** (1949).

According to Heiler, prayer is more than meditation, or adoration which is merely reverent contemplation, and it is more than devotion, though these are necessary elements in religious experience. The **essence of prayer** is intercourse with God; where fellowship with the Deity is lacking, prayer cannot be said to be taking place. Adoration is the "contemplative surrender to a supreme good," while prayer is "a living communion of the religious man with God . . . a communion which reflects the forms of the social relations of humanity."

67

FRIEDRICH HEILER

The Essence of Prayer[1]

Prayer appears in history in an astonishing multiplicity of forms; as the calm collectedness of a devout individual soul, and as the ceremonial liturgy of a great congregation; as an original creation of a religious genius, and as an imitation on the part of a simple, average religious person; as the spontaneous expression of upspringing religious experiences, and as the mechanical recitation of an incomprehensible formula; as bliss and ecstacy of heart, and as painful fulfilment of the law; as the voluntary concentration on a religious object; as loud shouting and crying, and as still, silent absorption; as artistic poetry, and as stammering speech; as the flight of the spirit to the supreme Light, and as a cry out of the deep distress of the heart; as joyous thanksgiving and ecstatic praise, and as humble supplication for forgiveness and compassion; as a childlike entreaty for life, health, and happiness, and as an earnest desire for power in the moral struggle of existence; as a simple petition for daily bread, and as an all-consuming yearning for God Himself; as a selfish wish, and as an unselfish solicitude for a brother; as wild cursing and vengeful thirst, and as heroic intercession for personal enemies and persecutors; as a stormy clamour and demand, and as joyful renunciation and holy serenity; as a desire to change God's will and make it chime with our petty wishes, and as a self-forgetting vision of and surrender to the Highest Good; as the timid entreaty of the sinner before a stern judge, and as the trustful talk of a child with a kind father; as swelling phrases of politeness and flattery before an unapproachable King, and as a free outpouring in the presence of a friend who cares; as the humble petition of a servant to a powerful master, and as the ecstatic converse of the bride with the heavenly Bridegroom.

[1] From *Prayer: A Study in the History and Psychology of Religion* by Friedrich Heiler, translated and edited by Samuel McComb. Oxford University Press, 1932. Reprinted by permission. Excerpt from chapter 13, "The Essence of Prayer," 353–363.

In considering these varied contrasts and in the survey of the different leading types of prayer, the problem emerges: what is common to all these diverse kinds of prayer, what underlies all these phenomenal forms, in a word, what is the essence of prayer? The answer to this question is not easy. There is the danger of fundamentally misinterpreting prayer by making its essence an empty abstraction. If we would understand the essence of prayer we must look attentively at those types in which we see it as the naïve, spontaneous utterance of the soul; we must, therefore, separate the primary types from the secondary. This separation is easily effected. The primary types which cannot be confounded with the others are these: — the naïve prayer of primitive man, the devotional life of men of religious genius, the prayers of great men, the common prayer of public worship in so far as it has not hardened into a stiff, sacrosanct institution. In all these instances prayer appears as a purely psychical fact, the immediate expression of an original and profound experience of the soul. It bursts forth with innate energy. Very different are the secondary types. They are no longer an original, personal experience, but an imitation or a congealment of such a living experience. The personal prayer of the average religious man is a more or less true reflection of the original experience of another; it remains inferior to the ideal model in power, depth, and vitality. The philosophical idea of prayer is a cold abstraction built up in harmony with metaphysical and ethical standards; by it living prayer is subjected to an alien law, to the principles of philosophy, and is transformed and revised in accordance with this law. The product of this amendment is no longer real prayer, but its shadow, an artificial, dead simulacrum of it. The ritual forms of prayer, the cultual hymn, liturgical common prayer as an institution of the cultus, all these types are phenomena of congelation in which the upspringing personal life has been transmuted into objective, impersonal forms and rules. The penetration into their inner meaning may indeed give rise in devout, susceptible souls to new experiences of prayer, their recitation in public or private worship may take place in a devotional mood, but they themselves are not the direct expression of a personal experience. The essential features of prayer are never visible in these disintegrated, dead, secondary forms, but only in unadulterated, simple prayer as it lives in unsophisticated, primitive human beings and in outstanding men of creative genius. In determining the essence of prayer, therefore, we must fix our attention exclusively on prayer in its primitive simplicity. Only then can we take into consideration the secondary types and inquire how far the essence of prayer is expressed by them.

To answer our question, we must first of all discover the essential motive of prayer, its common psychological root. What moves men to pray? What do men seek when they pray? Da Costa Guimaraens, a French psychologist, defined it thus: "To pray means to satisfy a psychical need." The definition is superficial and is, moreover, insipidly formulated, but it is on the track of a correct psychological motivation. Prayer is the expression of a primitive impulsion to a higher, richer, intenser, life. Whatever may be the burden of the prayer, to whatever realm of values it may be belong, whether to the eudaemonistic, the ethical, or the purely religious realm — it is always a great longing for life, for a more potent, a purer, a more blessed life. "When I seek Thee, my God," prays Augustine, "I seek a blessed life." His words uncover the psychical root of all prayer. The hungry pygmy who begs for food, the entranced mystic, absorbed in the greatness and beauty of the infinite God, the guilt-oppressed Christian who prays for forgiveness of sins and assurance of salvation — all are seeking life; they seek a confirmation and an enrichment of their realization of life. Even the Buddhist beggar-monk, who by mediation works himself up into a state of perfect indifference, seeks in the denial of life to attain a higher and purer life.

The effort to fortify, to reinforce, to enhance one's life is the motive of all prayer. But the discovery of the deepest root of prayer does not disclose its peculiar essence. In order to get to the bottom of this, we should not ask for the psychological motive of prayer; we must rather make clear the religious ideas of him who prays in simplicity, we must grasp his inner attitude and spiritual aim, the intellectual presuppositions which underlie prayer as a psychical experience. What does the simple, devout person, undisturbed by reflection, think when he prays? He believes that he speaks with a God, immediately present and personal, has intercourse with Him, that there is between them a vital and spiritual commerce. There are three elements which form the inner structure of the prayer-experience: faith in a living personal God, faith in His real, immediate presence, and a realistic fellowship into which man enters with a God conceived as present.

Every prayer is a turning of man to another Being to whom he inwardly opens his heart; it is the speech of an "I" to a "Thou." This "Thou," this other with whom the devout person comes into relation, in whose presence he stands as he prays, is no human being but a supersensuous, superhuman Being on whom he feels himself dependent, yet a being who plainly wears the features of a human personality, with thought, will, feeling, self-consciousness. "Prayer," says Tylor, "is the address of a personal spirit to a personal spirit." Belief in the personality of God is the necessary presupposition, the fundamental condition of all prayer. The anthropomorphism which is always found in primitive prayer and which often appears in the prayer of outstanding religious personalities, the prophets among them, is a coarsening and materialising of this belief in God's personality; it does not, however, belong to the essence of prayer as faith does. But wherever the vital conception of the divine personaliity grows dim, where, as in the philosophical ideal or in pantheistic mysticism, it passes over into the "One and All," genuine prayer dissolves and becomes purely contemplative absorption and adoration.

The man who prays feels himself very close to this personal God. Primitive man believes that God dwells in a visible place; to this place he hastens when he would pray, or he turns his eyes and hands towards it. The religious genius experiences the divine presence in the stillness of his own heart, in the deepest recesses of his soul. But it is always the reverential and trustful consciousness of the living presence of God, which is the keynote of the genuine prayer-experience. It is true that the God to whom the worshipper cries transcends all material things — and yet the pious man feels His nearness with an assurance as undoubted as though a living man stood before him.

Belief in God's personality and the assurance of His presence are the two presuppositions of prayer. But prayer itself is no mere belief in the reality of a personal God — such a belief underlies even a theistic metaphysic; — nor is it a mere experience of His presence — for this is the accompaniment of the entire life and thought of the great men of religion. Prayer is rather a living relation of man to God, a direct and inner contact, a refuge, a mutual intercourse, a conversation, spiritual commerce, an association, a fellowship, a communion, a converse, a one-ness, a union of an "I" and a "Thou." Only an accumulation of these synonyms which human speech employs to make clear the innermost relations of man to man, can give an appropriate picture of the realistic power and vitality of that relation into which the praying man enters with God. Since prayer displays a communion, a conversation between an "I" and a "Thou," it is a social phenomenon. The relation to God of him who prays always reflects an earthly social relation: that of servant or child or friend or bride. In the praying of primitive man, as in the devoutness of creative religious personalities, the religious bond is conceived after the analogy of human society. It is just this earthly social element that lends to natural prayer its dramatic vivacity. Wherever, as with many mystics, the religious relation no longer exhibits an analogy to social relations, prayer passes over from a real relation of communion to mere contemplation and adoration.

As anthropomorphism is only a crude form of belief in the personality of God, so belief in the real influence of prayer on the divine will, in the winning over of God to our side as it appears most clearly in primitive and prophetic prayer, is only a crude form of immediate, vital, and dynamic intercourse with God. It does not belong to the essence of prayer. The miracle of prayer does not lie in the accomplishment of the prayer, in the influence of man on God, but in the mysterious contact which comes to pass between the finite and the infinite Spirit. It is by this very fact that prayer is a genuine fellowship of man with God, that it is something not merely psychological, but transcendental and metaphysical, or as Tholuck has expressed it, "no mere earthly power but a power which reaches to the heavens." In the words of Söderblom: "in the depths of our inner life we have not a mere echo of our own voice, of our own being, resounding from the dark depths of personality, but a reality higher and greater than our own, which we can adore and in which we can trust."

Prayer is, therefore, a living communion of the religious man with God, conceived as personal and present in experience, a communion which reflects the forms of the social relations of humanity. This is prayer in essence. It is only imperfectly realised in the subordinate types of prayer. In ritual prayer, cultual hymn, in liturgical prayer, as in prayer regulated by law and deemed a thing in itself meritorious, the experience of the Divine presence is, for the most part, weak and shadowy. Here we have prayer as a more or less external action, not as an inner contact of the heart with God. But also in the philosophical ideal of prayer and in certain forms of mystical communion, we can discern but faintly the essence of prayer. If we are to distinguish clearly between the religious experiences and states of mind related to prayer, which play an important part in the religion of philosophers and mystics, and prayer itself considered simply from the point of view which makes it to be prayer, some elucidation of what we mean by "adoration" and "devotion" is necessary.

Adoration (or reverent contemplation) and devotion are absolutely necessary elements in religious experience. Both terms stand for conceptions much wider than that of prayer; both denote religious experiences and states, the nature of which is obviously different from that of prayer; nay, we may go further and say that they comprehend psychical events and experiences which belong to the "secular," not to the strictly religious realm, or are on the borderland of both.

Adoration is the solemn contemplation of the "Holy One" as the highest Good, unreserved surrender to Him, a mingling of one's being with His. We see this even in the religious life of primitive peoples. The awe which primitive man evinces by speech and gesture as he stands in the presence of a "holy object," that is, an object filled with supernatural and magical power, is "adoration," although in a crude and imperfect fashion. The "holy" object has for him ideal worth: yes, even supreme value in the moment when, overcome by awe and wonder, he sinks in the dust before it. But it is in the personal experience of the poet and the mystic that we find adoration in its absolute purity and perfection. It is the soul-satisfying contemplation of the highest good, the very climax of mystical prayer: it is the unreserved losing of one's self in the glory of Nature as seen in the sacred poetry of ancient peoples and in the aesthetic mysticism of modern poets. Compared with it primitive ceremonial adoration is but a preliminary form. Now, a personal God can be the object of this adoration, just as He is the object of prayer. The God whom primitive man worships is an anthropomorphic being; the *summum bonum* of a mysticism centering in a personal God shows the traits of a spiritual personality. But the note of personality is by no means essential to the object of adoration. Primitive cults knew not only spiritual beings made after man's image, but also lifeless objects which being "holy," that is, as *mana* and *tabu*, lay claim to worship. Moreover, the object in which the poetic spirit sinks in an ecstasy of adoration, is not personal: it is the lifegiving sun, creative and nurturing Mother Nature, the Alone and the Infinite as revealed in the beautiful. There is, nevertheless, something that is beyond experience, something which shines through Nature as through a translucent medium. Just as the God whom the worshipper invokes, is felt to be palpably near and immediately present, so also the object of adoration which the pious spirit regards with awe is felt to be equally near and present. The relation to God into which he who prays enters, resembles in its intimacy the relation which subsists between the adoring person and the object of his adoration.

Subsidiary to religious adoration is the "secular." Ordinarily we indicate by the word "adoration" the state of being laid hold of by a supreme good, the complete surrender to it, whether this good be religious (*numinous*) or "secular," natural or supernatural, earthly or heavenly. Everything which man experiences as a supreme good, whatever is the object of "love" — a person, an association of persons, an abstract idea — can also in the wider sense of the word be an object of adoration. The young lover adores his beloved, the patriotic citizen his fatherland, the loyal working man his class, the creative artist his muse, the high-minded philosopher the idea of the true and the good. If love means the belief of a man in his supreme good, adoration is the belief at its highest point of intensity, the culmination of love. The adoring person steadily contemplates his ideal object; he is filled with inspiration, admiration, rapture, yearning; all other thoughts and wishes have vanished; he belongs only to the one object, loses himself in it, and in it dissolves away. *Adoration is the contemplative surrender to a supreme good.*

Devotion (*Andacht*) is a necessary presupposition and foundation alike of prayer and adoration. The praying man who converses with God, the adoring man who is absorbed in his highest ideal — both are devout, self-collected, concentrated. But the state of a soul in contemplation can just as well dispense with every reference to God or a supreme good. Devotion is, to begin with, concentration of the mind on a definite point, a wide-awake state of consciousness whose field is greatly circumscribed. But the mathematician who solves a geometrical problem also experiences this state of concentration, or the designer who constructs a model. Devotion, as distinct from mere mental concentration, from intensity of attention, is a solemn, still, exalted, consecrated mood of the soul. The philosopher experiences devotion when the mystery of the human spirit rises up before him in its autonomy and freedom: the scholar when he deciphers ancient documents and recalls to life long-forgotten men and peoples; the lover of nature when he stands before some lofty mountain peak or when he delights in the contemplation of some modest wild flower; the artist when suddenly a new idea forces itself upon him; the lover of art when he admires Raphael's Madonna or listens to a Symphony of Beethoven; the man engaged in a moral struggle when he searches his conscience, judges himself, and sets before himself lofty aims and tasks; the pious man when he participates in a holy act of worship or ponders on a religious mystery; even the irreligious man when he enters into the still dimness of a majestic cathedral or witnesses the solemn high mass in a Roman Catholic church. Devotion may rise into complete absorption; the field of consciousness is narrowed, the intensity of the experience grows; the concrete perceptions and ideas which aroused the experience of devotion wave themselves in a mood that is at once deep and agreeable. The states of absorption appear in the religious as in the 'secular" experience. They meet us just as much in the mystical devotional life as in scientific investigation and artistic creation. In absorption the mystic experiences perfect stillness and serenity, holy joy and equanimity — all of them experiences which may be clearly distinguished from contemplative adoration. Yet in them there lives in some manner the thought of an ultimate and highest state, though not so vividly as in adoration. Even in Buddhist absorption the idea of an ultimate and a highest — Nirvana — is operative.

Devotion is, therefore, the quiet, solemn mood of the soul which is caused by the contemplation of ethical and intellectual, but especially of aesthetic and religious values, whether of external objects or of imaginative conceptions dominated by feeling. Whilst adoration is concerned inwardly with an ideal object and holds it fast with convulsive energy, the objective presupposition of the experience of devotion acts purely as a stimulus. Devotion itself tends to depart from its objective presupposition, and to become wholly subjective, concentrated, and absorbed. In short, adoration has an objective, devotion a subjective character.

The analysis of adoration and devotion enables us to set the essence of prayer in the clearest light. Prayer is no mere feeling of exaltation, no mere hallowed mood, no mere prostration before a supreme good. It is rather a real intercourse of God with man, a living fellowship of the finite spirit with the Infinite. And just because the modern has no correct conception of the immediacy and tenderness of the relation effected by prayer in which the simple and devout soul stands to God, he is constantly confusing with genuine prayer these more general religious phenomena — adoration and devotion — which have their analogies even outside the religious sphere. Because the man of to-day, entangled in the prejudices of a rationalistic philosophy, struggles against the primitive realism of frank and free prayer, he is inclined to see the ideal and essence of prayer in a vague, devotional mood and in aesthetic contemplation. But the essence of prayer is revealed with unquestionable clearness to penetrating psychological study, and it may be put thus: *to pray means to speak to and have intercourse with God,* as suppliant with judge, servant with master, child with father, bride with bridegroom. The severely non-rational character of religion nowhere makes so overwhelming an impression as in prayer. For modern thought, dominated by Copernicus and Kant, prayer is as great a stone of stumbling as it was for the enlightened philosophy of the Greeks. But a compromise between unsophisticated piety and a rational world-view obliterates the essential features of prayer, and the most living manifestation of religion withers into a lifeless abstraction. There are only two possibilities: either decisively to affirm prayer "in its entirely non-rational character and with all its difficulties," as Ménégoz says, or to surrender genuine prayer and substitute for it adoration and devotion which resemble prayer. Every attempt to mingle the two conceptions violates psychological veracity.

Religious persons and students of religion agree in testifying that prayer is the centre of religion, the soul of all piety. The definition of the essence of prayer explains this testimony; prayer is a living communion of man with God. Prayer brings man into direct touch with God, into a personal relation with Him. Without prayer faith remains a theoretical conviction; worship is only an external and formal act; moral action is without spiritual depth; man remains at a distance from God; an abyss yawns between the finite and the Infinite. "God is in heaven and thou art on the earth." "We cannot come to God," says Luther, "except through prayer alone, for He is too high above us." In prayer man rises to heaven, heaven sinks to earth, the veil between the visible and the invisible is torn asunder, man comes before God to speak with Him about his soul's welfare and salvation. "Prayer," says Mechthild of Magdeburg, "draws the great God down into a small heart; it drives the hungry soul up to God in His fulness." Similarly Johann Ardnt says: "In prayer the highest and the lowest come together, the lowliest heart and the most exalted God."

As the mysterious linking of man with the Eternal, prayer is an incomprehensible wonder, a miracle of miracles which is daily brought to pass in the devout soul. The historian and psychologist of religion can only be a spectator and interpreter of that deep and powerful life which is unveiled in prayer: only the religious man can penetrate the mystery. But in the final analysis scientific inquiry stands under the same overwhelming impression as living religion. It is compelled to agree with the confession of Chrysostom: "There is nothing more powerful than prayer and there is nothing to be compared with it."

GEORGE ARTHUR BUTTRICK

GEORGE ARTHUR BUTTRICK (1892-   ), born at Seaham Harbour Northumberland, England on March 23, 1892, was educated at Lancaster Independent College, Manchester, and Victoria University, winning honors in philosophy at the latter university. Coming to the United States, he was ordained a minister of the Congregational Church in 1915 and occupied the pulpit of the distinguished Madison Avenue Presbyterian Church in New York City from 1927 to 1954. Concurrent with his pastorate at the New York Church, he taught at Union Theological Seminary which has some affiliation with Columbia University. In 1954, Harvard University appointed him Plummer Professor of Christian Morals and Chairman of the Board of Preachers, a post he held until his retirement.

His publications include: **The Parables of Jesus** (1928), **Jesus Came Preaching** (1931), **The Christian Fact and Modern Doubt** (1934), **Prayer** (1942), **Christ and Man's Dilemma** (1946), **So We Believe, so We Pray** (1951), **Faith and Education** (1952), **Sermons Preached in a University Church** (1960). He was general editor of **The Interpreter's Bible,** and editor of **The Interpreter's Dictionary.**

A Neo-Orthodoxist, influenced by the Existentialist philosophy of Sören Kierkegaard, he is known for his homiletical technique and his prayers; the excerpt taken from his book, **Prayer,** is a forceful presentation in defence of the validity of prayer.

Buttrick contends that prayer is communion or comradeship with the Divine, not merely a subjective psychological experience, but a genuine objectively valid one. He examines interpretations of prayer as mere soliloquy, self-deception, autosuggestion, a "healthy lie," projection, wishful thinking, rationalization, and finds them inadequate objections and explanations which do not square away with the facts of experience. His defence of prayer in the present selection is basically negative, that is, he disproves and rebuts the arguments lodged against prayer, and offers only one positive argument in support of prayer, a pragmatic one, namely 'try it and see for yourself' that it is valid.

68

GEORGE ARTHER BUTTRICK

In Defence of Prayer[1]

It is not strange that prayer should draw the sharpest attacks of doubt, and that in every generation misgiving or scorn should allege that prayer is less than communion with the Divine. The spiritual fact, the world beyond our eyes, is always "our dearest faith; our ghastliest doubt;" and prayer, which goes behind argument to cry openly on God, is always the most daring assertion of that Unseen Realm. Thus prayer has defended the pass for all religion — since religion is conquered when prayer dies — and has gathered all the spears of skepticism into its own heart. How sharp the spears: "Perhaps prayer is a mere soliloquy, a self-deception, a cowardice that dare not face the unheeding world!"

· · · · ·

. . . Is prayer mere autosuggestion? A man need not be a theorist to feel this doubt. Who among praying folk has not sometimes said, "Perhaps I am only talking to myself"? Latterly the misgiving has gained standing as a full-grown skepticism. Prayer, we are told, is a soliloquy: its only objective answer is the echo of its soul. Not all the skeptics would therefore disavow prayer. Some would say that it is still valuable as a self-discipline. It is an inverted form of self-reliance; and beyond cavil the man who says, "I shall fail," is already half triumphant. So prayer, these critics would allow, is a "healthy lie of life" which pours new confidence into the reservoirs of the subconscious.

But again the theory breaks upon the rock of fact. In strict sense there is no autosuggestion, for whatever we propose to ourselves takes rise in some measure beyond ourselves. If in a dream we see our house attacked by green unicorns each with a tail like a meteor and eight legs shod with

[1] From *Prayer* by George A. Buttrick. Copyright 1942 by Whitmore & Stone (Abingdon Press). Excerpts from chapter 3 "Some Defective Theories of Prayer," 43, 48-53. Reprinted by permission.

lightning, the dream would still draw for its material upon a world beyond ourselves. The combination may be ours, but the ingredients: we have seen, in a picture or in actuality, green, lightning, meteors, and unicorns. It is not in man's power, even in his thoughts, to make something out of nothing. Autosuggestion is not an inner spring: it is the hidden channel of a river with far objective sources. As has been well said, it would be more accurate to affirm, not that prayer is autosuggestion, but that autosuggestion is a form of prayer. If a man suggests God to himself, presumably that august idea also had its fount beyond the pool of man's own life.

Furthermore, if prayer were only a "healthy lie" — supposing lies could ever be healthy — it would be detected, and noble spirits would renounce it. But prayer has been the central faith of many a noble spirit; and souls as realistic as Jesus, "brave Son of fact," have found in prayer their vital breath. "Murder will out." A lie, even "a healthy lie," cannot long pose as truth. The movement of the universe seems to be unfolding: it cannot keep a secret: "There is nothing . . . hid, that shall not be known." A modern proverb insists that "it is fun to be fooled," but it is fun only when we know we are being fooled, and then only as test of our defenses. Facts have their coercion, and human nature its fundamental honesty. If prayer were a pretense it might have endured a generation: it could hardly have been an agelong rapture. Many who have prayed would have repudiated instantly any self-deception: "Search me, O God, and know my heart; try me, and know my thoughts; and see if there be any wicked way in me, and lead me in the way everlasting." Thus prayer at its best is itself a fundamental honesty. It has had inward grace of redemption from lies. Age after age it is purified: the tribal deity of the early Old Testament becomes "the God and Father of our Lord Jesus Christ." To propose that the universal travail of prayer, with its throes of spirit and its issues in martyrdom, is only a man talking to himself is not a convincing theory. Jesus, with ethic gleaming white and courage unto a cross, prayed there, "Father, forgive them." Let the critic insist that he was talking only to a white-bearded imagining called God, or indulging a poor self-mumbling: the critic, not Jesus, is then under judgment. Shallowness could hardly be more shallow.

There is a further rejoinder. Mere autosuggestion, with no foundation in fact, would be a force for chaos; for it would be against the grain of reality. Unworthy forms of prayer — pleas merely cowardly or a private selfishness — *have* been chaotic, but worthy prayer has been an integration. Can there be any real doubt that nights spent on a mountainside in prayer sharpened the judgment of Jesus, granted him vision, and confirmed him in that courage and consecration which are the world-abiding miracle? Nor has this wholeness given by prayer been transitory, pending the detection of a self-deception: it is the testimony in word and life of all the saints. The ages have drunk of their loyalty and light. If this is prayer's issue how can prayer be dubbed a chimera? Would that we might all live beneath the mirage! A striking acknowledgment is given in Dr. J. A. Hadfield's "The Psychology of Power":

Speaking as a student of psychotherapy, who, as such, has no concern with theology, I am convinced that the Christian religion is one of the most valuable and potent influences that we possess for producing that harmony and peace of mind . . . . needed to bring health and power to a large proportion of nervous patients. In some cases I have attempted to cure nervous patients with suggestions of quietness and confidence, but without success until I have linked these suggestions on to that faith in the power of God which is the substance of the Christian's confidence and hope. Then the patient has become strong.

This is a fascinating paragraph: it bristles with interrogations. We would like to ask the author: "Then can you any longer have 'no concern with theology'? You would not suggest 'faith in the power of God' without believing in it? Can psychotherapy hope to be genuinely constructive without some basic faith?" But these questions do not impair the verdict. It is supported, as to physical and mental health, by increasing evidence. The integration wrought by prayer goes far beyond health of body and "mind" — as it must to be convincing, for all men must die: prayer grants wholeness of vision and motive. If there is any world-purpose, if Christ in any measure reveals it, and if prayer gathers life's unruly waters into the crystal precipitate of that purpose, how can prayer be merely man's self-proposal? If prayer were only autosuggestion it would be thistledown carried away by the wind, or wrecked like a boat defying the stars; whereas, at its best, it is deeply consonant with man's truest life. Why should we not believe that it is therefore the moving of a Cosmic Spirit?

One other defective theory, very characteristic of an age just dying, almost vocally demands examination. "Projection," "wishful thinking," "rationalization" are a new vocabulary, but they represent a potent and wide-spread doubt. This psychological onslaught on the citadel of faith did not arise of itself: it was enlisted to explain what skepticism termed the agelong aberration of religion. That is to say, a group of sincere critics, of whom, in America, Joseph Wood Krutch, Eustace Hayden, and Walter Lippmann may be regarded as types and leaders, determined on grounds other than psychological that faith in God is folly. Then, confronted by the immemorial phenomenon of faith, they turned to psychology to account for this "blunder" of the generations. With the skepticism itself we are not now concerned. We have tried elsewhere to trace the natural history of modern doubt. It arose from an overweening and unwarranted reliance on the "scientific" view. It arose from the ancient doubt concerning an apparently unheeding universe, a doubt older than Omar Khayyám but never stated more persuasively than in the *Rubáiyát*. It arose, perhaps mainly, from the pagan life of the modern world, since life shapes our creeds even as our creeds shape life. Our inquiry will lead us again to explore this ground of modern skepticism, but we are presently concerned only with a certain psychological account of prayer. Some account had to be given: if there is no God why have the journeying generations believed in Him? Why have men prayed? The critics enlisted psychological reinforcements, and marched forth to hurl charges of "projection," "wishful thinking," and "rationalization." The contention in brief is this: God, if He exists, is as inert as the moon. But most of the race, too timid to face the fact of a world "blind and deaf to our beseeching," invented a man-in-the-moon — who is really a dried-up ocean bed — to whom age after age prayers have been offered for man's timid comfort.

It might be enough to answer that this view, laid alongside the agelong travail of prayer, has all the marks of a hasty glance and a clever guess. But the view has gained such wide currence that answer must be more specific. Let us admit that there *is* "rationalization" in religion and in every realm. Men have always been tempted to "make the worse appear the better reason" — because of some basic optimism, or for fear's sake, or for quick advantage. There *is* "projection": men have imprinted on the sky for worship many a god made only in man's image. There *is* "wishful thinking": "the wish is father to the thought." That these subtle self-deceptions infect the whole range of man's life — his psychologies and skepticisms, for instance, as well as his religion — no honest man can doubt. In every prayer a man must be on guard, and is perhaps never quite unscathed. But the question is this: can prayer, in its whole sweep and at its best, be stigmatized as a whistling in the dark? For instance, can the prayer of Jesus for his murderers, "Father, forgive them, for they know not what they do," be dismissed as a timid plea to the man in the moon? When the question is thus sharply stated, the answer is not long in doubt. The projection theory has no grace of profundity. The original skepticisms were weighty and honorable, but the psychological ally is bedraggled and thin.

Man has always wondered if his world is real. The misgiving arises, from the days of the Greek sophists to our day, even of tangible and visible things. It is the more acute of "things unseen." Trees are in doubt: they may exist only behind the optic and tactile nerves. Love is in double doubt. Not strangely solipsism is a recurrent theory, but not strangely its force is soon spent. How do we know that sunrise or great music has its own reality? First, it is faithfully recurrent. If it were a private vagary it would hardly keep its own characteristics. It is doubtful, for example, if the sunrise would always occur in the east. Second, it is attested by the group; and though great music has a different meaning for each different hearer — being one thing to a radio engineer, another to an acoustician, another to a composer, and still another to a music printer — it is yet its "own" in sufficient measure to make a common cause for all hearers. Third, it takes us by surprise. It has its own initiatives. We are sure by some instant tang of consciousness it comes from "out there" as well as from "in here." The same argument holds of man's ideals: they also are faithfully recurrent, socially attested, and have their own instigations and demands. Dr. David S. Cairns has recently written: "In the last resort the great issue as to whether the universe . . . . is fundamentally sub-moral, sub-human, and sub-rational, because impersonal and unconscious, seems to me to turn, above all, on the question of whether I ought to do the highest that I know." "I ought to do the highest that I know" is faithfully recurrent, socially attested, and has its own benign coercions. We no more made "the best that I know" than we made ourselves. How, then, can it be mere "projection" — however locally distorted — mere "rationalization," or mere "wishful thinking"?

There is ultimately no argument for prayer except praying, but there is an argument to rebut the arguments leveled against prayer. Furthermore, there is a basic matter-of-factness, a substratum of sanity, which approves of itself when left to itself the record concerning Jesus: "And it came to pass in those days, that he went into a mountain to pray, and continued all night in prayer *to God*." Prayer in its essence is neither fear, nor social control, nor autosuggestion, nor rationalization. The certitude abides that it is comradeship with God.

Part Ten: RELIGIOUS FAITH
AND KNOWLEDGE
The Problem of Religious
Knowledge

HANS VAIHINGER

HANS VAIHINGER (1852-1933) was born in a Swabian parsonage near Tübingen, and at twelve years of age was placed under the tutelege of Sauer in Leonberg. Subsequently, he was educated at Stuttgart Grammar School and the University of Tübingen, where he undertook theological studies. While a student at this latter institution, he wrote a prize winning essay, **Recent Theories of Consciousness** (1873). Graduating from Tubingen in 1874, Vaihinger furthered his education at Leipzig, where a number of celebrated philosophers had collected. In 1876, his first philosophical work was published, **Hartmann, Duhring and Lange,** a critical treatment of Nineteenth Century philosophy, consisting of lectures delivered in the Academic Philosophical Society at Leipzig. In 1876, his inaugural dissertation, **Logical Studies. Part I: The Theory of Scientific Fictions,** appeared in published form in 1911 as "Part I: Basic Principles" of **The Philosophy of 'As If'.** In 1884, his **Commentary on Kant** won him the appointment as Professor at Halle, and at that institution, he founded the **Kantstudien** (a journal) and the Kant Society.

Vaihinger, whose philosophical thought was markedly influenced by Kant and Schopenhauer, identifies his position as **Positivist Idealism** or **Idealistic Positivism,** which represents a synthesis of Idealism and Positivism. For the propagation of this school of thought, he founded, in 1919, the journal: **Annalen der Philosophie.** The selection chosen for the present text is from his classic **The Philosophy of 'As If'.**

69

HANS VAIHINGER

The Philosophy of 'As If'[1]

Kant once more repeats expressly and distinctly that "we observe a certain organization of the practical reason in which (1) the subject of universal legislation, as originator of the world, (2) the object of the will of mundane beings, as conforming in their end to the subject, (3) the condition of these beings, in which alone they are capable of attaining that end [God, freedom and immortality] — are in the practical aspect self-made ideas." In other words, these concepts are and remain — self-made ideas.

Here too we see clearly the immeasurable difference between the Kantian justification of religious ideas and that of the pre-and-post Kantians. The Kantian justification of religious ideas is a purely fictive, or better perhaps, a fictionalistic one. They are for him practical, expedient fictions, whereas the pre- and post-Kantian justification of religious concepts and judgments is a rationalistic one; they are rationally grounded hypotheses. A variety only of this rationalism is the *Kantianismus vulgaris*, the popular version of Kant's doctrine, which represents Kant as justifying the principal ideas of religion on the basis of moral facts; for according to the presentation of this popular Kantianism that has become customary since Reinhold, theoretical inferences have been drawn from moral phenomena as to the existence of God, etc., i.e. we are again making hypotheses. The real and genuine Kantian criticism draws no theoretical inferences whatever, but says: You must act *as* you would *if* a God existed, etc. Therein lies Kant's critical Pragmatism.

A very important passage for the elucidation of Kant's meaning is contained in the treatise *Von einem neuerdings erhobenen vornehmen Ton in der Philosophi*e (1796). There we find the expression "belief"

[1] H. Vaihinger, *The Philosophy of 'As If'*, tr. C. K. Ogden (London: Routledge & Kegan Paul, Ltd., 1924, 1935, and New York: Barnes & Noble, Inc.), 304–307. Reprinted by permission.

fully explained in a note: Taken theoretically "to believe" means, "to regard a thing as likely," and is "something half-way between thinking and
knowing." With regard to empirical things and empirical evidence such
theoretical belief is a fact, but with regard to the supersensuous no
judgment whatever is possible and, therefore, no judgment of probability:
"there is therefore no such thing as theoretical belief in the supersensuous."

"But from the practical (moral-practical) point of view, not only is
such a belief in the supersensuous possible. It is inevitable." For the
categorical commands of the "voice of morality within me" require of
us that we should co-operate in realizing the unconditioned purpose of
the highest good (which, of course, is only an idea): "To believe in such
a ruler practically and morally, does not mean first to assume his reality
as true, in order that we may realize the end imposed. For that purpose
the law of reason is in itself objectively sufficient. No, it means that, in
accordance with the ideal of that purpose, we are to act as we should if
such a world-government really existed." "This is an imperative which
enjoins not belief, but action." In other words, in the Kantian sense, in the
sense of the Critical Philosophy, the expression, "I believe in God," means
simply that "I act *as if* a God really existed." As a moral agent the man
who thinks in the Kantian, the critical manner, acts *as if* the Good possessed an unconditioned value, such as to render it the decisive factor
in the world; and the Good would be the decisive factor in the world if
there were a world-government to bring about its final triumph. In spite
of the fact that my theoretical reason *forbids* me to assume such a moral
world-order — this concept would have no content — I yet act as if such
a moral world-order might exist, since my practical reason *bids* me do
good unconditionally. In following this command of practical reason I
am, in strict theory, acting irrationally, for my theoretical reason tells me
that such a moral world-order is merely an empty, even if a beautiful,
concept. But I do actually find within me the command of practical
reason to do good, and this command impresses me as though it were
something sublime. I act according to this command. But in acting thus,
I am, at the same time, acting as if I did make this assumption of a moral
world-order which I recognize to be theoretically impossible, nay even
contradictory. Not in the sense of supposing that it is the assumption
which gives the command; far from it; my soul does not think of that at
all. The command meets with our approval and impresses us for its own
sake; it is indeed part of the content of my practical reason. In other
words, to the normal moral man, the moral world-order and the author
of the moral order of the world, God, are not in the least a presupposition
necessary to his voluntary submission to the moral commandment. On

the contrary, in obeying the moral commandment Kant's normal man not only behaves just *as if* this obedience had not only to a certain extent empirical consequences in time and in the phenomenal world, but as if this moral action of his extended into an intelligible supersensuous world and, on the one hand, helped toward the attainment of a general eternal supreme good and, on the other, were incorporated by a divine power, as an expedient element in a system of purposes. Such is always and everywhere the nature of unconditioned, ethically-good action; for to act morally means, in contradistinction to the empirical conditions, to act *as if* it had the power to extend into a super-empirical world in which a supreme ruler provided for the harmonizing of good and evil. In this sense good action is identical with a belief in God and immortality. In this sense the atheist who acts morally also believes *practically* in God and immortality, since he acts *as if* God and immortality existed. All ethical conduct, therefore, involves the fiction of God and immortality — this is the meaning of the practical rational belief in God and immortality. In this sense, too, and only in this sense, must we understand the conclusion elsewhere established by Kant regarding "a morally earnest and therefore religious endeavour towards good." The morally-good can say to himself and to his kind: "Your acts are good and, for that reason, you are, in your way, a believer, for you act as though a God existed: in short, your actions are good and therefore you believe." This Kantian *recte agis, ergo credis* is the basic axiom of Descartes' theoretical philosophy as rightly understood: *cogito, ergo sum.*

A. J. AYER

ALFRED JULES AYER (1910-   ), elected Fellow of the British Academy in 1952, is currently Professor of Logic in the University of Oxford, a post he assumed in 1959. His education was at Eton College, and Christ Church, Oxford University, the latter school granting him his M.A. in 1936. His professional career commenced at Christ Church, where from 1932 to 1935 he was Lecturer in Philosophy. Subsequent appointments were: Research Student from 1935 to 1944; Fellow of Wadham College, Oxford University, from 1944 to 1946, and Dean for the 1945-1946 school season. From 1946 to 1959, he assumed the post of Grote Professor of Mind and Logic at the University of London before returning to Oxford, his present position.

Among his publications are his much contested book which earned him fame as philosopher and chief exponent of Logical Positivism, **Language, Truth and Logic** (1936, rev. ed. 1946), **The Foundations of Empirical Knowledge (1940), Thinking and Meaning** (1947, his inaugural lecture), **British Empirical Philosophers** (1952, ed. with Raymond Winch), **Philosophical Essays** (1954), **The Problem of Knowledge** (1956), **Logical Positivism** (1959).

70

A. J. AYER

God as Unverifiable[1]

This mention of God brings us to the question of the possibility of religious knowledge. We shall see that this possibility has already been ruled out by our treatment of metaphysics. But, as this is a point of considerable interest, we may be permitted to discuss it at some length.

It is now generally admitted, at any rate by philosophers, that the existence of a being having the attributes which define the god of any non-animistic religion cannot be demonstratively proved. To see that this is so, we have only to ask ourselves what are the premises from which the existence of such a god could be deduced. If the conclusion that a god exists is to be demonstratively certain, then these premises must be certain; for, as the conclusion of a deductive argument is already contained in the premises, any uncertainty there may be about the truth of the premises is necessarily shared by it. But we know that no empirical proposition can ever be anything more than probable. It is only *a priori* propositions that are logically certain. But we cannot deduce the existence of a god from an *a priori* proposition. For we know that the reason why *a priori* propositions are certain is that they are tautologies. And from a set of tautologies nothing but a further tautology can be validly deduced. It follows that there is no possibility of demonstrating the existence of a god.

What is not so generally recognised is that there can be no way of proving that the existence of a god, such as the God of Christianity, is even probable. Yet this also is easily shown. For if the existence of such a god were probable, then the proposition that he existed would be an empirical hypothesis. And in that case it would be possible to deduce from it, and other empirical hypotheses, certain experiential propositions

[1] A. J. Ayer, *Language, Truth and Logic* (London: Victor Gollancz, 1936, and New York: Dover Publications, Inc.), 114–120. Reprinted through the permission of the publishers.

which were not deducible from those other hypotheses alone. But in fact this is not possible. It is sometimes claimed, indeed, that the existence of a certain sort of regularity in nature constitutes sufficient evidence for the existence of a god. But if the sentence "God exists" entails no more than that certain types of phenomena occur in certain sequences, then to assert the existence of a god will be simply equivalent to asserting that there is the requisite regularity in nature; and no religious man would admit that this was all he intended to assert in asserting the existence of a god. He would say that in talking about God, he was talking about a transcendent being who might be known through certain empirical manifestations, but certainly could not be defined in terms of those manifestations. But in that case the term "god" is a metaphysical term. And if "god" is a metaphysical term, then it cannot be even probable that a god exists. For to say that "God exists" is to make a metaphysical utterance which cannot be either true or false. And by the same criterion, no sentence which purports to describe the nature of a transcendent god can possess any literal significance.

It is important not to confuse this view of religious assertions with the view that is adopted by atheists, or agnostics. For it is characteristic of an agnostic to hold that the existence of a god is a possibility in which there is no good reason either to believe or disbelieve; and it is characteristic of an atheist to hold that it is at least probable that no god exists. And our view that all utterances about the nature of God are nonsensical, so far from being identical with, or even lending any support to, either of these familiar contentions, is actually incompatible with them. For if the assertion that there is a god is nonsensical, then the atheist's assertion that there is no god is equally nonsensical, since it is only a significant proposition that can be significantly contradicted. As for the agnostic, although he refrains from saying either that there is or that there is not a god, he does not deny that the question whether a transcendent god exists is a genuine question. He does not deny that the two sentences "There is a transcendent god" and "There is no transcendent god" express propositions one of which is actually true and the other false. All he says is that we have no means of telling which of them is true, and therefore ought not to commit ourselves to either. But we have seen that the sentences in question do not express propositions at all. And this means that agnosticism also is ruled out.

Thus we offer the theist the same comfort as we gave to the moralist. His assertions cannot possibly be valid, but they cannot be invalid either. As he says nothing at all about the world, he cannot justly be accused of saying anything false, or anything for which he has insufficient grounds. It is only when the theist claims that in asserting the existence of a transcendent god he is expressing a genuine proposition that we are entitled to disagree with him.

It is to be remarked that in cases where deities are identified with natural objects, assertions concerning them may be allowed to be significant. If, for example, a man tells me that the occurrence of thunder is alone both necessary and sufficient to establish the truth of the propositions that Jehovah is angry, I may conclude that, in his usage of words, the sentence "Jehovah is angry" is equivalent to "It is thundering." But in sophisticated religions, though they may be to some extent based on men's awe of natural process which they cannot sufficiently understand, the "person" who is supposed to control the empirical world is not himself located in it; he is held to be superior to the empirical world, and so outside it; and he is endowed with super-empirical attributes. But the notion of a person whose essential attributes are non-empirical is not an intelligible notion at all. We may have a word which is used as if it named this "person," but, unless the sentences in which it occurs express propositions which are empirically verifiable, it cannot be said to symbolize anything. And this is the case with regard to the word "god," in the usage in which it is intended to refer to a transcendent object. The mere existence of the noun is enough to foster the illusion that there is a real, or at any rate a possible entity corresponding to it. It is only when we enquire what God's attributes are that we discover that "God," in this usage, is not a genuine name.

It is common to find belief in a transcendent god conjoined with belief in an after-life. But, in the form which it usually takes, the content of this belief is not a genuine hypothesis. To say that men do not ever die, or that the state of death is merely a state of prolonged insensibility, is indeed to express a significant proposition, though all the available evidence goes to show that it is false. But to say that there is something imperceptible inside a man, which is his soul or his real self, and that it goes on living after he is dead, is to make a metaphysical assertion which has no more factual content than the assertion that there is a transcendent god.

It is worth mentioning that, according to the account which we have given of religious assertions, there is no logical ground for antagonism between religion and natural science. As far as the question of truth or falsehood is concerned, there is no opposition between the natural scientist and the theist who believes in a transcendent god. For since the religious utterances of the theist are not genuine propositions at all, they cannot stand in any logical relation to the propositions of science. Such antagonism as there is between religion and science appears to consist in the fact that science takes away one of the motives which make men religious. For it is acknowledged that one of the ultimate sources of religious feeling lies in the inability of men to determine their own destiny; and science tends to destroy the feeling of awe with which men regard an alien world, by making them believe that they can understand and anticipate the course of natural phenomena, and even to some extent control it. The fact that it has recently become fashionable for physicists themselves to be sympathetic towards religion is a point in favour of this hypothesis. For this sympathy towards religion marks the physicists' own lack of confidence in the validity of their hypotheses, which is a reaction on their part from the anti-religious dogmatism of nineteenth-century scientists, and a natural outcome of the crisis through which physics has just passed.

It is not within the scope of this enquiry to enter more deeply into the causes of religious feeling, or to discuss the probability of the continuance of religious belief. We are concerned only to answer those questions which arise out of our discussion of the possibility of religious knowledge. The point which we wish to establish is that there cannot be any transcendent truths of religion. For the sentences which the theist uses to express such "truths" are not literally significant.

An interesting feature of this conclusion is that it accords with what many theists are accustomed to say themselves. For we are often told that the nature of God is a mystery which transcends the human understanding. But to say that something transcends the human understanding is to say that it is unintelligible. And what is unintelligible cannot significantly be described. Again, we are told that God is not an object of reason but an object of faith. This may be nothing more than an admission that the existence of God must be taken on trust, since it cannot be proved. But it may also be an assertion that God is the object of a purely mystical intuition, and cannot therefore be defined in terms which are intelligible to the reason. And I think there are many theists who would assert this. But if one allows that it is impossible to define God in intelligible terms, then one is allowing that it is impossible for a sentence both to be significant and to be about God. If a mystic admits that the object of his vision is something which cannot be described, then he must also admit that he is bound to talk nonsense when he describes it.

For his part, the mystic may protest that his intuition does reveal truths to him, even though he cannot explain to others what these truths are; and that we who do not possess this faculty of intuition can have no ground for denying that it is a cognitive faculty. For we can hardly maintain *a priori* that there are no ways of discovering true propositions except those which we ourselves employ. The answer is that we set no limit to the number of ways in which one may come to formulate a true proposition. We do not in any way deny that a synthetic truth may be discovered by purely intuitive methods as well as by the rational method of induction. But we do say that every synthetic proposition, however it may have been arrived at, must be subject to the test of actual experience. We do not deny *a priori* that the mystic is able to discover truths by his own special methods. We wait to hear what are the propositions which embody his discoveries, in order to see whether they are verified or confuted by our empirical observations. But the mystic, so far from producing propositions which are empirically verified, is unable to produce any intelligible propositions at all. And therefore we say that his intuition has not revealed to him any facts. It is no use his saying that he has apprehended facts but is unable to express them. For we know that if he really had acquired any information, he would be able to express it. He would be able to indicate in some way or other how the genuineness of his discovery might be empirically determined. The fact that he cannot reveal what he "knows," or even himself devise an empirical test to validate his "knowledge," shows that his state of mystical intuition is not a genuinely cognitive state. So that in describing his vision the mystic does not give us any information about the condition of his own mind.

These considerations dispose of the argument from religious experience, which many philosophers still regard as a valid argument in favour of the existence of a god. They say that it is logically possible for men to be immediately acquainted with God, as they are immediately acquainted with a sense-content, and that there is no reason why one should be prepared to believe a man when he says that he is seeing a yellow patch, and refuse to believe him when he says that he is seeing God. The answer to this is that if the man who asserts that he is seeing God is merely asserting that he is experiencing a peculiar kind of sense-content, then we do not for a moment deny that his assertion may be true. But, ordinarily, the man who says that he is seeing God is saying not merely that he is experiencing a religious emotion, but also that there exists a transcendent being who is the object of this emotion; just as the man who says that he sees a yellow patch is ordinarily saying not merely that his visual sense-field contains a yellow sense-content, but also that there exists a yellow object to which the sense-content belongs. And it is not irrational to be prepared to believe a man when he asserts the existence of a yellow object, and to refuse to believe him when he asserts the existence of a transcendent god. For whereas the sentence "There exists here a yellow-coloured material thing" expresses a genuine synthetic proposition which could be empirically verified, the sentence "There exists a transcendent god" has, as we have seen, no literal significance.

We conclude, therefore, that the argument from religious experience is altogether fallacious. The fact that people have religious experiences is interesting from the psychological point of view, but it does not in any way imply that there is such a thing as religious knowledge, any more than our having moral experiences implies that there is such a thing as moral knowledge. The theist, like the moralist, may believe that his experiences are cognitive experiences, but, unless he can formulate his "knowledge" in propositions that are empirically verifiable, we may be sure that he is deceiving himself. It follows that those philosophers who fill their books with assertions that they intuitively "know" this or that moral or religious "truth" are merely providing material for the psycho-analyst. For no act of intuition can be said to reveal a truth about any matter of fact unless it issues in verifiable propositions. And all such propositions are to be incorporated in the system of empirical propositions which constitutes science.

JOHN WISDOM

ARTHUR JOHN TERANCE DIBBER WISDOM (1904-   ), the son of a clergyman, was educated at Aldeburgh Lodge School and Fitzwilliam House, Cambridge, receiving his B.A. in 1924, and his M.A. in 1934. He is currently Professor of Philosophy, Cambridge University, a post he assumed in 1952; he is also a Member of the Senate, and a Fellow of Trinity College, Cambridge.

His publications include: "Logical Constructions" in **Mind** (1931-1933), "Is Analysis a Useful Method in Philosophy" in **Proceedings of the Aristotelian Society,** Supplementary Volume (1931), "Philosophical Perplexity" in **Proceedings of the Aristotelian Society** (1936-1937), "Metaphysics and Verification" in **Mind** (1938), "Gods" in **Proceedings of the Aristotelian Society** (1944-1945), "Philosophy, Metaphysics, and Psycho-Analysis" in **Philosophy and Psycho-Analysis** (1957), and the following books: **Problems of Mind and Matter** (1934), **Other Minds** (1952), and **Philosophy and Psycho-Analysis** (1953).

71

JOHN WISDOM

Gods[1]

1. *The existence of God is not an experimental issue in the way it was.* An atheist or agnostic might say to a theist "You still think there are spirits in the trees, nymphs in the streams, a God of the world." He might say this because he noticed the theist in time of drought pray for rain and make a sacrifice and in the morning look for rain. But disagreement about whether there are gods is now less of this experimental or betting sort than it used to be. This is due in part, if not wholly, to our better knowledge of why things happen as they do.

It is true that even in these days it is seldom that one who believes in God has no hopes or fears which an atheist has not. Few believers now expect prayer to still the waves, but some think it makes a difference to people and not merely in ways the atheist would admit. Of course with people, as opposed to waves and machines, one never knows what they won't do next, so that expecting prayer to make a difference to them is not so definite a thing as believing in its mechanical efficacy. Still, just as primitive people pray in a business-like way for rain, so some people still pray for others with a real feeling of doing something to help. However, in spite of this persistence of an experimental element in some theistic belief, it remains true that Elijah's method on Mount Carmel of settling the matter of what god or gods exist would be far less appropriate today than it was then.

2. *Belief in gods is not merely a matter of expectation of a world to come.* Someone may say "The fact that a theist no more than an atheist expects prayer to bring down fire from heaven or cure the sick does not mean that there is no difference between them as to the facts, it does not mean that the theist has no expectations different from the atheist's. For very often those who believe in God believe in another world and

[1] John Wisdom, "Gods," *Proceedings of the Aristotelian Society* (1944-1945). Reprinted by the courtesy of the Editor of the Aristotelian Society.

believe that God is there and that we shall go to that world when we die."

This is true, but I do not want to consider here expectations as to what one will see and feel after death nor what sort of reasons these logically unique expectations could have. So I want to consider the differences between atheists and theists insofar as these differences are not a matter of belief in a future life.

3. *What are these differences? And is it that theists are superstitious or that atheists are blind?* A child may wish to sit awhile with his father and he may, when he has done what his father dislikes, fear punishment and feel distress at causing vexation, and while his father is alive he may feel sure of help when danger threatens and feel that there is sympathy for him when disaster has come. When his father is dead he will no longer expect punishment or help. Maybe for a moment an old fear will come or a cry for help escape him, but he will at once remember that this is no good now. He may feel that his father is no more until perhaps someone says to him that his father is still alive though he lives now in another world and one so far away that there is no hope of seeing him or hearing his voice again. The child may be told that nevertheless his father can see him and hear all he says. When he has been told this the child will still fear no punishment nor expect any sign of his father, but now, even more than he did when his father was alive, he will feel that his father sees him all the time and will dread distressing him and when he has done something wrong he will feel separated from his father until he has felt sorry for what he has done. Maybe when he himself comes to die he will be like a man who expects to find a friend in the strange country where he is going, but even when this is so, it is by no means all of what makes the difference between a child who believes that his father lives still in another world and one who does not.

Likewise one who believes in God may face death differently from one who does not, but there is another difference between them besides this. This other difference may still be described as belief in another world, only this belief is not a matter of expecting one thing rather than another here or hereafter, it is not a matter of a world to come but of a world that now is, though beyond our senses.

We are at once reminded of those other unseen worlds which some philosophers "believe in" and others "deny," while non-philosophers unconsciously "accept" them by using them as models with which to "get the hang of" the patterns in the flux of experience. We recall the timeless entities whose changeless connections we seek to represent in symbols, and the values which stand firm amidst our flickering satisfaction and remorse, and the physical things which, though not beyond the corruption of moth and rust, are yet more permanent than the shadows they throw upon the screen before our minds. We recall, too, our talk of souls and of what lies in their depths and is manifested to us partially and intermittently in our own feelings and the behaviour of others. The hypothesis of mind, of other human minds and of animal minds, is reasonable because it explains for each of us why certain things behave so cunningly all by themselves unlike even the most ingenious machines. Is the hypothesis of a world mind reasonable for like reasons — someone who adjusts the blossom to the bees, someone whose presence may at times be felt — in a garden in high summer, in the hills when clouds are gathering, but not, perhaps, in a cholera epidemic?

4. *The question "Is belief in gods reasonable?" has more than one source.* It is clear now that in order to grasp fully the logic of belief in divine minds we need to examine the logic of belief in animal and human minds. But we cannot do that here and so for the purposes of this discussion about divine minds let us acknowledge the reasonableness of our belief in human minds without troubling ourselves about its logic. The question of the reasonableness of belief in divine minds then becomes a matter of whether there are facts in nature which support claims about divine minds in the way facts in nature support our claims about human minds.

In this way we resolve the force behind the problem of the existence of gods into two components, one metaphysical and the same which prompts the question "Is there *ever any* behaviour which gives reason to believe in any sort of mind?" and one which finds expression in "are there other mind-patterns in nature beside the human and animal patterns which we can all easily detect, and are these other mind-patterns superhuman?"

Such overdetermination of a question syndrome is common. Thus, the puzzling questions "Do dogs think?" "Do animals feel?" are partly metaphysical puzzles and partly scientific questions. They are not purely metaphysical; for the reports of scientists about the poor performances of cats in cages and old ladies' stories about the remarkable performances of their pets are not irrelevant. But nor are these questions purely scientific; for the stories never settle them and therefore they have other sources. One other source is the metaphysical source we have already noticed, namely, the difficulty about getting behind an animal's behaviour to its mind, whether it is a non-human animal or a human one.

But there's a third component in the force behind these questions, these disputes have a third source, and it is one which is important in the dispute which finds expression in the words "I believe in God," "I do not." This source comes out well if we consider the question "Do flowers feel?" Like the questions about dogs and animals this question about flowers comes partly from the difficulty we sometimes feel over inference from *any* behaviour to thought or feeling and partly from ignorance as to what behaviour is to be found. But these questions, as opposed to a like question about human beings, come also from hesitation as to whether the behaviour in question is *enough* mind-like, that is, is it enough similar to or superior to human behaviour to be called "mind-proving"? Likewise, even when we are satisfied that human behaviour shows mind and even when we have learned whatever mind-suggesting things there are in nature which are not explained by human and animal minds, we may still ask "But are these things sufficiently striking to be called a mind-pattern? Can we fairly call them manifestations of a divine being?"

"The question," someone may say, "has then become merely a matter of the application of a name. And 'What's in a name?' "

5. *But the line between a question of fact and question or decision as to the application of a name is not so simple as this way of putting things suggests.* The question "What's in a name?" is engaging because we are inclined to answer both "Nothing" and "Very much." And this "Very much" has more than one source. We might have tried to comfort Heloïse by saying "It isn't that Abelard no longer loves you, for this man isn't Abelard"; we might have said to poor Mr. Tebrick in Mr. Garnet's *Lady into Fox* "But this is no longer Silvia." But if Mr. Tebrick replied "Ah, but it is!" this might come not at all from observing facts about the fox which we have not observed, but from noticing facts about the fox which we had missed, although we had in a sense observed all that Mr. Tebrick had observed. It is possible to have before one's eyes all the items of a pattern and still to miss the pattern. . . .

Things are revealed to us not only by the scientists with microscopes, but also by the poets, the prophets, and the painters. What is so isn't merely a matter of "the facts." For sometimes when there is agreement as to the facts there is still argument as to whether defendant did or did not "exercise reasonable care," was or was not "negligent."

And though we shall need to emphasize how much "There is a God" evinces an attitude to the familiar, we shall find in the end that it also evinces some recognition of patterns in time easily missed and that, therefore, difference as to there being any gods is in part a difference as to what is so and therefore as to the facts, though not in the simple ways which first occurred to us.

6. *Let us now approach these same points by a different road.*

6.1 *How it is that an explanatory hypothesis, such as the existence
of God, may start by being experimental and gradually become something quite different can be seen from the following story*:

Two people return to their long neglected garden and find among the
weeds a few of the old plants surprisingly vigorous. One says to the other
"It must be that the gardener has been coming and doing something about
these plants." Upon inquiry they find that no neighbor has ever seen anyone at work in their garden. The first man says to the other "He must
have worked while people slept." The other says "No, someone would
have heard him and besides, anybody who cared about the plants would
have kept down these weeds." The first man says "Look at the way these
are arranged. There is purpose and feeling for beauty here. I believe
that someone comes, someone invisible to mortal eyes. I believe that the
more carefully we look the more we shall find confirmation of this." They
examine the garden ever so carefully and sometimes they come on new
things suggesting the contrary and even that a malicious person has been
at work. Besides examining the garden carefully they also study what
happens to gardens left without attention. Each learns all the other
learns about this and about the garden. Consequently, when after all
this, one says "I still believe a gardener comes" while the other says
"I don't," their different words now reflect no difference as to what they
have found in the garden, no difference as to what they would find in
the garden if they looked further and no difference about how fast un-
tended gardens fall into disorder. At this stage, in this context, the
gardener hypothesis has ceased to be experimental, the difference between one who accepts and one who rejects it is now not a matter of
the one expecting something the other does not expect. What is the
difference between them? The one says "A gardener comes unseen and
unheard. He is manifested only in his work with which we are all familiar," the other says "There is no gardener" and with this difference in
what they say about the gardener goes a difference in how they feel
towards the garden, in spite of the fact that neither expects anything of
it which the other does not expect.

But is this the whole difference between them — that the one calls
the garden by one name and feels one way towards it, while the other
calls it by another name and feels in another way towards it? And if this
is what the difference has become then is it any longer appropriate to
ask "Which is right?" or "Which is reasonable?"

And yet surely such questions *are* appropriate when one person says to
another "You still think the world's a garden and not a wilderness, and
that the gardener has not forsaken it" or "You still think there are nymphs

of the streams, a presence in the hills, a spirit of the world." Perhaps when a man sings "God's in His heaven" we need not take this as more than an expression of how he feels. But when Bishop Gore or Dr. Joad write about belief in God and young men read them in order to settle their religious doubts the impression is not simply that of persons choosing exclamations with which to face nature and the "changes and chances of this mortal life." The disputants speak as if they are concerned with a matter of scientific fact, or of trans-sensual, trans-scientific and metaphysical fact, but still of fact and still a matter about which reasons for and against may be offered, although no scientific reasons in the sense of field surveys of fossils or experiments on delinquents are to the point.

6.2. *Now can an interjection have a logic?* Can the manifestation of an attitude in the utterance of a word, in the application of a name, have a logic? When all the facts are known how can there still be a question of fact? How can there still be a question? Surely as Hume says ". . . after circumstance, every relation is known, the understanding has no further room to operate."

6.3. When the madness of these questions leaves us for a moment *we can all easily recollect disputes which though they cannot be settled by experiment are yet disputes in which one party may be right and the other wrong* and in which both parties may offer reasons and the one better reasons than the other. *This may happen in pure and applied mathematics and logic.* Two accountants or two engineers provided with the same data may reach different results and this difference is resolved not by collecting further data but by going over the calculations again. Such differences indeed share with differences as to what will win a race, the honour of being among the most "settlable" disputes in the language.

6.4. *But it won't do to describe the theistic issue as one settlable by such calculation,* or as one about what can be deduced in this *vertical* fashion from the facts we know. No doubt dispute about God has sometimes, perhaps especially in mediaeval times, been carried on in this fashion. But nowadays it is not and we must look for some other analogy, some other case in which a dispute is settled, but not by experiment.

6.5. *In courts of law* it sometimes happens that opposing counsel are agreed as to the facts and are not trying to settle a question of further fact, are not trying to settle whether the man who admittedly had quarrelled with the deceased did or did not murder him, but are concerned with whether Mr. A who admittedly handed his long-trusted clerk signed blank checks did or did not exercise reasonable care, whether a ledger is or is not a document, whether a certain body was or was not a public authority.

In such cases we notice that the process of argument is not a *chain* of demonstrative reasoning. It is a presenting a re-presenting of those features of the cases which *severally cooperate* in favour of the conclusion, in favour of saying what the reasoner wishes said, in favour of calling the situation by the name by which he wishes to call it. The reasons are like the legs of a chair, not the links of a chain. Consequently although the discussion is a priori and the steps are not a matter of experience, the procedure resembles scientific argument in that the reasoning is not *vertically* extensive but *horizontally* extensive — it is a matter of the cumulative effect of several independent premises, not of the repeated transformation of one or two. And because the premises are severally inconclusive the process of deciding the issue becomes a matter of weighing the cumulative effect of one group of severally inconclusive items against the cumulative effect of another group of severally inconclusive items, and thus lends itself to description in terms of conflicting "probabilities." This encourages the feeling that the issue is one of fact — that it is a matter of guessing from the premises at a further fact, at what is to come. But this is a muddle. *The dispute does not cease to be a priori because it is a matter of the cumulative effect of severally inconclusive premises.* The logic of the dispute is not that of a chain of deductive reasoning as in a mathematic calculation. But nor is it a matter of collecting from several inconclusive items of information an expectation as to something further, as when a doctor from a patient's symptoms guesses at what is wrong, or a detective from many clues guesses the criminal. It has its own sort of logic and its own sort of end — the solution of the question at issue is a decision, a ruling by the judge. But it is not an arbitrary decision, though the rational connections are neither quite like those in vertical deductions nor like those in inductions in which from many signs we guess at what is to come; and though the decision manifests itself in the application of a name it is no more merely the application of a name than is the pinning on of a medal merely the pinning on of a bit of metal. . . .

6.7.   *And if we say, as we did at the beginning, that when a difference as to the existence of a God is not one as to future happenings then it is not experimental and therefore not as to the facts, we must not forthwith assume that there is no right and wrong about it,* no rationality or irrationality, no appropriateness or inappropriateness, no procedure which tends to settle it, *nor even that this procedure is in no sense a discovery of new facts.* After all even in science this is not so. Our two gardeners, even when they had reached the stage when neither expected any experimental result which the other did not, might yet have continued the dispute, each presenting and re-presenting the features of the garden favouring his hypothesis, that is, fitting his model for describing the accepted fact; each emphasizing the pattern he wishes to emphasize. True, in science, there is seldom or never a pure instance of this sort of dispute, for nearly always with difference of hypothesis goes some difference of expectation as to the facts. But scientists argue about rival hypotheses with a vigour which is not exactly proportioned to difference in expectations of experimental results.

The difference as to whether a God exists involves our feelings more than most scientific disputes and in this respect is more like a difference as to whether there is beauty in a thing. . . .

. . . . .

10. *Now what happens, what should happen, when we inquire in this way into the reasonableness, the propriety of belief in gods?* The answer is: A double and opposite-phrased change. Wordsworth writes:

> . . . And I have felt
> A presence that disturbs me with the joy
> Of elevated thoughts; a sense sublime
> Of something far more deeply interfused,
> Whose dwelling is the light of setting suns,
> And the round ocean and the living air,
> And the blue sky, and the mind of man:
> A motion and a spirit, that impels
> All thinking things, all objects of all thought,
> And rolls through all things. . . .[2]

We most of us know this feeling. But is it well placed like the feeling that here is first-rate work, which we sometimes rightly have even before we have fully grasped the picture we are looking at or the book we are reading? Or is it misplaced like the feeling in a house that has long been empty that someone secretly lives there still. Wordsworth's feeling *is* the feeling that the world is haunted, that something watches in the hills and manages the stars. The child feels that the stone tripped him when he stumbled, that the bough struck him when it flew back in his face. He has to learn that the wind isn't buffeting him, that there is not a devil in it, that he was wrong, that his attitude was inappropriate. And as he learns that the wind wasn't hindering him so he also learns it wasn't helping him. But we know how, though he learns, his attitude lingers. It is plain that Wordsworth's feeling is of this family.

[2] *Tintern Abbey.*

Belief in gods, it is true, is often very different from belief that stones are spiteful, the sun kindly. For the gods appear in human form and from the waves and control these things and by so doing reward and punish us. But varied as are the stories of the gods, they have a family likeness and we have only to recall them to feel sure of the other main sources which cooperate with animism to produce them. . . .

JACQUES MARITAIN

JACQUES MARITAIN (1882-   ) was born in Paris on November 18, 1882, and educated in Paris, Rome, and Heidelberg. From the University of Paris, he received the degree Agrégé de Philosophie; from Roman Universities, the Doctor of Philosophy. In 1904, he married a Russian Jewess, Raissa Ousmanoff, who, with him in 1906, became converted to Catholicism. In 1914, he was appointed Professor of Philosophy at the Institut Catholique de Paris, and in 1923 founded the Bibliothèque Française de Philosophie. Subsequently, he held appointments at Louvain, Geneva, Fribourg, Milan, Bonn, Oxford, Santander, Chicago, Angelicum in Rome, Institute of Mediaeval Studies in Toronto, Canada, and from 1948 to 1953 held a Professorship at Princeton University. From 1945 to 1948, he served in the post of French Ambassador to the Vatican.

Maritain is regarded as the most influential philosopher of Thomism and contemporary Catholicism's most famous one. His publications include: **La Philosophie Bergsonienne** (1913), **The Degrees of Knowledge** (1932), **Science and Wisdom** (1935), **Integral Humanism** (1936), **Ransoming the Time** (1941), **Existence and the Existent** (1948), **Man and the State** (1950), **The Range of Reason** (1952), **Creative Intuition in Art and Poetry** (1953), **Approaches to God** (1954), **On the Philosophy of History** (1957), **Reflections on America** (1958), **Moral Philosophy: An Historical and Critical Survey of the Great Systems** (1964).

72

JACQUES MARITAIN

A New Approach to God[1]

The dialectics of anthropocentric humanism developed within three centuries. Man's approach to God changed accordingly. For the notion of God — to the extent that it ceases to be encompassed and kept pure by revelation — is linked to culture and its fate is comfortable to that of culture. At the first moment of humanistic dialectics, God, as we noted above, became the assurance of man's domination over matter. He was a transcendent God, but closed up in His transcendence and forbidden to interfere in human affairs. He became a decorative God, the God of the classical bourgeois world. At the second moment, with romanticist philosophy and the great idealist metaphysicians, God became an idea. He was an immanent God, engulfed in the dialectical progress of the self-asserting Idea and evolving world. This God of pantheism and of the romanticist bourgeois world was but the ideal borderline of the development of mankind. This God was also the absolute, basic and unbending justification of good and evil, of all crimes, oppressions, iniquities, as well as of conquests and the money-making progress of history.

At a third moment, Feuerbach was to discover that God — such a God — alienates man from himself. Marx was to declare that He is but an ideological mirror of the alienation of man accomplished by private property. And Nietzsche was exhilarated by the mission with which he felt himself endowed, namely, to proclaim the death of God. How could God still live in a world from which His image, that is, the free and spiritual personality of man, seems definitely destined to vanish away? God as dead, God in the grave, was the God of the final agony and self-destruction of an age of civilization which is now at its end. Atheism is the final end of the inner dialectics of anthropocentric humanism.

Thus we are confronted with the problem of atheism, the significance

[1] Jacques Maritain, "A New Approach to God," Our Emergent Civilization, ed. Ruth Nanda Anshen (New York: Harper & Row), 1947. Reprinted by permission.

of which for culture and for the emergent civilization must be scrutinized. There are many kinds of atheism. There are pseudo atheists who believe that they do not believe in God and who in reality unconsciously believe in Him, because the God whose existence they deny is not God but something else. There are practical atheists who believe that they believe in God but who in reality deny His existence by each one of their deeds. Out of the living God they have made an idol. There are absolute atheists who actually deny the existence of the very God in whom the believers believe and who are bound to change their entire scale of values and to destroy in themselves everything that connotes His name.

Practical atheism does not pose any special problem for the philosopher, except the problem of the possibility of cleavage between the intellect and the will, theoretical belief and actual behavior, or, in theological terms, between faith (dead faith) and charity. Dead faith is faith without love. The practical atheist accepts the fact that God exists — and forgets it on all occasions. His case is a case of voluntary, stubborn forgetting.

Quite different is the case of the absolute atheist. He does not forget God, he steadily thinks of Him — in order to free himself from Him. When he has acquired the intellectual persuasion that God does not exist, his task and endeavor is not finished; this very negation delivers him over to an inner dialectic which obliges him ceaselessly to destroy any resurgence in himself of what he has buried. For in denying God he has explicitly denied Transcendence. But in actual fact the good which everyone desires, even without knowing it, is finally self-subsisting Good; and thus, in actual fact, the dynamism of human life, because it tends toward good and happiness, even if their true countenance is not recognized, tends implicitly toward Transcendence. Doubtless the absolute atheist may ascribe to superstition or human stupidity or human "alienation" every vestige or trace of Transcendence he contemplates in the common behavior and beliefs, individual or social life, of men. Yet within himself is the real drama. In proportion as the dialectic of atheism develops in his mind, — each time he is confronted with the natural notion of and natural tendency to an ultimate End, or with the natural notion of and natural attention to absolute values or unconditioned standards, or with any metaphysical anxiety — he will discover in himself vestiges of Transcendence which have not yet been abolished. He must get rid of them. God is a perpetual threat to him. His case is not a case of practical forgetting, but a case of deeper and deeper commitment to refusal and fight.

What is the meaning of this absolute atheism? It is in no way a mere absence of belief in God. It is rather a refusal of God, a fight against God, a challenge to God. And when it achieves victory it innerly changes man, it gives man a kind of stolid solidity, as if the spirit of man had been stuffed with dead substance, and his organic tissues turned into stone. Atheism begins with a kind of new start in moral activity, a determination to confront good and evil in an absolutely free experience by casting aside any ultimate end — a determination which is mistaken for moral maturity and boils down in reality to the complete giving of self to some human, concrete "Great Being." For Auguste Comte it was Mankind; for others a Work to be done or a Party to serve. At the same time the relation to the absolute Good which the moral good essentially implies is abolished, and as a result the very nature of the moral good vanishes away. In the true atheist, duty or virtue necessarily becomes a requirement of his own perfection accepted as a supreme cult, or as a hopeless rite of his own greatness, or as an attribute of his deified will. The thunder-like appearance of absolute atheism in human history has been the conclusion of a progressive degradation of the idea of God and has meant the beginning of a new age in which the process of death and the process of resurrection will develop together, confronting each other and struggling with each other.

With regard to culture, atheism is a mirror, a true and faithful mirror, of the state to which the human being has been reduced. For man being the image of God, he naturally thinks of Him according to the state in which the image presents itself at a given moment of culture. Absolute atheism means that the personality of man is definitely endangered; and that all the masks, the words, the façades, the palliatives, the plasters and cosmetics with which human conscience tries to deceive itself and to give us the appearance of man are henceforth useless and will be cast away. Picasso's art, in its present character, is the true art of atheism; I mean of that thorough defacement of contemporary man, which is mirrored in atheism. We are no more persons that the distorted, imbecile faces of those ferocious females. We no longer possess true, human faces.

Absolute atheism is also a translation into crude and inescapable terms, a ruthless counterpart, an avenging mirror, of the practical atheism of too many believers who do not actually believe — Christians who keep in their minds the stage-set of religion, especially because of the class or family advantages that religion seems to them to protect. But they deny the gospel and despise the poor. They pass through the tragedy of their time only with resentment for the loss of their social and political privileges and fear for their own prestige or possessions. They contemplate without flinching every kind of injustice or atrocity if it does not threaten their own way of life. They scorn their neighbor, scorn the Jew, scorn the Negro, scorn their own nation if it ceases to be the "good nation" of their old dreams, worship force and brand as "subhuman" the peoples, races or classes they fear or do not understand. They have a clear conscience and live and act as if God did not exist. Such men and women invoke the name of God and do not really believe in Him. They live on empty formulas and stereotyped phrases, on mental clichés. They cherish every kind of sham that will soothe and deceive them. They await the deceivers. They are famished for deception.

In their own existence absolute atheists have dehumanized life and the claims of the soul. They have replaced human receptivity to transcendence and the vital, unsatisfied needs of personality by the cosmic dynamism of nature. They present the appearance of corpses. In some of them, moreover, the process of death is not achieved; there still remains a hidden germ of life, a living thirst. And this subsisting germ, thwarted, denudated, stripped of every rational support, becomes all the more genuine and alive as it resists the destruction and havoc which atheism has brought on all sides into the spiritual substance of man. Such atheists, if they receive the grace of faith, will become men for whom nothing is of account except God and the gospel. For them atheism has been a sort of hellish purification.

Practical atheists also have dehumanized life and the claims of the soul in their own existence. They nurture nothingness. But they have the appearance and colors of life although they are dead within. They are whited sepulchers. They are perfumed with all the fragrance of self-righteousness; there is no substance in them. It would be too optimistic to pretend that their time has passed. Yet it seems probable that they will be of no use in the new age of civilization, in the emergent civilization of revolution and change that is already upon us.

Atheists and believers will live together in this new age. They will walk a long way, each asserting his own position against the other, each endeavoring to have the human mind and civilization inspired by his respective philosophy. Under penalty of spiritual death civilization will have to overcome atheism and free itself of its inspiration. This cannot be done by machine guns, police forces and dictators. If it is true that absolute atheism is primarily the fruit and condemnation of practical atheism and is its reflected image in the mirror of divine wrath, then it must be said that the only way of getting rid of absolute atheism is to get rid of practical atheism. Decorative Christianity is nowadays not enough. Living Christianity is necessary to the world. Faith must be actual, practical, existential faith. To believe in God must mean to live in such a manner that life cannot be lived if God does not exist. Gospel justice, gospel attentiveness to everything human must inspire not only the deeds of the saints, but the structures and institutions of common life, must penetrate to the depths of social, terrestrial existence.

This is not possible, even in the imperfect ways of humanity and among the hard conflicts of the coming age, if in those who believe in God the true sources are not alive, and if the life they must give to the world does not flow down into them from the heights of God-given wisdom. A great deal of wisdom, a great deal of contemplation will be required in order to render the immense technological developments of the emergent civilization truly human and liberating. At this point one should recall Henri Bergson's observations on the mutual need which "mystics" and "mechanics" have of each other, and on the *supplément d'âme* that must vivify the body, now become too large, of our civilization. Contemplative life, perhaps in new forms, and made available not only to the chosen few but to the common man if he actually believes in God, will be the prerequisite of that very activity which tries to spread the gospel leaven all over the world.

As I have endeavored to emphasize for many years, the deepest requirement of a new age of civilization will be the sanctification of secular life. For pagan antiquity, *holy* was synonymous with *sacred;* that is, with what had been set apart to be physically, visibly, socially at the service of God. And it was only to the extent that sacred rites and symbols ruled human life that the latter could externally please God. The gospel has deeply changed all that by interiorizing moral life and the sanctity in the hearts of men, in the secret of the invisible relations between the divine Personality and the human personality.

Henceforth what is secular or "profane" is not to be distinguished from what is sacred in the sense that what is impure is differentiated from what is pure; but rather as a certain order of human activity, the aim of which is temporal, is distinguished from another order of human activity which is socially constituted to assure spiritual aims by preaching the Word of God and ministering to the soul. And both, the one involved in the secular or temporal order and the other involved in the sacred order, must tend to the perfection of human life; that is, to inner sanctity.

Now it can be observed that this evangelical principle has been progressively realized and manifested in human conscience and behavior, but that its process of spiritual development is far from being achieved on earth.

In these perspectives we may understand that a new "style" of sanctity, a new step in the sanctification of secular life, will be demanded by the new age. Not only will the spirit of Christ spread into secular life, seek for witnesses among those who labor in yards and factories, in social work, politics or poetry, as well as among monks dedicated to the search for perfection; but a kind of divine simplification will help people to realize that the perfection of human life does not consist in a stoical athleticism of virtue nor in a bookish and humanly calculated application of holy recipes, but rather in a ceaselessly increasing love, despite our mistakes and weaknesses, between the Uncreated Self and the created Self. There will be a growing consciousness that everything depends on that descent of the divine plenitude into the human being of which I spoke above, and which performs in man death and resurrection. There will be a growing consciousness that man's sanctification has its touchstone in neighborly love, requiring him to be always ready to give what he has, especially himself, and finally to die in some manner for those he loves.

PAUL TILLICH

PAUL JOHANNES TILLICH (1886-   ) was born in Starzeddel, Kreis Guben, Prussia, on August 20, 1886. His education was obtained from the University of Berlin (1904-1905), University of Tübingen (1905), University of Halle (1905-1907), University of Berlin (1908), and the University of Breslau, where, in 1911, he earned his degree of Doctor of Philosophy. His professional career began as Privatdozent of Theology at the University of Berlin in 1919, and in 1924, he resigned the post to accept an appointment as Professor of Theology at the University of Marburg. His professorships continued: University of Dresden (1925-1929), University of Leipzig (1928-1929), and from 1929 to 1933, he served as Professor of Philosophy at the University of Frankfurt-am-Main. In 1933, he came to America to accept an appointment as Professor of Philosophy and Theology at Union Theological Seminary, New York, a post he held until 1955 when he left Union for Harvard University where he remained until his retirement.

Many scholars regard Tillich as America's most influential theologian. Many honors have been accorded him, including at least a dozen honorary doctoral degrees. His publications include: **The Interpretation of History** (1936), **The Shaking of the Foundations** (1948), **The Protestant Era** (1948), **Systematic Theology** (vol. I, 1951, vol. II, 1957), **The Courage to Be** (1952), **Love, Power, and Justice** (1954), **The New Being** (1955), **Biblical Religion and the Search for Ultimate Reality** (1955), **The Religious Situation** (1956), **Dynamics of Faith** (1957), **Theology of Culture** (1959).

73

PAUL TILLICH

Faith and the Courage to Be[1]

THE COURAGE TO BE AS THE KEY TO BEING-ITSELF

Nonbeing Opening Up Being

The courage to be in all its forms has, by itself, revelatory character. It shows the nature of being, it shows that the self-affirmation of being is an affirmation that overcomes negation. In a metaphorical statement (and every assertion about being-itself is either metaphorical or symbolic) one could say that being includes nonbeing but nonbeing does not prevail against it. "Including" is a spatial metaphor which indicates that being embraces itself and that which is opposed to it, nonbeing. Nonbeing belongs to being, it cannot be separated from it. We could not even think "being" without a double negation: being must be thought as the negation of the negation of being. This is why we describe being best by the metaphor "power of being." Power is the possibility a being has to actualize itself against the resistance of other beings. If we speak of the power of being-itself we indicate that being affirms itself against nonbeing. In our discussion of courage and life we have mentioned the dynamic understanding of reality by the philosophers of life. Such an understanding is possible only if one accepts the view that nonbeing belongs to being, that being could not be the ground of life without nonbeing. The self-affirmation of being without nonbeing would not even be self-affirmation but an immovable self-identity. Nothing would be manifest, nothing expressed, nothing revealed. But nonbeing drives being out of its seclusion, it forces it to affirm itself dynamically. Philosophy has dealt with the dynamic self-affirmation of being-itself wherever it spoke dialectically, notably in Neoplatonism, Hegel, and the philosophers of life and process. Theology has done the same whenever it took

[1] Paul Tillich, *The Courage to Be* (New Haven: Yale University Press, 1952), 178-190. Reprinted by permission.

the idea of the living God seriously, most obviously in the trinitarian symbolization of the inner life of God. Spinoza, in spite of his static definition of substance (which is his name for the ultimate power of being), unites philosophical and mystical tendencies when he speaks of the love and knowledge with which God loves and knows himself through the love and knowledge of finite beings. Nonbeing (that in God which makes his self-affirmation dynamic) opens up the divine self-seclusion and reveals him as power and love. Nonbeing makes God a living God. Without the No he has to overcome in himself and in his creature, the divine Yes to himself would be lifeless. There would be no revelation of the ground of being, there would be no life.

But where there is nonbeing there is finitude and anxiety. If we say that nonbeing belongs to being-itself, we say that finitude and anxiety belong to being-itself. Wherever philosophers or theologians have spoken of the divine blessedness they have implicitly (and sometimes explicitly) spoken of the anxiety of finitude which is eternally taken into the blessedness of the divine infinity. The infinite embraces itself and the finite, the Yes includes itself and the No which it takes into itself, blessedness comprises itself and the anxiety of which it is the conquest. All this is implied if one says that being includes nonbeing and that through nonbeing it reveals itself. It is a highly symbolic language which must be used at this point. But its symbolic character does not diminish its truth; on the contrary, it is a condition of its truth. To speak unsymbolically about being-itself is untrue.

The divine self-affirmation is the power that makes the self-affirmation of the finite being, the courage to be, possible. Only because being-itself has the character of self-affirmation in spite of nonbeing is courage possible. Courage participates in the self-affirmation of being-itself, it participates in the power of being which prevails against nonbeing. He who receives this power in an act of mystical or personal or absolute faith is aware of the source of his courage to be.

Man is not necessarily aware of this source. In situations of cynicism and indifference he is not aware of it. But it works in him as long as he maintains the courage to take his anxiety upon himself. In the act of the courage to be the power of being is effective in us, whether we recognize it or not. Every act of courage is a manifestation of the ground of being, however questionable the content of the act may be. The content may hide or distort true being, the courage in it reveals true being. Not arguments but the courage to be reveals the true nature of being-itself. By affirming our being we participate in the self-affirmation of being-itself. There are no valid arguments for the "existence" of God, but there are acts of courage in which we affirm the power of being, whether we know it or not. If we know it, we accept acceptance consciously. If we do not know it, we nevertheless accept it and participate in it. And in our acceptance of that which we do not know the power of being is manifest to us. Courage has revealing power, the courage to be is the key to being-itself.

Theism Transcended

The courage to take meaninglessness into itself presupposes a relation to the ground of being which we have called "absolute faith." It is without a *special* content, yet it is not without content. The content of absolute faith is the "God above God." Absolute faith and its consequences, the courage that takes the radical doubt, the doubt about God, into itself, transcends the theistic idea of God.

Theism can mean the unspecified affirmation of God. Theism in this sense does not say what it means if it uses the name of God. Because of the traditional and psychological connotations of the word God such an empty theism can produce a reverent mood if it speaks of God. Politicians, dictators, and other people who wish to use rhetoric to make an impression on their audience like to use the word God in this sense. It produces the feeling in their listeners that the speaker is serious and morally trustworthy. This is especially successful if they can brand their foes as atheistic. On a higher level people without a definite religious commitment like to call themselves theistic, not for special purposes but because they cannot stand a world without God, whatever this God may be. They need some of the connotations of the word God and they are afraid of what they call atheism. On the highest level of this kind of theism the name of God is used as a poetic or practical symbol, expressing a profound emotional state or the highest ethical idea. It is a theism which stands on the boundary line between the second type of theism and what we call "theism transcended." But it is still too indefinite to cross this boundary line. The atheistic negation of this whole type of theism is as vague as the theism itself. It may produce an irreverent mood and angry reaction of those who take their theistic affirmation seriously. It may even be felt as justified against the rhetorical-political abuse of the name God, but it is ultimately as irrelevant as the theism which it negates. It cannot reach the state of despair any more than the theism against which it fights can reach the state of faith.

Theism can have another meaning, quite contrary to the first one: it can be the name of what we have called the divine-human encounter. In this case it points to those elements in the Jewish-Christian tradition which emphasize the person-to-person relationship with God. Theism in this sense emphasizes the personalistic passages in the Bible and the

Protestant creeds, the personalistic image of God, the word as the tool of creation and revelation, the ethical and social character of the kingdom of God, the personal nature of human faith and divine forgiveness, the historical vision of the universe, the idea of a divine purpose, the infinite distance between creator and creature, the absolute separation between God and the world, the conflict between holy God and sinful man, the person-to-person character of prayer and practical devotion. Theism in this sense is the nonmystical side of biblical religion and historical Christianity. Atheism from the point of view of this theism is the human attempt to escape the divine-human encounter. It is an existential — not a theoretical — problem.

Theism has a third meaning, a strictly theological one. Theological theism is, like every theology, dependent on the religious substance which it conceptualizes. It is dependent on theism in the first sense insofar as it tries to prove the necessity of affirming God in some way, it usually develops the so-called arguments for the "existence" of God. But it is more dependent on theism in the second sense insofar as it tries to establish a doctrine of God which transforms the person-to-person encounter with God into a doctrine about two persons who may or may not meet but who have a reality independent of each other.

Now theism in the first sense must be transcended because it is irrelevant, and theism in the second sense must be transcended because it is one-sided. But theism in the third sense must be transcended because it is wrong. It is bad theology. This can be shown by a more penetrating analysis. The God of theological theism is a being beside others and as such a part of the whole of reality. He certainly is considered its most important part, but as a part and therefore as subjected to the structure of the whole. He is supposed to be beyond the ontological elements and categories which constitute reality. But every statement subjects him to them. He is seen as a self which has a world, as an ego which is related to a thou, as a cause which is separated from its effect, as having a definite space and an endless time. He is a being, not being-itself. As such he is bound to the subject-object structure of reality, he is an object for us as subjects. At the same time we are objects for him as a subject. And this is decisive for the necessity of transcending theological theism. For God as a subject makes me into an object which is nothing more than an object. He deprives me of my subjectivity because he is all-powerful and all-knowing. I revolt and try to make *him* into an object, but the revolt fails and becomes desperate. God appears as the invincible tyrant, the being in contrast with whom all other beings are without freedom and subjectivity. He is equated with the recent tyrants who with the help of terror try to transform everything into a mere object, a thing among things, a cog in the machine they control. He becomes the model of everything against which Existentialism revolted. This is the God Nietzsche said had to be killed because nobody can tolerate being made into a mere object of absolute knowledge and absolute control. This is the deepest root of atheism. It is an atheism which is justified as the reaction against theological theism and its disturbing implications. It is also the deepest root of the Existentialist despair and the widespread anxiety of meaninglessness in our period.

Theism in all its forms is transcended in the experience we have called absolute faith. It is the accepting of the acceptance without somebody or something that accepts. It is the power of being itself that accepts ánd gives the courage to be. This is the highest point to which our analysis has brought us. It cannot be described in the way the God of all forms of theism can be described. It cannot be described in mystical terms either. It transcends both mysticism and personal encounter, as it transcends both the courage to be as a part and the courage to be as oneself.

The God Above and the Courage to Be

The ultimate source of the courage to be is the "God above God"; this is the result of our demand to transcend theism. Only if the God of theism is transcended can the anxiety of doubt and meaninglessness be taken into the courage to be. The God above God is the object of all mystical longing, but mysticism also must be transcended in order to reach him. Mysticism does not take seriously the concrete and the doubt concerning the concrete. It plunges directly into the ground of being and meaning, and leaves the concrete, the world of finite values and meanings, behind. Therefore it does not solve the problem of meaninglessness. In terms of the present religious situation this means that Eastern mysticism is not the solution of the problems of Western Existentialism, although many people attempt this solution. The God above the God of theism is not the devaluation of the meanings which doubt has thrown into the abyss of meaninglessness; he is their potential restitution. Nevertheless absolute faith agrees with the faith implied in mysticism in that both transcend the theistic objectivation of a God who is a being. For mysticism such a God is not more real than any finite being, for the courage to be such a God has disappeared in the abyss of meaninglessness with every other value and meaning.

The God above God of theism is present, although hidden, in every divine-human encounter. Biblical religion as well as Protestant theology are aware of the paradoxical character of this encounter. They are aware that if God encounters man God is neither object nor subject and is therefore above the scheme into which theism has forced him. They are aware that personalism with respect to God is balanced by a transpersonal presence of the divine. They are aware that forgiveness can be accepted only if the power of acceptance is effective in man — biblically speaking, if the power of grace is effective in man. They are aware of the paradoxical character of every prayer, of speaking to somebody to whom you cannot speak because he is not "somebody," of asking somebody of whom you cannot ask anything because he gives or gives not before you ask, of saying "thou" to somebody who is nearer to the I than the I is to itself. Each of these paradoxes drives the religious consciousness toward a God above the God of theism.

The courage to be which is rooted in the experience of the God above the God of theism unites and transcends the courage to be as a part and the courage to be as oneself. It avoids both the loss of oneself by participation and the loss of one's world by individualization. The acceptance of the God above the God of theism makes us a part of that which is not also a part but is the ground of the whole. Therefore our self is not lost in a larger whole, which submerges it in the life of a limited group. If the self participates in the power of being-itself it receives itself back. For the power of being acts through the power of the individual selves. It does not swallow them as every limited whole, every collectivism, and every conformism does. This is why the Church, which stands for the power of being-itself or for the God who transcends the God of the religions, claims to be the mediator of the courage to be. A church which is based on the authority of the God of theism cannot make such a claim. It inescapably develops into a collectivist or semicollectivist system itself.

But a church which raises itself in its message and its devotion to the God above the God of theism without sacrificing its concrete symbols can mediate a courage which takes doubt and meaninglessness into itself. It is the Church under the Cross which alone can do this, the Church which preaches the Crucified who cried to God who remained his God after the God of confidence had left him in the darkness of doubt and meaninglessness. To be as a part in such a church is to receive a courage to be in which one cannot lose one's self and in which one receives one's world.

Absolute faith, or the state of being grasped by the God beyond God, is not a state which appears beside other states of the mind. It never is something separated and definite, an event which could be isolated and described. It is always a movement in, with, and under other states of the mind. It is the situation on the boundary of man's possibilities. It *is* this boundary. Therefore it is both the courage of despair and the courage in and above every courage. It is not a place where one can live, it is without the safety of words and concepts, it is without a name, a church, a cult, a theology. But it is moving in the depth of all of them. It is the power of being, in which they participated and of which they are fragmentary expressions.

One can become aware of it in the anxiety of fate and death when the traditional symbols, which enable men to stand the vicissitudes of fate and the horror of death have lost their power. When "providence" has become a superstition and "immortality" something imaginary that which once was the power in these symbols can still be present and create the courage to be in spite of the experience of a chaotic world and a finite existence. The Stoic courage returns but not as the faith in universal reason. It returns as the absolute faith which says Yes to being without seeing anything concrete which could conquer the nonbeing in fate and death.

And one can become aware of the God above the God of theism in the anxiety of guilt and condemnation when the traditional symbols that enable men to withstand the anxiety of guilt and condemnation have lost their power. When "divine judgment" is interpreted as a psychological complex and forgiveness as a remnant of the "father-image," what once was the power in those symbols can still be present and create the courage to be in spite of the experience of an infinite gap between what we are and what we ought to be. The Lutheran courage returns but not supported by the faith in a judging and forgiving God. It returns in terms of the absolute faith which says Yes although there is no special power that conquers guilt. The courage to take the anxiety of meaninglessness upon oneself is the boundary line up to which the courage to be can go. Beyond it is mere non-being. Within it all forms of courage are re-established in the power of the God above the God of theism. The *courage to be is rooted in the God who appears when God has disappeared in the anxiety of doubt.*

INDEX

473